ZAGAT®

Chicago
Restaurants
2011/12

Including
Milwaukee

LOCAL EDITORS
Alice Van Housen and Ann Christenson
STAFF EDITORS
Emily Rothschild with Cynthia Kilian

Published and distributed by
Zagat Survey, LLC
4 Columbus Circle
New York, NY 10019
T: 212.977.6000
E: chicago@zagat.com
www.zagat.com

ACKNOWLEDGMENTS

We thank Jennifer Olvera, Steven Shukow, Ian Turner, Thomas Van Housen and Donna Marino Wilkins, as well as the following members of our staff: Caitlin Eichelberger (senior associate editor), Anna Hyclak (editorial assistant), Brian Albert, Sean Beachell, Maryanne Bertollo, Danielle Borovoy, Reni Chin, Larry Cohn, Nicole Diaz, Kelly Dobkin, Alison Flick, Jeff Freier, Matthew Hamm, Justin Hartung, Marc Henson, Aynsley Karps, Natalie Lebert, Mike Liao, James Mulcahy, Polina Paley, Josh Rogers, Chris Walsh, Jacqueline Wasilczyk, Art Yaghci, Sharon Yates, Anna Zappia and Kyle Zolner.

The reviews in this guide are based on public opinion surveys. The ratings reflect the average scores given by the survey participants who voted on each establishment. The text is based on quotes from, or paraphrasings of, the surveyors' comments. Phone numbers, addresses and other factual data were correct to the best of our knowledge when published in this guide.

Contents

Ratings & Symbols

Zagat Top Spot	Name	Symbols		Cuisine	Zagat Ratings			
					FOOD	DECOR	SERVICE	COST

Area, Address & Contact

Z Tim & Nina's ◑ *Pizza*   ▽ 23 | 9 | 13 | $15

Hyde Park | 456 E. Chicago Ave. (Division St.) | 312-555-3867 | www.zagat.com

Review, surveyor comments in quotes

Hordes of "unkempt" U of C students have gone nuclear over this "low-budget" cafeteria-style "24/7 dive", which "single-handedly" started the "deep-dish sushi pizza craze" that's "sweeping the Windy City like a lake-effect tsunami"; "try the to-die-for eel-pepperoni-wasabi-mozzarella or Osaka-Napolitano pies" – but be patient, since "T & N never heard of service."

Ratings

Food, Decor & **Service** are rated on a 30-point scale.

0	–	9	poor to fair
10	–	15	fair to good
16	–	19	good to very good
20	–	25	very good to excellent
26	–	30	extraordinary to perfection
▽			low response	less reliable

Cost

The price of dinner with a drink and tip; lunch is usually 25% less. For unrated **newcomers** or **write-ins,** the price range is as follows:

I	$25 and below	E	$41 to $65
M	$26 to $40	VE	$66 or above

Symbols

Z highest ratings, popularity and importance
◑ serves after 11 PM
Ⓢ Ⓜ closed on Sunday or Monday
⊄ no credit cards accepted

About This Survey

This **2011/12 Chicago Restaurants Survey** is an update reflecting significant developments since our last Survey was published. It covers 1,339 restaurants in the Chicago area and Milwaukee, including 188 important additions. We've also indicated new addresses, phone numbers, chef changes and other major alterations. Like all our guides, this one is based on input from avid local consumers – 5,701 all told. Our editors have synopsized this feedback, highlighting representative comments (in quotation marks within each review). To read full surveyor comments – and share your own opinions – visit **ZAGAT.com,** where you'll also find free restaurant news, special events, deals, reservations, menus, photos and lots more.

ABOUT ZAGAT: In 1979, we started asking friends to rate and review restaurants purely for fun. The term "user-generated content" had not yet been coined. That hobby grew into Zagat Survey; 32 years later, we have over 375,000 surveyors and cover everything from airlines to hotels, nightlife and shopping around the world. Along the way, we evolved from being a print publisher to a digital content provider, e.g. **ZAGAT.com** and Zagat mobile apps (for iPad, iPhone, Android, BlackBerry, Windows Phone 7 and Palm webOS). We also produce marketing tools for a wide range of corporate clients. And you can find us on Twitter (twitter.com/zagat), Facebook and just about any other social media network.

THREE SIMPLE PREMISES underlie our ratings and reviews. First, we believe that the collective opinions of large numbers of consumers are more accurate than those of any single person. (Consider that our surveyors bring some 830,000 annual meals' worth of experience to this survey, visiting Chicago restaurants year-round, anonymously – and on their own dime.) Second, food quality is only part of the equation when choosing a restaurant, thus we ask surveyors to separately rate food, decor and service and report on cost. Third, since people need reliable information in a fast, easy-to-digest format, we strive to be concise and we offer our content on every platform – print, online and mobile. Our Top Ratings lists (pages 7–16) and indexes (starting on page 212) are also designed to help you quickly choose the best place for any occasion, be it business or pleasure. Milwaukee's Top Ratings and indexes start on pages 273 and 292, respectively.

THANKS: We're grateful to our local editors, Alice Van Housen, a freelance writer and editor; and Ann Christenson, the dining critic for *Milwaukee Magazine.* We also sincerely thank the thousands of surveyors who participated – this guide is really "theirs."

JOIN IN: To improve our guides, we solicit your comments; it's vital that we hear your opinions. Just contact us at **nina-tim@zagat.com.** We also invite you to join our surveys at **ZAGAT.com.** Do so and you'll receive a choice of rewards in exchange.

New York, NY
June 15, 2011

Nina and Tim Zagat

What's New

Economic indicators notwithstanding, new restaurants are popping up all over Chicago at a robust rate. Fine-dining destinations are fewer – with the notable exception of Grant Achatz's daring **Alinea** follow-up, **Next,** and upscale steakhouses **Chicago Cut** and **Mastro's** – but chefs of all stripes continue to create casual concepts featuring burgers, barbecue and more. That's welcome news, since the average Chicago dinner tab, $36.97, is higher than the national average of $35.52.

SPIN-OFFS: A number of newcomers have been so successful that they're already planning spin-offs. Stephanie Izard's thriving **Girl & The Goat** will give birth to **The Little Goat** in the fall; **Gilt Bar**'s Brendan Sodikoff plans to open **Ox Diner** this summer on the heels of his über-chic **Maude's Liquor Bar**; and also this summer, Graham Elliot Bowles' sandwich spot, **Grahamwich,** will get wheels as **Grahambulance.**

HONK HONK: Speaking of wheels, this year brought a flotilla of food trucks: Bucktown's **The Southern** debuted a mac 'n' cheese mobile; Phillip Foss (recently of Lockwood) launched **Meatyballs Mobile** (serving, yes, meatballs); and Matt Maroni – a founding father of Chicago's food truck movement – got rolling with his **Gaztro-Wagon** serving 'naan-wiches' all over town.

CHEF SHUFFLE: Several seemingly entrenched chefs decamped, with Laurent Gras leaving **L2O,** Jason McLeod exiting **Ria,** Martial Noguier quitting **Café des Architectes** for **Bistronomic,** Todd Stein fleeing theWit Hotel's **Cibo Matto** for **The Florentine,** and Ryan Poli proving not to be **Perennial** – its new incarnation, **Perennial Virant,** will be helmed by **Vie**'s Paul Virant. Jackie Shen (ex **Red Light**) now cooks at **Chicago Cut,** Jeremy Lycan left his **Niche** and Christophe David is no more at **Nomi Kitchen.**

FAREWELLS: We said so longs to **Army & Lou's, Brasserie Jo, Café Matou, Eve, Mado, Marché, May Street Market, Opera, Otom** (which Homaro Cantu replaced with **Ing**), **Red Light, Shikago** and **Spring.** Other places temporarily closed for revamps: **Nomi,** in the Gold Coast's Park Hyatt, was to reopen at press time with a new look and expanded menu; **Bice** will set up shop in a new location with extensive outdoor seating; and **The Pump Room** is aiming for a fall comeback.

MILWAUKEE MATTERS: Notable openings ranged from **Harbor House,** a high-end Downtown seafooder, to breakfast specialists **Blue's Egg,** on the West Side, and Bay View's **Honeypie.** Red meat remains a draw, as shown by the success of Downtown's **Ward's House of Prime.** And locavores got a boost from Brookfield's **Parkside 23,** which specializes in locally sourced eats, including vegetables and herbs grown on its adjacent plot.

Chicago, IL
Milwaukee, WI
June 15, 2011

Alice Van Housen
Ann Christenson

Most Popular

Plotted on the map at the back of this book.

1. Frontera Grill | *Mexican*
2. Alinea | *American*
3. Topolobampo | *Mexican*
4. Charlie Trotter's | *American*
5. Gibsons | *Steak*
6. Joe's Sea/Steak | *Seafood/Steak*
7. Blackbird | *American*
8. Wildfire | *Steak*
9. Morton's | *Steak*
10. Tru | *French*
11. Spiaggia | *Italian*
12. Everest | *French*
13. Avec | *Mediterranean*
14. Shaw's | *Seafood*
15. Lou Malnati's | *Pizza*
16. MK | *American*
17. Chicago Chop House | *Steak*
18. L2O | *Seafood*
19. Capital Grille | *Steak*
20. Giordano's | *Pizza*
21. Gene & Georgetti | *Steak*
22. Publican | *American*
23. Maggiano's | *Italian*
24. Hugo's | *Seafood*
25. Bob Chinn's | *Seafood*
26. Hot Doug's | *Hot Dogs*
27. Café Spiaggia | *Italian*
28. Ruth's Chris* | *Steak*
29. Original Gino's | *Pizza*
30. Gage | *American*
31. Orig./Walker Pancake | *Amer.*
32. Les Nomades | *French*
33. Japonais | *Japanese*
34. Coco Pazzo | *Italian*
35. Catch 35 | *Seafood*
36. Cheesecake Factory | *American*
37. Arun's | *Thai*
38. Rosebud* | *Italian*
39. David Burke's | *Steak*
40. Francesca's | *Italian*
41. Cafe Ba-Ba-Reeba! | *Spanish*
42. Naha | *American*
43. Bistro 110 | *French*
44. Harry Caray's* | *Italian/Steak*
45. Heaven/Seven* | *Cajun/Creole*
46. Pizzeria Uno/Due | *Pizza*
47. North Pond | *American*
48. Le Colonial | *Vietnamese*
49. Atwood Cafe | *American*
50. Mercat | *Spanish*

Many of the above restaurants are among the Chicago area's most expensive, but if popularity were calibrated to price, a number of other restaurants would surely join their ranks. To illustrate this, we have added two lists comprising 80 Best Buys on page 16.

* Indicates a tie with restaurant above

KEY NEWCOMERS

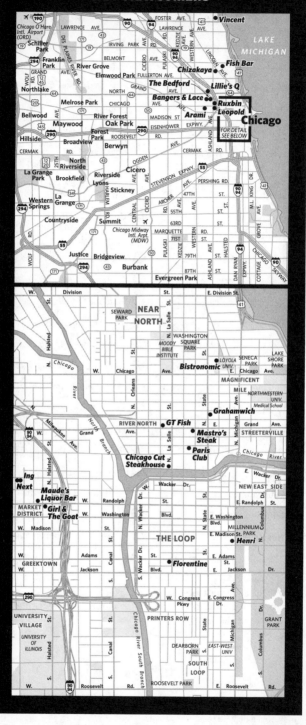

Key Newcomers

Our editors' favorites among this year's arrivals. See a full list on page 244.

Arami | *Japanese* | Innovative sushi in a serene West Town setting

Bangers & Lace | *Pub Food* | Gourmet sausages and brew in Wicker Park

Bedford | *American* | Artisanal dishes in a former Wicker Park bank

Bistronomic | *French* | Seasonal plates du jour in the Gold Coast

Chicago Cut | *Steak* | A handsome River North steakhouse with a view

Chizakaya | *Japanese* | Locally sourced small plates in Lakeview

Fish Bar | *Seafood* | Lakeview fish shack sibling to DMK Burger Bar

Florentine | *Italian* | Contemporary Loop dining in an elegant hotel setting

Girl & The Goat | *American* | West Loop entry from a *Top Chef* champion

Grahamwich | *Sandwiches* | Graham Elliot–created 'wiches in River North

GT Fish | *Seafood* | Ocean-centric eats from the Boka crew in River North

Henri | *American* | Luxe South Loop counterpart to The Gage

Ing | *American* | West Loop Moto spin-off with more mass appeal

Leopold | *Belgian* | Hearty grub in a Noble Square watering hole

Lillie's Q | *BBQ/Southern* | Beyond-the-basics BBQ house in Bucktown

Mastro's Steak | *Steak* | Glitzy Arizona import in River North

Maude's Liquor Bar | *French* | Hip West Loop boîte via Brendan Sodikoff

Next | *Eclectic* | Grant Achatz's West Loop follow-up to Alinea

Paris Club | *French* | Updated classics in a rustic River North locale

Ruxbin | *Eclectic* | Funky Noble Square BYO with global accents

Vincent | *American* | Andersonville charmer with Dutch influences

---

ON THE HORIZON: Notable upcoming openings include **The Black Sheep** from James Toland, in Noble Square, and the **Old Town Social** set's still-unnamed makeover of the West Loop's **Marché**. River North will welcome two newcomers: **Slurping Turtle** from Takashi Yagihashi (**Takashi**), and the **Mercadito** crew's **Tavernita**. On the hotel dining front, expect **Tribute,** serving American comfort food in the South Loop's Essex Inn, and **Michael Jordan's Steak House** in Streeterville's InterContinental.

Top Food

BY CUISINE

Excludes places with low votes

ECLECTIC

27 Moto
26 Lula Cafe
22 Uncommon Ground
21 Zed 451
   Hub 51

FRENCH

29 Les Nomades
28 Michael
   Tallgrass
   Tru
27 Oceanique

FRENCH (BISTRO)

25 Barrington Country
   Bistro Campagne
   Kiki's
24 Cafe Central
   Le Bouchon

GREEK

22 Artopolis
   Costa's
21 Parthenon
   Santorini
   Roditys

HOT DOGS/BURGERS

27 Hot Doug's
23 Al's Beef
22 DMK Burger
   Epic Burger
21 Wiener's Circle

INDIAN

25 India House
23 Marigold
22 Hema's Kitchen
   Gaylord
   Vermilion

ITALIAN

27 Riccardo
   Spiaggia
26 A Tavola
   Mia Francesca
25 Coco Pazzo

JAPANESE

27 Katsu
   Sushi Wabi
25 Yoshi's Café
   Mirai Sushi
   Sai Café

MEDITERRANEAN

26 Avec
24 Pita Inn
23 Turquoise
20 A La Turka

MEXICAN

28 Topolobampo
27 Frontera Grill
26 Cafe 28
   Salpicón
25 Mixteco Grill

MIDDLE EASTERN

24 Pita Inn
23 Turquoise
20 A La Turka
18 Andies
   Aladdin's Eatery

PIZZA

24 Lou Malnati's
23 Aurelio's
   Piece
   Chicago Pizza/Oven
   Spacca Napoli

SEAFOOD

27 Oceanique
26 Joe's Sea/Steak
24 Catch 35
   Shaw's Crab
   Hugo's

SMALL PLATES

26 Avec
   Green Zebra
25 Boka
24 Browntrout
21 Quartino

SPANISH/TAPAS

26 Mercat
24 Emilio's Tapas
   La Tasca
   Tapas Gitana
23 Mesón Sabika

STEAKHOUSES

26 Joe's Sea/Steak
   Morton's
   Gibsons
25 Capital Grille
   Rosebud Prime/Steak

THAI

28	Arun's
23	Thai Pastry
22	Butterfly
20	Star of Siam

VEGETARIAN

26	Green Zebra
23	Ethiopian Diamond
22	Hema's Kitchen
	Chicago Diner
21	Blind Faith

BY SPECIAL FEATURE

BREAKFAST

26	Lula Cafe
25	M Henry/Henrietta
24	Bongo Room
23	Lou Mitchell's
	Ina's

BRUNCH

27	Frontera Grill
26	Cafe 28
	Salpicón
25	Yoshi's Café
	North Pond

BUSINESS DINING

29	Les Nomades
	Alinea
28	Topolobampo
	Michael
27	Blackbird

CHILD-FRIENDLY

27	Hot Doug's
26	Smoque BBQ
24	Lou Malnati's
	Lawry's
	Original/Walker Pancake

HOTEL DINING

27	Seasons (Four Seasons)
26	Avenues (Peninsula)
	Mercat (Blackstone)
	Gibsons (Doubletree)
25	Shanghai Terrace (Peninsula)

LATE DINING

26	Avec
	Kuma's Corner
	Gibsons
24	Coast Sushi/South Coast
	Ai Sushi
	Itto Sushi*

LIVE ENTERTAINMENT

25	Chicago Chop
24	Catch 35
	Smoke Daddy
23	Nacional 27
22	Uncommon Ground

MEET FOR A DRINK

26	Joe's Sea/Steak
	Gibsons
25	Publican
24	Japonais
	Nine Steak

PEOPLE-WATCHING

27	Blackbird
	Naha
	MK
26	Avec
–	Girl & The Goat

WINNING WINE LISTS

29	Les Nomades
	Alinea
28	Arun's
	Topolobampo
	Michael

WORTH A TRIP

28	Michael | Winnetka
	Tallgrass | Lockport
27	Oceanique | Evanston
	Carlos' | Highland Park
	Vie | Western Springs
26	Le Titi/Paris | Arlington Hts.
25	Barrington Country | Barrington
	Campagnola | Evanston

Vote at ZAGAT.com

BY LOCATION

ANDERSONVILLE/ EDGEWATER

25 M Henry/Henrietta
Anteprima
23 Ethiopian Diamond
Hopleaf
Jin Ju

BUCKTOWN

26 Takashi
24 Coast Sushi
Hot Chocolate
Le Bouchon
23 Bristol

CHINATOWN

24 Lao
23 Phoenix
Emperor's Choice
Al's Beef
21 Three Happiness

GOLD COAST

27 Spiaggia
Seasons
26 Morton's
Gibsons
25 Café Spiaggia

GREEKTOWN

23 Giordano's
22 Artopolis
21 Parthenon
Santorini
Roditys

LAKEVIEW

26 Mia Francesca
25 Yoshi's Café
Mixteco Grill
Sola
24 Tango Sur

LINCOLN PARK

29 Alinea
27 Charlie Trotter's
Riccardo
25 Boka
North Pond

LINCOLN SQUARE/ UPTOWN

25 Bistro Campagne
24 Agami

23 Pizza D.O.C.
Marigold
Tank Sushi

LITTLE ITALY

24 Chez Joël
23 Al's Beef
22 Francesca's
Rosebud
Tuscany

LOOP

27 Everest
26 Morton's
25 Rosebud Prime
24 Catch 35
Palm

RIVER NORTH

28 Topolobampo
27 Naha
Frontera Grill
26 Joe's Sea/Steak
Avenues

STREETERVILLE

29 Les Nomades
28 Tru
25 Capital Grille
Rosebud Steak
24 Emilio's Tapas

SUBURBS

28 Michael
Tallgrass
27 Oceanique
Carlos'
Vie

WEST LOOP

27 Blackbird
Sushi Wabi
Moto
26 Avec
One Sixtyblue

WICKER PARK

29 Schwa
25 Mirai Sushi
24 Smoke Daddy
Bongo Room
Bob San

Top Decor

28 L2O	Vie
Shanghai Terrace	33 Club
	Nine Steak
27 Avenues	Café/Architectes
Alinea	
Sixteen	24 Mercat
Les Nomades	Il Mulino
Tru	Naha
Everest	Sunda
Spiaggia	Alhambra Palace
	SushiSamba Rio*
26 Signature Room	Zealous*
North Pond	Topolobampo
Cibo Matto	Atwood Cafe
Japonais	One Sixtyblue
RL	Capital Grille
Carlos'	Zed 451
	MK
25 Carnivale	Le Titi/Paris
Seasons	Sepia
Charlie Trotter's	
Le Colonial	23 Custom House
Lovells/Lake Forest	

OUTDOORS

Athena	Park Grill
Big Star	Piccolo Sogno
Fulton's	Purple Pig
Japonais	Shanghai Terrace
Mia Francesca	Smith & Wollensky

ROMANCE

Cibo Matto	Japonais
Everest	Le Colonial
Geja's Cafe	Les Nomades
Henri	Maude's Liquor Bar
Il Mulino	Sunda

ROOMS

Alinea	Next
Henri	Paris Club
Mastro's Steak	Ria
Maude's Liquor Bar	Sixteen
Mercat	Terzo Piano

VIEWS

Everest	Signature Room
North Pond	Sixteen
Park Grill	Smith & Wollensky
Riva	Spiaggia
Shanghai Terrace	Terzo Piano

Top Service

<u>28</u> Alinea
Les Nomades
Tru
Vie

<u>27</u> L2O
Carlos'
Moto
Arun's
Shanghai Terrace
Charlie Trotter's
Oceanique
Everest
Avenues
Michael
Spiaggia
Seasons

<u>26</u> Topolobampo
MK

<u>25</u> Naha
Gabriel's

Blackbird
Le Titi/Paris
Crofton on Wells
Bonsoirée
Capital Grille
A Tavola
Adelle's
Joe's Sea/Steak
Morton's
One Sixtyblue
Schwa
Yoshi's Café
Custom House
Café Spiaggia
Barrington Country
Boka

<u>24</u> Tallgrass
Cafe Central
Fogo de Chão
Green Zebra

Best Buys

In order of Bang for the Buck rating.

1. Superdawg
2. Hot Doug's
3. Margie's Candies
4. Potbelly Sandwich
5. Wiener's Circle
6. 90 Miles
7. Al's Beef
8. Mr. Beef
9. Hannah's Bretzel
10. Pita Inn
11. Five Guys
12. Gold Coast Dogs
13. Epic Burger
14. Belly Shack
15. Yolk
16. Billy Goat Tavern
17. Julius Meinl
18. Aurelio's
19. Lou Mitchell's
20. Original/Walker Pancake
21. Art of Pizza
22. Breakfast Club
23. M Henry/Henrietta
24. Penny's Noodle
25. Pompei Pizza
26. Ann Sather
27. Artopolis
28. Toast
29. Bongo Room
30. Xoco
31. Nookies
32. Milk & Honey
33. Irazu
34. Hamburger Mary's
35. Counter
36. Kuma's Corner
37. Kitsch'n
38. Aladdin's Eatery
39. DMK Burger
40. Piece

OTHER GOOD VALUES

Andies
Bagel
Ba Le Sandwich
Birchwood Kitchen
Chicago Diner
Chicago Pizza/Oven
Chickpea
Crêpe Crave
Depot
Edzo's
Frances' Deli
Hot Woks
Icosium
Joy Yee
Kroll's
Las Tablas
Leo's Coney Island
Lou Malnati's
Maiz
Nosh
Old Oak Tap
Orange
Over Easy
Pasta Palazzo
Perry's Deli
Phò Xe Tång
Pomegranate
Reza's
Roti
Russell's BBQ
Smak-Tak
Smoque BBQ
Taco Fuego
Tango Sur
Thai Classic
Tre Kronor
Tweet
Victory's Banner
Vito & Nick's
Wishbone

Vote at ZAGAT.com

CHICAGO
RESTAURANT
DIRECTORY

Abigail's 🅈Ⓜ *American*

24 | 20 | 19 | $40

Highland Park | 493 Roger Williams Ave. (St. Johns Ave.) | 847-849-1009 | www.abigails493.com

"Surprisingly fresh and interesting" fare displaying "some actual risks being taken" lures North Suburbanites to this "reasonably priced" seasonal New American "hot spot" in Highland Park; the "small space" results in "crowds" (summer sidewalk tables help) and some say the "terrible acoustics" make it "too noisy to digest" – but friends note "they're working on it."

NEW Abiquiù Cafe 🅈Ⓜ *New Mexican*

- | - | - | I

Lakeview | 1034 W. Belmont Ave. (Kenmore Ave.) | 773-577-3917 | www.abiquiucafe.com

At this affordable Lakeview BYO, expect New Mexican fare such as enchiladas, tamales, chiles rellenos and daily specials; the intimate setting features a desert-and-turquoise color scheme, evocative artwork, a beehive fireplace and seasonal outdoor dining.

NEW A 'Cappella Bistro *American*

- | - | - | I

South Loop | 1301 S. Michigan Ave. (13th St.) | 312-922-0600 | www.acappellabistro.com

This BYO neighborhood bistro hopes to harmonize with the South Loop with its menu of unpretentious, affordable American comfort food – think flatbread pizzas, breakfast classics, lunchtime sandwiches and a Sunday brunch buffet (it also makes custom cakes); the cozy setting is dressed up in green and earth tones with well-spaced tables, soft lighting and traditional artwork.

Accanto *Italian*

- | - | - | E

Logan Square | 2171 N. Milwaukee Ave. (Talman Ave.) | 773-227-2727 | www.accanto-chicago.com

Respected Milan-born chef Domenico Acampora oversees the contemporary, fusion-style Italian menu at this destination-dining (read: expensive) spot in Logan Square; the modern, intimate milieu is done up in sophisticated neutral tones, and also features leather seating, rustic wood beams and stainless dome light fixtures.

NEW Ace Bar *Burgers*

- | - | - | I

Lincoln Park | 1505 W. Fullerton Ave. (bet. Bosworth & Greenview Aves.) | 312-970-1505

A bountiful burger menu – 20 preps, nine proteins – plus a craft beer selection boost this Lincoln Park bar above its wings 'n' nachos brethren; leather booths, a vintage bar, live music (the wall of speakers promises big sound) and low prices help fuel the party vibe; P.S. it serves lunch on weekends.

NEW Acre ● *Pub Food*

- | - | - | M

(fka Charlie's Ale House)

Andersonville | 5308 N. Clark St. (bet. Berwyn & Summerdale Aves.) | 773-334-7600 | www.acrerestaurant.com

The former Charlie's Ale House in Andersonville has been transformed by the team behind Anteprima into this farm-focused, seasonal American gastropub serving housemade charcuterie, pasta and breads and wood-grilled specialties in a stylish but cozy dining room with two fireplaces; a separate menu (including lunch) of 'samiches', soups and salads is served in the Tap Room, which houses the original booths and bar (expect a craft beer emphasis, along with wines and house cocktails).

NEW Act One Pub Ⓜ American

- | - | - | M

Rogers Park | 1330 W. Morse Ave. (Wayne Ave.) | 773-381-4550 | www.actonepub.com

Jimmy Madla of Coobah (and onetime Veruca Salt drummer) cooks creative American comfort food and regional specialties (including a weekend brunch buffet) in a casual, vintage pub setting in Rogers Park; the wood-on-wood interior includes a massive carved oak bar issuing draft microbrews for a refreshing quaff before or after a music show at the adjacent Mayne Stage (formerly the Morse Theatre).

Adelle's Ⓜ American

25 | 23 | 25 | $42

Wheaton | 1060 College Ave. (bet. President St. & Stoddard Ave.) | 630-784-8015 | www.adelles.com

"Fresh", "consistent", "well-prepared" New American "comfort food with character" woos West Suburbanites to this "quaint" Wheaton "getaway" that's "worth seeking out" "for a special night" ("you'd go twice a week if it weren't as pricey"); additional assets include a "wonderfully accommodating staff" and a "pleasant" ambiance with a gas fireplace when it's cold and "gorgeous outside terrace" "when it's warm"; N.B. there's live jazz most Thursdays.

Adobo Grill Mexican

21 | 19 | 20 | $32

Old Town | 1610 N. Wells St. (North Ave.) | 312-266-7999 | www.adobogrill.com

"Colorful surroundings" add to the "festive atmosphere" at this Old Town favorite that amigos call a "solid choice for upper-scale Mexican" fare with "occasional flashes of wonderful" ("tableside guacamole" and "premium tequila cocktails" are "highlights"); while party-poopers snipe it's "living on reputation", "hand-shaken margaritas" and "easy-to-swallow prices" "are worth the negatives"; P.S. it's "ideally close to Second City", and offers outdoor dining.

Agami Japanese

24 | 23 | 21 | $43

Uptown | 4712 N. Broadway (Leland Ave.) | 773-506-1845 | www.agamisushi.com

"Innovative rolls" are an "unexpected" find in the "restaurant-barren" Uptown location of this "spacious" Japanese "lifesaver" that also pours an "exciting sake" selection amid its "entertaining" "underwater fantasy decor"; while service can be "a bit uneven", it's still "perfect for dinner before a concert at the Green Mill or Riviera."

Ai Sushi Lounge ◑ Japanese

24 | 21 | 20 | $43

River North | 358 W. Ontario St. (Orleans St.) | 312-335-9888 | www.aichicago.us

"Creative sushi" with "beautiful presentations" (plus a "small number of exciting entrees") pair with an "extensive selection of sakes" at this "romantic" River North Japanese from the owners of Ringo and Tsuki; the "knowledgeable" staff and "modern, trendy" decor are pluses – and an improved Food score indicates it "just keeps getting better" – so even if it's a "little pricey", most "would return, especially for drinks in the back lounge" or the "Sunday all-you-can-eat" special.

Aja *Asian*

`- | 22 | 20 | M`

River North | Dana Hotel & Spa | 660 N. State St. (Erie St.) | 312-202-6050 | www.danahotelandspa.com

Changing to a "less-expensive format", the Dana Hotel's former pricey steakhouse is now this midpriced Asian small plates and sushi specialist offering "unique flavor combinations" plus weekend brunch, sakes by the glass and signature cocktails; the bar area's seating includes a communal table, otherwise the "fabulous decor" remains the same – soaring walls of windows, a steel mesh scrim and silk wall treatments plus two gas fireplaces, an outdoor patio and a rooftop lounge – all perfect for "people-watching."

Akai Hana *Japanese*

`21 | 14 | 17 | $28`

Wilmette | 3223 W. Lake Ave. (Skokie Rd.) | 847-251-0384 | www.akaihanasushi.com

"Hidden in a Wilmette strip mall", this "solid" North Suburban "player" serves "straightforward sushi" and Japanese "cooked dishes" ("don't look for gourmet touches, but everything is fresh and tasty") in a "spartan", "kid-friendly" "barn" (the "decor needs some work"); tipsters deem it "dependable" (though not quite the "deal it was"), and though service can be "perfunctory", it's so "popular" there's sometimes a "wait on weekend nights."

Aladdin's Eatery *Mideastern*

`18 | 13 | 18 | $17`

Lincoln Park | 614 W. Diversey Pkwy. (Clark St.) | 773-327-6300 | www.aladdinseatery.com

Along with a "large variety" of "fresh, reliable Middle Eastern fare" including vegetarian dishes, this "casual", "reasonably priced" Lincoln Park outpost of a "popular chain" also offers "fast and efficient" service (plus beer and wine) beneath its pita bread–shaped fixtures; even detractors dubbing it merely "decent" deem it "fine to grab a bite before or after a movie" and "for lunch or takeout."

A La Turka *Turkish*

`20 | 18 | 20 | $27`

Lakeview | 3134 N. Lincoln Ave. (bet. Barry & Belmont Aves.) | 773-935-6101 | www.alaturkachicago.com

Enthusiasts who "have enjoyed" this midpriced Lakeview Turkish "place to eat and be entertained" "for years" are "sure to go" Friday or Saturday "when the belly dancers are there"; the "whimsical", "romantic setting" works "best for a group" or as a "date spot", and though some call it "predictable", it's "charming in its own way."

Al Bawadi Grill *Mideastern*

`- | - | - | M`

Bridgeview | 7216 W. 87th St. (bet. Harlem & Oketo Aves.) | 708-599-1999 | www.albawadigrill.com

This unassuming South Suburban Middle Eastern offers an array of moderately priced, authentic specialties, from eggplant relish and sour pickles to charcoal-fired kebabs and falafel with garlicky *motawma* dip; despite its location in a Bridgeview strip-mall parking lot, it has an *Arabian Nights* vibe, with ornate lanterns and colorful tapestries setting a festive mood that's perfect for groups.

Alhambra Palace Restaurant *Mideastern* 16 | 24 | 16 | $34

West Loop | 1240 W. Randolph St. (bet. Elizabeth St. & Racine Ave.) | 312-666-9555 | www.alhambrapalacerestaurant.com

It's "welcome to the Arabian Nights" for adventurers "entertained" by the Middle Eastern "dinner and a show" at this "over-the-top" West Looper with "fanciful, opulent decor", a "huge menu and por- tions", and a "belly-dancing spectacle" on weekends; faulters find "better and cheaper" chow elsewhere, and gripe that they "cannot service the large space" ("lots of drinks" help); P.S. "diners are in- vited to join in the belly dancing" though "some should decline."

Z Alinea **M** *American* 29 | 27 | 28 | $199

Lincoln Park | 1723 N. Halsted St. (bet. North Ave. & Willow St.) | 312-867-0110 | www.alinearestaurant.com

"World-famous for its vision and creativity", "genius" Grant Achatz's "progressive" New American "gastronirvana" provides "amazing" "avant-garde food" in a "labor-intensive" multicourse "wild ride" that "incorporates all the senses" and includes cleverly "engineered" serving pieces ("acupuncture needles", "trapezes", "pillows", "branches", "rubber tablecloths"); *Get Smart* automatic doors" give way to the "luxurious, minimalistic" Lincoln Park setting where a "professional" staff (rated No. 1 for Service) provides "per- sonal" attention "with some humor", completing an "unforgetta- ble", "shock-and-awe experience" – albeit a "fiscally challenging" one that's "not for the faint of culinary heart"; P.S. "if you can afford it", choose the "incredible wine pairings."

Al Primo Canto *Brazilian/Italian* 24 | 23 | 25 | $40

River North | 749 N. Clark St. (bet. Chicago Ave. & Superior St.) | 312-280-9090
Northwest Side | 5414 W. Devon Ave. (Central Ave.) | 773-631-0100 **M**
www.alprimocanto.com

"Brazilian meets Italian in an unlikely setting" at this "friendly", "family-run" Northwest Side spot (with a River North sibling) where specialties such as rotisserie chicken are a "deal"; "old-world service" operates under a domed wooden ceiling in a "huge room" that's "a bit too noisy at times" – especially when the "live music" kicks up on Fridays and Saturdays; P.S. an à la carte menu has been added.

Z Al's Beef *Sandwiches* 23 | 9 | 17 | $11

NEW Loop | 28 E. Jackson Blvd. (bet. State St. & Wabash Ave.) | 312-461-9292
NEW Loop | 601 W. Adams St. (Jefferson St.) | 312-559-2333
River North | 169 W. Ontario St. (Wells St.) | 312-943-3222 ☻
NEW Wrigleyville | 3420 N. Clark St. (Sheffield Ave.) | 773-935-2333 ☻
Chinatown | 5441 S. Wentworth Ave. (Garfield Blvd.) | 773-373-4700 ☻

(continued)

(continued)

Al's Beef

Little Italy/University Village | 1079 W. Taylor St. (Aberdeen St.) | 312-226-4017 ⬛⇥
Niles | 5948 W. Touhy Ave. (Lehigh Ave.) | 847-647-1577
Park Ridge | 1036 W. Higgins Rd. (Cumberland Ave.) | 847-825-2345
Chicago Heights | 551 W. 14th St. (Division St.) | 708-748-2333
Tinley Park | 7132 183rd St. (Harlem Ave.) | 708-444-2333
www.alsbeef.com
Additional locations throughout the Chicago area

"Get it dipped with hot peppers, eat, repeat" instruct devotees of the Windy City's "champ of beef on a bun", a "cheap and fast" chain also prized for "sausage sandwiches", "fabulous" "hand-cut french fries" and "classic Chicago dogs"; though locations vary, overall they leave chompers cheering for their "messy, sloppy, fabulous" eats and advising "if you want decor, take it home with you."

Amber Cafe ⬛Ⓜ *American*   22 | 20 | 20 | $41

Westmont | 13 N. Cass Ave. (Burlington Ave.) | 630-515-8080 | www.ambercafe.net

Westmont's "snazzy" "local spot for fish" and more presents "an interesting twist on New American" while offering "quality" fare and service in a woody, brick-walled setting; though "often crowded" and "perhaps a bit overpriced", it's a "reasonable choice" that devotees dub "among the best" in the area; P.S. the "outside is hopping in the summertime" for cocktails and "alfresco dining."

American Girl Place Cafe *American*   16 | 22 | 21 | $29

Streeterville | American Girl Place, Water Tower Place Mall | 835 N. Michigan Ave. (bet. Chestnut & Pearson Sts.) | 312-943-9400 | www.americangirlplace.com

"Take your little girl and her favorite doll" to Streeterville's "charming" "fairyland" where each "gets their own place setting" for a "tea" of "dainty sweets and sandwiches"; service is "efficient", but some "squealing" and merely "decent" fare are to be expected, and if it's a bit "pricey", just "watch the delight in the kids' eyes."

Amitabul ⬛Ⓜ *Korean*   21 | 11 | 19 | $21

Northwest Side | 6207 N. Milwaukee Ave. (Huntington St.) | 773-774-0276 | www.amitabulvegan.com

"Unique" "vegan fusion" fare is dished out at this BYO Northwest Side Korean that "operates under a spiritual [Buddhist] theme" while delivering "mammoth portions" of "fresh", affordable organic eats with "fast service"; some snipe the "extremely casual" space is "quite uninviting", and a few earnest omnivores who "want to like it" "find it wanting", but all agree it's a "must try for vegetarians."

Andalous *Moroccan*   22 | 17 | 20 | $23

Lakeview | 3307 N. Clark St. (Aldine Ave.) | 773-281-6885 | www.andalous.com

"Terrific" tagines meet up with a smattering of Spanish and Middle Eastern–accented specialties at this Lakeview Moroccan, also beloved for its wallet-friendly BYO policy; fans find it a refreshing "change from the ordinary", with "welcoming", if occasionally "slow", service, and a lively, artifact-decked interior completing the package.

Andies *Mediterranean/Mideastern*

18 | 15 | 18 | $22

Andersonville | 5253 N. Clark St. (Berwyn Ave.) | 773-784-8616
Ravenswood | 1467 W. Montrose Ave. (Greenview Ave.) |
773-348-0654
www.andiesres.com

"Reliable" is the word on these "friendly" "neighborhood" twins in Andersonville and Ravenswood turning out "tasty" Middle Eastern and Mediterranean eats, with plenty of vegetarian options; though some find the fare "nothing to write home about", both earn kudos for their "cheap" tabs and "quick" service, as well as a "casual" atmosphere kicked up by patio seating that's especially pleasant in "summer."

Angelina Ristorante *Italian*

21 | 19 | 21 | $30

Lakeview | 3561 N. Broadway (Addison St.) | 773-935-5933 |
www.angelinaristorante.com

A "charming" stop on the Lakeview dining circuit, this longtime "favorite" "holds up well" what with its "authentic" Southern Italian cuisine served in a "quaint" candlelit interior; "bargain prices" sweeten the deal, as do weeknight specials like Monday's half price wine and Wednesday's locals' discount.

Angin Mamiri Ⓜ *Indonesian*

- | - | - | I

West Rogers Park | 2739 W. Touhy Ave. (bet. California &
Washtenaw Aves.) | 773-262-6646 | www.anginmamirichicago.com

"If you're jonesing for Jakarta", this inexpensive West Rogers Parker "fills the bill" with "authentic" Indonesian delicacies like sates, curries and gado gado; the pale-green space doesn't offer much in the way of atmosphere, so "bring some friends" to liven things up, and bring a bottle too, as it's BYO.

Anna Maria Pasteria *Italian*

24 | 17 | 22 | $31

Ravenswood | 4400 N. Clark St. (Montrose Ave.) | 773-506-2662 |
www.annamariapasteria.com

"Just what you want" in a "neighborhood" restaurant, this Ravenswood entry charms guests with "excellent" takes on "traditional" Italian recipes; the "warm" atmosphere is helped along by modest tabs, Tuscan-style furnishings and a "friendly" staff that "makes you feel at home."

Ann Sather *American/Swedish*

21 | 15 | 20 | $18

Andersonville | 5207 N. Clark St. (Foster Ave.) | 773-271-6677
Lakeview | 909 W. Belmont Ave. (Clark St.) | 773-348-2378

Ann Sather Café *American/Swedish*

Lakeview | 3411 N. Broadway (Roscoe St.) | 773-305-0024
Lakeview | 3416 N. Southport Ave. (Roscoe St.) | 773-404-4475
www.annsather.com

A Chicago brunchtime "icon", this "bustling" daytime chainlet is famed for its "addictive", "ooey gooey" cinnamon buns that kick off "huge" helpings of "fantastically caloric" Swedish-American "comfort food"; even if some score the sustenance "pedestrian", it remains an area "standby", with "prompt" service and "reasonable" tabs making the perpetual "waits" on weekends easier to stomach.

Anteprima *Italian*

25 | 19 | 22 | $38

Andersonville | 5316 N. Clark St. (bet. Berwyn & Summerdale Aves.) | 773-506-9990 | www.anteprimachicago.net

"Inspired" Italian cooking with a "farm-to-table" bent awaits at this "destination"-worthy Andersonville "treasure", also cherished for its "outstanding", "affordable" stash of wines; "crowds" are a regular occurrence, but a "knowledgeable" staff keeps the mood "homey" no matter how "cramped" and "noisy" it gets.

Antica Pizzeria *Pizza*

23 | 15 | 22 | $25

Andersonville | 5663 N. Clark St. (Hollywood Ave.) | 773-944-1492 | www.anticapizzeriachicago.com

"Delicious", "thin-crust" "Neapolitan-style" pizzas transport you right "back to Italy" at this Andersonville BYO also pumping out "well-made" pastas, salads and such at "great-value" tabs; it's not fancy, but the "small", rustic space is made more "cozy" by a wood-burning oven and an affable owner chock-full of "old-world charm."

NEW Antico *Italian*

- | - | - | M

Bucktown | 1946 N. Leavitt St. (Armitage Ave.) | 773-489-4895 | www.anticochicago.com

At this Euro-style Bucktown cafe, hearty Italian fare made with fresh ingredients (there's a seasonal kitchen garden) includes house-made salumi and gnocchi three ways; there's also house-roasted coffee, a Boot-focused wine list and warm modern digs with wood floors and tables, industrial ductwork and seasonal outdoor seating.

Antico Posto *Italian*

22 | 20 | 21 | $30

Oak Brook | Oakbrook Center Mall | 118 Oakbrook Ctr. (Rte. 83) | 630-586-9200 | www.leye.com

Weary shoppers rely on this "suburban" Italian outpost in the Oakbrook Center, a "relaxing find" for an "eclectic" array of well-priced wines, pastas and other "consistently good" nibbles capped by housemade gelato; if "nothing's ever bad", it's "not ever outstanding" either, though it works for a "reliable" bite at the mall.

NEW Aquitaine *American/French*

- | - | - | M

Lincoln Park | 2221 N. Lincoln Ave. (bet. Belden & Webster Aves.) | 773-698-8456 | www.aquitainerestaurant.com

Seasonal American-French bistro fare featuring local ingredients at moderate prices – plus full bar service including a handpicked wine list focused on small producers – finds a home at this cozy Lincoln Parker; the quaint setting boasts traditional wallpaper and white table-cloths, and the front windows open onto the street in warm weather.

NEW Arami Ⓜ *Japanese*

- | - | - | M

West Town | 1829 W. Chicago Ave. (bet. Wolcott Ave. & Wood St.) | 312-243-1535 | www.aramichicago.com

Two brothers and a pedigreed Asian sushi chef are behind this dinner-only West Town Japanese with a straightforward, midpriced menu of cold and hot apps, nigiri and maki (along with an omakase option at the sushi bar); the serene setting features moss gardens in the front windows, an atrium dining room with stands of fresh bamboo outside the windows and a mural of a Japanese landscape.

NEW Ara On 🖂 Asian

- - - M

Loop | 190 S. LaSalle Bldg. | 160 W. Adams St. (LaSalle St.) | 312-781-7300 | www.ara-on.com

If you seek chic Asian cuisine (Japanese, Korean, banh mi, sushi and more) in the Loop, consider this swanky, midpriced arrival in the former home of Shikago; the vast, striking space includes a sushi bar that's claimed to be the city's longest, and there's also a lounge, outdoor seating, seductive low lighting and plasma TVs.

Aria Asian

24 23 23 $53

Loop | Fairmont Chicago Hotel | 200 N. Columbus Dr. (bet. Randolph St. & Wacker Dr.) | 312-444-9494 | www.ariachicago.com

"They strive for excellence and it shows" at this "upscale" enclave "hidden inside" the Loop's Fairmont Hotel and turning out "excellent", "innovative" Asian cuisine with a focus on fine sushi; the "sophisticated" surroundings make it a natural for "business lunches", and the "pricey" tabs mean it's "best on an expense account."

Aroy Thai

- - - I

Lincoln Square | 4654 N. Damen Ave. (bet. Eastwood & Leland Aves.) | 773-275-8360

This humble Lincoln Square venture from a Siam Noodle vet pleases locals with its BYO policy and affordable Thai classics; but it's the pungent Thai-language-menu offerings and its location steps from the Brown Line that lure expats and adventurous culinari to the 'hood.

Art of Pizza Pizza

22 7 15 $13

Lakeview | 3033 N. Ashland Ave. (Nelson St.) | 773-327-5600

Patrons choose from "mouthwatering" "slices or full pizzas" ("deepdish, thin-crust or in-between") at this "reasonably priced", "laidback" Lakeview "self-serve", where fans swear "some of the best" pie is served; those deeming the "zero ambiance" "painful" simply "fly in and fly out" – while a few wonder "what all the fuss is about."

Artopolis ❶ Greek/Mediterranean

22 20 17 $19

Greektown | 306 S. Halsted St. (Jackson Blvd.) | 312-559-9000 | www.artopolischicago.com

Regulars "relax" over "wonderful" breads, "satisfying" salads, sandwiches and "fresh-baked" pastries at this "casual" Greektown purveyor of "affordable" Hellenic-Med eats; occasionally "haphazard" service is a drawback, but it's open into the wee hours, making it well suited for a "late-night" bite.

❷ Arun's 🅜 Thai

28 23 27 $96

Northwest Side | 4156 N. Kedzie Ave. (bet. Irving Park Rd. & Montrose Ave.) | 773-539-1909 | www.arunsthai.com

"Who says Thai can't be upscale?" ask admirers of Arun Sampanthavivat's "unforgettable" Northwest Side jewel where a

	FOOD	DECOR	SERVICE	COST

"top-notch" staff rolls out "exquisite" prix fixe meals composed of "unusual", "delicious little dishes" that "just keep on coming"; it's set in "simple" digs, although more than a few "wish they'd upgrade the space" to match the "splurge"-worthy prices.

☒ A Tavola ☒ Italian `26` `20` `25` `$44`

Ukrainian Village | 2148 W. Chicago Ave. (bet. Hoyne Ave. & Leavitt St.) | 773-276-7567 | www.atavolachicago.com

It's "like eating at someone's home" at this "wonderfully cozy" Ukrainian Village "gem" turning out "fabulous" Northern Italian dishes including some "amazing" gnocchi ("like eating a cloud"); "reasonable" prices and "attentive" service suit the overall "low-key" vibe, and there's also a "lovely" patio in summer.

Athena ◑ Greek `21` `19` `20` `$32`

Greektown | 212 S. Halsted St. (Adams St.) | 312-655-0000 | www.athenarestaurantchicago.com

Amid a gaggle of Greektown eateries, this "family-owned" Hellenic stands out for its "authentic" eats served on a "lush", landscaped patio in summer; inside sports two fireplaces, lots of candles and a bustling bar so you can really "eat well" here for cheap any time of year.

Atwater's American/French `20` `22` `21` `$44`

Geneva | Herrington Inn | 15 S. River Ln. (State St.) | 630-208-7433 | www.herringtoninn.com

Guests laud this "romantic" respite in the Herrington Inn with a "cozy, old-fashioned" feel and linen-topped tables overlooking the Fox River; even if the tasty" New American–French menu is "not too adventurous" (and on the pricey side to boot), it offers loads of "choices" for diners, and service sometimes "shines" too.

Atwood Cafe American `22` `24` `22` `$39`

Loop | Hotel Burnham | 1 W. Washington St. (State St.) | 312-368-1900 | www.atwoodcafe.com

"Comforting" Traditional American fare including Sunday brunch (and holiday season tea service) befits the Loop's "beautifully restored" "historic" Hotel Burnham, where the "quirky", "whimsical decor" "feels old-Chicago and very now all at once"; "shoppers", "theater or CSO" patrons and "hotel guests" fill the "odd chairs" (which some find "uncomfortable") while dining on midpriced fare with service that's "gracious" but "inconsistent"; P.S. a chef change is not reflected in the Food score.

Aurelio's Pizza Pizza `23` `15` `20` `$17`

Loop | Holiday Inn Chicago Downtown | 506 W. Harrison St. (Canal St.) | 312-994-2000

Addison | Centennial Plaza | 1455 W. Lake St. (Lombard Rd.) | 630-889-9560

Chicago Heights | 1545 Western Ave. (15th St.) | 708-481-5040
Homewood | 18162 Harwood Ave. (183rd St.) | 708-798-8050
South Holland | 601 E. 170th St. (Park Ave.) | 708-333-0310
Palos Heights | 6543 W. 127th St. (Ridgeland Ave.) | 708-389-5170

(continued)

Aurelio's Pizza

Tinley Park | 15901 Oak Park Ave. (Rte. 6) | 708-429-4600
Downers Grove | 940 Warren Ave. (Highland Ave.) | 630-810-0078
Naperville | 931 W. 75th St. (Plainfield-Naperville Rd.) |
630-369-0077
Oak Brook | 100 E. Roosevelt Rd. (Summit Rd.) | 630-629-3200
www.aureliospizza.com
Additional locations throughout the Chicago area

"Real no-nonsense pizza" at these wallet-loving South Suburban "joints" is "a religion" to disciples who "remember" "growing up with" the "sweet and tangy sauce" of the "killer" "thin-crust, deep-dish and individual" pies; service is "friendly and efficient" and there's a "basic", "family-oriented" feel to some, but the Homewood "original" really seems "like home" to regulars who ask for their order "baked in the old oven" for optimal "crispness"; P.S. some of the franchised locations are pickup and delivery only.

☑ Avec ◐ *Mediterranean*

26 | 21 | 23 | $44

West Loop | 615 W. Randolph St. (Jefferson St.) | 312-377-2002 | www.avecrestaurant.com

Blackbird's vino-focused "casual yet classy" next-door cafe is a West Loop "chef hangout" where surveyors say Koren Grieveson's "imaginative", "chef-driven" Mediterranean small plates and "gourmet charcuterie" feature "flavor combinations that make you rethink life"; while some who "wish the prices were as minimal as the portions" "could do without cuddling up to a stranger" in the "uncomfortable", "communal" setting reminiscent of a "Swedish sauna", "extroverts" "squeeze in and have a ball" with "wonderful wine experiences" prompted by "savvy servers."

☑ Avenues ⌧Ⓜ *American*

26 | 27 | 27 | $102

River North | Peninsula Hotel | 108 E. Superior St. (bet. Michigan Ave. & Rush St.) | 312-573-6754 | www.peninsula.com/chicago

Curtis Duffy's "superb, creative" New American "cuisine with artful design and surprising flavor combinations" meets "sublime service" in the "beautifully serene atmosphere" of the Peninsula Hotel's "formal" dining room at this "understated, elegant" River North "special-occasion" place; an "excellent view" featuring the historic Water Tower and "impressive wine list" add to an "experience" that's "simply stunning" and "tremendously expensive."

NEW Aviary, The ⌧Ⓜ *Eclectic*

− | − | − | E

West Loop | 955 W. Fulton Mkt. (bet. Morgan & Sangamon Sts.) | 312-226-0868

Taking flight adjacent to sister restaurant Next, Grant Achatz's swanky bar/lounge makes an artful science out of eye-popping presentations, from the inventive molecular cocktails to the edgy, Alinea-inspired single bites of Eclectic fare; the airy West Loop setting features modern torchère lighting, undulating banquettes that form an operatic sea of waves and a standing area near the open kitchen.

	FOOD	DECOR	SERVICE	COST

NEW Awash Ethiopian Restaurant *Ethiopian*

| - | - | - | I |

Edgewater | 6322 N. Broadway (bet. Devon & Rosemont Aves.) | 773-274-0784 | awashethiopian.angelfire.com

This utensil-free Edgewater eatery serves inexpensive Ethiopian eats (it's named for one of that country's major rivers), delivered via covered basket trays in a setting dressed up with bright-green walls, charcoal portraits and elaborately carved wood chairs; it also serves house juices and grain-based nonalcoholic drinks.

Azucar ◑Ⓜ *Spanish*

| ▽ 22 | 18 | 20 | $42 |

Logan Square | 2647 N. Kedzie Ave. (Milwaukee Ave.) | 773-486-6464 | www.azucartapasrestaurant.com

Raters "run to this" "tiny" Logan Square "treasure" for "fresh, inventive and lovingly prepared" if slightly "pricey" Spanish tapas with "big flavor" and specialty drinks wielded by a "warm staff"; P.S. there's also late-night service (till 2 AM on weekends) and sidewalk seating.

Bacchanalia ⌷ *Italian*

| 24 | 16 | 23 | $33 |

Southwest Side | 2413 S. Oakley Ave. (bet. 24th & 25th Sts.) | 773-254-6555 | www.bacchanaliainchicago.com

"True" "homestyle Italian" earns enthusiasts for this "old-school" Southwest Side "favorite" with a "menu selection from North to South" of "simple", "refreshing" fare; tables are "packed in tightly" under the big mural of Bacchus, but "fair prices" for generous portions and "warm welcomes" make fans "feel like family"; P.S. it's convenient "before or after White Sox games."

Bacino's *Italian*

| 22 | 15 | 19 | $25 |

Lincoln Park | 2204 N. Lincoln Ave. (Webster Ave.) | 773-472-7400
West Loop | 118 S. Clinton St. (Adams St.) | 312-876-1188 Ⓢ
www.bacinos.com

Bella Bacino's *Italian*

Loop | 75 E. Wacker Dr. (Upper Michigan Ave.) | 312-263-2350
La Grange | 36 S. La Grange Rd. (Harris Ave.) | 708-352-8882 Ⓜ
www.bellabacinos.com

"Loyal"-ists "keep going back" to this "casual", "friendly" and affordable Italian quartet that's a "dependable" choice for "delicious deep-dish", thin-crust and "personal"-size pizzas; though some dub them "ordinary", most find them "perfect" "for large groups with children"; P.S. the Bellas "concentrate more on pasta and 'fancier' fare", with a "good wine selection for this sort of eatery."

Bad Apple *Pub Food*

| - | - | - | I |

North Center/St. Ben's | 4300 N. Lincoln Ave. (Cullom Ave.) | 773-360-8406 | www.badapplebar.com

Brew-themed pub fare – think a beer-can chicken sandwich and steak frites with 'beer-naise' – pairs with an extensive draft and bottle selection, plus funky cocktails, at this North Center spot; set in a vintage corner brick-and-stone building, it boasts jewel-toned walls, glowing globe lighting, stained glass, a tin ceiling with fans over the bar area and shady sidewalk dining in season.

Bagel, The Deli

| | 19 | 12 | 18 | $18 |

Lakeview | 3107 N. Broadway (Belmont Ave.) | 773-477-0300
Skokie | Westfield Shoppingtown | 4999 Old Orchard Ctr. (Skokie Blvd.) |
847-677-0100
www.bagelrestaurant.com

Among "the few genuine delis left" in Chicago, these Skokie and Lakeview contenders "fill a need" "when you're hankering for a shmear" and other "old-time favorites" like "chopped liver, gefilte fish and chocolate phosphates" ("free pickles don't hurt either"); "witty servers", "matzo ball soup that heals all ills" and "comically large portions" for which the "price is right" find more fans than foes, so just "ignore" the "time-warp decor."

Bakin' & Eggs American

| | 19 | 21 | 18 | $16 |

Lakeview | 3120 N. Lincoln Ave. (bet. Barry & Belmont Aves.) |
773-525-7005 | www.bakinandeggschicago.com

Lakeview's "upscale" American diner with "modernistic decor" featuring "bright turquoise walls" and reclaimed church pews projects a "lively", "youthful feel" and lives up to its name with "inventive", "well-flavored egg dishes" and a "bacon flight", plus a "bakery and espresso counter"; even those joking it "needs a few more minutes in the oven" acknowledge it has "a lot of potential"; P.S. it's BYO and closes at 3 PM daily with weekends offering brunch-only and lunch served weekdays.

Ba Le Sandwich &

Bakery Sandwiches/Vietnamese

| | - | - | - | I |

Uptown | 5014 N. Broadway (bet. Argyle St. & Winnemac Ave.) |
773-561-4424 | www.balesandwich.com

French-inspired Vietnamese banh mi sandwiches, spring rolls and pastries are washed down with exotic smoothies and *chè* (a sweet dessert beverage made with seeds, beans and other ingredients) at this inexpensive Uptown quick-serve; the glass-enclosed digs have a modern, industrial vibe, with menus on giant screens, an open kitchen and a handful of space-age molded tables and chairs; P.S. there's no alcohol, but there is free WiFi.

Balsan European

| | - | - | - | E |

Gold Coast | The Elysian | 11 E. Walton St. (bet. Rush & State Sts.) |
312-646-1400 | www.balsanrestaurant.com

"Upscale" yet "informal", this Modern European bistro in the Gold Coast's "stunning Elysian hotel" provides "pricey", "refined rustic" fare (including charcuterie, raw bar items and "tarte flambé almost too good to be true") with "sharp service" amid "chic decor" recalling 1920s Paris; surveyors suggest it's "way better than it needs to be", drawing a "hip and interesting crowd" while also offering a late-night menu and weekend brunch; P.S. Sunday supper is a prix fixe bargain.

Bandera American

| | 22 | 20 | 20 | $35 |

Streeterville | 535 N. Michigan Ave., 2nd fl. (bet. Grand Ave. & Ohio St.) |
312-644-3524 | www.hillstone.com

Southwestern-style American "comfort food" with "just enough of a twist" meets "attentive service without the 'tude" at this Streeterville "oasis" that fans claim "sets the standard for chain" links; a "limited menu" that's "a little pricey" is trumped by "live nightly jazz" and "low lighting", creating a "cozy, warm atmosphere" and making it "so worth it"; P.S. "get there early for a window seat" "overlooking the Magnificent Mile."

NEW Bangers & Lace ● *Pub Food* — | — | — | I

Wicker Park | 1670 W. Division St. (Paulina St.) | 773-252-6499 | www.bangersandlacechicago.com

Gourmet bangers and brew star at this Wicker Park gastropub offering more than two dozen draft choices, a cicerone (beer sommelier), on-site brewing and 'keggers' shared at a communal table, rounded out with tarted-up snacks like bacon-roasted peanuts, chile corn nuts and even a chocolate-stout float; despite the British overtones in the name, the rustic-modern setting evokes a beer hall–cum-lodge, with brick and stone walls, a long front bar and funky leather sofas.

Bank Lane Bistro ⧄ *American* 23 | 21 | 22 | $45

Lake Forest | 670 N. Bank Ln. (bet. Deerpath Rd. & Market Sq.) | 847-234-8802 | www.banklanebistro.com

Boosters bank on a "well-prepared, thoughtful meal" of "ambitious" New American fare "that mostly meets its mark" and is served by a "pleasant staff" at this North Suburban "quaint little getaway in Lake Forest" complete with a wood-burning oven for fresh bread; though foes find it "overpriced", friends advise "ask for a table on the balcony for a view" of the "historic market square."

Bar Louie ● *Pub Food* 16 | 15 | 16 | $22

NEW O'Hare Area | Holiday Inn Chicago O'Hare Airport | 5615 N. Cumberland Ave. (Bryn Mawr Ave.) | 773-332-8029
Hyde Park | 5500 S. Shore Dr. (55th St.) | 773-363-5300
Printer's Row | 47 W. Polk St. (Dearborn St.) | 312-347-0000
Evanston | 1520 Sherman Ave. (Grove St.) | 847-733-8300
NEW Skokie | Holiday Inn North Shore | 5300 Touhy Ave. (Niles Center Rd.) | 847-763-3056
NEW Mt. Prospect | Holiday Inn Mount Prospect | 200 E. Rand Rd. (Kensington Rd.) | 847-394-3456
Naperville | 22 E. Chicago Ave. (Washington St.) | 630-983-1600
Oak Park | 1122 Lake St. (Harlem Ave.) | 708-725-3300
www.barlouieamerica.com

"Decent" American "bar grub" "without a huge price tag" draws "friends" who "hang out" from lunch to "happy hour" to "late-night" for "people-watching" or "watching sports" at this chain that "always manages to net a good time"; the fare and "service is consistently average", and some who say there are "better local places" only "go for the drinks", which include "excellent" "monster martinis"; N.B. outdoor seating and entertainment vary by location.

⧉ Barrington Country Bistro ⧄ *French* 25 | 23 | 25 | $46

Barrington | Foundry Shopping Ctr. | 718 W. Northwest Hwy. (Hart Rd.) | 847-842-1300 | www.barringtoncountrybistro.com

"It's worth the drive to Barrington" for "French fare better than at pricier" places assure *amis* of this "surprise find" that rates as the "best bistro in the Chicago area"; a "lovely country setting" (despite being "in a shopping mall"), "gracious service" and seasonal "outdoor seating" all contribute to the feeling of "a little slice of France."

Basil Leaf Café *Italian*
18	17	18	$29

Lincoln Park | 2465 N. Clark St. (Fullerton Pkwy.) | 773-935-3388 | www.basilleaf.com

Lincoln Parkers satisfied by this "reliable", "standard neighborhood Italian" cite its "friendly staff", "unpretentious", "rustic-chic" "charm" and "European bistro feel"; the less-smitten call the fare "unimaginative – although there is a lot of it" at "reasonable" prices.

NEW Bauer's Brauhaus ● Ⓜ *German*
-	-	-	M

Palatine | 45 W. Slade St. (bet. Bothwell & Brockway Sts.) | 847-991-1040 | www.bauersbrauhaus.com

This Palatine arrival slings midpriced German fare (sauerbraten and schnitzel, sausages and liver-dumpling soup), plus American bar food (soft pretzels, fried pickles and cheese curds) and über-hearty breakfasts; the cozy tavern setting boasts traditional elements like a tin ceiling, wood pillars with carved heads, servers in risqué costumes and a hand-carved wood bar outfitted with numerous handles of Teutonic brews.

NEW Bedford, The Ⓢ *American*
-	-	-	M

Wicker Park | 1612 W. Division St. (Ashland Ave.) | 773-235-8800 | www.bedfordchicago.com

Mark Steuer (ex Hot Chocolate, The Gage) pairs artisanal American eats inspired by the Midwest with local beers, boutique wines and craft cocktails at his midpriced Wicker Parker that also serves a lighter menu for late-night weekend munching; set in a former bank, it boasts design touches such as elaborate terrazzo floors, the original vault, a wall of fireplaces and safe deposit boxes surrounding sofas in the lounge.

Bella Notte *Italian*
21	16	21	$35

Noble Square | 1374 W. Grand Ave. (Noble St.) | 312-733-5136 | www.bellanottechicago.com

"Be prepared to share or to have lots of leftovers", because the "solid", midpriced "traditional" Southern Italian dishes come in "enormous portions" at this "lively", "family-owned" Noble Square spot that lures the faithful "off the beaten path" (especially "before United Center games"); the mahogany-accented setting is "relaxing" with "attentive service", just "don't bring a crowd on a Saturday night."

Belly Shack Ⓜ *Asian*
23	16	18	$16

Humboldt Park | 1912 N. Western Ave. (Homer St.) | 773-252-1414 | www.bellyshack.com

The "Urban Belly gang" begat this "fast", "zingy" Asian with "Latin-fusion" touches that's "always interesting" ("where else can you get a bulgogi sandwich with an order of tostones") in a "casual, hip" Humboldt Park setting with "industrial decor" that's "gritty on purpose"; "low prices and BYO attract a young crowd" – as if "soft-serve ice cream" isn't "reason enough."

	FOOD	DECOR	SERVICE	COST

Benihana *Japanese/Steak* 18 | 18 | 20 | $36

Wheeling | 150 N. Milwaukee Ave. (Dundee Rd.) | 847-465-6021
Schaumburg | 1200 E. Higgins Rd. (bet. Meacham Rd. & National Pkwy.) | 847-995-8201
Lombard | 747 E. Butterfield Rd. (Meyers Rd.) | 630-571-4440
www.benihana.com

"Bring on the onion volcano" clamor customers who count on an "entertaining" "show" for "all ages" at this Japanese steakhouse chain where tableside teppanyaki chefs perform "knife-juggling" feats while delivering "reliable" eats, including sushi and other "updated" items; critics call it "tired", "tacky" and "overpriced", but it's a good place to "take the kids and still have an edible meal."

Benny's Chop House *Steak* - | - | - | E

River North | 444 N. Wabash Ave. (bet. Hubbard & Illinois Sts.) | 312-626-2444 | www.bennyschophouse.com

From the owner of Volare, this upscale steakhouse in River North offers a pricey menu that includes prime beef, seafood and raw-bar selections, the requisite sides and a handful of pastas and lunch sandwiches; the white-tablecloth setting boasts rich, traditional decor with warm lighting, a champagne cart, live piano on weekends and a handsome bar issuing elaborate cocktails and an affordable wine list.

Ben Pao *Chinese* 21 | 22 | 21 | $34

River North | 52 W. Illinois St. (Dearborn St.) | 312-222-1888 | www.benpao.com

Lettuce Entertain You's "upscale" River Norther offers a "carefully thought-out and well-prepared" blend of China's regional cuisines plus "delicious cocktails" amid "soothing", "stylish" "decor that avoids the most hackneyed clichés" with its huge pillars and waterfalls; while some pout about "tourist-friendly" "Americanized" dishes that are "slightly overpriced", others say the "homemade ginger ale" alone is "worth the trip", adding "if you want authentic, go to Chinatown."

NEW Bento Box *Asian* - | - | - | I

Bucktown | 2246 W. Armitage Ave. (bet. Leavitt St. & Oakley Ave.) | 773-278-3932 | www.artisancateringchicago.com

Born of an existing catering outfit, this humble counter-service BYO in Bucktown offers a weekly changing chalkboard menu of affordable mixed Asian fare served in, yes, bento boxes, which can be taken out or enjoyed at a handful of tables; P.S. it's open for lunch and dinner, Wednesday–Saturday only.

Berghoff Restaurant/Cafe  *German* 18 | 16 | 17 | $25

Loop | 17 W. Adams St. (bet. Dearborn & State Sts.) | 312-427-7399
Berghoff Cafe *German*
O'Hare Area | O'Hare Int'l Airport | Concourse C (I-190) | 773-601-9180
www.theberghoff.com

"You can still" "enjoy" a "truncated menu" of "standard German fare" "or choose from more modern (lighter) items" and a "great selection of suds" amid "old-world decor" at this redo of the former

Loop "landmark" ("owned by an actual Berghoff"); "nostalgic" nosh-ers "miss" the "grumpy Teutonic waiters" and contend that this "shadow" of the "historic site" is "banking on the reputation" (and "higher prices", though there is a weekday-only "lunch deal" in the downstairs Cafe); P.S. the O'Hare outpost is "better than most air-port eateries, but not like the real one."

NEW Bia for Mia *Italian*
- | - | - | M

River West | 1147 W. Grand Ave. (bet. May St. & Racine Ave.) | 312-226-0312

Mel Markon (ex Dixie Que) returns to the scene with this vibrant River West Italian offering whacked-out, moderately priced takes on bar bites (Sardinian-style sushi, a toasted spaghetti-topped burger) as well as more classic pasta, pizza and panini-type fare; the art-adorned, purple-and-orange setting makes sense too, once rounds of funky cocktails – including one that promises eternal love – arrive.

Big & Little's 🗷🎏 *Seafood*
- | - | - | I

River North | 939 N. Orleans St. (bet. Oak & Walton Sts.) | 312-943-0000

Former Hell's Kitchen contestant Tony D'Alessandro and partner Gary Strauss lure Near North Side fin fans to this quick-serve, cash-only seafooder for the likes of fresh fish 'n' chips as well as more ambitious eats like crab tostadas, grilled fish tacos and foie gras fries (burgers too); the basic, fluorescent-lit setting is dressed up with little more than yellow walls and counter seating.

Big Bowl *Asian*
20 | 18 | 20 | $25

River North | 60 E. Ohio St. (Rush St.) | 312-951-1888
Gold Coast | 6 E. Cedar St. (State St.) | 312-640-8888
Lincolnshire | 215 Parkway Dr. (Milwaukee Ave.) | 847-808-8880
Schaumburg | 1950 E. Higgins Rd. (Rte. 53) | 847-517-8881
www.bigbowl.com

"Fast and easy" Asian fare with a "contemporary" spin includes "noodles your way" from the "compose-it-yourself stir-fry bar" and other "tasty", "solid performers" at this "busy" sustainable-leaning Lettuce Entertain You chainlet that "satisfies" "families", "groups" and "out-of-town guests"; the "theme" decor is "cute" and the out-lay "can be cost-effective", plus even those who find it "unremark-able" admit "the housemade ginger ale rocks."

Big Jones *Southern*
21 | 19 | 21 | $32

Andersonville | 5347 N. Clark St. (bet. Balmoral & Summerdale Aves.) | 773-275-5725 | www.bigjoneschicago.com

For an "upscale", "coastal" "Southern fix" built around "hospitality, flair" and a "seasonal" menu "without too much fried" fare, survey-ors head to this midpriced Andersonviller that's "devoted to sus-tainable products" served in a room that's airy and contemporary; weekend brunch is "fabulous" (the weekday version offers a smaller menu), so even diners who "don't know if it's authentic" wash it all down with "syrupy sweet tea" and agree it's "never boring"; P.S. it recently added a landscaped outdoor patio.

Big Star ● ⊄ *Mexican*

23 | 17 | 17 | $26

Wicker Park | 1531 N. Damen Ave. (bet. Pierce & Wicker Park Aves.) | 773-235-4039 | www.bigstarchicago.com

"Quality" tacos plus "tequila and whiskey" have surveyors asking "where do I sign up" for this cash-only, budget-loving Wicker Park Mexican from Paul Kahan (Blackbird, The Publican) that's "more of a bar" with "outstanding" fare backing up "unique cocktails" and "minimalist decor"; it's "consistently packed" and "noisy" (the seasonal patio should help), but provides some of the "best people-watching" around; P.S. there's a "take-out window" too and a food truck in the works.

NEW Big Stuff ⊠ *Pizza/Sandwiches*

- | - | - | M

Lincoln Park | 2312 N. Lincoln Ave. (bet. Belden & Fullerton Aves.) | 773-472-7795 | www.bigstufftoeat.com

Prodigious thin-crust pizza, piled-high sandwiches and build-your-own salad bowls sustain Lincoln Parkers at this funky counter-service cafe with an open kitchen, acid-green storefront facade and – despite no alcohol service or BYO – night-owl hours on weekends.

Bijan's Bistro ● *American*

19 | 17 | 19 | $31

River North | 663 N. State St. (Erie St.) | 312-202-1904 | www.bijansbistrochicago.com

"In a town that closes up a bit too early", this midpriced River North "neighborhood hangout" "mix of bistro and sports bar" is "almost always open" serving New American fare that's "a smidgen above bar food" (though most takers are "too tired to care what they're eating at 3 AM"); there's also "super-late – or is it early" – "people-watching" and if you're up, lunch and weekend brunch.

Billy Goat Tavern *American*

17 | 12 | 15 | $12

Loop | 309 W. Washington St. (Franklin St.) | 312-899-1873 ⊠⊄

Loop | 330 S. Wells St. (Van Buren St.) | 312-554-0297 ⊠

River North | Merchandise Mart | 222 Merchandise Mart (bet. Orleans & Wells Sts.) | 312-464-1045

River North | 430 N. Lower Michigan Ave. (bet. Hubbard & Illinois Sts.) | 312-222-1525 ●⊄

Streeterville | Navy Pier | 700 E. Grand Ave. (Lake Shore Dr.) | 312-670-8789

O'Hare Area | O'Hare Field Terminal 1 | Concourse C (I-190) | 773-462-9368

West Loop | 1535 W. Madison St. (Ogden Ave.) | 312-733-9132 ⊄ www.billygoattavern.com

"Characters abound" at these "quintessential Chicago" "greasy spoons" "famous" for their "*SNL* legacy", "cheap" "hangover" grub, "verbal abuse" and an "owner who perpetrated the 'curse of the goat' on the Cubs"; the newer locations made to "look like old-school neighborhood dives" don't compare to the "delightful" 1934 "dungeon" "under the sidewalk" in River North, and butt-inskis bleat that there's "more bun" than beef on this "cheezborger."

Bin 36 *American*

21 | 20 | 21 | $40

River North | 339 N. Dearborn St. (Kinzie St.) | 312-755-9463 |
www.bin36.com

Bin Wine Cafe *American*

Wicker Park | 1559 N. Milwaukee Ave. (Damen Ave.) | 773-486-2233 |
www.binwinecafe.com

Champions of this River North American/wine shop with a Wicker
Park sibling cite the "chic" confines "convenient for breakfast, lunch,
drinks and dinner" plus "fabulous flights" of vino and "sublime"
choices for the "cheese obsessed", all at "fair prices" – though sour
grapes include "excessive noise" and service that veers from
"knowledgeable" to a "mixed bag"; the more casual cafe serves as a
"pleasant" "date spot or after-work hangout", while the original also
offers classes for budding oenophiles and fromage fiends.

Birchwood Kitchen Ⓜ *Sandwiches*

23 | 16 | 19 | $16

Bucktown | 2211 W. North Ave. (bet. Bell Ave. & Leavitt St.) |
773-276-2100 | www.birchwoodkitchen.com

They "take pride in what they do" at this "welcoming", "bright and
airy" counter-service Bucktown BYO offering "truly unique sandwiches" on the "limited menu" of "comfy meals" (including weekend
brunch), all "lovingly prepared" from "locally sourced ingredients";
add "accommodating" service and "reasonable prices" and wags
"wish they would open a place in my kitchen"; P.S. it "gets crowded",
but there's a "lovely courtyard" patio in warm weather.

Bistro Bordeaux *French*

- | - | - | E

Evanston | 618 Church St. (Chicago Ave.) | 847-424-1483 |
www.lebistrobordeaux.com

"Interesting" "classic bistro dishes" delivered by a "knowledgeable"
staff under the "watchful eye of an enthusiastic owner" make this
French spot a "keeper" on the "Evanston dining scene"; the "warm,
intimate space" features burgundy velvet curtains, leather banquettes and vintage posters, and additional assets include Sunday
brunch and sidewalk seating.

🅩 Bistro Campagne *French*

25 | 22 | 23 | $42

Lincoln Square | 4518 N. Lincoln Ave. (bet. Sunnyside & Wilson Aves.) |
773-271-6100 | www.bistrocampagne.com

You can go "light and subtle" or "decadent" at Lincoln Square's
"charming little bistro" where chef-owner Michael Altenberg's "locally
grown" approach results in "good value" for "high-quality" French
fare with "seasonal specials" that are especially "lovely"; an "outstanding beer menu", sustainable-minded wine list and "personable"
staff add to the allure, and while some call the "warm" quarters "intimate" and others say "crowded", all agree the "garden" is "magical."

NEW Bistronomic *French*

- | - | - | M

Gold Coast | 840 N. Wabash Ave. (bet. Chestnut & Pearson Sts.) |
312-944-8400 | www.bistronomic.net

At this Gold Coast arrival (in the digs that once housed Eve), chef
Martial Noguier (ex one sixtyblue, Café des Architectes) is whip-

ping up grilled cheese, tartines and variably sized, French-forward seasonal plates; a midpriced wine list gives Gallophiles plenty to quaff, though the moodily lit, burgundy-tinged setting, with dark-wood tables and slate-gray banquettes, spells romance regardless of what's sipped.

Bistro 110 *French*

21 | 20 | 21 | $42

Gold Coast | 110 E. Pearson St. (bet. Michigan Ave. & Rush St.) | 312-266-3110 | www.bistro110restaurant.com

"After two decades", this French "standby" still delivers "delicious" "everyday" "bistro fare" to patrons who "love the roasted garlic with crusty bread", "relaxing" Sunday "jazz brunch", "wonderful bar" and "Magnificent Mile milieu"; if the resistance reckons it's "tired, touristy" and "a bit pricey", others find the tabs "reasonable", service "competent" and note "in summer, you can sit outside and watch the beautiful people walk by."

NEW Bistro One West 🍽 Ⓜ *American*

- | - | - | M

St. Charles | 1 W. Illinois St. (bet. 1st St. & Riverside Ave.) | 630-444-0600 | www.bistro1west.com

Vets from the Loop's Trattoria No. 10 are behind this upscale New American in St. Charles that feels anything but suburban thanks to its loftlike, exposed-brick digs in a former factory; a spacious patio on the banks of the Fox River featuring live music in season and a 100-label wine list round out the savvy, yet family-friendly, experience.

Bistrot Margot *French*

20 | 20 | 20 | $39

Old Town | 1437 N. Wells St. (bet. North Ave. & Schiller St.) | 312-587-3660 | www.bistrotmargot.com

Supporters of this "cozy Old Town institution" with "classic French bistro cooking" "swear by" its "pleasant", "reliable" fare and staff, "neighborhood" vibe, "reasonably priced wine list" and "lunch and brunch"; frustrated followers feel it "could be better", but the "friendly bar for after work" and "one of the best sidewalk cafes" draw an "interesting clientele."

Bistrot Zinc *French*

21 | 21 | 21 | $38

Gold Coast | 1131 N. State St. (bet. Cedar & Elm Sts.) | 312-337-1131 | www.bistrotzinc.com

"Authentic" "Parisian ambiance" starts with the titular zinc bar at this "consistent" Gold Coast "neighborhood" "oasis" for "well-made" French bistro "comfort food" including "weekend brunch" and "amazing lunch specials"; "friendly service" adds to the "value in an area where most choices are expensive", and people-watchers note that come summer, "window walls are opened right onto State Street."

Bite Cafe *American*

- | - | - | I

Ukrainian Village | 1039 N. Western Ave. (Cortez St.) | 773-395-2483 | www.bitecafechicago.com

Longman & Eagle's owners have upgraded this long-standing Ukrainian Village eatery adjacent to their Empty Bottle nightclub, where an affordable, amped-up American 'diner' menu includes many globally accented dishes (burritos, bibimbop, falafel) as well as brunch; the spruced-up space is now an earthy, modern milieu with brown banquettes and sky-blue chairs plus counter seating, while the background music is tuned to the performance schedule next door.

NEW Bivona Ristorante-Pizzeria Ⓜ *Italian* — | — | — | M

Lincoln Park | 2506 N. Clybourn Ave. (bet. Fullerton & Wrightwood Aves.) | 773-525-2100 | www.bivonaristorante.com
Old-school, moderately priced Sicilian fare (including housemade pasta) and stone-baked pizzas made with fresh ingredients are dished out for dinner and weekend lunch at this Lincoln Park arrival; the cozy digs include a dining room with a brick fireplace and peach artwork (a nod to the signature fried pizza dough dessert with peach-caramel sauce), and there's also a barroom with a few tables.

Ⓩ Blackbird Ⓩ *American* 27 | 22 | 25 | $66

West Loop | 619 W. Randolph St. (bet. Desplaines & Jefferson Sts.) | 312-715-0708 | www.blackbirdrestaurant.com
The West Loop's "bold" "destination" "flagship of the [Paul] Kahan empire" flies an "outstanding", "ever-changing menu" that's "crafted in the finest tradition of New American" cuisine and coupled with an "unbelievable wine list" and "skillful service" in "sleek, stark" surroundings; while "priced for a special occasion", it delivers a vaunted "value-quality ratio" (wallet-watchers might "come for lunch"), and if the other "diners are so close you're practically wearing each other's clothes", the "high noise and energy level is part of the plan", so just "eat" and "talk later."

Blind Faith Café Ⓜ *Vegetarian* 21 | 16 | 19 | $22

Evanston | 525 Dempster St. (bet. Chicago & Hinman Aves.) | 847-328-6875 | www.blindfaithcafe.com
"Tasty", "healthy" meals make this Evanston's "solid" "old faithful" – "especially for vegans and vegetarians" – where affordable tabs meet a "comfortable", certified green setting and a staff that's "genuinely interested in pleasing"; P.S. omnivores not sharing the "spirit" bet on the "bakery" and weekend brunch.

NEW Blokes & Birds ● *British* — | — | — | M

Lakeview | 3343 N. Clark St. (bet. Roscoe & School Sts.) | 773-472-5252 | www.blokesandbirdschicago.com
Lakeview lays claim to this British 'public house' offering beyond-the-basics bar food (lobster-stuffed deviled eggs, chicken tikka masala) and a bevy of domestic and imported craft brews; mixed seating (communal, bar, high-tops and even leaning counters) is well spaced throughout the comfy digs, which have been done up in wood, wood and more wood and boast two fireplaces and a billiard table.

Bluebird, The ● *American* 20 | 21 | 19 | $31

Bucktown | 1749 N. Damen Ave. (Willow St.) | 773-486-2473 | www.bluebirdchicago.com
New American small plates like "cheese and charcuterie" and "flatbreads that rule" served amid "cool decor" featuring "repurposed doors and windows" and a fireplace make this midpriced Bucktown

"neighborhood hangout" a "cozy" "place for an early evening date" or "late-night dining"; P.S. service can be spotty, so "locals in-the-know" eat "at the bar" and order from the "extensive wine and beer list."

Blue Ocean *Japanese* ▽ 23 | 22 | 24 | $42

Ravenswood | 4650 N. Clark St. (Leland Ave.) | 773-334-6288 | www.blueoceanchicago.com

Tucked into the corner of a Ravenswood residential complex, this storefront "neighborhood gem" serves signature rolls in full and half sizes (including creative vegetarian options) "always with a twist" plus Japanese small plates; its eye-popping, psychedelic-colored setting includes 'tinsel' ball light fixtures, a sushi bar and swanky banquette seating.

Blue 13 ●Ⓜ *American* 24 | 23 | 25 | $44

River North | 416 W. Ontario St. (bet. Kingsbury & Orleans Sts.) | 312-787-1400 | www.blue13chicago.com

"Creative" New American dishes are partnered with service that's "attentive (in a good way)" at this upscale, "cozy" River Norther decked out with exposed brick and candlelight; it's "hip, but never tries to be hipper than its customers", with a house "filthy martini", selection of beers and "reasonably priced wine list" keeping fans lubricated till "late night."

NEW Bluette Ⓜ⇄ *French* - | - | - | M

Wilmette | 1162 Wilmette Ave. (Central Ave.) | 847-853-8988 | www.bluettecafe.com

Expect French classics like salad Lyonnaise and steak frites, plus some unexpected fusion dishes and vegetarian options at this North Suburban cash-only BYO serving lunch and dinner; true to its name, the sleek, chic setting features Wedgewood blue walls and a blue awning over the front picture windows.

Z Bob Chinn's Crab House *Seafood* 23 | 14 | 20 | $40

Wheeling | 393 S. Milwaukee Ave. (bet. Dundee & Willow Rds.) | 847-520-3633 | www.bobchinns.com

"Fresh" fanatics can "check the air bills on the wall" at this "longtime" North Suburban "standard" for "amazing seafood" that has "little sophistication" but comes with moderate prices and "powerful cocktails"; expect a "rowdy", "efficient" "production line", "plastic plates" and "wharfish 1980s seaside" surroundings, plus you may have to "control your server" to not feel "rushed"; but while some who tag it "tired" and "overpriced" don't get the "hype", the fact is "people have been waiting in line since the day they opened."

Bob San ● *Japanese* 24 | 19 | 21 | $36

Wicker Park | 1805 W. Division St. (Wood St.) | 773-235-8888 | www.bob-san.com

Wicker Park's "warm and welcoming" midpriced Sushi Naniwa sibling is a Japanese "mainstay" offering "so many options" of "fresh" sushi and sashimi (the best of which can "stop all conversation") served in "generous portions"; an "understated atmosphere" and "courteous service" are additional reasons it suits for a "casual date."

	FOOD	DECOR	SERVICE	COST

NEW Boiler Room ●⊄ *Pizza* | – | – | – | M |

Logan Square | 2210 N. California Ave. (bet. Milwaukee Ave. & Palmer St.) | 773-276-5625 | www.boilerroomlogansquare.com

This cash-only hipster hangout in Logan Square pairs cocktails and craft brews with chef-driven pizza in whole pies or by the slice, with toppings like PBR-braised meatballs, pulled pork with mole and Thai barbecue chicken with bean sprouts and peanuts; the retro-industrial setting offers booth, bar and patio seating, and there's a vintage boiler on display, along with salvaged materials (scrap metal, subway doors, airline cargo strapping), funky light fixtures and solar panels.

Boka *American* | 25 | 23 | 25 | $58 |

Lincoln Park | 1729 N. Halsted St. (Willow St.) | 312-337-6070 | www.bokachicago.com

"Talented" chef Giuseppi Tentori has turned this "casually elegant" Lincoln Park "escape" "near the Halsted theater" into a "distinctive fine-dining" destination featuring "cutting-edge" New American cuisine "from raw to small plates to entrees" and "some of the best desserts" in a "cool" setting with "sails" on the ceiling and "a great buzz" (plus an "adorable" enclosed patio); a few reticent raters say some of the "very creative presentations" "work better than others" and it's "a bit pricey" – but all agree it's still "special" (wallet-watchers might try the "early prix fixe" Sunday–Thursday).

Bolat African Cuisine Ⓜ *African* | – | – | – | I |

Lakeview | 3346 N. Clark St. (bet. Buckingham Pl. & Roscoe St.) | 773-665-1100 | www.bolatrestaurant.com

Thanks to a "makeover", this former "cabbie-style Lakeview joint is now a hip, contemporary" and "authentic" regional African eatery with "bold", "delicious" fare (emphasis on small plates and sustainable seafood); the "tastefully done" setting with "traditional art painted on the walls" and affordable tabs help surveyors to "overlook" the "somewhat unprofessional service."

Bombon Café Ⓩ *Mexican* | – | – | – | I |

West Loop | 36 S. Ashland Ave. (Monroe St.) | 312-733-8717

This West Loop counter-service cafe from the Bombon Bakery family specializes in affordable Mexican sandwiches (choose from 16 combos or create your own) served on housemade artisanal breads, and also offers tamales, salads, baked goods and more; the family-friendly storefront, done up in warm wood and bright ochre, serves early morning to early evening.

Bongo Room *American* | 24 | 16 | 18 | $19 |

Wicker Park | 1470 N. Milwaukee Ave. (Honore St.) | 773-489-0690
South Loop | 1152 S. Wabash Ave. (Roosevelt Rd.) | 312-291-0100
www.thebongoroom.com

Fans are "bonkers" about "some of the best breakfast eats in town" (plus "interesting salads and sandwiches" for lunch) at this "reasonably priced" Wicker Park "crack pancake" palace and its South Loop sister that are "a cut above the usual diner"; weekend brunch "crowds" and occasional "rude service" deter some, but most deem the "decadent" "twists on savory and sweet" sustenance "worth the wait"; P.S. they don't serve dinner, but with these "portions", "you won't need it."

Bonsai Café *Asian*

- - - I

Evanston | 2916 Central St. (Lincolnwood Dr.) | 847-866-7498

"Well-prepared", "affordable Asian specialties" – from potstickers and crab Rangoon to Thai curry to sushi – come at "very reasonable prices" and pair with beverages including fresh ginger ale and bubble tea at this "cozy" BYO corner storefront in Evanston; while doubters "aren't sure about the authenticity, there's a wide variety" and "portions tend toward the generous"; P.S. a patio is open in season.

☑ Bonsoirée Ⓜ *American/French*

26 19 25 $76

Logan Square | 2728 W. Armitage Ave. (Fairfield Ave.) | 773-486-7511 | www.bon-soiree.com

Initiates insist a "terrific", "strictly degustation" New American–New French "sensory adventure" awaits at this "tiny", "onetime secret" Logan Square "storefront" where "you can wear jeans and have truffles shaved over your plate" by "thoughtful servers"; Saturday dinners are invitation-only through the website, Sunday's menu is a market-driven surprise, and while it's prix fixe only and on the "pricey" side, most feel it's a "bargain" considering the no-corkage BYO policy ("bring your best vino" or arrange for delivery).

Boston Blackies *Burgers*

19 14 18 $20

Loop | 120 S. Riverside Plaza (bet. Adams & Monroe Sts.) | 312-382-0700 Ⓢ
Deerfield | 405 Lake Cook Rd. (Rte. 43) | 847-418-3400
www.bostonblackies.com

"Reliable for burgers and affordable American" fare (with kudos for the "garbage salad", "onion rings" and "coleslaw"), the remaining members of this "decent chain" of "busy pubs" also offer a "selection of brews" and "no-nonsense service" "from central casting" to go along with a "typically Chicago atmosphere" and dose of "nostalgia."

Bourgeois Pig *Coffeehouse/Sandwiches*

- - - I

Lincoln Park | 738 W. Fullerton Ave. (bet. Burling & Halsted Sts.) | 773-883-5282 | www.bpigcafe.com

Literati from nearby DePaul rub elbows at this exposed-brick-and-book-trimmed Lincoln Park nook, where vintage furniture, a fireplace and crystal chandeliers ooze bygone charm; the affordable, cafe-style eats – all-day breakfast, sandwiches, salads and housemade sweets – are complemented by up to 100 teas, classic and contemporary coffee concoctions and hot chocolate.

Branch 27 *American*

17 20 20 $36

Noble Square | 1371 W. Chicago Ave. (Noble St.) | 312-850-2700 | www.branch27.com

Noble Square's "cozy", "casual" New American in a "converted former branch of the Chicago Public Library" wields "upscale bar food" and "brews" that are "priced appropriately" ("nothing extraordinary, but there's something for everyone"); a "twenty-thirtysomething crowd" in "groups" or with "dates" fills the brick-lined space and "back atrium with beautiful lighting from the glass ceiling"; P.S. the Food score may not reflect recent chef changes.

Breakfast Club *American* | 20 | 13 | 21 | $16 |

Near West | 1381 W. Hubbard St. (Noble St.) | 312-666-2372 | www.chicagobreakfastclub.com

Near West "locals" laud this "out-of-the-way", "old-school" "breakfast joint" for its American fare including "excellent omelets", "killer" "stuffed French toast" and "Bloody Marys" served by a "pleasant staff" in a "homey atmosphere" with "pink accents" reminiscent of a "grandma's country kitchen"; it all adds up to "great value" – in other words, "be prepared to wait awhile on the weekends" (though "tables turn fairly quickly").

Bricks *Pizza* | 22 | 15 | 17 | $22 |

Lincoln Park | 1909 N. Lincoln Ave. (Wisconsin St.) | 312-255-0851

Bricks on the Run *Pizza*

Bucktown | 1940 N. Elston Ave. (bet. Armitage Ave. & Homer St.) | 773-252-2220
www.brickschicago.com

Fans "forget the basement" "dungeonlike location" with the "first bite" of this Lincoln Park pizzeria's "creative concoctions" made with "not-too-thick, not-too-thin crusts" that are "right on the mark" "when you don't want a manhole-cover–size pie"; "long waits" are endurable thanks to a "friendly staff", "reasonably priced" "craft beers" and an "inexpensive wine list"; P.S. the Bucktown location serves takeout only, and a Lakeview expansion will add barbecue.

Briejo 🅑Ⓜ *American/Eclectic* | ▽ 14 | 18 | 15 | $38 |

Oak Park | 211 Harrison St. (Lombard Ave.) | 708-848-2743 | www.briejo.com

Hopefuls had "high expectations" for this midpriced Eclectic–New American "tucked away" in "Oak Park's cool little art district", given its pedigree (one of the owners is from the former Tomboy), "interesting" menu and "wonderful ambiance" with warm tones and low lighting; so while some are "disappointed" with "mediocre" fare and "service that could use better training", they add that it's "trying" and "not bad for the neighborhood."

Brio Tuscan Grille *Italian* | 22 | 23 | 21 | $33 |

Lombard | Shops on Butterfield | 330 Yorktown Ctr. (Butterfield Rd.) | 630-424-1515 | www.brioitalian.com

"Varied and tasty" Italian menu choices including weekend brunch "at a decent price" sate Butterfield shoppers at this "lively", "comfortable" and "kid-friendly" Lombard chain link; "when you get the right service person", it's an even better "experience", enhanced by a "warm" Tuscan villa setting that includes two fireplaces in the lounge.

	FOOD	DECOR	SERVICE	COST

Bristol, The *American*
23 | 19 | 21 | $40

Bucktown | 2152 N. Damen Ave. (bet. Shakespeare & Webster Aves.) | 773-862-5555 | www.thebristolchicago.com

"Believers" in Bucktown's "worthy", "locavore" New American gastropub say it "cranks out" an "ever-changing seasonal menu" including "delectable and distinctive dishes" in the "nose-to-tail" "school of cooking" ("eat parts you never knew were edible") ferried by a "welcoming", "informed staff"; naysayers note it's "noisy" with "packed tables" and "communal seating" that's "not for everyone", plus the "no-reservations policy is the pits" – but "phenomenal" "custom" cocktails and "many beers and ales" help "while you wait."

Broadway Cellars *American*
21 | 17 | 20 | $32

Edgewater | 5900 N. Broadway (Rosedale Ave.) | 773-944-1208 | www.broadwaycellars.net

Edgewater denizens "date and dine" at this "jazzy", "comfortable" "neighborhood" "brick-exposed cellar" with "consistently" "delicious" New American fare (including "excellent brunch"), "pick-your-own wine flights" from a "creative list" and a "welcoming staff"; added attractions are "occasional live music", seasonal outdoor seating and weeknight deals for "specials, wine-flight dinners and prix fixe."

Browntrout *American*
24 | 17 | 22 | $35

North Center/St. Ben's | 4111 N. Lincoln Ave. (bet. Belle Plaine & Warner Aves.) | 773-472-4111 | www.browntroutchicago.com

"It's worth swimming upstream" for this midpriced North Center contemporary American where the "delicious, creative" "farm-to-table" fare comes in "small and large plates" with "big flavors"; fans of "communal tables" find the warm-hued modern digs "tastefully decorated" while others peg it as "plain Jane", though most are "impressed" by the "sustainable", "green approach" and "heartfelt chef-iness"; P.S. there's also Sunday brunch and sidewalk seating.

Bruna's Ristorante *Italian*
26 | 12 | 21 | $32

Southwest Side | 2424 S. Oakley Ave. (24th Pl.) | 773-254-5550

"One of Chicago's oldest continuously operated restaurants" (opened 1933), this moderately priced Southwest Side "neighborhood stalwart" is an "oasis" of "classic family Italian" dining complete with an "old-world staff"; it may "look like a typical red-sauce" place "but the quality is much better" say aficionados who aver it's "always a pleasure (despite the ancient decor)", plus it's "not a tourist" spot.

Buona Terra Ristorante Ⓜ *Italian*
24 | 17 | 22 | $31

Logan Square | 2535 N. California Ave. (bet. Fullerton Ave. & Logan Blvd.) | 773-289-3800 | www.buona-terra.com

"*Va bene*" cheer champions of this "unpretentious", "popular" Logan Square haunt offering "enjoyable" Northern Italian fare "with some unusual touches" and "caring service" in a "homey" surround including a mural of a Tuscan scene; regulars especially "love the spread for the bread" and the "Thursday prix fixe" "bargain" that offers the run of the menu; N.B. there's garden dining in summer.

NEW Burger Bar *Burgers*

- | - | - | I

Lincoln Park | 1578 N. Clybourn Ave. (bet. Dayton & Halsted Sts.) |
312-255-0055 | www.burgerbarchicago.com

Build your own half-pound burger or choose from creative topping
combos like prosciutto-fried egg-mozzarella at this Lincoln Parker
where several fry and sauce options, salads, handspun shakes
(in flavors like cheesecake and malted milk ball), craft brews and
bargain wines round out the menu; located right next door to sister
pizzeria Sono Wood Fired, the wood-and-brick, warehouse-chic setting features industrial lighting and ductwork, local artwork and
a photo booth.

NEW Burger Boss *Burgers*

- | - | - | I

Elmwood Park | 7512 W. North Ave. (Jackson Ave.) | 708-452-7288 |
www.theburgerboss.com

Whether you opt for Angus, chicken or portobello, the burgers are
indeed boss at this West Suburban counter-service stand where patrons choose their bread, cheese, sauce and other toppings – or opt
for one of a half-dozen signature combos; fresh cut fries with dipping sauces plus hand-packed shakes, smoothies, beer and wine
round out a wallet-friendly menu that's served amid colorful tiles,
mod metal chairs and multiple TVs.

Butterfly Sushi Bar & Thai Cuisine *Japanese/Thai*

22 | 16 | 19 | $23

Noble Square | 1156 W. Grand Ave. (bet. May St. & Racine Ave.) |
312-563-5555
NEW West Loop | 1131 W. Madison St. (bet. Aberdeen St. &
Racine Ave.) | 312-997-9988
West Town | 1421 W. Chicago Ave. (bet. Bishop & Noble Sts.) |
312-492-9955
www.butterflysushibar.com

A "young, hip crowd" flits to these "lively", often "packed" West
Town and Noble Square favorites (now with a West Loop sibling too)
for a "diverse menu" of "fresh, tasty" "Thai and sushi classics" including a "dizzying array of rolls" at "fair prices" with a "no-corkage"
"BYO to boot"; but while some praise "quick service", others feel
"rushed out the door."

Cab's Wine Bar Bistro *American*

24 | 21 | 25 | $40

Glen Ellyn | 430 N. Main St. (Duane St.) | 630-942-9463 |
www.cabsbistro.com

Situated in "old Downtown Glen Ellyn", this midpriced "casual"
"neighborhood" "landmark" offers seasonal New American "fine
dining" with "wonderful wine" (focusing on Cal Cabernets) and a
"friendly" vibe in an "unassuming storefront"; though some lobby for
"more specials", live music most weekends strikes the right chord.

Café Absinthe M *American/French*

23 | 18 | 21 | $42

Bucktown | 1958 W. North Ave. (Damen Ave.) | 773-278-4488

To absinthe-minded admirers of this "charming" Bucktown "old
standard", the seasonal American-French cuisine is "consistently

interesting and delicious" (if "a bit pricey") and the confines confer a "cool vibe" for "dressed-up or casual" occasions; diners taking a dimmer view suggest bringing a "flashlight" for the "dark" ambiance and mention the "noise" factor, though a "wine list with some boutique options" might help you "tolerate" that.

Cafe Ba-Ba-Reeba! *Spanish*

22 | 19 | 20 | $32

Lincoln Park | 2024 N. Halsted St. (Armitage Ave.) | 773-935-5000 | www.cafebabareeba.com

After more than 25 years, LEYE's Lincoln Park "pioneer" of the genre still serves "some of the most reliable" "tapas (small dishes) and pinxtos (even smaller dishes)" in a "lively", "loud" setting (where "varieties" of "sangria make everyone even louder"); service is usually "active and efficient", but nitpickers note "some highlights and some mediocre" menu options, and warn it "can get expensive" ("$3 tapas at the bar is a great bargain" at varying times); P.S. "unique Sunday brunch", "three-bite desserts" and "outdoor seating" are added lures.

Café Bernard *French*

19 | 15 | 20 | $41

Lincoln Park | 2100 N. Halsted St. (Dickens Ave.) | 773-871-2100 | www.cafebernard.com

A Lincoln Park "institution" since 1972 for "well-prepared" "traditional French cooking" including "game specials", this "dimly lit", "tried-and-true" "favorite" is also appreciated for its "terrific, well-priced wine list"; a few who feel it's "faded from its former glory" note it "needs a makeover", while others prefer the "atmosphere" of the less-expensive back-room wine bar and cafe called the Red Rooster.

Café Bionda *Italian*

22 | 17 | 20 | $31

South Loop | 1924 S. State St. (Archer Ave.) | 312-326-9800

Amici of this "cozy" South Loop Italian are drawn to its "hearty" "traditional" fare dished out in "large quantities" with "friendly service" amid a "neighborhood ambiance"; "fair prices" add to the allure, including the Sunday platter that's a "terrific bargain" of meatballs, sausages and veal braciole.

Cafe Central ⓜ *French*

24 | 19 | 24 | $38

Highland Park | 455 Central Ave. (bet. Linden & St. Johns Aves.) | 847-266-7878 | www.cafecentral.net

Highland Park's "unpretentious" "kissing cousin" to the "extremely upscale Carlos'" is the "go-to place" for "consistent", "classic [French] bistro" fare in a "casual" setting; though the "tables are close" there's "outdoor seating in summer", plus tabs are "reasonable" and kids are welcome – just allow for "no reservations after 6:30."

Café des Architectes *French*

24 | 25 | 24 | $53

Gold Coast | Sofitel Chicago Water Tower | 20 E. Chestnut St. (Wabash Ave.) | 312-324-4063 | www.cafedesarchitectes.com

"Seasonal, local and flavorful" New French meals with "beautiful presentations" come with "excellent service to match" (that's earned a ratings boost) at this *"très European"* eatery in the Sofitel Chicago Water Tower; the "civilized" setting projects "modern luxury" through vibrant colors and mood lighting, and if "prices can be a bit high", the "prix fixe special is a steal" and the "fantastic breakfast" is a "great value"; P.S. the Food score doesn't reflect a chef change post-Survey.

Café Iberico ● *Spanish* | 22 | 16 | 18 | $29 |

River North | 737 N. LaSalle Dr. (bet. Chicago Ave. & Superior St.) | 312-573-1510 | www.cafeiberico.com

Boosters of this "boisterous" River North taparia cheer the "well-rounded selection" of "tasty" Spanish "small plates to share" plus "some of the best paella" around, all at "recession-proof prices" that "pack" the large, "cafeteria-like" digs with "groups" and other diners "on a budget"; just expect "deafening" "noise" and "prepare to drink a lot of sangria while waiting for your table", as reservations are only accepted for parties of six or more.

Café Marbella Ⓜ *Spanish* | - | - | - | I |

Jefferson Park | 5527 Milwaukee Ave. (bet. Bryn Mawr & Catalpa Aves.) | 773-853-0128 | www.cafemarbella.com

Relocated from its former Peterson Avenue digs, this budget-friendly Jefferson Park BYO turns out an extensive menu of hot and cold Spanish tapas and a fair number of entrees beyond the usual paella, all served in modest digs with booths and cafe tables, tile floor and arched windows; N.B. during the fixed-price Spanish 'dim sum' brunch, available all day Sunday, bring bubbly and the restaurant will squeeze the OJ.

Café 103 ⓍⓂ *American/Eclectic* | - | - | - | E |

Far South Side | 1909 W. 103rd St. (Walden Pkwy.) | 773-238-5115 | www.cafe103.com

"Small and intimate", this "upscale" bistro is a "wonderful Far South Side treat" in an "otherwise food-challenged" area; New American-Eclectic eats arrive by "attentive" servers for lunch and dinner, and the alcohol policy is BYO only, with a small corkage fee.

Cafe Pyrenees Ⓜ *French* | 21 | 19 | 20 | $36 |

Libertyville | Adler Square Shopping Plaza | 1762 N. Milwaukee Ave. (Buckley Rd./Rte. 137) | 847-362-2233 | www.cafepyrenees.com

Libertyville locals laud this "lovely", "family-run" "traditional French bistro" for its "simple but tasteful" midpriced menu (with some American additions), "interesting", "affordable wines" and "warm" "cafe atmosphere" where "once inside, you quickly forget you're in a strip mall"; some gripe that service can be "standoffish", but positives include patio seating and periodic live music.

Café Selmarie *American* | 23 | 17 | 19 | $26 |

Lincoln Square | 4729 N. Lincoln Ave. (bet. Lawrence & Leland Aves.) | 773-989-5595 | www.cafeselmarie.com

Patrons of this "neighborhood" "favorite" praise its "mom-and-pop air" yet "professional" service while dishing out "well-prepared" New American "comfort food" and "fantastic desserts" at moderate

FOOD | DECOR | SERVICE | COST

prices; it offers "wonderful summer dining outside on Lincoln Square" and is a "quick place for afternoon tea", weekend brunch, lunch or light dinner – and some surveyors suggest it's an even "better bakery."

☑ Café Spiaggia *Italian*

25 | 23 | 25 | $56

Gold Coast | 980 N. Michigan Ave., 2nd fl. (Oak St.) | 312-280-2750 | www.cafespiaggia.com

"More intimate" than its "formal" and "more-expensive big brother" "next door", this "lively", "upscale" Gold Coast cafe lures "Magnificent Mile cruisers" with "luscious", "slightly more rustic" Italian fare ("particularly the fresh pastas"), a "top-notch wine list" and "warm but professional service"; add in a "chichi" setting "overlooking Michigan Avenue" and cafe-goers say that it "never fails to please", just expect a "hefty bill."

Café Touché ⓂFrench

▽ 25 | 23 | 22 | $36

Edison Park | 6731 N. Northwest Hwy. (Oshkosh Ave.) | 773-775-0909 | www.cafetouche.com

Situated "in a neighborhood full of" dining "hits" on "Edison Park's Restaurant Row", this Northwest Side "casual French bistro" "find" is becoming a "local favorite" for its "flavorful", "quality" fare "at reasonable prices"; a dark-wood and brick-lined room plus seasonal sidewalk seating and free valet parking stoke the "terrific" vibe.

Cafe 28 *Cuban/Mexican*

26 | 20 | 22 | $30

North Center/St. Ben's | 1800-1806 W. Irving Park Rd. (Ravenswood Ave.) | 773-528-2883 | www.cafe28.org

North Center's "neighborhood" "treasure" earns enthusiasm for its "well-seasoned", "well-priced" and "mouthwatering" Cuban and Mexican fare with a "contemporary twist" that's built with "extremely fresh ingredients" and delivered by a "dedicated staff"; a "wonderful brunch", "house mojitos" and "big-city buzz" heighten the appeal; P.S. "when the weather's nice, try the patio seating."

NEW Calabruzzi's Café *Italian*

- | - | - | I

Bridgeport | 3302-04 S. Halsted St. (bet. 33rd Pl. & 33rd St.) | 773-247-9999

This bargain-priced Far South Side Italian cafe combines classic starters, pastas and entrees with a big list of panini and pizza two ways (thin or double dough); the cozy setting includes a tin ceiling, exposed brick and Italy-themed artwork, plus a granite bar dispensing beer, wine and spirits.

NEW Caminito Argentinean Grill Ⓜ *Argentinean*

- | - | - | M

Lincoln Park | 1629 N. Halsted St. (bet. North Ave. & Willow St.) | 312-846-6911 | www.caminitoargentiniangrill.com

Midpriced Argentinean classics (empanadas, parrilladas) and the influence of Italian *cucina* (pizza, pasta, pollo) define the dinner-only menu at this low-profile, intimate Lincoln Park BYO; the space's casual cafe tables are surrounded by primary-colored walls, a ceramic tile floor and a wall mural of tango dancers hinting at the live music played on Saturdays.

	FOOD	DECOR	SERVICE	COST

Campagnola *Italian* | 25 | 20 | 23 | $45 |

Evanston | 815 Chicago Ave. (Washington St.) | 847-475-6100 |
www.campagnolarestaurant.com

"Upscale but not fancy", this Evanston Italian with rustic decor and
"lots of character" is a "date-night locale" that draws a "devoted following" for its seasonal, "unique takes on typical" fare with a focus
on "sustainable" and "locally grown" ingredients; if it's a bit "expensive", a "modest yet excellent wine list" and "friendly, competent
staff" (with improved Service scores) add to the "value"; P.S. the patio is popular in summer.

Cantonesia *Chinese* | - | - | - | I |

Chinatown | 204 W. Cermak Rd. (Wentworth Ave.) | 312-225-0100 |
www.cantonesia.com

Since 1969, this long-standing Chinatown chowhouse has offered
Cantonese and Mandarin fare at affordable prices; tropical tiki drinks
and mai tais issuing from the full bar contribute to a relaxing vibe in the
warmly lit, black-and-gold space scattered with decorative screens.

Cape Cod Room *Seafood* | 22 | 22 | 23 | $60 |

Streeterville | Drake Hotel | 140 E. Walton St. (Michigan Ave.) |
312-787-2200 | www.thedrakehotel.com

Serving Streeterville since 1933, this "dark, clubby" "institution"
"tucked away in the Drake Hotel" offers "classy seafood" to "sentimental" types who recall its "historical" heyday and appreciate "old-
time classics" such as "Bookbinder's soup with sherry on the side"
served by "seasoned professionals"; naysayers knock the "nautical
decor" as "stuffy" "in spite of an update", but old salts find it "elegant
yet comfortable", adding it's "expensive" and "worth every penny."

☒ Capital Grille *Steak* | 25 | 24 | 25 | $63 |

Streeterville | 633 N. St. Clair St. (Ontario St.) | 312-337-9400
Rosemont | 5340 N. River Rd. (Balmoral Ave.) | 847-671-8125
Lombard | 87 Yorktown Shopping Ctr. (Highland Ave.) | 630-627-9800
www.thecapitalgrille.com

Fans "feel like power brokers" after being "fortified" by "stellar"
steaks (and "getting lubricated at the wonderful bar pre-dinner") at
these "heavyweight" contenders among the "big hunka meat restaurants" situated in Chicago's city and suburbs as well as
Downtown Milwaukee; they remain "true to the national brand with
highly professional service and reliable menus" of "traditional steakhouse fare" served in a "clubby", "upscale atmosphere", though a
few carnivores call them "somewhat corporate" with "no differenti-
ating features"; P.S. if you're not on an "expense account", "lunch is
the best bet pricewise."

☒ Carlos' *French* | 27 | 26 | 27 | $92 |

Highland Park | 429 Temple Ave. (Waukegan Ave.) | 847-432-0770 |
www.carlos-restaurant.com

"Still near the top of the charts" after some 30 years, Highland
Park's New French "destination" offers "amazing, approachable
gourmet" cuisine and an "incredible, if pricey, wine list" accompa-

FOOD | DECOR | SERVICE | COST

nied by service "with grace and a sense of humor"; the "conversation-friendly", "intimate space" adds to the feeling of "understated elegance" (jackets are required), and while "you pay a premium", it's "perfect" for even the "most special of occasions."

Carlucci *Italian*

19 | 21 | 19 | $36

Downers Grove | 1801 Butterfield Rd. (I-355) | 630-512-0990 | www.carluccirestaurant.com

This Downers Grove Italian provides a "wide variety of classics" plus some "inventive" dishes in a pleasant (even "romantic") modern setting; maybe it's "not gourmet" but it's "solid", with "good service and value", "great outdoor seating" and occasional live entertainment.

Carlucci *Italian*

20 | 19 | 20 | $41

Rosemont | Riverway Complex | 6111 N. River Rd. (Higgins Rd.) | 847-518-0990 | www.carluccirosemont.com

Expect "well-prepared" Northern Italian fare, "both traditional and with small twists", at this "upscale" Rosemont fixture with a Tuscan-style interior plus patio seating; it's "convenient to O'Hare" and a "safe bet" for business meals with "perfectly timed" service, though a few critics find it "predictable" and geared for "expense accounts."

Carmichael's Chicago Steak House *Steak*

22 | 19 | 20 | $50

West Loop | 1052 W. Monroe St. (bet. Aberdeen & Morgan Sts.) | 312-433-0025 | www.carmichaelsteakhouse.com

Carnivores come to this "solid" West Loop "neighborhood" meatery for a "business lunch" or a "classic Chicago-style steak dinner" with "large portions" but "without the attitude"; the clubby "old-school masculine decor" features large booths, and there's also outdoor seating; P.S. it's "convenient for United Center games."

Carmine's ● *Italian*

22 | 18 | 20 | $43

Gold Coast | 1043 N. Rush St. (bet. Bellevue Pl. & Cedar St.) | 312-988-7676 | www.rosebudrestaurants.com

"Step past the Lamborghinis, Hummers and Ferraris" to enter this Gold Coast Italian of the "Rosebud franchise" that's "popular" for "generous" "portions of red-sauce goodness"; even those who warn of a "Viagra Triangle" vibe and a "cookie-cutter" menu that "costs too much" admit the scene at the "huge bar", "live piano" and "patio" perch for "people-watching" the "Rush Street crowd" "can't be beat."

⦿ Carnivale *Nuevo Latino*

23 | 25 | 21 | $41

Loop | 702 W. Fulton Mkt. (Union Ave.) | 312-850-5005 | www.carnivalechicago.com

Jerry Kleiner's "extravagant", "slightly pricey" Nuevo Latino on the fringe of the Loop boasts "bright" "flavors and even brighter decor" for a "wonderful sensory overload" fueled by "funky servers" and "daring drinks"; just know the "atmosphere is true to its name" (it can be "deafening"), though there is seasonal dining on the patio.

Carson's *BBQ*

22 | 16 | 20 | $34

River North | 612 N. Wells St. (Ontario St.) | 312-280-9200

(continued)

Carson's

Deerfield | 200 Waukegan Rd. (bet. Kates & Lake Cook Rds.) | 847-374-8500

www.ribs.com

"One of the Chicago originals", this River North rib "reliable" and its Deerfield double have their boosters for "some of the best" babyback barbecue, "fabulous, artery-clogging potato sides" and "free chopped liver" served in confines that are "comfortable" if "nothing fancy"; some find the fare "a bit pricey" and sour on the "sweet sauce", but at least service is "speedy"; P.S. the Decor score does not reflect extensive remodeling of the Wells Street flagship done post-Survey.

☑ Catch 35 *Seafood*   24 | 23 | 23 | $49

Loop | Leo Burnett Bldg. | 35 W. Wacker Dr. (bet. Dearborn & State Sts.) | 312-346-3500

Naperville | 35 S. Washington St. (bet. Benton & Van Buren Aves.) | 630-717-3500

www.catch35.com

Fish fans are hooked on "wonderfully fresh seafood" "with an Asian twist" at the "high-volume" Loop "location by the Chicago River" (also offering "enjoyable" "live entertainment") and its Naperville schoolmate; finicky types label the "casual modern" settings "cold" and find it a bit "overpriced", but service that's "attentive to time issues" makes Downtown a "staple" for a "business lunch" or "pre-theater dining."

Cellar at The Stained Glass *Eclectic*   ▽ 21 | 21 | 18 | $36

Evanston | 820 Clark St. (bet. Benson & Sherman Aves.) | 847-864-8678 | www.thecellarevanston.com

Valued for its "varied", "generous and tasty" Eclectic small plates and wine offerings both "priced and sized right", this "baby-bistro of the Stained Glass" in Evanston is "not too formal nor too casual" and "cozier than" its parent "around the corner" in its brown-hued digs with plaid banquettes; P.S. bargain specials include two-for-one micro burgers and $1 mini fish tacos after 9 PM Sunday–Thursday.

Ceres' Table ☒ *American*   - | - | - | M

Uptown | 4882 N. Clark St. (bet. Ainslie St. & Lawrence Ave.) | 773-878-4882 | www.cerestable.com

Named for the Roman goddess of agriculture, this smart, stylish Uptown New American features seasonal fare crafted by Giuseppe Scurato (ex Boka, Topaz Café) from local and imported ingredients; the spartan-chic space is decked out in slate-gray and light-blue walls, with a bar, banquette and table seating and romantic pendant lighting – decidedly upscale considering the moderate prices.

Chalkboard *American*   22 | 19 | 21 | $42

Lakeview | 4343 N. Lincoln Ave. (bet. Montrose & Pensacola Aves.) | 773-477-7144 | www.chalkboardrestaurant.com

"Creative" chef-owner Gilbert Langlois writes his "changing menu" of "slightly exotic" New American "comfort food" "across a chalkboard" at this "cozy", kid-friendly Lakeview spot that also serves weekend "afternoon tea" and Sunday brunch; even if it's "a bit over-priced for the neighborhood", surveyors note a "local, organic" bent plus "welcoming service" and say it's "lovely" "for a special night out."

Chama Gaucha *Brazilian/Steak*

| - | - | - | E |

Downers Grove | 3008 Finley Rd. (bet. Branding Ln. & Butterfield Rd.) | 630-324-6002 | www.chamagaucha.com

Skewer-wielding, bombacha-clad gauchos carve a succession of charcoal-fired meats tableside at this fixed-price Brazilian meatery imported from Texas; the masculine, wood-heavy dining room, anchored by an expansive salad bar in the round, draws expense-accounters and celebratory Downers Grove suburbanites.

☒ Charlie Trotter's 🅂 Ⓜ *American*

| 27 | 25 | 27 | $140 |

Lincoln Park | 816 W. Armitage Ave. (bet. Dayton & Halsted Sts.) | 773-248-6228 | www.charlietrotters.com

Regulars revere "the original celebrity chef's palace of haute cuisine" as the "pinnacle" of "precision", where a "memorable" "three-hour homage" to New American "gastronomic bliss" "showcases flavors in new intensities and sometimes surprising combinations" alongside selections from an "encyclopedic wine list"; "formal", "professional service" befits the "staid" Lincoln Park setting, and though some patrons are "put off" by "pretense" and "petite portions", the faithful insist "go at least once in your lifetime", especially if you can "find someone with an expense account."

☒ Cheesecake Factory *American*

| 19 | 19 | 18 | $28 |

Streeterville | John Hancock Ctr. | 875 N. Michigan Ave. (bet. Chestnut St. & Delaware Pl.) | 312-337-1101 ◗

Lincolnshire | Lincolnshire Commons | 930 Milwaukee Ave. (Aptakisic Rd.) | 847-955-2350

Skokie | Westfield Shoppingtown | 4999 Old Orchard Ctr. (Skokie Blvd.) | 847-329-8077

Schaumburg | Woodfield Shopping Ctr. | 53 Woodfield Rd. (Golf Rd.) | 847-619-1090

Oak Brook | Oakbrook Center Mall | 2020 Spring Rd. (bet. Harger Rd. & 22nd St.) | 630-573-1800

www.thecheesecakefactory.com

With outposts in Chicago and Milwaukee, this "raucous" Traditional American chain offers "one of the largest menus known to man" and "serving sizes" that "never fail to amaze"; boosters bet "you could eat here every day and get something different" "without breaking the bank", praising the "offbeat decor" and "enthusiastic staff", and though haute culinary types call it "hyper-commercialized", "tacky and touristy", masses willingly brave the "two-hour waits", "loud" conditions with "cranky kids" and service that's "slow when busy."

🆕 Chef Amaury's
Epicurean Affair Ⓜ *American*

| - | - | - | E |

Aurora | 33 W. New York St. (Commons Dr.) | 630-375-0426 | www.chefamaury.com

The eponymous chef has relocated his fine-dining beacon to new digs in Downtown Aurora, where he's attracting both locals and urbanites

	FOOD	DECOR	SERVICE	COST

for a New American menu emphasizing local produce and meats; the sleek white-tablecloth setting boasts river views and a wood-trimmed bar, while occasional live music and wine tastings are added boons.

Chef's Station ⓂAmerican

| | 24 | 20 | 22 | $51 |

Evanston | Davis Street Metro Station | 915 Davis St. (Church St.) | 847-570-9821 | www.chefs-station.com

"Hidden away" in a 1920 building "under the tracks" of the Davis Street Metro is where fans find this New American "gem" with an "enthusiastic" "host-proprietor" and chef who always has "something different to look forward to" on his menu; "personal service", "inventive, comfortable" decor and a seasonal patio add to the "quality-to-value quotient", though it's "not cheap."

Chens Asian

| | 22 | 17 | 18 | $23 |

Wrigleyville | 3506 N. Clark St. (Addison St.) | 773-549-9100 | www.chenschicago.com

Wrigleyville's "civilized" "local" Chinese-Japanese-Thai hybrid offers a "quality" menu that "works for even the pickiest of eaters" (and includes "fresh sushi") plus an "impressive martini and cocktail list"; the "decor and music are not exactly what you'd expect, but that's a good thing" – as are affordable prices.

Chez Joël Ⓜ French

| | 24 | 20 | 22 | $43 |

Little Italy/University Village | 1119 W. Taylor St. (May St.) | 312-226-6479 | www.chezjoelbistro.com

"Right at home in Little Italy", this "welcome exception" of a French "charmer" features a "classic bistro experience" with "authentic" fare and "friendly, helpful service" in a "comfortable neighborhood setting"; it's considered a "value" by surveyors who also note an "outdoor space that's quite special."

🆕 Chez Violette Ⓜ Haitian

| | - | - | - | I |

Rogers Park | 2311 W. Howard St. (bet. Claremont & Oakley Aves.) | 773-961-7275 | www.chezviolette.com

Rogers Park hosts this casual, BYO Haitian hangout offering all-day dining ranging from national classics like pâté patties, goat stew and griot (pork with plantains) to American comfort foods; the bright storefront includes bare tables and an open kitchen.

Chicago Burgerwurks 🅭 Burgers

| | - | - | - | I |

Brookfield | 8819 W. Ogden Ave. (Grove Ave.) | 708-387-2333

A ketchup-and-mustard-colored exterior sets the mood at this West Suburban hamburger stand, where gluttons gorge on elevated fast fare at a half-dozen stools or ramshackle picnic tables; its affordable menu includes 26 burger varieties (and corresponding chicken sammies), plus dogs, soups (available October–May) and gravy-topped fries.

🅩 Chicago Chop House Steak

| | 25 | 21 | 23 | $66 |

River North | 60 W. Ontario St. (bet. Clark & Dearborn Sts.) | 312-787-7100 | www.chicagochophouse.com

Carnivores concur "steak becomes an experience, not just a meal" at River North's "classic Chicago" "bastion of big beef" (and "fabulous fish") complete with a "piano player" and pictures of local celebrities "on the wall"; the "old men's-club vibe" may be better for "business" than "romance", especially given the "expense-account" tariff, and though most call the staff "professional", some say what's most "legendary" is the "wait" to be seated.

Chicago Curry House *Indian/Nepalese*   25 | 18 | 21 | $28
South Loop | 899 S. Plymouth Ct. (9th St.) | 312-362-9999 |
www.curryhouseonline.com

"Delicious" and "authentic", the Indian-Nepalese cuisine goes beyond "excellent curries" to include "some unusual dishes" (such as momo dumplings) say South Loopers who've sampled this "wonderful" "neighborhood" spot's midpriced menu with an "extra spin"; the "polite" staff "goes out of its way to please" in the "pleasant", "simple space", and the "lunch buffet is a fantastic value."

NEW Chicago Cut Steakhouse *Steak*   – | – | – | E
River North | 300 N. LaSalle St. (bet. Kinzie St. & Wacker Dr.) |
312-329-1800 | www.chicagocutsteakhouse.com

A pair of Chicago steakhouse veterans are behind this handsome white-tablecloth River North meatery where the prime dry-aged beef includes double cuts and the iPad wine list showcases multiple magnums (there's plenty of seafood too); the traditional upscale atmosphere features red velvet and leather seating and a wall of windows overlooking the patio and the Chicago River; P.S. Jackie Shen (ex-chef of the now defunct Red Light) came onboard post-opening.

Chicago Diner *Diner/Vegetarian*   22 | 14 | 19 | $21
Lakeview | 3411 N. Halsted St. (Roscoe St.) | 773-935-6696 |
www.veggiediner.com

"'Meat-free since '83' is the catchy slogan" at this Lakeview longtimer touted as a "safe haven" serving "innovative", "value"-priced vegetarian fare "with all sorts of dietary needs met" amid decor that "looks like a diner" because "that's what it is"; "servers are a little too cool for school" and omnivores opine "if you aren't vegan, it's hit-or-miss", but the "back patio is beautiful in the summer."

Chicago Firehouse *American*   20 | 21 | 21 | $45
South Loop | 1401 S. Michigan Ave. (14th St.) | 312-786-1401 |
www.chicagofirehouse.com

With its "unusual ambiance" "in a cleverly remodeled old firehouse" (circa 1905) as a "definite draw", this Traditional American "delivers" "one of the classiest" dining experiences "in the South Loop" to a brigade of believers who "enjoy" the "classic dishes" and "wonderful steaks"; though wet blankets deem it "just ok for the cost", generally "professional service" and a "summer patio" fan the flames.

Chicago Pizza &   23 | 16 | 20 | $22
Oven Grinder Co. ⌿ *Pizza*
Lincoln Park | 2121 N. Clark St. (bet. Dickens & Webster Aves.) |
773-248-2570 | www.chicagopizzaandovengrinder.com

"Pizza in a bowl? oh yes, my friend" affirm fans of Lincoln Park's "unique Chicago" "dive-gem" famed for its affordable "pot pie" 'za and "ginormous subs" with "fresh ingredients" served in a "cuckoo" "'70s ski lodge" setting; there are "no credit cards and no reservations, so come prepared to pay cash and wait" warn patient patrons who insist "that guy who remembers where we are in line 40 minutes later" must have a "photographic memory."

NEW Chicago Q *BBQ*

| - | - | - | M |

Gold Coast | 1160 N. Dearborn St. (bet. Division & Elm Sts.) | 312-642-1160 | www.chicagoqrestaurant.com

At this Gold Coaster, pedigreed pit-master Lee Ann Whippen wrangles upscale barbecue – from meaty regional favorites cooked with various woods to Kobe brisket – accompanied by sides like 'pig powder' chips and hominy with smoked corn and black beans, plus a generous wine selection, fresh juices, craft sodas and French press coffee; the stylish setting's refined furnishings, including stone floors and black-leather seating, put surprising polish on the notion of the neighborhood pit stop.

Chicago's Home of Chicken & Waffles *Southern*

| - | - | - | M |

River North | 3947 S. King Dr. (Oakwood Blvd.) | 773-536-3300
NEW **Oak Park** | 543 W. Madison St. (bet. Scoville & SE Aves.) | 708-524-3300
www.chicagoshomeofchickenandwaffles.com

The brick-trimmed, mahogany-hued River North original has been followed up with a swanky Oak Parker turning out generously portioned soul food – including renditions of the namesake – in an upscale, exposed-brick space with low lighting; a friendly air and down-home sides (collards, grits, mac 'n' cheese) further prove popular with the after-church crowd, who flood its mock 'gator banquettes – especially during weekend brunch.

Chickpea ⊭ *Mideastern*

| 22 | 18 | 19 | $15 |

West Town | 2018 W. Chicago Ave. (bet. Damen & Hoyne Aves.) | 773-384-9930 | www.chickpeaonthego.com

West Town's "friendly" oasis offers "healthy, delicious" "home-cooked" Middle Eastern and "authentic Palestinian" fare – prepared by the owner's mother – in a "cool space" with a "warm" vibe and budget-coddling prices (including the $1 BYO corkage fee); P.S. it's cash-only and there's no reserving, but delivery is now available.

Chief O'Neill's *Pub Food*

| 18 | 18 | 17 | $24 |

Northwest Side | 3471 N. Elston Ave. (Albany Ave.) | 773-583-3066 | www.chiefoneillspub.com

"Solid, hearty" fare – including "tasty, traditional" Emerald Isle favorites and a Sunday brunch buffet "deal" – goes down easy with a "terrific Guinness pour" and "Irish musical entertainment" (Sundays and Tuesdays) at this "comfortable", wallet-friendly Northwest Side "neighborhood pub"; a staff with "personality" and "one of the best beer gardens in the city" add to the allure; N.B. Saturday breakfast has been added.

NEW Chikurin Sushi & Asian Cuisines *Asian*

— | — | — | M

Wicker Park | 1811 W. North Ave. (bet. Honore & Wood Sts.) | 773-252-8880 | www.chikurinchicago.com

This subterranean strip-mall lair in Wicker Park offers sushi and maki along with a midpriced all-Asian menu (Thai, Chinese, Japanese and Korean) of stir-fries, curries and noodle dishes for lunch and dinner; the modern setting features well-spaced table and banquette seating, with abstract mirrored artwork inspired by bamboo (in a nod to the restaurant's name), and the free parking lot is an asset in this busy 'hood.

Chilam Balam 🗷 M ⊄ *Mexican*

25 | 14 | 21 | $31

Lakeview | 3023 N. Broadway (bet. Barry & Wellington Aves.) | 773-296-6901 | www.chilambalamchicago.com

Diners "crowd" into this "teeny" Lakeview "basement" for "adventurous", "delicious" "Mexican small plates" with "huge flavor" (plus some larger plates) served in a "funky" setting with "lively artwork"; "you may have to wait for a table" and it's "not cheap", but the "BYO policy helps keep the price down" (margarita mix and virgin sangria are available); P.S. it's "cash-only."

China Grill *Asian*

22 | 22 | 20 | $55

Loop | Hard Rock Hotel | 230 N. Michigan Ave. (Lake St.) | 312-334-6700 | www.chinagrillmgt.com

"Hip", "contemporary" and "loud", this Loop chain link in the Hard Rock Hotel dishes out a "diverse, upscale" Asian menu and "amazing concoctions at the bar" in a setting featuring red lacquer walls; while some surveyors are "pleasantly surprised" by the fare (if not so much the spotty service), others are "shocked by the price" and "eliminate it as an option" unless "with a group" so the "large portions" "can be shared."

Chinn's 34th St. Fishery *Seafood*

25 | 15 | 23 | $37

Lisle | 3011 W. Ogden Ave. (Fender Ave.) | 630-637-1777 | www.chinns-fishery.com

"Delicious fresh fish" (flown in daily) is "reasonably priced" at this "hopping" Lisle seafooder where "signature mai tais" and "addictive garlic rolls" add zest to a "bland" nautical setting; "service is always 'on'" and it's "kid-friendly", so most don't mind the lack of "inventive recipes" (as evidenced in improved scores across the board).

NEW Chizakaya ❶ 🗷 *Japanese*

— | — | — | M

Lakeview | 3056 N. Lincoln Ave. (bet. Barry & Wellington Aves.) | 773-697-4725 | www.chizakaya.com

Eliding 'Chicago' and 'izakaya', this Lakeview Japanese pub boasts two pedigreed chefs in the kitchen crafting a menu of elevated modern small plates (puffed pig ears, beef liver 'sashimi', hamachi with bone marrow) from local and sustainable sources, served along with plenty of sake, shochu, whiskey, beer and signature cocktails; the spare modern space sports an open kitchen, a mix of regular and communal tables and fantastical ceiling murals depicting a geisha and samurai.

	FOOD	DECOR	SERVICE	COST

Choppers *Burgers*

| - | - | - | I |

Wicker Park | 1659 N. Ashland Ave. (bet. North & Wabansia Aves.) | 773-227-7800 | www.choppers-chicago.com

This long-standing Wicker Park greasy spoon is known as much for its casual, retro vibe as for its Choppak – a classic double cheeseburger with fries and creamy slaw; other choices include Chicago-style dogs and Italian beef, plus ultrathick malts and shakes (try the cinnamon apple pie), the largest of which are served in a souvenir cup.

Cho Sun Ok *Korean*

| - | - | - | I |

North Center/St. Ben's | 4200 N. Lincoln Ave. (Berteau Ave.) | 773-549-5555 | www.chosunokrestaurant.com

North Center noshers have been cooking their own 'cue (meats, tripe, octopus) for over 30 years at this BYO Korean classic, where the rest of the menu offers a wide variety of authentic entrees (kimchi stew, bibimbop, various noodle dishes) and chef's specials served from early lunch to late dinner; the bustling, family-friendly setting is warmly lit and well ventilated and prices are low, which further explains why lines are not uncommon.

C-House *Seafood*

| 21 | 22 | 21 | $56 |

Streeterville | Affinia Chicago Hotel | 166 E. Superior St. (St. Clair St.) | 312-523-0923 | www.c-houserestaurant.com

Chef Marcus Samuelsson (NYC's Red Rooster) has "brought his skills to the Windy City" to a mixed reception at this Streeterville seafood house – one school calls the "creative fresh take on small plates" served amid "modern, simplistic" decor "wonderful and innovative", while another pegs the edibles "erratic" at prices that are "a bit much" (granted it's in an "expensive area"); service, however, is "welcoming."

Ciao Napoli Pizzeria *Pizza*

| - | - | - | M |

Logan Square | 2607 N. Milwaukee Ave. (Sawyer Ave.) | 773-278-7300 | www.ciaonapolipizzeria.com

A hand-built brick pizza oven fires the Neapolitan 'za crafted from imported ingredients by a native pizzaiolo at this midpriced Logan Square arrival also known for fresh pasta, Italian doughnuts and artful cocktails; the warm, urban-rustic setting combines exposed brick, wood, lots of windows and a bar where you can keep your eye on the pies.

Cibo Matto ⚿Ⓜ *Italian*

| 24 | 26 | 23 | $53 |

Loop | theWit Hotel | 201 N. State St. (Lake St.) | 312-239-9500 | www.eatcibomatto.com

"Trendy" types testify the "hype is justified" at this "elegant but happening" Loop Italian in theWit Hotel where "ultramodern decor" with "swanky booths" is the setting for "inventive", "beautifully presented" seasonal cuisine accompanied by "informed service"; while it may be "expensive", the "see-and-be-seen" atmosphere makes for a special "night out"; N.B. the Food score doesn't reflect a post-Survey chef change.

Cité *American*

20 | 26 | 20 | $71

Streeterville | Lake Point Tower | 505 N. Lake Shore Dr., 70th fl. (Navy Pier) | 312-644-4050 | www.citechicago.com

City-dwellers and "tourists" alike seek out this "quiet", "elegant" (jackets suggested) New American – towering 70 stories above Streeterville since 1969 – "for a romantic dinner or special occasion" complete with a "phenomenal" 360-degree panorama; grudging graders who call the service and "expensive" fare "not fantastic" grump "you can't eat the view."

CityGate Grille Ⓩ *American/Mediterranean*

– | – | – | M

Naperville | CityGate Ctr. | 2020 Calamos Ct. (Westings Ave.) | 630-718-1010 | www.citygategrille.com

West Suburban Naperville's LEED-certified CityGate Centre is home to this New American with Mediterranean underpinnings that serves lunch and dinner (there's a bar menu too), accompanied by signature cocktails and a Cal-Med wine list; the smart, handsome space boasts walls of windows and tiered pendant light fixtures, and there's live music on Fridays and Saturdays.

NEW City Provisions Deli Ⓜ *Deli*

– | – | – | I

Ravenswood | 1818 W. Wilson Ave. (bet. Ravenswood & Wolcott Aves.) | 773-293-2489 | www.cityprovisions.com

A catering company has expanded its operations to serve counter-service deli fare at a bright, casual Ravenswood storefront where it butchers, roasts and cures meats and bakes its own bread; most everything else is sourced close to home (including sustainable beer and wine and local dairy products), and salads, coffee and to-go dinners round out the affordable offerings.

Clubhouse, The *American*

21 | 21 | 20 | $40

Oak Brook | Oakbrook Center Mall | 298 Oakbrook Ctr. (Rte. 83) | 630-472-0600 | www.theclubhouse.com

Surveyors swinging into this "upscale American" in Oak Brook's mall for a "business lunch, happy hour" or "break from shopping" find "comfort food" in "large portions" (including "monster-sized salads" and "massive desserts"); service might be "hit-or-miss", but the place offers "something for everyone in both cuisine and price", including a Sunday brunch with "value"; P.S. the bar is "always buzzing" with "singles" but the "upstairs is quieter" and patio seating has expanded.

Club Lucky *Italian*

19 | 16 | 20 | $30

Bucktown | 1824 W. Wabansia Ave. (Honore St.) | 773-227-2300 | www.clubluckychicago.com

"Old-time homestyle Italian" fare "in a new-wave neighborhood" lures Bucktowners to this '40s-style "supper club" that pours some of the "best martinis in town"; service is "attentive", and while most call the "red-sauce" fare "satisfying" and "lots for the buck", even those "underwhelmed" by it admit the "red-checkered tablecloths and wall-to-wall cool vibe" "keep you coming back."

	FOOD	DECOR	SERVICE	COST

Coalfire Pizza Ⓜ *Pizza* | 23 | 13 | 18 | $20

Noble Square | 1321 W. Grand Ave. (bet. Ada & Elizabeth Sts.) |
312-226-2625 | www.coalfirechicago.com

"Excellent East Coast–style" pie wins "thin-crust" fans for this
"funky little" affordable Noble Square "joint" with a "kick-ass coal-
burning" oven "so hot the pizza always comes out a little" "charred"
(which some "love" and others call "burnt"); "now that they have
their liquor license" regulars reckon "the only thing holding them
back" is the somewhat "remote" locale.

Coast Sushi Bar ◑ *Japanese* | 24 | 20 | 18 | $36

Bucktown | 2045 N. Damen Ave. (bet. Dickens & McLean Aves.) |
773-235-5775 | www.coastsushibar.com

Southcoast *Japanese*

South Loop | 1700 S. Michigan Ave. (bet. 16th & 18th Sts.) |
312-662-1700 | www.southcoastsushi.com

Fin fans attest this Bucktown Japanese "BYO treasure" (with a South
Loop sibling that serves wine) offers "extremely fresh" fish and a
"wide variety" of "creative rolls" while "keeping costs down and
quality high"; it's not only a suitable "place for friends to eat" or a
"date", but even for losing one's "sushi virginity" – thanks to a
"knowledgeable staff" and "loungey" feel.

Ⓩ Coco Pazzo *Italian* | 25 | 22 | 24 | $52

River North | 300 W. Hubbard St. (Franklin St.) | 312-836-0900 |
www.cocopazzochicago.com

Surveyors are "still crazy after all these years" for this "sophisticated, simple and not snooty" River Norther whether "for business
dining, pre-theater" or a "quick and classy lunch" of "remarkable",
"*delizioso*" "seasonal" Northern Italian cuisine; the all-Italy "long
and varied wine list", "elegant" "loft" setting with "white tablecloths" and "consummately professional staff" complete a "Tuscan
experience" that's "expensive" and "worth it."

Coco Pazzo Café *Italian* | 22 | 19 | 20 | $40

Streeterville | Red Roof Inn | 636 N. St. Clair St. (Ontario St.) |
312-664-2777 | www.cocopazzocafe.com

Amici of "Coco Pazzo's unassuming but overachieving little brother"
consider it a Streeterville "gem" by virtue of its "simple", "moderately priced" menu including "authentic pastas" and "delicious antipasti" served in "smart casual" surroundings with a "contemporary
European feel" right down to the "alfresco" patio; if "service is a cut
below" its "upscale sibling" and one rater's "cozy" is another's
"crowded", most dub it "always satisfying."

Conoce Mi Panama Ⓜ *Central American* | - | - | - | I

Logan Square | 3054 W. Armitage Ave. (bet. Albany Ave. & Whipple St.) |
773-252-7440 | www.conocemipanama.weebly.com

Hearty plates of Panamanian cuisine with Costa Rican and
Caribbean accents lure Logan Square locals to this inexpensive BYO
(beer and wine only), which also offers vegetarian and vegan options plus nonalcoholic beverages and coffees; the little brick store-

front has a casual yet warm feel with hot-hued walls, photographs of Panama and catchy island background music.

Coobah *Filipino/Nuevo Latino*   17 | 17 | 17 | $32
Lakeview | 3423 N. Southport Ave. (bet. Newport Ave. & Roscoe St.) | 773-528-2220 | www.coobah.com
"Eclectic" Nuevo Latino–Filipino "flavor combinations" and "delicious" weekend brunch in a "sexy", "clubby" and "dark" setting are the draw at this midpriced Lakeview lair; though downbeat diners dish the "drinks are better than the food" and "service has opportunity for improvement", the "upbeat vibe" trumps all for many.

Corner 41 Bar & Grill *American*   - | - | - | M
North Center/St. Ben's | 4138 N. Lincoln Ave. (bet. Berteau & Warner Aves.) | 773-327-3500 | www.corner41.com
This upscale North Center bar and grill offers a midpriced American menu including prime beef, a lengthy sandwich list and some Italian-Med fare, plus full-bar service and local beers from Half Acre Brewery; there's a rustic-industrial feel to the open, loftlike room with open ductwork and warm lighting, and you can eat outdoors as well.

Co-Si-Na Grill Ⓜ *Mexican*   - | - | - | I
Andersonville | 1706 W. Foster Ave. (Paulina St.) | 773-271-7103 | www.co-si-na.com
"Authentic", affordable Mexican fare and "complex, flavorful moles" draw Andersonville denizens for lunch and dinner to this "appealing little storefront" with a simple, colorful interior including a painted concrete floor; P.S. "BYO is encouraged" (with virgin piña coladas plus strawberry daiquiri and flavored margarita mixes on hand).

Costa's *Greek*   22 | 19 | 20 | $37
Oakbrook Terrace | 1 S. 130 Summit Ave. (Roosevelt Rd.) | 630-620-1100 | www.costasdining.com
While the Greektown mainstay has closed due to a fire (repairs are pending), fans attest this midpriced Oakbrook Terrace outpost serves "traditional, satisfying" Greek fare along with a selection of wines from Greece in a "relaxed atmosphere" where "you'll be treated like family"; N.B. there's live entertainment on weekends.

Counter, The *Burgers*   20 | 15 | 19 | $19
Lincoln Park | 666 W. Diversey Pkwy. (bet. Clark & Orchard Sts.) | 773-935-1995 | www.thecounterburger.com
"Customize" your ("huge") burger and toppings from a "great variety" of "combinations" (including a "bunless bowl") at this Lincoln Park chain link that also offers "shakes and shareable sides of fries" in a "hip, dinerlike environment"; some think it's "overpriced for what it is" but the brew crew likes the "beers on tap."

Courtright's Ⓜ *American*   25 | 26 | 25 | $66
Willow Springs | 8989 S. Archer Ave. (Willow Springs Rd.) | 708-839-8000 | www.courtrights.com
"Overlooking a forest preserve", the "view is always spectacular" at this "upscale, pricey" Southwest Suburban "fine-dining spot" where

the "wonderful", "inventive" New American cuisine is accompanied by an "excellent wine list", all served by a "knowledgeable" staff; the Arts and Crafts setting contributes additional "warmth" and "elegance" to a "night to remember", "especially with the tasting menu."

Crêpe Crave *Crêpes*

FOOD	DECOR	SERVICE	COST
-	-	-	I

Wicker Park | 1752 W. North Ave. (bet. Hermitage Ave. & Wood St.) | 773-698-8783 | www.crepecrave.com

Wicker Park's affordable "neighborhood" "quick-service" BYO offers "tasty crêpes" and the option to choose "one of their suggested combos or make up your own"; add in a "personable" "counter staff", plus gelato and coffee, and it's suitable "for takeout or dine-in."

Crêpe Town *Crêpes*

FOOD	DECOR	SERVICE	COST
-	-	-	I

Lakeview | 3915 N. Sheridan Rd. (Dakin St.) | 773-248-8844
Creative crêpes make for budget-friendly bites at this upscale-casual Lakeview counter-service BYO with bright, modern decor; you can take out or grab a table to also enjoy a smoothie or coffee.

☑ Crofton on Wells ⊠ *American*

FOOD	DECOR	SERVICE	COST
26	21	25	$60

River North | 535 N. Wells St. (bet. Grand Ave. & Ohio St.) | 312-755-1790 | www.croftononwells.com

Suzy Crofton's "refined", "inventive" New American fare featuring "impressive local ingredients" (including "fabulous vegetarian options") compensates for the "drab decor" at this "steady" River North "treasure" tended by a "professional" staff; patrons who declare it "doesn't get the hype of others but is just as tasty" plead "please don't tell anyone"; P.S. it's "expensive, but worth the price."

Crust *Pizza*

FOOD	DECOR	SERVICE	COST
19	15	15	$23

Wicker Park | 2056 W. Division St. (Hoyne Ave.) | 773-235-5511 | www.crustorganic.com

Michael Altenberg's "cool", "casual" Wicker Park pizzeria turns out "gourmet" seasonal pies with a "special", "thin and crispy crust" for patrons who praise the "natural and organic offerings" in both the fare and the "many beers"; "infused vodkas" help take the edge off spotty service, and tabs are "quite reasonable"; P.S. fresh-air fiends gravitate to "one of the large outdoor spaces", front or back.

Cucina Paradiso *Italian*

FOOD	DECOR	SERVICE	COST
∇ 20	20	21	$36

Oak Park | 814 North Blvd. (Oak Park Ave.) | 708-848-3434 | www.cucinaoakpark.com

Oak Park's "neighborhood" *cucina* "charms" with "pasta classics with a twist" and other "delicious" Italian fare served in a warm, modern setting with brick and yellow walls hung with posters and photos; "accommodating" service adds to the "experience", and a patio and moderate prices help make it "worth a visit."

NEW Cumin *Nepalese*

FOOD	DECOR	SERVICE	COST
-	-	-	M

Wicker Park | 1414 N. Milwaukee Ave. (bet. Evergreen & Wolcott Aves.) | 773-342-1414 | www.cumin-chicago.com

This newcomer spices up Wicker Park with an exhaustive midpriced menu of contemporary Nepalese and Indian fare, accompanied by

	FOOD	DECOR	SERVICE	COST

selections from a full bar and exotic nonalcoholic drinks including shakes, lassis and juices; the trendy, white-tablecloth setting welcomes with bright walls, wood floors and landscape paintings – and despite the modern vibe, there's still a traditional bargain lunch buffet.

NEW Currents on the River ⌧ *American*   — | — | — | M

Loop | 200 S. Wacker Dr. (Adams St.) | 312-846-6692 | www.currentsontheriver.com

Open for breakfast, lunch and dinner on weekdays only, this American bistro in the Loop offers a midpriced menu showcasing local ingredients and global accents (think Thai katsu chicken satay and Moroccan vegetable stew) with full bar signature cocktails; the traditional masculine decor includes warm wood and carpeted floors, as well as an entryway aquarium and a sprawling riverside view.

Curry Hut Restaurant *Indian/Nepalese*   20 | 15 | 19 | $25

Highwood | 410 Sheridan Rd. (bet. Walker & Webster Aves.) | 847-432-2889 | www.curryhutrestaurant.com

Surveyors "welcome" the "change of taste" and "value" at this "kid-friendly" Highwood hut that offers a "unique combination of Nepal and India" and "even Indian wines" and beers; the "run-of-the-mill" decor doesn't need to impress given "attentive" service and an "extensive" "lunch buffet worth coming for" on the budget-loving scene.

Custom House Tavern *American*   25 | 23 | 25 | $58

Printer's Row | Wyndham Blake | 500 S. Dearborn St. (Congress Pkwy.) | 312-523-0200 | www.customhouse.cc

A broader menu of "wonderful new items" (including a tavern menu in the lounge) is replacing the former meat-centric concept at this Hotel Blake New American where "pleasant, efficient service" and a "wine list without the usual suspects" help make the "modern, elegant" quarters suitable "for a business lunch or dinner" and "well worth beating a path to" Printer's Row; N.B. the Food score may not reflect a recent chef change.

Cyrano's Bistrot & Wine Bar ⌧ *French*   22 | 19 | 20 | $42

River North | 546 N. Wells St. (Ohio St.) | 312-467-0546 | www.cyranosbistrot.com

"Authenticity has made" this River Norther a "keeper" for its "traditional" French bistro "favorites" ("chef Didier [Durand] cares") complete with "quaint" "character" and "streetscape sidewalk" seating; the "reasonable price lets you eat like a Frenchman without the airfare", making it "suitable for casual, business or romantic" meals.

Czech Plaza *Czech*   ▽ 22 | 8 | 18 | $19

Berwyn | 7016 W. Cermak Rd. (bet. Home & Wenonah Aves.) | 708-795-6555 | www.czechplaza.com

"Generous portions" of "inexpensive", "authentic" fare "not for" lightweights draw big eaters to Berwyn's Czech chowhouse where "meals include soup, dessert" and side dishes plus "good beer and broken English"; furthermore, "you can have supper with every grandma in the neighborhood" amid "simple" decor that "hasn't changed in decades" (possibly since 1962).

D & J Bistro ☒ *French*

24 | 19 | 23 | $43

Lake Zurich | First Bank Plaza Ctr. | 466 S. Rand Rd./Rte. 12 (Rte. 22) | 847-438-8001 | www.dj-bistro.com

Lake Zurich's "bustling" "charmer" is a "solid performer" that "belies its location" "in a strip mall" with a "wonderful", "authentic" "French bistro menu", "personal service" and "very European surroundings" including a "congenial bar area" – all of which make it a local "favorite" "in this price range."

Dan McGee ☒ *American*

– | – | – | M

Frankfort | 9975 W. Lincoln Hwy. (N. Locust St.) | 815-469-7750 | www.danmcgees.com

Champions cheer "chef Dan gets it" by dishing out "top-notch", "amply portioned" "American fare" (including "spot-on desserts") with "cocktails and service" to match at this Frankfort "find"; "comfortable" yet "sophisticated" "minimalist" decor "rounds out the experience", which South Suburbanites swear "saves the trip Downtown for comparable cuisine."

NEW Danzón ☒ *Nuevo Latino*

– | – | – | M

Logan Square | 2715 N. Milwaukee Ave. (Sawyer Ave.) | 773-698-6640 | www.danzonlatino.com

Geno Bahena's Logan Square BYO (named for a Cuban dance) offers the Mexican maven's modern take on mild to spicy Nuevo Latino comfort foods, e.g. carne asada, Creole hushpuppies, Colombian stuffed potatoes, all at moderate prices; the casual corner storefront is done in fiery reds and oranges, and the open kitchen includes both a slow-roasting oven and mesquite wood-burning grill; P.S. there's free WiFi.

NEW Davanti Enoteca *Italian*

– | – | – | M

Little Italy/University Village | 1359 W. Taylor St. (Loomis St.) | 312-226-5550 | www.davantichicago.com

Scott Harris is behind this stylish, moderately priced restaurant and wine bar, a neighbor to the Little Italy branch of Francesca's serving small shareable Italian plates, pizza and pasta for lunch and dinner daily (plus weekend brunch); the rustic-chic setting conjures a wine cellar, with exposed brick, reclaimed wood and floor-to-ceiling vino displays – in an unusual policy, patrons can buy wine at modest retail prices and drink it with their meal for a corkage fee or take it home to enjoy later.

Dave's
Italian Kitchen *Italian*

17 | 11 | 17 | $19

Evanston | 1635 Chicago Ave., downstairs (bet. Church & Davis Sts.) | 847-864-6000 | www.davesik.com

Boosters believe they're "back in college" at this "Evanston tradition" "run by really nice folks" "that keeps on keeping on" serving "standard, huge" "homestyle" Italian dishes "at giveaway prices" in a "casual" "basement" with "simple decor"; unconvinced eaters say it's not for "adults looking for real food" but "fine for family dining with the children."

	FOOD	DECOR	SERVICE	COST

☑ David Burke's Primehouse *Steak* — 25 | 22 | 23 | $71

River North | The James Chicago Hotel | 616 N. Rush St. (Ontario St.) |
312-660-6000 | www.davidburke.com

"Magnificent" meat praised for its "depth, power and tang" (including long-"aged masterpieces") plus an "excellent array of sides and desserts", "expansive wine list" and "wonderful" weekend brunch win fans for this "classy", "contemporary" River North "steakhouse with imagination" that's "more hip than its competitors"; the "prices can stop your heart quicker than the cholesterol will", and though a few have their "doubts", most agree that the fare and service "are worth it."

Davis Street Fishmarket *Seafood* — 19 | 16 | 18 | $38

Evanston | 501 Davis St. (Hinman Ave.) | 847-869-3474 |
www.davisstreetfishmarket.com

Evanston locals hit this "reliable" midpriced "neighborhood" seafooder for a "wealth of fish choices" (including Cajun) "in a casual atmosphere", "fresh raw oysters" and "lobster specials that can't be beat"; service can be "iffy" and nostalgists still "miss the old feel" from before "it made its upscale move", but they're outnumbered by those who find the nautical decor "attractive", thus it's "often crowded."

Deca Restaurant + Bar *French* — - | - | - | M

Streeterville | Ritz-Carlton Hotel | 160 E. Pearson St., 12th fl.
(Michigan Ave.) | 312-573-5160 | www.decarestaurant.com

As part of a multimillion-dollar renovation, the Ritz-Carlton has debuted this midpriced French brasserie concept featuring *fruits de mer* and classic dishes from locally sourced ingredients with 40 wines by the glass (half the list); the open setting in the 12th-floor lobby features multilevel seating, handsome art deco–inspired decor, adjustable lighting at each table and a chic bar with a sweeping city view situated by the famous fountain.

De Cero ⓜ *Mexican* — 21 | 17 | 16 | $32

West Loop | 814 W. Randolph St. (bet. Green & Halsted Sts.) |
312-455-8114 | www.decerotaqueria.com

Patrons praise this "modern" West Loop "taco shop" for its "excellent selection" of "tapas-style Mexican" fare, "outstanding cocktails" and "people-watching" amid "trendy", "design-savvy" digs; naysayers call the noshes "overpriced" and "don't understand why this place is so crowded" to which amigos answer "sitting outside in the summer sipping margaritas with duck nachos is the way to live."

Decolores *Mexican* — - | - | - | I

Pilsen | 1626 S. Halsted St. (17th St.) | 312-226-9886 | www.decolor.us

Fresh Mexican lunch and dinner fare – including traditional dishes, seafood specialties, housemade moles, three flavors of tres leches and agua frescas – comes at affordable prices at this Pilsen storefront BYO; past the charming brick facade, the simple interior is accented by a giant skull mural and other local artwork, plus skylights and ceiling fans.

	FOOD	DECOR	SERVICE	COST

Dee's *Asian*   19 | 16 | 18 | $29

Lincoln Park | 1114 W. Armitage Ave. (Seminary Ave.) | 773-477-1500 | www.deesrestaurant.com

"If you want sushi" plus Mandarin and Sichuan specialties all "in one restaurant", this "upscale" Lincoln Park "institution" fills the bill; its "attractive" space complete with roomy patio, "warm, charming" owner and "live jazz" on Wednesdays and Fridays have many calling it dee-lightful, but the less-impressed dismiss it as a "jack of all trades, master of none."

Dee's Place *Soul Food/Southern*   - | - | - | I

Wicker Park | 2114 W. Division St. (Hoyne Ave.) | 312-348-6117 | www.deesplacechicago.com

Not to be confused with Dee's in Lincoln Park, this neighborhood storefront BYO in Wicker Park dishes up hearty, inexpensive Southern and soul-food classics (barbecue from the house pit, fried chicken and catfish, greens, mac 'n' cheese); the funky, casual setting hosts a variety of weekend entertainment, including movies and live jazz and blues.

Deleece *Eclectic*   19 | 16 | 19 | $32

Lakeview | 4004 N. Southport Ave. (Irving Park Rd.) | 773-325-1710 | www.deleece.com

"For a regular night out", fans of this "welcoming" Lakeview veteran favor its "fresh, inventive" Eclectic dishes and "fantastic deals on Mondays and Tuesdays" (three courses for $20), not to mention its "pleasing contemporary" interior heavy on "exposed brick and wood" and "nice patio"; some "disappointed" dinner patrons claim its "aspirations are higher than its reach", but even they "recommend brunch"; P.S. a planned move is scheduled to take them a few blocks away (3747 North Southport Avenue) in summer 2011.

Deleece Grill Pub Ⓜ *American*   ▽ 20 | 15 | 18 | $25

Lakeview | 3313 N. Clark St. (bet. Aldine Ave. & Buckingham Pl.) | 773-348-3313 | www.deleecegrillpub.com

A casual counterpart to nearby Deleece, this Lakeview standby offers "tasty", "value"-priced steaks, chops and American "comfort" staples (e.g. "a variety of mac 'n' cheese" iterations), which go down well with its "fantastic" craft beers; "warm" decor "with lots of local art on the walls" is another reason locals keep coming back to this "friendly", pubbish place.

Del Rio Ⓢ Ⓜ *Italian*   20 | 15 | 21 | $39

Highwood | 228 Green Bay Rd. (Rte. 22) | 847-432-4608

It "hasn't changed in years" (possibly since 1923) and that pleases fans of this "Highwood stalwart", a fourth-generation family-owned "neighborhood red-sauce Italian" appreciated for its "predictable but good food at reasonable cost" ("when you do something right, stick to it") and "vast" wine cellar; ok, maybe it feels "a little tired", but to most it's a "North Shore classic" all the same; N.B. reservations taken for larger parties only.

	FOOD	DECOR	SERVICE	COST

𝐍𝐄𝐖 Del Seoul *Korean*

| - | - | - | I |

Lakeview | 2568 N. Clark St. (Wrightwood Ave.) | 773-248-4227 | www.delseoul.com

At this casual Lakeview noshery, plasma screens display the budget-friendly Korean menu, including decadent pork-belly kimchi french fries, along with a few classics like bibimbop and dumplings; the modern, no-frills setting sports bright colors, corrugated metal and tasteful lighting; P.S. it recently expanded into the space next door.

Demera Ethiopian *Ethiopian*

| - | - | - | I |

Uptown | 4801 N. Broadway (Lawrence Ave.) | 773-334-8787 | www.demeraethiopianrestaurant.com

Two colorful rooms decorated with African carvings and paintings set the tone at this fresh Ethiopian on a prime Uptown corner offering a well-priced menu featuring vegetarian and omnivore entrees served with traditional, hands-on breads; draws also include house-roasted coffee in clay pots (incense optional) and a weekday lunch buffet.

Depot American Diner *Diner*

| - | - | - | I |

Far West | 5840 W. Roosevelt Rd. (bet. Mayfield & Monitor Aves.) | 773-261-8422 | www.depotamericandiner.com

"Such a deal" swoon supporters of this Far West "pinnacle of diner dining" and its "fresh", low-priced, three-meals-a-day American "comfort" classics; regulars "really like their pot-roast sandwich" and "doughnuts to die for", and the "blue-plate specials", a BYO policy and nifty "'50s" decor are more reasons it's "worth going back to."

Depot Nuevo *Nuevo Latino*

| 18 | 18 | 18 | $30 |

Wilmette | 1139 Wilmette Ave. (bet. Central & Lake Aves.) | 847-251-3111 | www.depotnuevo.com

Surveyors split over the food at this Wilmette way station – literally, it's housed in a 100-year-old train depot – with some reporting "tasty, contemporary takes on" Nuevo Latino fare but others merely a "mediocre" "North Shore idea" of the same; however, all agree on the "fabulous" margaritas, "cute" decor and "pleasant porch dining."

Devon Seafood Grill *Seafood*

| 21 | 21 | 20 | $46 |

River North | 39 E. Chicago Ave. (Wabash Ave.) | 312-440-8660 | www.devonseafood.com

"Your choice of preparations" of fish ordered from a "diverse" menu is the deal at this "solid", "subtly elegant" River North link of an "upscale" seafood chain; the "main floor" and its "crowded" bar boasts plenty of "buzz", while the downstairs dining room's "cozy booths" are "better for conversation" – either way most rate the overall package "nicely done"; P.S. check out the "great happy-hour specials."

Dining Room at Kendall College 𝕊 𝕄 *French*

| 23 | 20 | 22 | $40 |

Near West | Kendall College | 900 N. North Branch St. (Halsted St.) | 312-752-2328 | www.kendall.edu

At this "special, hidden" Near West learning ground, Kendall College students prepare the New French "fine-dining" fare, which is served by "nervous, dewy-eyed" trainees in "simple, elegant" digs elevated by "sweeping" skyline views; it's a "nice deal" for lunch or dinner, and a "great way to support" the "next generation of American chefs"; P.S. it now has a full bar and wine list.

Dinotto Ristorante *Italian*   19 | 17 | 19 | $36

Old Town | 215 W. North Ave. (Wells St.) | 312-202-0302 | www.dinotto.com

Old Towners tout this "charming, comfortable neighborhood favorite" for its "tasty" Italian cooking at "reasonable prices", "great" wine list and "cozy", "traditionally appointed" space augmented with a "wonderful patio"; a few who feel it "needs new menu items" shrug "nothing special", but they're in the minority; P.S. it's well located for dining "pre–Second City or Zanies."

Di Pescara *Italian/Seafood*   19 | 16 | 19 | $36

Northbrook | Northbrook Court Shopping Ctr. | 2124 Northbrook Ct. (Lake Cook Rd.) | 847-498-4321 | www.leye.com

"Better-than-average mall grub" satisfies "shoppers", "families" and "ladies who lunch" at this Italian seafooder from the Lettuce group that's especially appreciated given "Northbrook Court's limited selection" of eating options; sure, plenty are "unimpressed", citing an "uninspired" menu and "uneven" service, but it's "always crowded" (and "noisy") nonetheless – so "come early or make a reservation."

NEW DiSotto Enoteca ● *Italian*   - | - | - | M

Streeterville | Francesca's on Chestnut | 200 E. Chestnut St. (bet. DeWitt Pl. & Mies van der Rohe way) | 312-482-8727

Scott Harris (Mia Francesca, Davanti Enoteca, The Purple Pig et al.) is behind this cavernous, vaulted subterranean wine bar – his fourth new venture within a month's time – beneath Francesca's on Chestnut in Streeterville; sidle up to the small bar or grab a table in the earth-toned hideaway for 35 wines by the glass and a modern Italian, small-plates lineup served until 2 AM on weekends.

Distinctive Cork ▣ *American*   ▽ 21 | 22 | 21 | $35

Naperville | 192 W. Gartner Rd. (Washington St.) | 630-753-9463 | www.distinctivecork.com

Naperville's "off-the-beaten-path" "gem" of a wine bar offers a "short menu" of "bistro-style" New American small plates and entrees, all designed to go well with the wines available "by the taste, glass, flight or bottle"; it's equally suited for a "light, casual" get-together with friends or a "quiet, romantic" dinner, with weekend jazz and sidewalk dining in summer to further boost the mood.

Ditka's *Steak*   22 | 21 | 21 | $50

Gold Coast | Tremont Hotel | 100 E. Chestnut St. (Michigan Ave.) | 312-587-8989

Oakbrook Terrace | 2 Mid America Plaza (bet. 16th & 22nd Sts.) | 630-572-2200

www.ditkasrestaurant.com

"Kudos to da coach" say supporters of these "upscale" Gold Coast and Oakbrook Terrace sports bars/steakhouses, where "everything

	FOOD	DECOR	SERVICE	COST

is big", "from the drinks to the sides" to the "juicy pork chops" and "thick" slabs of beef "worthy of a linebacker"; football fans who hail it as a "hall-of-fame experience" figure in the "entertainment upstairs" (in the Downtown location) and the "chance" to see "local sports celebrities" and even Mike himself, but the opposition throws a penalty flag on "overpriced", "ordinary" offerings and "spotty" service.

Dixie Kitchen & Bait Shop *Cajun/Southern* `19` `18` `19` `$23`

Evanston | 825 Church St. (bet. Benson & Sherman Aves.) | 847-733-9030
Lansing | 2352 E. 172nd St. (Torrence Ave.) | 708-474-1378
www.dixiekitchenchicago.com

"When a trip to New Orleans isn't in the cards", hit these "casual", "funky" Cajuns in Evanston and Lansing that are "reliable" sources for "Southern-style" sustenance in "generous", "low-priced" portions (including pleasingly "spiced-up breakfast"); the overall experience is "full of fun and flavor", enhanced by "super-kitschy" setups and "prompt", "friendly" service.

DMK Burger Bar *Burgers* `22` `17` `19` `$20`

Lakeview | 2954 N. Sheffield Ave. (Wellington Ave.) | 773-360-8686 | www.dmkburgerbar.com

Restaurateurs David Morton and Michael Kornick "take burgers to another level" at this "trendy" Lakeview spot whose "carefully sourced, grass-fed" beef patties (plus lamb, turkey and veggie versions) come with a bevy of "interesting" topping and fry options, as well as an "extensive craft beer list"; the majority declares it "awesome", but a few humbuggers aver "nothing special" and gripe about "loud" acoustics and "lackluster" service; P.S. "definitely try the milkshakes."

NEW D'Noche &
Café Con Leche *American/S. American* `-` `-` `-` `I`

Logan Square | 2710-14 N. Milwaukee Ave. (Sawyer Ave.) | 773-289-4274 | www.dnochechicago.com

At this double-duty Logan Square hipster hangout, a new restaurant, D'Noche, now joins its smaller coffee bar sibling next door, Café Con Leche, and adds South American dinner plates plus craft cocktails to the existing menu of Traditional American breakfasts, Latin sandwiches and house-blend Cuban joe; the dark, cozy setting features a fireplace and carved wood ceiling, plus a rear beer garden and front sidewalk seating; P.S. the D'Noche dinner menu is served starting at 4:30, when the cafe space generally shuts down (save for takeout).

NEW Donatella Mediterranean
Bistro *Italian/Mediterranean* `-` `-` `-` `M`

Evanston | 1512 Sherman Ave. (bet. Grove & Lake Sts.) | 847-328-7720

Donatella Majore returns following the closing of La Cucina di Donatella, this time with a chef-partner, at this midpriced Evanston BYO dishing up Italian and Med fare; the romantic neighborhood storefront is done up in ochre and brown, and also has outdoor seating; P.S. there's a wine list available 5–9 PM Monday–Saturday, with bottles delivered by a local store.

Don Juan's *Mexican*
20 | 14 | 19 | $31

Edison Park | 6730 N. Northwest Hwy. (Oshkosh Ave.) | 773-775-6438 |
www.donjuanschicago.com

An Edison Park "classic" for "many years now" (since 1984), this affordable Mexican is appreciated for its "killer margaritas", 40-plus-label tequila selection and "authentic", seasonal *comida* ordered from "two menus": one features "top-notch standards", the other more "distinctive, creative" dishes; the unenthused cite "dingy" digs and food they claim has gone "downhill" recently, but the fact that it's often "crowded" speaks for itself.

Dorado Ⓜ *French/Mexican*
23 | 13 | 19 | $36

Lincoln Square | 2301 W. Foster Ave. (bet. Claremont & Oakley Aves.) |
773-561-3780 | www.doradorestaurant.net

"Wonderful", "sophisticated" and definitely "not your run-of-the-mill Mexican", this colorful Lincoln Square standout offers "upscale" yet "reasonably priced" south-of-the-border fare with French influences; factor in the BYO policy, and you've got an "incredible value" – and even if there are often "waits" and service can be "slow", to most it's a "great find in the 'hood."

Dos Diablos ❶ *Tex-Mex*
- | - | - | I

River North | 15 W. Hubbard St. (bet. Dearborn & State Sts.) |
312-245-3100 | www.dosdiabloschicago.com

Devilish temptations at this River Norther include midpriced Tex-Mex fare for lunch, dinner and late-night, plus plenty of margaritas and other Mexican cocktails; the sprawling, clubby saloon setting features funky light fixtures and a big bar.

Double Li *Chinese*
- | - | - | I

Chinatown | 228 W. Cermak Rd. (bet. Archer & Wentworth Aves.) |
312-842-7818

A "good alternative" to the usual suspects, this under-the-radar player is touted as "one of the real treasures of Chinatown" by those few surveyors who've discovered it; the "genuine", "spicy" Sichuan fare prepared with "fresh ingredients" is delivered in unpretentious environs, and there's a BYO policy to keep the already-low price down.

Drake Bros.' *American*
- | - | - | M

Gold Coast | Drake Hotel | 140 E. Walton St. (Michigan Ave.) |
312-932-4626 | www.thedrakehotel.com

This former steakhouse inside the Drake Hotel has undergone some changes of late, and now serves a revamped menu of midpriced Traditional American fare during the day only (no dinner), including an "outstanding Sunday brunch buffet"; luckily the "fabulous" dark wood–lined setting retains its stellar views out over Lake Michigan.

Drawing Room ❶ⓏⓂ *American*
▽ 23 | 24 | 20 | $41

Gold Coast | 937 N. Rush St. (bet. Oak & Walton Sts.) | 312-266-2694 |
www.thedrchicago.com

Maybe "a restaurant attached to a club is the last place you'd expect to find good food", but this Gold Coast eatery connected to Le

Passage (and now owned by Three Headed Productions) exceeds expectations with its "innovative" New American cuisine matched with some of the "most creative cocktails in town", mixed "table-side" upon request; better still, this "place to chill" is open into the wee hours.

Duchamp Ⓜ American | 17 | 19 | 17 | $36

Bucktown | 2118 N. Damen Ave. (Charleston St.) | 773-235-6434 | www.duchamp-chicago.com

"Fun, creative" New American dishes with a "global reach" and "attitude-free" service are assets at this Bucktown gastropub, where the "cubist" confines are equipped with communal tables ("convivial" to some, "could be an issue" for others); the jury's still out on the kitchen's "inconsistent" output, however, but all agree that the terrace is "one of Chicago's most beautiful and inviting" outdoor dining options.

Duckfat Tavern & Grill American | - | - | - | M

Forest Park | 7218 Madison St. (Elgin Ave.) | 708-488-1493 | www.duckfatgrill.com

Named for its signature duckfat fries, this West Suburban neighborhood tavern serves a midpriced menu of Traditional American and pub food favorites with an upscale slant – think calamari with tequila cocktail sauce, Kobe sliders with truffle butter and four-cheese mac cooked in a skillet; the warm, wood-on-wood setting includes a big bar and seasonal outdoor seating.

Duck Walk Thai | 19 | 12 | 15 | $20

Lakeview | 919 W. Belmont Ave. (bet. Clark St. & Wilton Ave.) | 773-665-0455

Lincoln Park | 1217 W. Fullerton Ave. (bet. Racine Ave. & Surrey Ct.) | 773-327-6200

www.duckwalkchicago.com

"Good, cheap, basic" Thai fare and "sweet" service add up to "solid" neighborhood standby status for this "nothing-fancy" Lakeview original and its Lincoln Park sequel; "speedy delivery" ("it's like the food is beamed to you") and a BYO policy are icing on the cake.

NEW Due Lire Ⓜ Italian | - | - | - | M

Lincoln Square | 4520 N. Lincoln Ave. (bet. Sunnyside & Wilson Aves.) | 773-275-7878 | www.due-lire.com

A compact menu of authentic Italian fare (antipasti, crostoni, pasta and more) accompanied by a diverse wine list comes courtesy of a Bice alum at this moderately priced Lincoln Square storefront; the interior is simple but warm, with rustic wood chairs, colorful abstract artwork, a beamed ceiling and a copper bar.

Duke of Perth Scottish | 20 | 16 | 18 | $22

Lakeview | 2913 N. Clark St. (Oakdale Ave.) | 773-477-1741 | www.dukeofperth.com

Lakeview's longtime Scottish pub offers "authentic" eats (including an "all-you-can-eat fish fry" on Wednesdays and Fridays), "some exotic U.K. beers" and an "outstanding selection of single malts";

there's a "patio in the rear", and the "friendly corner bar atmosphere" with "no TV" and lots of antiques makes it ideal for a "blustery winter night", plus the "price is right."

NEW Eatt ◐ *American* | - | - | - | I |

River North | 6 W. Hubbard St. (State St.) | 312-494-3288 |
www.eattchicago.com

This River North entry from the Rosebud team issues classic, affordable American eats with some modern touches (Parmesan truffle tater tots, Kobe hot dogs) from early morning to late night; the one-time Vong space now sports a warm and stylish diner-inspired look with red booths, bare wood tables, quaint light fixtures and seasonal sidewalk seating, and there's a separate counter-service cafe for quick takeout.

Ed Debevic's *Diner* | 15 | 19 | 18 | $22 |

River North | 640 N. Wells St. (Ontario St.) | 312-664-1707 |
www.eddebevics.com

Good sports dutifully "doo-wop" at this "true-blue American" "classic diner" "serving burgers, fries and malts" in River North, where "service means the sassy waitress" gets "rude" and "dances on the countertop" ("be prepared to become part" of the "sideshow"); jaded jurors say the "'50s concept" makes for a "clichéd tourist trap" and call the prices "bloated", but others "never tire" of the "colorful" "shtick"; P.S. "bring the kiddies" – the "place will match their energy."

Edelweiss *German* | 19 | 21 | 22 | $32 |

Norridge | 7650 W. Irving Park Rd. (Overhill Ave.) | 708-452-6040 |
www.edelweissdining.com

"When it's good, it's wunderbar" at this "cozy", affordable Norridge German "neighborhood favorite" that's a "solid" option for "hearty" "schnitzel and wurst" plus "liters of brews" including Bavarian beers; the alpine-themed setting is complete with "oompahs from a live band" on weekends.

Edwardo's Natural Pizza *Pizza* | 20 | 11 | 15 | $19 |

Gold Coast | 1212 N. Dearborn St. (Division St.) | 312-337-4490
Lincoln Park | 2662 N. Halsted St. (Wrightwood Ave.) |
773-871-3400
Hyde Park | 1321 E. 57th St. (Kimbark Ave.) | 773-241-7960
South Loop | 521 S. Dearborn St. (bet. Congress Pkwy. & Harrison St.) |
312-939-3366
Skokie | 9300 Skokie Blvd. (Gross Point Rd.) | 847-674-0008
Wheeling | 401 E. Dundee Rd. (Milwaukee Ave.) | 847-520-0666
Oak Park | 6831 North Ave. (Grove Ave.) | 708-524-2400
www.edwardos.com

"Pie oh my" gush partial patrons of this chain they call "still one of the best" for "fresh", "flavorful" "stuffed or thin pizzas" plus a "nice selection of pasta and sandwiches"; the "digs are nothing special" but "you don't go for the ambiance or any other frills" – and some stick to "takeout" to bypass "questionable service" at some locations.

	FOOD	DECOR	SERVICE	COST

Edzo's Burger Shop ⓜ *Burgers* — — — I

Evanston | 1571 Sherman Ave. (bet. Davis & Grove Sts.) |
847-864-3396 | www.edzos.com

"Fresh-ground burgers" with a "variety of toppings" and hand-cut fries done 10 "different ways" "are the big draw" at this budget-loving lunch-only Evanston "burger joint" "with a little extra flair"; counter service is "friendly and efficient", "the milkshakes are for real" and "it's noisy, crowded and worth the trip."

Eggsperience Café *American* — — — I

NEW River North | Millennium Centre Condominiums |
35 W. Ontario St. (bet. Dearborn & State Sts.) | 312-870-6773
Bannockburn | Bannockburn Green Shopping Ctr. | 2545 Waukegan Rd.
(Half Day Rd.) | 847-940-8444
Glenview | 2000 Tower Dr. (Aviator Ln.) | 847-998-5111
NEW Park Ridge | 90 Northwest Hwy. (bet. Summit & Touhy Aves.) |
847-939-3976
Naperville | 2727 W. 75th St. (Beebe Dr.) | 630-548-1000
www.eggsperiencecafe.com

This low-cost chainlet whips up eggs in all their variations (omelets, skillets, Benedicts, scrambles and frittatas) along with pancakes and lunch fare like burgers, wraps, sandwiches, salads and panini, plus shakes and smoothies to top it all off; they close in the afternoon (though the River North branch is open later on weekends), and while the decor varies, all share a warm, cut-above-a-diner feel.

EJ's Place *Italian/Steak* 22 16 19 $49

Skokie | 10027 Skokie Blvd. (Old Orchard Rd.) | 847-933-9800 |
www.ejsplaceskokie.com

"Gene and Georgetti's north, if you will" ("the same family, the same meat"), this Skokie Italian steakhouse "standby" lures neighborhood loyalists who "love" its "terrific" beef and seafood and "Wisconsin roadhouse" atmosphere; penurious patrons would prefer "half the portions at half the price" but "brusque service seems to fit the setting."

Elate *American* ▽ 21 21 16 $41

River North | Hotel Felix | 111 W. Huron St. (Clark St.) | 312-202-9900 |
www.elatechicago.com

This "comfy bar/restaurant" in River North's Hotel Felix offers an "interesting menu" of "appealing" New American plates that most find "innovative yet not intimidating" served in an eco-friendly modern setting; prices are "reasonable" and service is "relaxed", but some say the "kitchen is slow", so it's best to be in "no rush."

Eleven City Diner *Diner* 19 17 17 $20

South Loop | 1112 S. Wabash Ave. (11th St.) | 312-212-1112 |
www.elevencitydiner.com

Surveyors "craving enormous deli sandwiches or matzo ball soup" head to this "cool, retro" "Jewish-American" "cross between a diner and a deli" that's a "welcome oasis in the South Loop" for the "comfort-food" "standards"; added treats are a full soda fountain

	FOOD	DECOR	SERVICE	COST

("Green River soda – enough said") and relatively late hours, though "Michigan Avenue pricing" and occasional "management attitude" influence "hit-or-miss" experiences.

☒ Emilio's Tapas *Spanish*

24	19	21	$32

Hillside | 4100 Roosevelt Rd. (Mannheim Rd.) | 708-547-7177

☒ Emilio's Tapas Sol y Nieve *Spanish*
Streeterville | 215 E. Ohio St. (St. Clair St.) | 312-467-7177
www.emiliostapas.com

Doling out an "interesting variety" of "well-prepared and flavorful" "traditional tapas" "to share with friends", these Streeterville and Hillside haunts appeal with "comfortable settings" (both also have a "nice patio") and "reasonable prices"; "unobtrusive, non-pushy service" enhances the experience, and "sangrias go down nicely" too; P.S. the Lincoln Park and Wheaton locations have closed.

Emperor's Choice ● *Chinese*

23	12	20	$27

Chinatown | 2238 S. Wentworth Ave. (Cermak Rd.) | 312-225-8800
"Sound Cantonese cooking" including "flawless seafood" and "unusual dishes" draws "gourmets" and adventurers alike to this Chinatown "haven" with a "quiet, intimate ambiance", "crisp white-linen tablecloths" and a saltwater fish tank; it might be "a bit pricier" than its neighbors, but "it's worth it"; P.S. open till midnight except Sunday (when it closes at 11 PM).

Epic ☒ *American*

-	-	-	E

River North | 112 W. Hubbard St. (bet. Clark St. & LaSalle Blvd.) | 312-222-4940 | www.epicrestaurantchicago.com

This swanky River Norther offers New American fine dining utilizing classic French technique and housemade ingredients; a winding staircase separates a second-floor dining room with soaring windows from an informal first-floor lounge (with a different menu) and seasonal outdoor dining on a vast rooftop.

Epic Burger *Burgers*

22	14	15	$13

Loop | 517 S. State St. (Congress Pkwy.) | 312-913-1373 | www.epicburger.com

"Eco-conscious" quick bites in the Loop earn enthusiasm for this "spacious, modern" "counter-service" concept where a "juicy", "delicious", "well-priced" "burger binge" involves "local ingredients" ("add a fried egg from a free-range chicken" or "nitrate-free bacon"), "sinful milkshakes" and "fast, friendly service"; patty partisans sniffing it's "not as 'epic' as depicted" are outnumbered by those who are "wow"-ed; P.S. a massive new Loop location is planned for summer 2011.

Erie Cafe *Italian/Steak*

22	19	23	$54

River North | 536 W. Erie St. (Kingsbury St.) | 312-266-2300 | www.eriecafe.com

"It may not be chic" but the "nothing-fancy" "solid steaks" and chops and "old-school staff" make this Italian "standby" "off the beaten path" in River North a "man's kind of place"; with its "pseudo" "Sinatra-era" vibe, "it's nostalgia on a plate, albeit a pricey one"; P.S. there's a "great view on the river[side] patio."

Erwin, An American Cafe & Bar M *American*

23 | 19 | 21 | $39

Lakeview | 2925 N. Halsted St. (Oakdale Ave.) | 773-528-7200 | www.erwincafe.com

Namesake chef Erwin Drechsler was "using local seasonal ingredients before it was cool" at his "reliable" contemporary American "Boys Town fixture" that's "popular with young and old alike" for its "tasty, inventive" dishes and "comfort-food" "favorites" (and "one of the best brunches"); it all comes at "value"-minded prices in a "warm and cozy" dining room with a "funky rooftop mural", where patrons happily "talk without shouting."

Essence of India *Indian*

21 | 19 | 20 | $30

Lincoln Square | 4601 N. Lincoln Ave. (Wilson Ave.) | 773-506-0002 | www.essenceofindiachicago.com

Though "south of Devon", this Lincoln Square subcontinental "does a good job" with its "traditional Indian dishes" (you can even "choose your own spice level") in a "cozy", "pleasing" setting hung with tapestries; quibblers peg it "on the pricier side for the portions", but on the plus side it serves beer and wine and has a summer patio.

Estrella Negra M *Mexican/Nuevo Latino*

- | - | - | I

Logan Square | 2346 W. Fullerton Ave. (bet. Oakley & Western Aves.) | 773-227-5993 | www.estrellanegra.com

From tacos to tamales, pozole to pomegranate-seed guacamole, this inexpensive, "funky, bohemian" Logan Square spot serves Mexican and "contemporary Latin cuisine with unexpected flair" (including brunch every day) in exposed-brick environs with "*Dia de los Muertos*–inspired art"; even those who find the decor "freaky weird" agree "there's nothing scary about the food or the BYO policy."

Z Ethiopian Diamond *Ethiopian*

23 | 16 | 20 | $24

Edgewater | 6120 N. Broadway (Glenlake Ave.) | 773-338-6100

Z Ethiopian Diamond II *Ethiopian*

Rogers Park | 7537 N. Clark St. (bet. Howard St. & Rogers Ave.) | 773-764-2200

www.ethiopiandiamondcuisine.com

"Still the spot" for "authentic" "finger food" (since "you eat with your hands"), this affordable Edgewater Ethiopian "diamond in the rough" is a "vegetarian's delight" while also "pleasing meat eaters"; it's a "great place for an introduction" to using "sour pancakelike" injera bread instead of utensils as "they will guide you" through the "experience", and live jazz most Fridays enhances the experience; P.S. there's a Rogers Park locale too.

Z Everest SM *French*

27 | 27 | 27 | $106

Loop | One Financial Pl. | 440 S. LaSalle St., 40th fl. (Congress Pkwy.) | 312-663-8920 | www.everestrestaurant.com

"High expectations" "reflect the name" of this Loop "special-occasion" French perched on the 40th floor of the Chicago Stock

Exchange that surveyors hail as the "summit" for "sublime", "classic white-linen" dining on the "inventive menus" of Jean Joho; an "unbelievable" ("in size and price") "wine binder" enhances an experience that's completed with "pomp", "formal" service and a "view that seems to stretch to Iowa"; P.S. jacket suggested.

NEW **Everest Burger** *Burgers*　　　- | - | - | I

Glencoe | 91 Green Bay Rd. (Linden Ave.) | 847-242-0909 |
www.everestburger.com

Numerous proteins (including organic hormone-free beef and vegetarian options) in globally inspired burger preps are paired with four renditions of fries at this health-conscious North Shore noshery that does all its baking in-house; the casual, modern strip-mall milieu features bright booths and bare tables, with a massive rock wall and mountainous mural nodding to the name.

Evergreen *Chinese*　　　∇ 23 | 16 | 21 | $33

Chinatown | 2411 S. Wentworth Ave. (24th St.) | 312-225-8898

"Excellent", "authentic" "mostly Cantonese cuisine with very fresh ingredients" is "prepared with imagination" at this Chinatown stalwart where "the Peking duck is something to quack about"; "good service" makes this "one of the better" choices in the area – and "one of the best values."

Fat Willy's Rib Shack *BBQ/Southern*　　23 | 11 | 16 | $22

Logan Square | 2416 W. Schubert Ave. (Western Ave.) | 773-782-1800 |
www.fatwillysribshack.com

"Satisfied" fans say this Logan Square Southern shack provides "authentic", "greasy" BBQ including "tasty, tangy" ribs "with a lot of verve" (and "don't forget the mac 'n' cheese") "in an appropriate dive setting"; patrons "never feel rushed" whether "inside or outside", plus it's "convenient" for a "movie across the street" and "carryout."

Feast *American*　　　19 | 16 | 17 | $29

Gold Coast | 25 E. Delaware Pl. (bet. State & Wabash Sts.) |
312-337-4001

Bucktown | 1616 N. Damen Ave. (North Ave.) | 773-772-7100
www.feastrestaurant.com

An "expansive menu of" "fresh, delicious" contemporary American fare, a "martini list" and "reasonable prices" lure feasters to these "casual" Bucktown and Gold Coast "hangouts" that are open all day and "accommodating to kids"; however, what some call "international dishes" are "all over the map" to others, who also suggest service can be "lacking"; P.S. both locations have "outdoor" settings "worth the wait" "in season."

Felony Franks ⊅ *Hot Dogs*　　　- | - | - | I

West Loop | 229 S. Western Ave. (Jackson Blvd.) | 312-243-0505 |
www.felonyfranks.com

It's cash only at this casual West Loop hot dogger where offerings include the Felony Frank and the Misdemeanor Weiner; loyalists who "like the concept a lot" attest "you'll get lunch" or budget-

	FOOD	DECOR	SERVICE	COST

friendly dinner while "supporting a business that helps a population so many ignore" – namely the ex-convicts providing the "good service."

Fifty/50, The ❶ *American*

| | 21 | 17 | 16 | $23 |

Wicker Park | 2047 W. Division St. (bet. Damen & Hoyne Aves.) | 773-489-5050 | www.thefifty50.com

"Bar food and outside dining" fill this "cool and entertaining" Wicker Park American with a drinking crowd aiming to "catch a game and grab a bite"; despite three levels and 18 flat-screens, it gets "crowded and loud", but service is "adequate" and affordable grub including "teriyaki boneless wings" and "fabulous sweet-potato fries" also has its fans.

Filippo's *Italian*

| | ▽ 24 | 18 | 23 | $40 |

Lincoln Park | 2211 N. Clybourn Ave. (Webster Ave.) | 773-528-2211 | www.filippos-chicago.com

Lincoln Parkers agree this "solid neighborhood Italian" is "still great after all these years" as they "chill out" while dining on "basic", "delicious" midpriced fare in the "cozy", rustic quarters; it can get "crowded" – "especially on weekends" – though there are "rarely ridiculous waits", and besides, a mostly Boot-centric wine list stokes the "sanctuary" vibe.

NEW Fin Sushi Bar Ⓜ *Japanese/Thai*

| | – | – | – | M |

Ravenswood | 1742 W. Wilson Ave. (Hermitage Ave.) | 773-961-7452 | www.finsushibar.com

A hip hybrid of sushi and Thai food rousts Ravenswood residents at this midscale BYO where 'regular' rolls are upstaged by 'irregular' rolls like tuna with garlic butter and honey-walnut shrimp tempura; the chic, modern corner storefront is done up with textured walls, bare tables, a sushi bar and a striking geometric banquette dividing the space.

Fiorentino's Cucina Italiana *Italian*

| | 22 | 17 | 21 | $36 |

Lakeview | 2901 N. Ashland Ave. (George St.) | 773-244-3026 | www.fiorentinoscucina.com

"Traditional" "Southern Italian cuisine" in "plentiful" portions combines with a "romantic atmosphere" to make this "off-the-beaten-track" Lakeview trattoria a "wonderful neighborhood" "gem"; P.S. "in the summer" patrons "welcome" the "outdoor patio option", and moderate prices add to reasons they "leave happy" year-round.

NEW Fish Bar Ⓜ *Seafood*

| | – | – | – | I |

Lakeview | 2956 N. Sheffield Ave. (Wellington Ave.) | 773-687-8177 | www.fishbarchicago.com

David Morton and Michael Kornick of Lakeview's DMK Burger Bar have taken over the space next door for this new-school version of an old-school shrimp shack where sustainable seafood and shellfish (including raw clams) are used for classics like lobster rolls, tartares, soups, po' boys and crab cakes; weather-beaten wood walls display funky boat and fish decor, while seating options include plaid booths and bars with mismatched stools – oh, and there are rolls of paper towels everywhere.

	FOOD	DECOR	SERVICE	COST

545 North ⊠ *American*
20 19 20 $35

Libertyville | 545 N. Milwaukee Ave. (Lake St.) | 847-247-8700 | www.545north.com

There's a "trendy city feeling" in the Northern Suburbs at this "intimate" midpriced Libertyville New American combining "small-scale charm" with "upscale touches" and "enjoyable" fare (including steaks), where "locals" linger and the "bar is usually packed with action"; entertainment "guarantees a lively weekend", and if some dub it "loud" and say service can be "lacking", others call it "happening" with its fireplace-equipped "summer patio" ("nirvana") and late bar hours (1 AM nightly, 3 AM Friday and Saturday).

Five Guys *Burgers*
20 10 16 $11

Lincoln Park | 2140 N. Clybourn Ave. (Wayne Ave.) | 773-327-5953

Lincoln Park | 2368 N. Clark St. (bet. Belden Ave. & Fullerton Pkwy.) | 773-883-8930

Rogers Park | The Morgan at Loyola Station | 6477 N. Sheridan Rd. (Arthur Ave.) | 773-262-9810

Naperville | 22 E. Chicago Ave. (Washington St.) | 630-355-1850

Oak Park | 1115 W. Lake St. (bet. Harlem Ave. & Marion St.) | 708-358-0856
www.fiveguys.com

"Juicy, greasy, tasty" burgers "with all the trimmings" "blow away" the competition according to fans of this "presidential favorite" that's also prized for its "farm-to-fryer" fries and "free peanuts while you wait"; so even if doubters "don't get the hype", these "bare-bones" but "clean and cheery" franchises are "taking the world by storm."

Flat Top Grill *Asian*
20 15 17 $21

Loop | 30 S. Wabash Ave. (bet. Madison & Monroe Sts.) | 312-726-8400

Lakeview | 3200 N. Southport Ave. (Belmont Ave.) | 773-665-8100

Old Town | 319 W. North Ave. (Orleans St.) | 312-787-7676

West Loop | 1000 W. Washington Blvd. (Carpenter St.) | 312-829-4800

Evanston | 707 Church St. (bet. Orrington & Sherman Aves.) | 847-570-0100

Lombard | Shops on Butterfield | 305 Yorktown Ctr. (Highland Ave.) | 630-652-3700

Naperville | 218 S. Washington St. (bet. Chicago & Jefferson Aves.) | 630-428-8400

Oak Park | 726 Lake St. (Oak Park Ave.) | 708-358-8200
www.flattopgrill.com

"Get exactly what you want" at this "fast-casual chain" by "creating a stir-fry" from a "stunning array" of "vegetables, protein and sauces" (or else "use their combinations") for dishes that are "cooked on a flat top"; holdouts hint it's best "if you're not too particular", but fans counter it can be "relatively healthy and cheap", adding "you don't come here for the service."

	FOOD	DECOR	SERVICE	COST

Fleming's Prime Steakhouse & Wine Bar *Steak*
23 | 23 | 22 | $60

Near North | 25 E. Ohio St. (bet. State & Wabash Sts.) | 312-329-9463
Lincolnshire | Lincolnshire Commons | 960 Milwaukee Ave. (Aptakisic Rd.) | 847-793-0333
www.flemingssteakhouse.com

"Swanky", "upscale" and "reliable", these city and suburban steakhouses, part of a national chain, please patrons who seek the classics "done well" along with an "enormous selection of wines by the glass" (100) and "happy hour in the bar"; "service is super", but since "everything is à la carte" it's best "on the company tab."

Flight ☒ *Eclectic*
17 | 16 | 17 | $38

Glenview | 1820 Tower Dr. (Patriot Blvd.) | 847-729-9463 | www.flightwinebar.com

Surveyors buckle up for Eclectic "small plates to pair" with an "excellent wine selection" (150 bottles, 80 by the glass) at this "refreshing" Glenview "independent in a land of chains"; but "downtown prices", "inconsistency" and "lackluster" decor leave undecideds up in the air.

Flo Ⓜ *American*
22 | 17 | 19 | $20

Noble Square | 1434 W. Chicago Ave. (bet. Bishop & Noble Sts.) | 312-243-0477 | www.eatatflo.com

Noble Square locals advise "run don't walk" to this "cozy, laid-back" "neighborhood joint" that's "designed like a rustic general store" and serves "dependable" Traditional and Southwestern American fare including weekend "brunch with a little kick"; prices are affordable and service is "accommodating and brisk" – but since "breakfast is a mob scene", less patient types "go for dinner."

Flo & Santos Pizza & Pierogi *Pizza/Pub Food*
– | – | – | I

South Loop | 1310 S. Wabash Ave. (bet. 13th & 14th Sts.) | 312-566-9817 | www.floandsantos.com

The likes of thin-crust pizzas, wings and a 'Polska sampler' meet on the menu at this South Loop amalgam of pub, pizzeria and Polish-Italian restaurant, with full bar service highlighting brews on tap and Polish vodkas; despite the culinary melting pot, the casual setting is industrial pub, with bare wood tables, open ductwork, dangling bulbs, multiple TVs and historic black-and-white photos of the bygone Chicago Coliseum.

🆕 Florentine, The *Italian*
– | – | – | E

Loop | JW Marriott Chicago | 151 W. Adams St. (bet. LaSalle & Wells Sts.) | 312-660-8866 | www.the-florentine.net

Todd Stein (ex Cibo Matto, MK) crafts upscale contemporary Italian cuisine from local ingredients for breakfast, lunch and dinner (plus Sunday brunch and separate pizza/crostini and lounge menus) at this arrival in the Loop's Marriott; the elegant setting features well-spaced tables, white linens, stately pillars, modern light fixtures and a white marble bar issuing seasonal cocktails and a Boot-focused wine list.

	FOOD	DECOR	SERVICE	COST

Fogo de Chão *Brazilian/Steak* | 24 | 20 | 24 | $59 |
River North | 661 N. La Salle Dr. (Erie St.) | 312-932-9330 |
www.fogodechao.com

"Serious carnivores" "pig out" at this River North churrascaria, a Brazilian "house of meat on a sword" offering an "obscene amount" of "grilled and BBQ" cuts plus an "off-the-charts salad bar"; it's "a little stagey", but service that's "fast and furious" from a "friendly staff" makes it "enjoyable" "especially for a group" – just come "hungry" as the tab "puts your cardiologist's kids through college."

NEW Fogón *Mexican* | - | - | - | M |
Noble Square | 1235 W. Grand Ave. (Ogden Ave.) | 312-421-2000 |
www.fogonchicago.com

To say that this midpriced Noble Square storefront serves Mexican cuisine doesn't tell the full story as many of the inventive dishes also reflect international influences; the upscale setting has a contemporary vibe, with big windows, sedate neutral colors and a black granite bar dispensing fruit-fusion margaritas and sipping tequilas; P.S. summer brings outdoor sidewalk seating.

Folklore ● *Argentinean/Steak* | - | - | - | M |
Ukrainian Village | 2100 W. Division St. (Hoyne Ave.) | 773-292-1600
A hipster version of Tango Sur hits Ukrainian Village, offering a similar affordable Argentinean steakhouse menu (with the addition of organic and grass-fed beef options) plus – unlike its BYO sibling – a full bar issuing specialty cocktails; the intimate, candlelit setting features a tin ceiling, reclaimed wood accents and a colorful exterior mural.

Fonda del Mar *Mexican/Seafood* | 25 | - | 20 | $33 |
Logan Square | 3749 W. Fullerton Ave. (bet. Hamlin & Ridgeway Aves.) |
773-489-3748 | www.fdmrestaurant.com

You might need a scorecard to keep up with this casual Mexican's location changes – it's now back in its original Logan Square home after a move to North Center – but whatever the address, it's appreciated for its "first-rate" "creative seafood combinations" and "genuinely pleasant servers"; "reasonable prices" don't hurt either.

Fonda Isabel *Mexican* | - | - | - | M |
Lombard | 18 W. 333 Roosevelt Rd. (bet. Church Ave. &
Westmore-Meyers Rd.) | 630-691-2222 | www.fondaisabel.com

Lombard lays claim to this traditional Mex whose midpriced lunch and dinner offerings are augmented by an all-inclusive set-price menu and a variety of signature margaritas, sangrias and tropical cocktails; painted in rich colors, its two cozy dining rooms are decorated with white tablecloths, vintage-inspired light fixtures and a few art objects.

Fontana Grill *Italian* | - | - | - | M |
Uptown | 1329 W. Wilson Ave. (bet. Beacon & Malden Sts.) |
773-561-0400 | www.fontanagrill.com

Dishing out moderately priced Italian fare including pizza, plus a "must-try" specialty of *cevapi* (Sarajevo-style grilled beef, lamb sau-

	FOOD	DECOR	SERVICE	COST

sages and onions in pita), this "cute place with friendly service" is a "treat to have Uptown" and a "hidden neighborhood gem" that "really shines in summer" with its "spacious, flower-lined patio"; P.S. there's also a "thoughtful list of wines" priced at $1 or $2 per ounce.

Foodlife *Eclectic* | 19 | 13 | 15 | $17 |

Streeterville | Water Tower Pl. | 835 N. Michigan Ave. (bet. Chestnut & Pearson Sts.) | 312-335-3663 | www.leye.com

Streeterville's Eclectic "self-serve" "world's fair" of fare is "what a mall food court should be", whether you're "shopping alone" at Water Tower Place or in a "group with no consensus on what to eat" seeking a "decent", "fast and efficient" solution; the "chaos" becomes somewhat "organized" with a "charge card" "payment concept" (you "settle up" on exiting) – still, despite "reasonable prices" you can "end up spending more" than planned.

NEW Fork ⓜ *Pub Food* | - | - | - | I |

Lincoln Square | 4600 N. Lincoln Ave. (Wilson Ave.) | 773-751-1500 | www.forkchicago.net

The owner of the former Fiddlehead Cafe in Lincoln Square has remodeled the space into this casual modern gastropub where guests can graze on an array of affordable cheese and charcuterie, plus New American noshes such as a house-smoked pork belly 'PBLT'; dishes can be paired with roughly 170 beers and 30 wines by the glass/flight, and it's all served in a rustic setting with brick-and-wood walls, leather lounge seating, tin ceilings and a glass-walled fireplace.

Fornetto Mei *Chinese/Italian* | 20 | 18 | 18 | $38 |

Gold Coast | Whitehall Hotel | 107 E. Delaware Pl. (bet. Michigan Ave. & Rush St.) | 312-573-6301 | www.thewhitehallhotel.com

Though it's "not on most people's radar", this "intimate, well-appointed" hotel eatery "close to Michigan Avenue shopping" "in the heart of the Gold Coast" offers an "interesting combination of Italian and Chinese" such as "thin-crust", "wood-fired pizza" plus "limited" Asian choices including potstickers and egg rolls – some say it's an "odd combo, but they do it well", with "attentive service" and at "decent prices."

Fountainhead *Pub Food* | - | - | - | M |

Ravenswood | 1970 W. Montrose Ave. (Damen Ave.) | 773-697-8204 | www.fountainheadchicago.com

Upscale American pub food pairs with a big list of draft microbrews (including two hand-pumped beer engines) and brown liquors at this cozy, midpriced Ravenswood corner spot where booths, a mahogany bar, a fireplace and warm lighting from vintage-inspired light fixtures create a rustic tavern feel; P.S. summer brings a sprawling seasonal roof garden with street lamps and a fountain.

1492 Tapas Bar *Spanish* | 21 | 19 | 20 | $35 |

River North | 42 E. Superior St. (Wabash Ave.) | 312-867-1492 | www.1492tapasbar.com

Surveyors explore an array of "flavorful", "authentic" tapas at this "cozy" "little" River North "hideaway" "in an old brownstone" where "not overly pricey" Spanish "small-ish plates" are washed down with "varieties of sangria"; though some find the "traditional" decor "nondescript" and service "somewhat spotty" and "slow", friends call the "sidewalk tables" "pleasant" for a "date during summer."

Francesca's Bryn Mawr Italian   22 | 19 | 21 | $35
Edgewater | 1039 W. Bryn Mawr Ave. (Kenmore Ave.) | 773-506-9261

Francesca's by the River Italian
St. Charles | 200 S. 2nd St. (Illinois St.) | 630-587-8221

Francesca's Campagna Italian
West Dundee | 127 W. Main St. (2nd St.) | 847-844-7099

Francesca's Famiglia Italian
Barrington | Cook Street Plaza | 100 E. Station St. (Hough St.) | 847-277-1027

Francesca's Fiore Italian
Forest Park | 7407 W. Madison St. (Harlem Ave.) | 708-771-3063

Francesca's Intimo Italian
Lake Forest | 293 E. Illinois Rd. (Western Ave.) | 847-735-9235

Francesca's North Italian
Northbrook | Northbrook Shopping Plaza | 1145 Church St. (Shermer Rd.) | 847-559-0260

Francesca's on Chestnut Italian
Streeterville | Seneca Hotel | 200 E. Chestnut St. (bet. Dewitt Pl. & Mies van der Rohe Way) | 312-482-8800

Francesca's on Taylor Italian
Little Italy/University Village | 1400 W. Taylor St. (Loomis St.) | 312-829-2828

La Sorella di Francesca Italian
Naperville | 18 W. Jefferson Ave. (bet. Main & Washington Sts.) | 630-961-2706
www.miafrancesca.com
Additional locations throughout the Chicago area

Regulars regard this "reliable", "growing" "local chain" (which is expanding nationally) as a "very satisfying experience" with its "rotating menu" of "simple, tasty" "less-traditional Italian" fare at "excellent-value" tabs, "better-than-average service" and "sophisticated, informal" "bistro"-like quarters; even if some locations at peak times "can be as noisy as a soccer match in Milan", fans feel there's "no downside."

Francesco's   24 | 13 | 20 | $34
Hole in the Wall Italian
Northbrook | 254 Skokie Blvd. (bet. Dundee & Lake Cook Rds.) | 847-272-0155 | www.francescosholeinthewall.com

Northbrook's "venerable", "one-of-a-kind local hangout" is known for "ample portions" of "excellent" "traditional Italian fare" "at very reasonable prices" from a "changing nightly menu", "chummy service" and "lines out the door" ("the trick to getting seated is to go early or late"); they still don't take reservations, but "good news, they are now accepting credit cards!"

	FOOD	DECOR	SERVICE	COST

Frances' Deli *Deli*
 — | — | — | I

Lincoln Park | 2552 N. Clark St. (bet. Deming Pl. & Wrightwood Ave.) | 773-248-4580 | www.francesdeli.com

Since 1938, this classic Lincoln Park deli has been dishing up three squares daily, offering jam-packed omelets, towering sandwiches and comfort-driven entrees (meatloaf, brisket), plus indulgences like thick shakes and sundaes; vinyl booths, Formica tables, old-fashioned diner accoutrements and a mural done up like a vintage postcard of Chicago landmarks lend the small space a retro air, while the sidewalk patio hops in warm weather.

Frankie's Scaloppine & 5th Floor Pizzeria *Italian/Pizza*
18 | 14 | 19 | $27

Gold Coast | 900 Shops | 900 N. Michigan Ave., 5th fl. (bet. Delaware & Walton Pls.) | 312-266-2500 | www.leye.com

"Exceeding expectations" "for mall eats", this "solid", "reasonably priced" Lettuce Entertain You Gold Coaster purveys "traditional, flavorful Italian fare" and "perfectly crispy", "thin-crust pizza" delivered by "friendly" staffers in a setting with "autographed dinner plates along the walls"; noshers naming it "nothing special" maintain it "will do when you're shopping", though boosters say it's "worth checking out" anytime.

Franks 'N' Dawgs   *Hot Dogs*
 — | — | — | I

Lincoln Park | 1863 N. Clybourn Ave. (bet. Kenmore & Sheffield Aves.) | 312-281-5187 | www.franksndawgs.com

Seasonal, foodie-friendly franks and sausages are offered in categories including 'wild', 'global' and 'haute' at this Lincoln Park dog house that also boasts artisanal French-style rolls, gourmet condiments and fresh hand-cut fries; the modern, casual diner setting features dark-wood booths, lots of quilted steel and funky artwork.

Frasca Pizzeria & Wine Bar *Pizza*
20 | 14 | 17 | $26

Lakeview | 3358 N. Paulina St. (Lincoln Ave.) | 773-248-5222 | www.frascapizzeria.com

"Better-than-average" "wood-fired", "brick-oven" pizza made with "high-end ingredients" lures Lakeview locals to this "neighborhood wine bar" that also offers "great antipasto" and other Italian fare in a setting with leather banquettes and large windows; "excellent" "drink and dinner specials" ("including two-for-one" pies on Wednesdays), "friendly service" and moderate prices make it a "repeat performer."

Fred's *American*
19 | 24 | 19 | $44

Gold Coast | Barneys New York | 15 E. Oak St. (Rush St.) | 312-596-1111 | www.barneys.com

"Well-heeled" "beautiful people" come to "see and be seen" at this "cosmopolitan" Gold Coast "fashionista capital of Chicago" where "accommodating service" accompanies New American fare that's "reasonably priced" "for the location" inside Barneys department store; additional assets include a "small but well-selected wine list", a "fabulous view" "down Oak Street to the lake" and outdoor terrace seating "on a beautiful day."

	FOOD	DECOR	SERVICE	COST

Froggy's French Cafe 🅢 *French* — 22 | 20 | 23 | $50

Highwood | 306 Green Bay Rd. (Highwood Ave.) | 847-433-7080 | www.froggysrestaurant.com

"They have maintained their Escoffier standards (and their butter content)" since 1980 at Highwood's "civilized" "traditional French restaurant" where "service is consistent and personable" and "kitschy paintings contribute" to the "old-style" ambiance; while "everything tastes the same as it has for years", diners divide on whether "that's a good thing" or it's "getting a little dated", but you can dine here "without breaking the bank."

❷ Frontera Grill 🅢🅜 *Mexican* — 27 | 22 | 23 | $45

River North | 445 N. Clark St. (bet. Hubbard & Illinois Sts.) | 312-661-1434 | www.fronterakitchens.com

"Magnificent" Mexican cuisine from celebrity chef Rick Bayless is a "revelation" at this River North "temple", voted Chicago's Most Popular and touted for its "bold", "complex flavors" ("he won *Top Chef Masters* for a reason"), "drinks as spectacular as" the fare and "colorful decor" with "museum-quality artwork"; the "crowds can be daunting" (it's mostly "first-come, first-served") but "it's worth the wait" to a "cultish following" that boasts "you have to believe Mexico is jealous" and calls the prices "totally reasonable"; P.S. "hint: sit at the bar for the same food but faster service."

❗NEW❗ Frontier ☀ *American/Pub Food* — - | - | - | M

Noble Square | 1072 N. Milwaukee Ave. (bet. Noble & Thomas Sts.) | 773-772-4322 | www.thefrontierchicago.com

A large taxidermy bear presides over this saloonlike Noble Square gastropub from the owners of Lottie's and the Pony Inn bars, where offerings include hearty game and oyster-centric eats, as well as whole animal feasts by advance order, augmented by over a dozen drafts and specialty cocktails; the warm, wood-beam setting features a long, communal table, and there's a seasonal beer garden for imbibing.

Fuego Mexican Grill & Margarita Bar 🅜 *Mexican* — 24 | 19 | 23 | $30

Logan Square | 2047 N. Milwaukee Ave. (Armitage Ave.) | 773-252-1122 | www.fuegomexicangrill.com

"Upscale" and "large", this midpriced Logan Square cantina is a "notch above your average Mexican" say locals who promise it "will exceed your expectations" for service and food with its "sophisticated moles and seafood preparations"; "outstanding margaritas" are also in the mix, and it's all served in an "upbeat, lively yet not-too-crowded atmosphere"; P.S. there's a lounge and nightclub upstairs.

Fulton's on the River 🅢 *Seafood/Steak* — 19 | 20 | 18 | $47

River North | 315 N. La Salle Dr. (Wacker Dr.) | 312-822-0100 | www.fultonsontheriver.com

Fin fans are lured to River North's "solid corporate seafood cousin of Disney's Orlando place" with its "excellent variety" of "fresh" fish, "tender steaks" and "classy decor" featuring a "big bar" and a "beautiful setting on the river"; the less-enchanted cite "inconsistent service" and "pretty standard fare", saying it's best "in the summer if you can sit outside", while wallet-watchers recommend lunch as "more affordable"; P.S. the Bridge Bar addition upstairs serves craft cocktails and upscale bar bites.

☒ Gabriel's ⌧Ⓜ *French/Italian*   `25` `23` `25` `$72`

Highwood | 310 Green Bay Rd. (Highwood Ave.) | 847-433-0031 | www.egabriels.com

Gabriel Viti "runs a hands-on operation" at his "intimate", "romantic" Highwood restaurant, which devotees dub a "mecca for exceptional eats" for its "wonderful take on Italian" with an "obvious French influence", "outstanding wine list" and "excellent", "personal service"; though some surveyors call it "too pricey", and others lobby for "some new dishes", all agree it's a "first-class night out."

Gaetano's ⌧ *Italian*   `24` `19` `23` `$48`

Forest Park | 7636 Madison St. (bet. Ashland & Lathrop Aves.) | 708-366-4010 | www.gaetanos.us

"Bringing Italy to the western suburbs", this Forest Park "surprise" offers "imaginative, tradition-based *cucina*" with "fresh ingredients" that's "reasonably priced", along with an excellent selection of wines; the "small" setting with art-adorned walls can be "a bit cramped, but it's lovely" and the "staff is friendly and professional."

☒ Gage, The *American*   `22` `22` `22` `$40`

Loop | 24 S. Michigan Ave. (bet. Madison St. & Monroe Dr.) | 312-372-4243 | www.thegagechicago.com

"Inventive" New American "comfort food" at "upscale prices" stays "in step with the season" at this gastropub "gem along Michigan Avenue" that's set in a "historic" Loop building with "beautiful decor and details" "right across from Millennium Park"; "servers know their stuff", and there's a "sidewalk cafe" and a "fantastic" "beer and spirits selection" plus a "lively" 50-ft. mahogany bar – just know it's "hard to park" and the "acoustics" can be "deafening."

Gale Street Inn *American*   `22` `15` `21` `$30`

Jefferson Park | 4914 N. Milwaukee Ave. (Lawrence Ave.) | 773-725-1300 | www.galestreet.com
Mundelein | 935 Diamond Lake Rd. (Rte. 45) | 847-566-1090 | www.galest.com Ⓜ

Rib wranglers feel like they're "in a supper club" when they "walk through the door" of these separately owned "old-school" Americans in Jefferson Park and Mundelein "famous for" "reasonably priced", "perfectly seasoned" "fall-off-the-bone" meat and "fantastic sides"; fans say the fare and "friendly service" "will keep you coming back."

Gaylord Fine Indian Cuisine *Indian*   `22` `19` `21` `$34`

Gold Coast | 100 E. Walton St. (bet. Michigan Ave. & Rush St.) | 312-664-1700
Schaumburg | 555 Mall Dr. (Higgins Rd.) | 847-619-3300 www.gaylordil.com

"Lots of interesting", "delicious" Indian dishes "that aren't too spicy" – plus an "inexpensive lunch buffet" with an "often-changed

FOOD | DECOR | SERVICE | COST

NEW Gaztro-Wagon 🗺️Ⓜ️ *Eclectic* — | — | — | I

Edgewater | 5973 N. Clark St. (Peterson Ave.) | 773-942-6152 |
www.gaztro-wagon.com

Food-truck founding father Matt Maroni offers his signature 'naan-wiches' (sandwiches on naan, in eclectic versions such as wild boar, pork shoulder and lobster roll) plus sweets from Fritz Pastry at both his casual Edgewater storefront home base as well as via a former postal wagon that travels around town dispensing the affordable eats; the truck can be tracked via the website, Facebook and Twitter.

Geja's Cafe *Fondue* 21 | 20 | 20 | $50

Lincoln Park | 340 W. Armitage Ave. (Orleans St.) | 773-281-9101 |
www.gejascafe.com

Lincoln Parkers liken this "folksy" fondue "throwback" to "'60s-era" spots "where romance blossomed in the dark" while dunking into melted "wonderful chocolate" and classic "Gruyère cheese" (plus a "variety of seafood and meat"); it's "a little pricey", but there are "well-chosen" wines (50 by the glass), and daters declare "if couples can't enjoy soft lights and live flamenco guitar" (weekends only) while dipping dinner, "it's breakup time"; P.S. no kids under age 10.

Gemini Bistro Ⓜ️ *American* 21 | 20 | 20 | $39

Lincoln Park | 2075 N. Lincoln Ave. (Dickens Ave.) | 773-525-2522 |
www.geminibistrochicago.com

Patrons of this "quality neighborhood Lincoln Park bistro" situated on a "desolate stretch of Lincoln Avenue" praise Jason Paskewitz's "well-prepared", moderately priced New American fare, "ever-changing menu" and "lively atmosphere" in a "mature", "glamorous yet understated" setting; a few note service, while "accommodating", is "less than polished" and it's "hard to hear at peak dining hours", "still", it's "worth a visit."

🅩 Gene & Georgetti 🗺️ *Steak* 24 | 17 | 22 | $63

River North | 500 N. Franklin St. (Illinois St.) | 312-527-3718 |
www.geneandgeorgetti.com

Carnivores who "like their steak with a step back in time" plead "save me a seat" at River North's "Chicago cow classic" "under the el tracks" – a "masculine" meatery with "melt-in-your-mouth" beef, "garbage salad and strong drink"; sentimental surveyors "savor" the "old-school" decor "untouched by interfering interior decorators" and "grumpy service that's part of the shtick", but modernists who muse it "must have been something in its day" mostly leave it to the "regulars who get special treatment."

Gene & Jude's Red Hot Stand ●📅 *Hot Dogs* — | — | — | I

O'Hare Area | 2720 River Rd. (Grand Ave.) | 708-452-7634

Old-school dogs and no new tricks make this anachronistic old-timer ('relished since 1946' as its sign proclaims) a popular O'Hare

Area landmark; tamales and fresh-cut fries round out the budget-friendly menu, which is served inside a ketchup-free, squat brick building with no-frills counter service (stand-up dining only) and frequent long lines.

NEW George Street Pub ● *Pub Food* | - | - | - | I |
Lakeview | 2858 N. Halsted St. (George St.) | 773-915-5005 | www.gspchicago.com

At this Lakeview pub, American bar food rooted in seafood and burgers is paired with 50-plus craft brews and served until late nightly; the stylish setting, done up with reclaimed vintage materials and a tin ceiling, includes WiFi and a big outdoor beer garden.

☑ Gibsons Bar & Steakhouse ● *Steak* | 26 | 21 | 24 | $64 |
Gold Coast | 1028 N. Rush St. (Bellevue Pl.) | 312-266-8999
Rosemont | Doubletree O'Hare | 5464 N. River Rd. (bet. Balmoral & Bryn Mawr Aves.) | 847-928-9900
NEW Oak Brook | 2105 S. Spring Rd. (22nd St.) | 630-954-0000
www.gibsonssteakhouse.com

"Waiters show you the slabs before they're cooked" at these "brash" city and suburban "speakeasy-styled steakhouses" serving "big", "succulent" steaks, "big side dishes" and "big desserts" at "big prices"; the "professional service" is "terrific" and "they pour a righteous drink", while the "people-watching" is peppered with "celebrities", "pro athletes", "cougars and sugar daddies" (especially in the "piano bar"), and if the Rosemont offshoot is "not quite the same" as the "Rush Street cornerstone", on the plus side it's also open till midnight most nights; P.S.an Oak Brook outpost opened post-Survey.

Gilt Bar ●☒Ⓜ *American* | - | - | - | M |
River North | 230 W. Kinzie St. (Franklin St.) | 312-464-9544 | www.giltbarchicago.com

Elevated New American gastro grub fashioned from artisanal ingredients gives new life to the former Aigre Doux space in River North, where French Laundry and Alain Ducasse veteran Brendan Sodikoff is turning out a midpriced menu complemented by classic cocktails, microbrews and a compact global wine list; the funky-chic surroundings are adorned with ornate antique mirrors, a hammered brass bar and vintage streetlamps.

Gioco *Italian* | 25 | 21 | 22 | $42 |
South Loop | 1312 S. Wabash Ave. (13th St.) | 312-939-3870 | www.gioco-chicago.com

For "quality" dining in the South Loop, surveyors look to the "excellent" seasonal Northern Italian fare ("nothing trendy or silly") including "heavenly pasta with wild boar sauce" at this "happening" "former speakeasy" from Jerry Kleiner (Marché, Red Light, 33 Club); "it's a little expensive", but the "warm", "urban" "exposed-brick decor" with "open kitchen" is home to a "noisy fun atmosphere" and "friendly, competent service"; P.S. it's also "near the Convention Center."

	FOOD	DECOR	SERVICE	COST

☑ Giordano's *Pizza* `23` `15` `18` `$22`

Loop | 135 E. Lake St. (Upper Michigan Ave.) | 312-616-1200 ◐
Loop | 225 W. Jackson Blvd. (Franklin St.) | 312-583-9400
River North | 730 N. Rush St. (Superior St.) | 312-951-0747 ◐
Lakeview | 1040 W. Belmont Ave. (Kenmore Ave.) | 773-327-1200
Logan Square | 2855 N. Milwaukee Ave. (Wolfram St.) | 773-862-4200
Northwest Side | 5927 W. Irving Park Rd. (Austin Ave.) | 773-736-5553
Hyde Park | 5311 S. Blackstone Ave. (53rd St.) | 773-947-0200
Southwest Side | 5159 S. Pulaski Rd. (Archer Ave.) | 773-582-7676 ◐
Southwest Side | 6314 S. Cicero Ave. (63rd St.) | 773-585-6100 ◐
Greektown | 815 W. Van Buren St. (Halsted St.) | 312-421-1221
www.giordanos.com
Additional locations throughout the Chicago area

"Stuffed and satisfied customers" of "all ages" crave the "delicious prototypical" "Chicago deep-dish" at this family of affordable local pie palaces, which is "why there's usually a wait"; those who claim the spots are "unfairly maligned by pizza snobs" add so what if "service and decor are unremarkable" – you're "there for" the pie.

NEW Girl & The Goat *American* `-` `-` `-` `M`

West Loop | 809 W. Randolph St. (Halsted St.) | 312-492-6262 |
www.girlandthegoat.com

Top Chef winner (and former Scylla chef-owner) Stephanie Izard is behind this midpriced West Loop arrival offering seasonal contemporary American sharing plates with Mediterranean influences, accompanied by Three Floyds brews on tap and Izard's own wine blend; the rustic-meets-industrial aesthetic mixes woods and vintage metalwork, and there's a long open kitchen, numerous seating options (including bar, lounge and outdoor) and, naturally, goat *objets d'art*; P.S. The Little Goat diner was in the works at press time.

☑ Glenn's Diner and Seafood House *Diner* `24` `14` `21` `$29`

Ravenswood | 1820 W. Montrose Ave. (Honore St.) | 773-506-1720 |
www.glennsdiner.com

An "eclectic crowd" gathers for "bargains on excellent fresh fish" that's "well prepared with restraint" plus Traditional American diner fare including "breakfasty meals" served all day at this Ravenswood "local dive" and "hidden treasure" where "service is attentive and friendly" and "fair corkage for BYO is a bonus" (it has "limited bar offerings"); gregarious graders suggest it for "some old-fashioned noise and prices", while conspiratorial types whisper "let's keep this" "a secret"; P.S. Tuesday's "all-you-can-eat crab legs is a steal" (Thursday offers the same deal but with peel-and-eat shrimp).

Glen Prairie *American* `23` `21` `21` `$34`

Glen Ellyn | Crowne Plaza Glen Ellyn | 1250 Roosevelt Rd. (Finley Rd.) |
630-613-1250 | www.glenprairie.com

"Surprising for a suburban hotel restaurant", this "green"-minded "find" in the Crowne Plaza Glen Ellyn incorporates "fresh selections from local purveyors" in its "reasonably priced" New American cuisine and offers a "modest", "interesting wine list with organic selections"; a "knowledgeable staff" and "beautiful" "prairie-style decor"

	FOOD	DECOR	SERVICE	COST

featuring recycled wood and earth tones underscore the "sustainable" scene, even if "they're not reinventing the wheel."

Gold Coast Dogs *Hot Dogs*

| 19 | 6 | 13 | $10 |

Loop | 159 N. Wabash Ave. (bet. Lake & Randolph Sts.) | 312-917-1677

Loop | Union Station | 225 S. Canal St. (bet. Adams St. & Jackson Blvd.) | 312-258-8585

Loop | Ogilvie Transportation Ctr. | 500 W. Madison St. (Canal St.) | 312-715-9488 🗵

Rogers Park | 2349 W. Howard St. (Asbury Ave.) | 773-338-0900

O'Hare Area | O'Hare Int'l Airport | Concourse L (I-190) | 773-462-7700 ❶

O'Hare Area | O'Hare Int'l Airport | Terminal 3 (I-190) | 773-462-9942

O'Hare Area | O'Hare Int'l Airport | Terminal 5 (I-190) | 773-462-0125

Rosemont | Rosemont Market Pl. | 7084 Mannheim Rd. (Touhy Ave.) | 847-759-1520

Southwest Side | Midway Int'l Airport | 5700 S. Cicero Ave. (55th St.) | 773-735-6789 ❶

www.goldcoastdogs.net

Patrons "woof!" their approval for this "quintessential" series of "stands" dispensing the "true Chicago dog" – "and don't forget the peppers" – "at a good price"; admirers warn "service with a smile this is not" and suggest "forget the decor" (just "what do you expect?"), and though some surveyors report "underwhelming" eats at what was once their "go-to", most insist it's "a must when you're in town."

Goose Island Brewing Co. *Pub Food*

| 17 | 16 | 18 | $23 |

Wrigleyville | 3535 N. Clark St. (Addison St.) | 773-832-9040
Lincoln Park | 1800 N. Clybourn Ave. (Sheffield Ave.) | 312-915-0071
www.gooseisland.com

"You can't beat their brews" and the "basket of homemade chips" at these affordable "local" Lincoln Park and Wrigleyville "staple stop-off" microbreweries appealing to "young singles, families and beer snobs" alike; even if the suds "outshine" the "upscale bar food" and "service could use some work", it's a "must" for "all pub crawls" – tip: have the "sampler if someone else is driving."

Gordon Biersch
Brewery Restaurant *Pub Food*

| 16 | 17 | 18 | $27 |

Bolingbrook | Promenade Bolingbrook | 639 E. Boughton Rd. (Janes Ave.) | 630-739-6036 | www.gordonbiersch.com

"If you can't find a true local microbrewery", this affordable Bolingbrook chain link is a "fine substitute" serving up "delicious" "craft beers" that "beat" the "decent" American pub grub (though all hail the "amazing" garlic fries); an "enjoyable happy-hour kinda place", it's not particularly "exciting", but the "relaxed" atmosphere is well suited to "kicking back with friends."

	FOOD	DECOR	SERVICE	COST

NEW Gosu *Japanese/Korean* — | — | — | M

Logan Square | 2515 N. California Ave. (bet. Altgeld St. & Logan Blvd.) | 773-276-7330 | www.gosurestaurant.com

Korean barbecue meets sushi – including 50 elaborately presented maki – and other midpriced Japanese fare at this Logan Square BYO in the former Rustik space; flagstone accents, elaborate globe chandelier lighting and 'flying' fish windsocks add visual appeal.

Graham Elliot ⛨Ⓜ *American* — 24 | 22 | 22 | $70

River North | 217 W. Huron St. (bet. Franklin & Wells Sts.) | 312-624-9975 | www.grahamelliot.com

"Cult followers" who favor Graham Elliot Bowles' "trendy" "deconstructed" New American "comfort" cuisine "mingling junk food and high ingredients" laud his "low-key" River North "passion project" as "kooky, innovative and totally delicious"; with its hefty tabs, some pan it as "pretentious" and say "substance" is often "drowned out by style" and "deafening music", but proponents of the "warm, inviting" setting and "down-to-earth staff" dub it "fantastic in every way."

NEW Grahamwich *Sandwiches* — | — | — | I

River North | 615 N. State St. (bet. Ohio & Ontario Sts.) | 312-265-0434 | www.grahamwich.com

Star chef Graham Elliot Bowles' counter-service concept in River North's historic Tree Studios offers eight 'wiches, crafted with his typical mix of whimsy and culinary commitment, as well as housemade sodas, seasonal gourmet ice cream flavors and some breakfast fare (but no decaf!); the casual setting features retro-inspired wallpaper, a large communal table and a bathroom with blackboard walls where you can channel your inner artist; P.S. the 'Grahambulance' will take the concept to the streets.

Grand Lux Cafe *Eclectic* — 20 | 21 | 19 | $29

River North | 600 N. Michigan Ave. (Ontario St.) | 312-276-2500 | www.grandluxcafe.com

Offering "pages and pages of options", this "classier counterpart" to the Cheesecake Factory located in River North serves "nicely done" Eclectic dishes in a "loud", somewhat "over-the-top" "high-ceilinged" environment that's inspired by European grand cafes; portions are as "ridiculously large" as the original's (but a bit "more expensive"), so there's still "no room" for the "decadent" desserts.

Great Lake ⛨Ⓜ *Pizza* — 23 | 11 | 11 | $22

Andersonville | 1477 W. Balmoral Ave. (bet. Clark St. & Glenwood Ave.) | 773-334-9270

Andersonville's "cramped", controversial "artisanal pizza" "hole-in-the-wall" divides diners into fans who warrant it's "worth the wait" for pies that are "more of an art form than most" with "daily choices reflecting local foods", and doubters who claim it may be "above-average" but is "overpriced" with "inflexible" service and "does not live up to the hype"; it's open only for dinner Wednesday through Saturday, and if you go, "don't forget a bottle of wine as it's BYO"; P.S. the menu is now 100% organic, and breakfast is in the works.

	FOOD	DECOR	SERVICE	COST

Greek Islands *Greek* 21 | 19 | 21 | $31

Greektown | 200 S. Halsted St. (Adams St.) | 312-782-9855 ●
Lombard | 300 E. 22nd St. (Highland Ave.) | 630-932-4545
www.greekislands.net

"Jovial crowds" cheer this "anchor of Greektown" (with a Lombard sibling) as "authentic to a degree" with "consistently well-prepared" "Greek favorites" and "fresh seafood that lifts it" "above most of its *'opa!'*-shouting neighbors"; "flaming cheese and people-watching" in "friendly" if somewhat "kitschy" confines are additional pluses, even as contrarians call out "standard" sustenance and service that swings from "speedy" to "slow."

Z Green Zebra *Vegetarian* 26 | 23 | 24 | $53

Noble Square | 1460 W. Chicago Ave. (Greenview Ave.) |
312-243-7100 | www.greenzebrachicago.com

"No one will miss the meat" with the "best vegetarian dining in Chicago" at Shawn McClain's "brilliant" Noble Square "innovator" where the "high-end", "creative, edgy" small plates are "almost totally veggie" and boast "plenty of flavors, a variety of influences" and "seasonal ingredients"; specialty "libations", "excellent brunch" and a "lovely staff" complete the "satisfying" supping in this "soothing", "subdued" sage-colored modern setting.

Grill on the Alley, 21 | 21 | 21 | $48
The *American*

Streeterville | Westin Michigan Ave. | 909 N. Michigan Ave.
(Delaware Pl.) | 312-255-9009 | www.thegrill.com

"Traditional" American chophouse fare and "comfort food in large quantities" – like "delicious steak, seafood", pot pie and "cobbler that's pure joy" – satisfy diners at this somewhat pricey Streeterville branch of the Beverly Hills original set in the Westin Michigan Avenue; the dark-wood and leather dining room is "quiet" with "usually knowledgeable, caring service", while a "warm and comfortable", "lively bar" area adds to the bonhomie.

Grillroom, The *Steak* 15 | 16 | 17 | $42

Loop | 33 W. Monroe St. (bet. Dearborn & State Sts.) | 312-960-0000 |
www.restaurants-america.com

"A wide range" of "typical steakhouse choices with some salads" delivered with "quick service" in a "modern ambiance" makes this Loop lair from the Midtown Kitchen folks the "place for a power lunch" or other "business dining"; "it's pleasant" and "perfectly adequate", though some say it's "pricey for dinner."

Gruppo di Amici ◪ *Italian* ▽ 16 | 16 | 18 | $31

Rogers Park | 1508 W. Jarvis Ave. (Greenview Ave.) | 773-508-5565 |
www.gruppodiamici.com

"Thin-crust", "wood-fired pizza" and "modern Italian-style entrees" draw "value"-minded Rogers Park regulars to this "warm", "cozy" "neighborhood place"; true, "there aren't a lot of other options" nearby, but "friendly service offsets the average" fare, and "terrific martinis" don't hurt either.

NEW GT Fish & Oyster *Seafood*

| | - | - | - | M |

River North | 531 N. Wells St. (Grand Ave.) | 312-929-3501

The crew behind Boka and other favorites strikes again, this time with Giuseppe Tentori's highly anticipated River North seafood sophisticate offering oysters and other moderately priced, ocean-centric hot and cold plates with sharing appeal (plus a few seafood-free choices); a striking boomerang-shaped table stands out among the nautical trappings, and the bar offers craft cocktails as well as extra seating; P.S. look for a sidewalk patio in season.

NEW Gyu-Kaku *Japanese*

| | - | - | - | M |

Streeterville | 210 E. Ohio St. (St. Clair St.) | 312-266-8929 | www.gyu-kaku.com

At this Streeterville outpost of an upscale international yakiniku chain, diners charcoal-grill their own Japanese meals at the table (smoke ventilation hopefully reduces dry-cleaning bills), choosing from ingredients that go above and beyond the usual – think prime and Kobe beef cuts, lamb, offal, pork jowl and duck – with rice and noodle dishes and desserts on offer too; the hip, Asian-industrial setting features exposed brick and ductwork, bamboo booths and a cozy second-floor lounge-library with full bar service.

Habana Libre *Cuban*

| | ▽ 22 | 10 | 18 | $24 |

Noble Square | 1440 W. Chicago Ave. (bet. Bishop St. & Greenview Ave.) | 312-243-3303 | www.habanalibrerestaurant.com

"Tasty pork preparations", empanadas and other "authentic" fare make diners "dream of Cuba" at this Noble Square "BYO neighborhood joint"; an "attentive staff" and "good value" add to reasons it also suits "for a weeknight date" or a "big group."

Hachi's Kitchen *Japanese*

| | - | - | - | M |

Logan Square | 2521 N. California Ave. (bet. Logan Blvd. & Fullerton St.) | 773-276-8080 | www.hachiskitchen.com

Sushi so "fresh" it's "like it swam to your plate" (including "delicious original rolls") joins "other Japanese specialties" in luring Logan Square locals to this "beautiful", "high-ceilinged" sibling of Sai Café; acolytes applaud the staff and say there's "rarely a wait", which along with moderate prices and a seasonal patio make it suitable "for friends or a date."

Hackney's *Burgers*

| | 18 | 15 | 19 | $22 |

Printer's Row | 733 S. Dearborn St. (bet. Harrison & Polk Sts.) | 312-461-1116
Glenview | 1241 Harms Rd. (Lake Ave.) | 847-724-5577
Glenview | 1514 E. Lake Ave. (bet. Sunset Ridge & Waukegan Rds.) | 847-724-7171
Lake Zurich | 880 N. Old Rand Rd. (Rand Rd.) | 847-438-2103
Palos Park | 9550 W. 123rd St. (La Grange Rd.) | 708-448-8300
www.hackneys.net

At this local chain of "good-old burger-joint" "time capsules" (Printer's Row is newer), hankerers hail the "huge" "Hackney-burger" "on dark rye" and "onion rings fried as a brick" as a "guilty pleasure" supplying "all the grease you need for a year"; the "road-house atmosphere" and service vary by location, but there's an option to "sit outside" and a "decent beer selection" at all, and though modernists sniff it's just plain "old", it's also "held the line on price."

Hai Yen *Chinese/Vietnamese* 21 | 13 | 18 | $23

Lincoln Park | 2723 N. Clark St. (Diversey Pkwy.) | 773-868-4888
Uptown | 1055 W. Argyle St. (B'way) | 773-561-4077
www.haiyenrestaurant.com

It's "definitely not high-end" joke fans of this duo's "authentic Vietnamese cuisine" that's mixed with Mandarin Chinese choices and "amazing fresh bubble teas" – all at "reasonable prices"; "bland but pleasant decor" and "so-so service" come with the territory, though cognoscenti call the Uptown location (which is closed Wednesdays) more culinarily "adventurous" than Lincoln Park.

Half Shell ●♥ *Seafood* 24 | 7 | 16 | $37

Lakeview | 676 W. Diversey Pkwy. (bet. Clark & Orchard Sts.) | 773-549-1773 | www.halfshellchicago.com

Fish lovers fancy this Lakeview "basement" seafooder, a no-reservations "madhouse" where "amazing crab legs and raw bar" options, "beer by the pitcher", "unfriendly service and cheap decor" converge for some of the "best value" dining in town ("just bring cash", they don't take cards); P.S. those not feeling the "dark", "dive" digs are "part of the charm" head for the "outdoor terrace in the summer."

Hamburger Mary's *Burgers* 17 | 16 | 20 | $18

Andersonville | 5400 N. Clark St. (Balmoral Ave.) | 773-784-6969 | www.hamburgermaryschicago.com

"Mixed crowds" of "all ages, genders and sexual orientation" convene at Andersonville's "kitsch" "center of activity" for "terrific burgers" and "interesting twists on traditional bar" bites plus "housemade microbrews"; seating includes a "playhouse upstairs" and "outdoor dining", and if it's "a little bit pricey for what you get", it's also "enjoyable dinner theater" – "how can you beat" having your bill "delivered in a slipper?"; P.S. the adjacent Rec Room serves the full menu.

Hana Restaurant ⓈJapanese - | - | - | M

Rogers Park | 6803 N. Sheridan Rd. (Pratt St.) | 773-338-8815
This affordable, family-owned neighborhood Japanese in Rogers Park specializes in sushi and teriyaki, plus bargain lunch specials, all served in a casual, no-frills storefront space with bare tables, bare walls and bright lighting; P.S. there's no booze, and no BYO.

Ⓩ Hannah's Bretzel Ⓢ *Sandwiches* 23 | 13 | 19 | $13

NEW **Loop** | 131 S. Dearborn St. (bet. Adams St. & Marble Pl.) | 312-621-1111
Loop | 180 W. Washington St. (bet. La Salle & Wells Sts.) | 312-621-1111
Loop | Illinois Ctr. | 233 N. Michigan Ave. (bet. Lake St. & Wacker Pl.) | 312-621-1111
www.hannahsbretzel.com

Some of the "best and freshest-tasting sandwiches in the Loop" are served at these "Downtown workday spots" that heap "high-end in-

FOOD | DECOR | SERVICE | COST

gredients" on "delicious" "pretzel bread" and offer a "wall" of "fancy chocolate bars" "for dessert"; while the budget brigade bristles that it's "expensive for what you get", most "don't mind paying a bit more" for organic ingredients; P.S. Washington Street has limited seating and Dearborn has the most.

Han 202 Ⓜ *Asian/Eclectic*

▽ 25 | 25 | 25 | $25

Bridgeport | 605 W. 31st St. (bet. Lowe Ave. & Wallace St.) | 312-949-1314 | www.han202.com

Near South Siders have taken to this Asian-Eclectic BYO, finding "excellent value" in its prix fixe menu of "interesting, flavorful" fare served by a "friendly", "attentive staff" amid "crisp decor"; P.S. there's "limited seating", but "it's well worth planning ahead."

Happ Inn Bar & Grill *American*

17 | 19 | 17 | $30

Northfield | 305 S. Happ Rd. (Willow Rd.) | 847-784-9200 | www.thehappinn.com

Kindred spirits are "rooting for" this midpriced Carlos' spin-off concept in Northfield that's a "comfortable setting" for American "comfort food" (plus some Mexican touches) with a "nice outdoor seating area"; some who are "not happy" guess it might be "too popular" (and "noisy") resulting in "uneven" fare and "rocky service", but repeat customers contend it's "getting better."

Hard Rock Cafe ◑ *American*

12 | 20 | 14 | $29

River North | 63 W. Ontario St. (bet. Clark & Dearborn Sts.) | 312-943-2252 | www.hardrockcafe.com

"Rock memorabilia" is the claim to fame of this "noisy", "nostalgic", music-driven American chain link in River North, and if the food doesn't exactly rock, it's fine for "enjoying a burger and a beer"; but those who deem the concept "so yesterday" ("does anyone still think this is cool?") feel it may be best left to "headbangers", "tourists" and youngsters who "love" those T-shirts.

Harry Caray's *Italian/Steak*

20 | 20 | 20 | $42

River North | 33 W. Kinzie St. (Dearborn St.) | 312-828-0966
Rosemont | O'Hare International Ctr., Holiday Inn | 10233 W. Higgins Rd. (Mannheim Rd.) | 847-699-1200
Lombard | Westin Lombard | 70 Yorktown Shopping Ctr. (Butterfield Rd.) | 630-953-3400

Harry Caray's Seventh Inning Stretch *Italian/Steak*

Southwest Side | Midway Int'l Airport | 5757 S. Cicero Ave. (55th St.) | 773-948-6300
www.harrycarays.com

To fans who "feel the presence of Harry himself", this phalanx of "fancy sports bars" is "exciting, noisy" and "less stuffy" than the steakhouse staples, with "enjoyable and tasty" (if "not gourmet") "steaks and oversize Italian specialties" plus "great baseball memorabilia" (including the "Bartman ball" Downtown); underwhelmed umps "go for the kitsch" and the "bar scene, especially when the Cubs are on TV", knocking the "overpriced", "mediocre food" and "touristy" tone.

	FOOD	DECOR	SERVICE	COST

Havana ⬚ *Nuevo Latino*

| - | - | - | M |

River North | 412 N. Clark St. (bet. Hubbard & Kinzie Sts.) | 312-644-1900 | www.havanachicago.com

River North's former Mambo Grill space houses this Nuevo Latino with a similar midpriced menu, served for lunch and dinner, along with a slew of specialty cocktails; aglow in natural light by day and golden lighting by night, the setting features dark wood, mirrors, stone tiles and a display of dining-related words snaking around the ceiling edge; P.S. there's also seasonal sidewalk seating.

NEW Haymarket Pub & Brewery ● *Pub Food*

| - | - | - | I |

West Loop | 737 W. Randolph St. (Halsted St.) | 312-638-0700 | www.haymarketbrewing.com

On the site of the historic Haymarket Square Riot in the West Loop, this pub pulls 32 handles (10 or so house-brewed) and boasts a big bottle selection as well, all the better to enjoy an artisanal menu of comfort food; dark wood, brick and low lighting create an upscale tavern feel, with TVs in the main bar and a view into the glass-encased brewery from the dining room; P.S. a weekday morning and afternoon coffee and pastry cafe is also on-site.

HB Home Bistro Ⓜ *American*

| 25 | 20 | 25 | $35 |

Lakeview | 3404 N. Halsted St. (Roscoe St.) | 773-661-0299 | www.homebistrochicago.com

Lakeview locals "keep coming back" to Joncarl Lachman's "small" New American BYO for its "good vibe" and "excellent fine dining" featuring "glorious" "seasonal" "combinations in every dish" served by an "accommodating", "enthusiastic" staff; it's so "affordable" that surveyors say "for the price, we ripped them off"; P.S. "make reservations as the few tables fill up fast."

Heartland Cafe *Eclectic/Vegetarian*

| 16 | 13 | 18 | $21 |

Rogers Park | Heartland Bldg. | 7000 N. Glenwood Ave. (Lunt Ave.) | 773-465-8005 | www.heartlandcafe.com

Opened in 1976, this "vegetarian-friendly" Rogers Park "throwback" is an "unwavering institution of hippiedom" offering affordable, "organic and delicious" Eclectic eats plus a "wonderful" "selection of draft beers"; though antis call the fare "hit-or-miss" ("except for breakfast") and declare service "a bit slow", it's an "experience on many levels" with "lots of outdoor seating", entertainment such as music Wednesday–Saturday and "incense-scented shopping in the extreme left-wing gift shop."

Hearty Ⓜ *American*

| - | - | - | M |

Lakeview | 3819 N. Broadway (Grace St.) | 773-868-9866 | www.heartychicago.com

Food Network stars the Hearty Boys dish out "updated" New American "comfort food" for dinner and brunch along with midpriced wines and creative cocktails at this "cozy", "friendly" Lakeview haunt with exposed brick and bright walls, glass artwork and a "scene" at the mahogany and tile bar; P.S. there's outdoor dining.

☑ Heaven on Seven *Cajun/Creole* 23 | 17 | 19 | $26

Loop | Garland Bldg. | 111 N. Wabash Ave., 7th fl. (Washington Blvd.) | 312-263-6443 ☒ ⊐

River North | AMC Loews | 600 N. Michigan Ave., 2nd fl. (bet. Ohio & Ontario Sts.) | 312-280-7774

Naperville | 224 S. Main St. (bet. Jackson & Jefferson Aves.) | 630-717-0777

www.heavenonseven.com

"Soul-satisfied" surveyors swear by the "modestly priced", "comprehensive menu of well-prepared Cajun and Creole specialties" and "hot-sauce kitsch atmosphere" featuring "rows of bottles on the wall" at this "taste of New Orleans in Chicago"; "service isn't much", but a consensus claims the "cash-only" Loop "original" (that's not open for dinner) offers "better" fare and "funkier atmosphere than the spin-offs", hence its "lines down the hall."

Hecky's Barbecue *BBQ* 20 | 5 | 14 | $18

Evanston | 1902 Green Bay Rd. (Emerson St.) | 847-492-1182 | www.heckys.com

"Barbecue as good as it gets" "for miles around" "hits the spot" for most meat eaters at this Evanston BYO that's "been there forever and is usually consistent" for "smoked ribs and sausages", "turkey legs" and "sauce that's not too sweet"; since there's "no decor" and "no real sit-down option", "takeout is the way" to go, but "delivery is a nice touch" too.

Hema's Kitchen *Indian* 22 | 12 | 16 | $22

Lincoln Park | 2411 N. Clark St. (Fullerton Pkwy.) | 773-529-1705

West Rogers Park | 2439 W. Devon Ave. (Artesian Ave.) | 773-338-1627

www.hemaskitchen.com

With kitchens in Lincoln Park and West Rogers Park, this "no-frills" BYO duo issues an "extensive menu" of "authentic dishes from various regions of India" that are "not too spicy unless you want it that way"; some call it "nothing special" with service that "can be too relaxed" and "decor that's lacking", "but the real attraction" is the fare, which is also a "godsend for vegetarians."

Hemmingway's Bistro *American/French* 21 | 19 | 21 | $39

Oak Park | Write Inn | 211 N. Oak Park Ave. (Ontario St.) | 708-524-0806 | www.hemmingwaysbistro.com

"Warm and welcoming", this three-meal-a-day "neighborhood spot" in the Write Inn is "in keeping with the Oak Park vibe" and a "comfortable" contender offering "Parisian" "flair" and a "selection of French bistro" and Traditional American fare along with a bar and "attentive service"; P.S. it's "perfect for a cold winter evening", and there's jazz on Wednesday nights and at the Sunday brunch buffet.

NEW Henri *American* - | - | - | E

South Loop | 18 S. Michigan Ave. (Monroe St.) | 312-578-0763 | www.henrichicago.com

This luxe South Loop counterpart to The Gage (named after architect Louis Henri Sullivan) serves American fare with classic French underpinnings – think rabbit consommé and pissaladière – accompanied by a boutique wine list and crafty cocktails; the upscale, white-tablecloth setting boasts crystal chandeliers, elaborate crown molding, leather and mohair upholstery and a mahogany bar, plus seasonal outdoor seating overlooking Millennium Park.

Holy Mackerel!
American Fish House *Seafood*

∇ 21 | 18 | 18 | $58

Lombard | Westin Lombard | 70 Yorktown Ctr. (Butterfield Rd.) | 630-953-3444 | www.holymackerelseafood.com

"There's a lot" of "good seafood" on the menu at this seafaring spin-off of the Harry Caray's clan located in the Westin Lombard and deemed "above average for a suburban hotel restaurant"; some who suggest the "city prices" "may not quite be justified" by the "portion size and quality" or "slower-than-expected service" prefer "sticking to" the steakhouse sibling "next door."

Honey 1 BBQ Ⓜ *BBQ*

20 | 8 | 15 | $20

Bucktown | 2241 N. Western Ave. (Lyndale St.) | 773-227-5130 | www.honey1bbq.com

"Serious barbecue" boosters praise the "pure, smoky, porky goodness" ("especially the ribs and tips" and "hot links") at this budget-loving Bucktown 'cue contender; "accommodations are sparse" and the meals "messy", so it might "not be the place for a first date", but who needs romance when "you're there for the food."

Hop Häus ◐ *Burgers*

19 | 15 | 17 | $21

River North | 646 N. Franklin St. (Erie St.) | 312-467-4287
Rogers Park | 7545 N. Clark St. (Howard St.) | 773-262-3783
www.thehophaus.com

"Burgers and more burgers" both "mini" and "tall" are on a "selection worth seeing" (including exotic game) along with "super-large salads", "tons of beers from around the world" and weekend brunch at these sometimes "noisy" "sports bars" with "TVs galore and friendly staff"; P.S. Rogers Park has a "lovely outdoor setting."

Hopleaf *Belgian*

23 | 18 | 18 | $27

Andersonville | 5148 N. Clark St. (Foster Ave.) | 773-334-9851 | www.hopleaf.com

A "hip crowd" (21 and older only) haunts this "authentic" gastro-pub, a "little bit of Belgium in Andersonville" that "sets the standard for others" say surveyors who explore a "dizzying array of beers" and "unique, delicious" midpriced fare ("don't miss" the moules frites) amid a "biergarten" atmosphere with a "fabulous patio in the summer"; the only complaints concern "staff attitude" and that it's "too popular", thus "hard to get in", but a second location is planned.

Hot Chocolate Ⓜ *American*

24 | 19 | 21 | $33

Bucktown | 1747 N. Damen Ave. (Willow St.) | 773-489-1747 | www.hotchocolatechicago.com

"Don't let the name fool you into thinking it's just sweets" at Mindy Segal's "unique", "crowded and loud" Bucktown "locavore" that's "trendy, upscale and down-home all at once; yes, the "decadent" desserts are "mind-blowing" and the "hot chocolate orgasmic", but the American "savory items are equally delicious" and the "tabs reasonable", making it a "top-to-bottom favorite" despite reports of "average service"; P.S. "take home a box of her cookies."

☑ Hot Doug's ⑤⌿ Hot Dogs   27 | 13 | 20 | $12

Northwest Side | 3324 N. California Ave. (Roscoe St.) | 773-279-9550 | www.hotdougs.com

"Believe what you read" woof wiener hounds hooked on the "mind-boggling" "gourmet" "encased meat" and "amazing fries" (sometimes "fried in duck fat") at this Northwest Sider – voted tops for hot dogs in this Survey – dispensing everything from the "classic" Chicago-style to "adventures in sausageology" including specials such as spicy alligator; "Doug [Sohn] is a mini-celebrity who still mans" the cash-only counter "with a smile", and though "lines are incredibly long" at this colorful space with hot dog memorabilia and outdoor seating, "they keep it moving" and "it's worth the wait"; P.S. open till 4 PM.

Hot Woks Cool Sushi   Asian   23 | 18 | 23 | $22

Loop | 30 S. Michigan Ave. (bet. Madison & Monroe Sts.) | 312-345-1234
NEW Loop | 312 W. Adams St. (bet. Franklin St. & Wacker Dr.) | 312-220-0011 ⑤
Northwest Side | 3930 N. Pulaski Rd. (Dakin St.) | 773-282-1818
NEW Roscoe Village | 2032 W. Roscoe St. (Seeley Ave.) | 773-880-9800
www.hotwokscoolsushi.com

"Decently priced", "dependable sushi, Thai food", "noodle dishes" and other Asian fare make these joints "welcome" additions to their neighborhoods, even if service can be slow; P.S. the Northwest Side outpost is BYO, but the others serve beer and wine.

House of Fortune   Chinese   23 | 13 | 17 | $23

Chinatown | 2407 S. Wentworth Ave. (24th St.) | 312-225-0880
Considered a "safe bet, both culinarywise and for overall service", this "consistent" Chinatowner is the choice of those who "know freshness, authenticity and quality"; its "low-key" atmosphere, "affordable" pricing and some of the "best Peking duck in the neighborhood" (which "you don't have to order in advance") are additional "incentives" bringing patrons back "again and again."

NEW Hoyt's   American   - | - | - | M

Loop | Hotel 71 | 71 E. Wacker Dr. (bet. Clark & Dearborn Sts.) | 312-346-7100 | www.hoytschicago.com
After a long restaurant hiatus, Hotel 71 now plays host to this moderately priced American serving contemporary comfort food (e.g. deep-fried deviled eggs, lamb leg Reuben, steak frites, designer chocolate pudding served in mason jars) for breakfast, lunch and dinner; the masculine, modern space is all angles and neutrals with natural stone and wood, sophisticated textures, dramatic lighting, a large bar and seasonal outdoor seating on the river.

🆕 Hubbard Inn ●☒ *American*

– **–** **–** **M**

River North | 110 W. Hubbard St. (bet. Clark & LaSalle Sts.) | 312-222-1331 | www.hubbardinn.com

This multilevel River North American – a restau-tap from the LaSalle Power Co. and English crew – takes decor cues from Hemingway's travels, featuring Moroccan tiles and a book-trimmed, first-floor library; the moderately priced menu (also served in the upstairs lounge) is anchored by snacks and small plates, with a selection of craft brews and global whiskeys and bourbons to wash it down.

Hub 51 ● *American/Eclectic*

21 **20** **19** **$34**

River North | 51 W. Hubbard St. (Dearborn St.) | 312-828-0051 | www.hub51chicago.com

"Trendy" "urban" "twentysomethings" tout the New American–"Eclectic food in an electric room" ("where else can you get sushi and Mexican in one place?"), "fabulous cocktails and moderate prices" at this "lively" River North noshery "from the sons of [Lettuce Entertain You] impresario Rich Melman"; it "turns into a nightclub later in the evening" (via downstairs lounge Sub 51) with DJs Thursday–Saturday, and "service is appropriate for the venue", but more staid types chalk up the lure to the "cool scene", "not the grub."

☑ Hugo's Frog Bar & Fish House ● *Seafood*

24 **21** **23** **$50**

Gold Coast | 1024 N. Rush St. (bet. Bellevue Pl. & Oak St.) | 312-640-0999
Naperville | Main Street Promenade Bldg. | 55 S. Main St. (Van Buren Ave.) | 630-548-3764
www.hugosfrogbar.com

"Where the locals eat in the Gold Coast", this "hoppin'" "fish companion to Gibsons" "delivers top (albeit pricey) seafood" including "amazing frogs' legs" ("plus steaks" from "next door"), piano nightly and "people-watching"; service is generally "professional", but many experience a "delay even with a reservation" especially "on weekends" (Naperville is somewhat less "noisy" than Downtown).

Icosium Kafe *African*

19 **15** **19** **$19**

Andersonville | 5200 N. Clark St. (Foster Ave.) | 773-271-5233
Lincoln Park | 2433 N. Clark St. (bet. Arlington Pl. & Fullerton Pkwy.) | 773-404-1300
www.icosiumkafechicago.com

"The lamps, mint tea" and "interesting decor and seating" "practically transport you to North Africa" at this Andersonville Algerian "surprise" (with a Lincoln Park sibling) serving "delicious" "twists" on "hot crêpes all day" (including build-your-own options and "dessert" "variations") at an "excellent price"; P.S. service can be "slow, so don't go if you're in a hurry."

Il Mulino New York *Italian*

25 **24** **24** **$77**

Gold Coast | 1150 N. Dearborn St. (bet. Division & Elm Sts.) | 312-440-8888 | www.ilmulino.com

Offering "fine Italian dining" complete with a "very good wine list", this Gold Coast "New York import" set in the "intimate", "beautiful

Biggs mansion" also boasts an "expert staff" that pleased patrons liken to "flawless performers on stage" delivering a "special evening"; the less-impressed say service "can be overwhelming" and find it all "outrageously expensive", but those seated next to one of the "fireplaces" just call it "wonderful."

Il Poggiolo *Italian*   19 | 21 | 19 | $40

Hinsdale | 8 E. First St. (bet. Garfield Ave. & Washington St.) | 630-734-9400 | www.ilpoggiolohinsdale.com

Beyond its red-and-white entrance canopy, Jerry Kleiner's "hopping" West Suburban seasonal Italian located in a former silent movie theater is "better than expected for a trendy Hinsdale spot", turning out "quality" fare "at reasonable prices"; though some call the service "consistently inconsistent", the "open environment" wins compliments for its "bar setup" and decor featuring a vaulted-ceiling dining room, photography and plush red upholstery.

Ina's *American*   23 | 16 | 22 | $23

West Loop | 1235 W. Randolph St. (Elizabeth St.) | 312-226-8227 | www.breakfastqueen.com

"Chicago icon" Ina Pinkney "makes you feel like a guest in her home" at her West Loop New American that's beloved for "breakfast with passion" and "tasty" "comfort food" ("go for the fried chicken") for lunch (hours vary seasonally); "warm service" amid a "collection of funky salt and pepper shakers" adds to the allure, so expect "long lines" at peak hours (however they "move quickly"); P.S. "you can't beat the free parking in the lot outside the door."

☒ India House *Indian*   25 | 18 | 19 | $29

River North | 59 W. Grand Ave. (bet. Clark & Dearborn Sts.) | 312-645-9500

NEW Arlington Heights | 721 W. Golf Rd. (bet. Algonquin Rd. & Fernandez Ave.) | 847-278-0760

Buffalo Grove | Buffalo Grove Town Ctr. | 228-230 McHenry Rd. (Lake Cook Rd.) | 847-520-5569

Schaumburg | 1521 W. Schaumburg Rd. (Springinsguth Rd.) | 847-895-5501 Ⓜ

Oak Brook | 2809 Butterfield Rd. (Meyers Rd.) | 630-472-1500 www.indiahousechicago.com

"Excellent, authentic Indian dishes" keep surveyors "satisfied" at these subcontinentals with "accommodating service", where the "delicious, beautifully presented lunch buffets" (price varies by location but they're all a "value") are one reason why regulars say "face it, you are going to overeat" so "enjoy it"; P.S. the Arlington Heights outpost also houses Bombay Chopsticks, an Indo-Chinese bistro.

Indian Garden *Indian*   21 | 15 | 18 | $27

Streeterville | 247 E. Ontario St., 2nd fl. (Fairbanks Ct.) | 312-280-4910 | www.indiangardenchicago.com

West Rogers Park | 2546 W. Devon Ave. (Rockwell St.) | 773-338-2929 | www.indiangardendevon.com

Surveyors "step into India" at these "reliable standbys" for a "variety of tasty", "decently spiced" midpriced "standards" and lunch "buffet extravaganzas"; they're separately owned, which might account for service that gets mixed marks and settings that rank somewhere between "nice" and merely "satisfactory."

Indie Cafe   *Japanese/Thai* | 24 | 18 | 20 | $22 |

Edgewater | 5951 N. Broadway (bet. Elmdale & Thorndale Aves.) | 773-561-5577 | www.indiecafe.us

"They are striving to be different" at this "low-key" Edgewater indie with an "extensive menu" of "creative sushi" and other "outstanding" Japanese bites, "luscious curries and Thai dishes", all "presented with a stunning sense of plating aesthetics"; so if the service is "somewhat random" and an "elegant" "city" feel to some is a "lack of decor" to others, everyone agrees you "go for" the "fantastic" fare.

NEW Ing   *American* | - | - | - | E |

West Loop | 951 W. Fulton Mkt. (Morgan St.) | 855-834-6464 | www.ingrestaurant.com

Homaro Cantu's second Moto spin-off, this West Loop arrival strikes a balance between the molecular mother ship and the bygone Otom with pricey, Asian-inflected New American plates small and large, available à la carte or in a dine-by-the-hour concept; the minimalist Fulton Market setting with oak walls and red sofa seating houses a noodle station up front and cold station in back, while an extravagant degustation is served at the chef's kitchen table.

Inovasi ⌀ *American* | - | - | - | M |

Lake Bluff | 28 E. Center Ave. (Scranton Ave.) | 847-295-1000 | www.inovasi.us

At this Lake Bluff New American, John Des Rosiers (ex Bank Lane Bistro) delivers creative, midpriced lunches and dinners in a variety of portion sizes (plus a kids' menu) using local and sustainable seasonal ingredients; the brick corner storefront sets a chic but casual mood with handsome wood and neutral-and-smoky-blue tones.

NEW IPO Restaurant   *American* | - | - | - | E |

Loop | W City Center Hotel | 172 W. Adams St. (bet. LaSalle & Wells Sts.) | 312-917-5608 | www.iporestaurant.com

This arrival in the Loop's W Chicago City Center (whose name does indeed stand for 'initial public offering') serves upscale, creative contemporary American fare for breakfast, lunch and dinner (and brunch on the weekends), along with inventive post-work cocktails; done up in rich neutrals and subdued lighting, the polished modern setting is bisected by a dramatic wood grid divider flanked by banquettes, with curved booths and the swanky, low-lit Living Room Bar as additional seating options.

Irazu ⌀⊄ *Costa Rican* | 22 | 10 | 18 | $17 |

Bucktown | 1865 N. Milwaukee Ave. (Western Ave.) | 773-252-5687 | www.irazuchicago.com

"Now known by more than [just] the locals", Bucktown's Costa Rican BYO and cash-only "neighborhood gem" dishes out "tasty", "unique" fare that's "super cheap"; it's "casual" and "family-friendly",

FOOD | DECOR | SERVICE | COST

but there are no reservations and fans say the "only downside is that the space is way too small for its justified popularity" – though you can sometimes "eat outside"; P.S. a recent patio update added more seating.

Irish Oak Pub & Grille *Pub Food*

▽ 19 | 24 | 22 | $23

Wrigleyville | 3511 N. Clark St. (Addison St.) | 773-935-6669 | www.irishoak.com

"Guinness and a burger is the name of the game" at this "real", affordable "old-fashioned" "Irish pub" located next to Wrigley Field that "knows how to pour a pint" – and where it's "always a great time for a drinking session"; the decor from the floors up "was brought over from the old sod", and there's live music Thursday through Saturday nights.

Isacco Kitchen Ⓜ *Italian*

- | - | - | M

St. Charles | 210 Cedar St. (bet. 2nd & 3rd Sts.) | 630-444-0202 | www.isaccokitchen.com

Globe-trotting chef Isacco Vitali presides over this affordable West Suburban spot where Northern Italian culinary concepts get creative, contemporary treatments; a former barbecue hut has been transformed into an intimate white-tablecloth dining room with modern Italian furnishings, splashes of bright color, funky art and a variety of seating including a small lounge area and patio.

Isla Filipino
Restaurant Ⓜ *Filipino*

- | - | - | I

Lincoln Square | 2501 W. Lawrence Ave. (Campbell Ave.) | 773-271-2988 | www.islapilipina.com

The extensive, budget-friendly Filipino menu "has far more hits than misses" at this "no-frills Lincoln Square BYO" situated in a strip mall; a "sweet staff", local art on the walls and bargain lunch specials add to the appeal.

ItaliAsia *Asian/Italian*

- | - | - | M

River North | Holiday Inn Chicago Mart Plaza | 350 W. Mart Center Dr., 15th fl. (Orleans St.) | 312-836-5000 | www.italiasiarestaurant.com

Italian and Asian cuisine combine at this midpriced River North aerie, where entrees run from chicken Vesuvio to seafood tempura, sweets include won ton cannoli and spumoni, and champagne and sake star on the drink list; its handsome modern setting sports distinctive geometric floor, wall and lighting treatments, and the adjacent Cityscape Bar offers great skyline views.

Itto Sushi ●Ⓩ *Japanese*

24 | 14 | 21 | $33

Lincoln Park | 2616 N. Halsted St. (Wrightwood Ave.) | 773-871-1800 | www.ittosushi.com

Regulars "welcome" this "completely unpretentious" Lincoln Park "respite from the trendy sake bars", an "old" (since the '80s) "traditional sushi" "standby" that's "reasonably priced" and the "real deal" for "authentic Japanese" fare served in a simple setting by a "friendly staff"; P.S. late hours (open till midnight) are a plus.

	FOOD	DECOR	SERVICE	COST

Jack's on Halsted *American*

21 | 17 | 19 | $34

Lakeview | 3201 N. Halsted St. (Belmont Ave.) | 773-244-9191 | www.jacksonhalsted.com

Halsted Street's New American "mainstay" is a "cozy", mid-priced Lakeview "neighborhood place" with an urban look as a backdrop for a "solid menu", special martinis and "pleasant service"; a "diverse, hipper-than-usual clientele" adds to the "city atmosphere", and it "gets pretty crowded most nights with the Boys Town crew" and other fans; P.S. it's "well located for dinner before Briar Street Theatre."

Jacky's on Prairie Ⓜ *Eclectic*

21 | 20 | 20 | $48

Evanston | 2545 Prairie Ave. (Central St.) | 847-733-0899 | www.jackysonprairie.com

Though former chef-owner "Jacky [Pluton] doesn't run the place anymore", this "intimate, unpretentious" Evanston homage is still gaining followers with its "delightful" seasonal Eclectic fare (even if it is "a little pricey"); the verdict on the "vibe is more neighborhood cafe than night on the town", though some say the "updated decor" is "less homey" than before.

Ja' Grill Restaurant & Lounge *Jamaican*

- | - | - | I

Lincoln Park | 1008 W. Armitage Ave. (Sheffield Ave.) | 773-929-5375 | www.jagrill.com

Inexpensive curries, jerks, whole fish and rum punch star on the menu at this upscale-casual Lincoln Park Jamaican where conversation-friendly reggae music (and weekend DJs) sets the mood; focal points of its brick-and-wood space are a red-glowing bar and huge mural of Bob Marley, plus there's a comfy lower-level lounge.

Jaipur *Indian*

- | - | - | M

West Loop | 847 W. Randolph St. (bet. Green & Peoria Sts.) | 312-526-3655 | www.jaipurchicago.com

For a "taste of real Indian on Restaurant Row", surveyors seek out the "honest", "wonderful" midpriced fare full of "fresh ingredients" at this West Loop eatery where the "service is great" and the "room is quite comfortable"; P.S. a patio and prix fixe all-you-can-eat lunch (not buffet) add to the "great deal."

J. Alexander's *American*

20 | 20 | 20 | $32

Lincoln Park | 1832 N. Clybourn Ave. (bet. Willow & Wisconsin Sts.) | 773-435-1018
Northbrook | 4077 Lake Cook Rd. (bet. I-294 & Sanders Rd.) | 847-564-3093
Oak Brook | 1410 16th St. (Rte. 83) | 630-573-8180
www.jalexanders.com

This "dependable" Lincoln Park and suburban trio is considered a "competent chain" for its "decent" "all-around" chophouse and Traditional American fare "at less-than-steakhouse prices" and in a "variety pleasing to all palates"; a "welcoming" staff and "warm", "comfortable" dark-wood confines have commenters noting "no surprises, no complaints."

	FOOD	DECOR	SERVICE	COST

Jam ⊉ *American*
▽ 21 | 16 | 24 | $19

Ukrainian Village | 937 N. Damen Ave. (bet. Augusta Blvd. & Walton St.) | 773-489-0302 | www.jamrestaurant.com

Ukrainian Villagers note that the "innovative, delicious" breakfast, brunch and lunch fare at this New American is "made with trendy ingredients" and "served by hipsters for hipsters" in a "nondescript" minimalist room with an "open kitchen" and sometimes "loud rock 'n' roll music playing in the background"; P.S. a Logan Square location is set to open in summer 2011.

Jane's Ⓜ *American/Eclectic*
22 | 16 | 18 | $29

Bucktown | 1655 W. Cortland St. (Paulina St.) | 773-862-5263 | www.janesrestaurant.com

Situated "off the beaten path" in a revamped old house, this "cozy", "adorable" New American–Eclectic "neighborhood joint" is a "long-time Bucktown favorite" rated "reliable" for "consistent, creative and comforting" midpriced comestibles and "friendly service"; P.S. it offers weekend brunch and seasonal outdoor dining.

⊠ Japonais *Japanese*
24 | 26 | 20 | $59

River North | 600 W. Chicago Ave. (Larrabee St.) | 312-822-9600 | www.japonaischicago.com

"Lots of young, beautiful people" come to "eat and be seen" at this "swanky", "pricey" River North Japanese with "excellent sushi", a "variety" of "inventive" entrees and "lethal signature martinis"; "service is what you'd expect" (some say "aloof"), but most maintain it's "managed to stay trendy" while providing "consistent" fare "for quite some time", plus the "neo-Asian decor" is an "architectural dream" – especially the "sexy downstairs bar with a river view."

Jerry's *Sandwiches*
22 | 16 | 20 | $24

Wicker Park | 1938 W. Division St. (Damen Ave.) | 773-235-1006 | www.jerryssandwiches.com

A Wicker Park "winner" for "super", "interesting sandwiches" from a long "menu that goes for days" and includes a "selection of microbrews" and wines by the glass, this inexpensive entry also claims a "convenient location" with a fireplace and sidewalk seating plus a "pleasant staff"; though it "can get a bit loud and crowded on weekends", fans say "during the week it's an extremely relaxing experience."

Jilly's Cafe Ⓜ *American/French*
21 | 19 | 21 | $42

Evanston | 2614 Green Bay Rd. (Central St.) | 847-869-7636 | www.jillyscafe.com

Fans of the "nicely frilly" New American–New French "bistro cuisine" (and brunch with a prix fixe champagne option) at this "quaint little" spot in Evanston call it an "undiscovered gem" that "doesn't look like much from the street" but is "charming" and "homelike" inside; service adds to the "dependable" experience that's perhaps "a little pricey"; P.S. "only wine and beer" (and champagne) are served.

Jin Ju *Korean*

23 | 20 | 22 | $31

Andersonville | 5203 N. Clark St. (Foster Ave.) | 773-334-6377 | www.jinjuchicago.com

"It's rare to find a high-end Korean restaurant", and while this "fantastic part of the Andersonville scene" is "not particularly authentic", "it's a pleasure to visit" for its "mouthwatering", "modern take" on the "classics" and "fabulous flavors" of soju martinis that "go down too easily"; add in "casual service" and a weekend back-room lounge and you have a potential "date place."

☒ Joe's Seafood, Prime Steak & Stone Crab *Seafood/Steak*

26 | 22 | 25 | $64

River North | 60 E. Grand Ave. (Rush St.) | 312-379-5637 | www.joes.net

Surveyors "look forward to" meals at Lettuce Entertain You's "sophisticated", "supper club"-like River Norther – the No. 1 chophouse in this Survey – that emulates the "famous" "Miami original" by serving "extra-fresh seafood in traditional and contemporary dishes" (of course, "stone crabs are the showstopper", even if they're "frozen" when "out of season") but also "outstanding steaks" and "Key lime pie for dessert"; "spot-on service" is "well trained" to handle "families and businessmen alike", and "it's jumping every night" due to "large crowds", the "high density of tables" and the "busy bar" – all in all, "a real treat and worth every wildly expensive penny."

NEW Joey's Shrimp House *Seafood*

– | – | – | I

Humboldt Park | 1432 N. Western Ave. (bet. Hirsch & Le Moyne Sts.) | 773-772-1400

Chefs from Japonais go downscale at this casual Humboldt Park seafooder where the open kitchen whips up a budget-friendly, ocean-centric menu; it sports an island-shack vibe with a seaside mural, nautical ephemera and TVs broadcasting sporting events, and night owls can munch till 2 AM (12 AM in the winter) on weekends.

John's Place Ⓜ *American*

18 | 14 | 19 | $23

Lincoln Park | 1200 W. Webster Ave. (Racine Ave.) | 773-525-6670

Roscoe Village | 2132 W. Roscoe St. (Hamilton Ave.) | 773-244-6430 | www.johnsplace.com

Somehow "family-friendly but still vaguely hip", this Lincoln Park "staple" and its Roscoe Village sibling serve "tasty" Traditional American "comfort food" including a "delicious" weekend brunch at "value" prices; the atmosphere is "pleasant", especially "outdoors in the summer", just be aware that there are usually "lots of young children"; P.S. sometimes "lines aren't as long" on Roscoe Street.

Joy Yee's Noodle Shop *Asian*

20 | 12 | 15 | $18

Chinatown | 2139 S. China Pl. (Archer Ave.) | 312-328-0001

South Loop | 1335 S. Halsted St. (bet. Liberty & W. Maxwell Sts.) | 312-997-2128

Evanston | 521 Davis St. (bet. Chicago & Hanman Aves.) | 847-733-1900

(continued)

Joy Yee's Noodle Shop
Naperville | Iroquois Ctr. | 1163 E. Ogden Ave. (Iroquois Ave.) |
630-579-6800
Joy Yee Plus Shabu Shabu *Asian*
Chinatown | 2159 S. China Pl. (Archer Ave.) | 312-842-8928
www.joyyee.com
"Expansive", "inexpensive" Asian menus "encourage experimenta-
tion" at this local chain of "quick-fix" BYO "favorites" known for "giant
portions" of multicultural "noodle choices for everyone" and "excellent
bubble teas and smoothies"; curmudgeons call it a "case of quantity
over quality (but the prices are sure right)", plus the speed of service varies by location and the "cafeteria-style" settings "discourage
lingering"; P.S. Chinatown's Plus focuses on shabu-shabu and sushi.

Julius Meinl *Austrian*
| 21 | 20 | 18 | $17 |

Lakeview | 3601 N. Southport Ave. (Addison St.) | 773-868-1857
Lincoln Square | 4363 N. Lincoln Ave. (Montrose Ave.) |
773-868-1876
Julius Meinl Coffee Bar &
Patisserie *Austrian*
Lakeview | 1416 W. Irving Park Rd. (Southport Ave.) |
773-883-1864
www.meinl.com
Surveyors seeking a "tranquil", "civilized" "oasis" find it at these
Lakeview and Lincoln Square "continental" "*konditoreis*" noted for
their "fabulous pastries" and "perfectionist coffee" plus a "surprising
variety" of "coffeehouse" and "authentic Austrian fare" for breakfast, lunch and dinner; it's a little "pricey", and the "European atmosphere" includes "weak service" but also "wonderful live music that
is not overwhelming" on weekend nights; P.S. the coffee bar/patisserie
outpost is geared more for takeout with no sit-down service.

Jury's *Pub Food*
| 18 | 12 | 19 | $21 |

North Center/St. Ben's | 4337 N. Lincoln Ave. (Montrose Ave.) |
773-935-2255 | www.jurysrestaurant.com
The verdict is in on this "upscale" North Center "neighborhood bar"
where the "simple, excellent burger" causes sold surveyors to forget
they "serve something else" – namely American "standards" and
"solid steaks and seafood"; decor and service are "old-school" with a
"welcoming atmosphere" some liken to "going home for dinner (or
lunch) – except you agree to pay the bill"; P.S. there's "outdoor dining."

J. Wellington's *Burgers*
| - | - | - | I |

Wicker Park | 2045 W. North Ave. (bet. Damen & Hoyne Aves.) |
773-687-9142
A wallet-friendly Wicker Parker, this quick-serve offers a variety of
burger combos (or a build-your-own option), along with fries,
Traditional American comfort foods like chili and mac 'n' cheese,
and traditional and craft sodas (you can also BYO); the interior is
smart for the category, with warm, earthy colors, wood tables, a
leather banquette and soft lighting.

NEW Kai Sushi *Japanese* — | — | — | M

West Town | 1406 W. Grand Ave. (Noble St.) | 312-733-9083 |
www.kaisushichicago.com

This West Town sushi specialist serves a slew of signature rolls but
no cooked fare (only a few salads round out the menu); besides a
small sushi bar, its midsize, minimal setting features low lighting
and bare wood tables, with free WiFi and no-corkage BYO (there's a
purveyor right next door) as perks.

Kamehachi *Japanese* 21 | 16 | 18 | $38

Loop | 311 S. Wacker Dr. (bet. Jackson Blvd. & Van Buren St.) |
312-765-8700 🛇

River North | Westin River North | 320 N. Dearborn St. (Kinzie St.) |
312-744-1900

Streeterville | 240 E. Ontario St. (bet. Fairbanks Ct. & St. Clair St.) |
312-587-0600

Old Town | 1400 N. Wells St. (Schiller St.) | 312-664-3663 ◑

Northbrook | Village Green Shopping Ctr. | 1320 Shermer Rd.
(bet. Meadow & Waukegan Rds.) | 847-562-0064
www.kamehachi.com

"One of the original Japanese restaurants in the city" (the Old Town
location) is the founding member of this chainlet where "traditional
sushi" and "light fare" including "teriyaki and tempura dishes" are
"well priced" and "consistently delicious", and come with "good service" "regardless of location" (unlike the variable decor); even adventurous eaters who deem it "unimaginative" vet it as "solid."

NEW Kanela Breakfast Club *American* — | — | — | M

Lakeview | 3231 N. Clark St. (bet. Aldine & Belmont Aves.) |
773-248-1622 | www.kanelacafe.com

This Lakeview nook serves a Greek-inflected American breakfast
menu until 3 PM daily – expect the likes of unusual fritters, beyond-
basic Benedicts and sweet or savory French toast; located in the
space that once housed bruncher Orange, the cinnamon-scented digs
feature exposed-brick walls, banquettes and a tile-fronted juice bar.

Kansaku *Japanese* ▽ 22 | 18 | 18 | $42

Evanston | 1514 Sherman Ave. (Grove St.) | 847-864-4386 |
www.kansakusushi.com

"Top-quality fish" in "fresh, inventive and tasty" presentations
paired with a "list of premium sakes" have fin fans flagging this
dimly lit, slightly pricey Evanston Japanese as a "place to wind down
as well as to celebrate" (especially with saketinis) seven days a
week; P.S. it's now also "open for lunch [and dinner] on weekends."

Kan Zaman *Lebanese* — | — | — | I

River North | 617 N. Wells St. (Ontario St.) | 312-751-9600 |
www.kanzamanchicago.com

"If you like to eat while sitting on pillows", this budget-friendly River
North Lebanese BYO has got the goods (and table seating too) for
dining on "tasty" "Middle Eastern meals" at lunch or dinner; on
weekend nights, the "enjoyable experience is highlighted by
live belly dancing."

	FOOD	DECOR	SERVICE	COST

Karma *Asian*
23 | 27 | 23 | $46

Mundelein | Doubletree Libertyville-Mundelein | 510 E. Il. Rte. 83 (Rte. 45) | 847-970-6900 | www.karmachicago.com

"Surprised" surveyors swear "you'd never guess that this gorgeous" "oasis of Zen" is in Mundelein's Doubletree Hotel, what with its Asian "fine" dining and "awesome cocktails" amid "darkly miminalist", "romantic" surroundings; it's a little pricey but "has that edge you're looking for when it's a special occasion."

Karyn's Cooked *Vegan/Vegetarian*
20 | 16 | 20 | $28

River North | 738 N. Wells St. (Superior St.) | 312-587-1050

Karyn's Fresh Corner *Vegan/Vegetarian*
Lincoln Park | 1901 N. Halsted St. (Armitage Ave.) | 312-255-1590
www.karynraw.com

"Vegans and vegetarians" vouch for this "friendly" "midpriced" duo's "refined", "savory cuisine" "for the compassionate eater" accompanied by a "selection of healthy nonalcoholic drinks", all brought by a "helpful staff"; River North's "modern yet cozy" Cooked fits the bill "whenever you need to get your 'veg' on" (it also offers organic wine and beer), and though fans of Lincoln Park's fountain-adorned Fresh say "raw never tasted so good", the less adventurous "really want to like it but . . ."

Karyn's on Green Ⓜ *American/Vegan*
- | - | - | M

Greektown | 130 S. Green St. (bet. Adams & Monroe Sts.) | 312-226-6155 | www.karynsongreen.com

Raw-foodist Karyn Calabrese (Karyn's Cooked, Karyn's Fresh Corner) has given Greektown an organic-chic dining destination with an all-vegan New American menu – some raw items, some reinterpreted comfort food – plus a bar program of sustainable sips and spirits; the modern setting has an open, airy feeling with a lofty mezzanine, waterfall sculpture and communal table, and there's also a small take-out and retail area.

🄩 Katsu Japanese Ⓜ *Japanese*
27 | 16 | 23 | $52

Northwest Side | 2651 W. Peterson Ave. (bet. Talman & Washtenaw Aves.) | 773-784-3383

Fish fanatics "skip the tony and more-publicized sushi boutiques and head" to the Northwest Side's "hidden gem", the "best Japanese restaurant in Chicago" where "caring owners" offer the "freshest", "most delectable" seafood and "traditional" hot fare that's "often exquisite", accompanied by "attentive service" and an "excellent sake selection" in a "conversation-friendly", "elegant" atmosphere; cost is also "top of the line" but most maintain it's "worth the money."

Katy's Dumpling House *Chinese*
- | - | - | I

Naperville | 790 Royal St. George Dr. (bet. Ogden Ave. & Pacific Dr.) | 630-416-1188 Ⓜ

Westmont | 665 N. Cass Ave. (Ogden Ave.) | 630-323-9393 ⊅
www.katysdumpling.com

This low-cost Chinese duo draws fans for its chewy, hand-pulled noodles, savory dumplings and potstickers; while foodies are especially fond of the spartan, cash-only location in an alcove of a Westmont strip mall, the Naperville outpost is decidedly glossier.

☑ Keefer's ☒ *American* | 25 | 22 | 24 | $59

River North | 20 W. Kinzie St. (Dearborn St.) | 312-467-9525 | www.keefersrestaurant.com

A "favorite" for many chop lovers, this "high-end", "adult" River Norther offers "consistent", "excellent" Traditional American steakhouse cuisine (chef "John Hogan does wonders with meat") and seafood (including "some of the best Dover sole") paired with a winning "wine list" and "warm yet professional" service; add the "contemporary, comfortable decor" and "summer patio" and it's "worth the trip" and "expense-account" tabs.

Kiki's ☒ *French* | 25 | 22 | 24 | $48

Near North | 900 N. Franklin St. (Locust St.) | 312-335-5454 | www.kikisbistro.com

"When the mood for country bistro food hits", "satisfied" Francophiles swear by the "fine traditional" fare and "affordable French wine" at this "adult" Near North "stalwart" where the atmosphere "oozes cozy" and service is "excellent under the watchful eye of owner" Georges 'Kiki' Cuisance; though a few nigglers say it "needs some spunk", for most, this "perennial winner" is "reassuring" "like a favorite pair of jeans."

NEW Kinderhook Tap ● *American* | - | - | - | M

Oak Park | 800 S. Oak Park Ave. (Van Buren St.) | 708-434-0373 | www.kinderhooktap.com

This West Suburban gastropub's midpriced, organic-leaning menu is chock-full of farmer's market finds and accompanied by a small, rotating selection of cocktails and local microbrews; neighborhood types fill the cozy setting with pressed tin ceilings, exposed brick and ductwork, copper-topped tables and a warm wood bar.

NEW Kingfisher Seafood Restaurant *Seafood* | - | - | - | M

Andersonville | 5721 N. Clark St. (Edgewater Ave.) | 773-506-7014 | www.kingfisheronclark.com

Expect fresh, simply prepared underwater delights – along with a handful of meat entrees and several 'duets' (think surf 'n' turf) – at this Andersonville incarnation of the former Pier 5736; set in a century-old building, it features exposed brick, arched windows, well-spaced tables and a vintage photo mural of Belmont Harbor, and while there's no outdoor seating, the front wall opens for fresh-air dining in season.

Kin Sushi & Thai Cuisine *Japanese/Thai* | - | - | - | I

Noble Square | 1132 N. Milwaukee Ave. (bet. Haddon Ave. & Thomas St.) | 773-772-2722

Kin Japanese Cuisine *Japanese*

NEW **Noble Square** | 933 N. Ashland Ave. (Walton St.) | 773-227-7758 www.kinchicago.com

Sushi stars at both of these affordable Noble Square BYO siblings, but the original (on North Milwaukee) also throws Thai classics into the Japanese mix; that location boasts a hip, modern, black-and-blond-wood setting complete with a lounge area featuring plastic bubble seats and a clubby decibel level, while the North Ashland spin-off has a more intimate, calm atmosphre.

Kinzie Chophouse *Steak*   22 | 19 | 22 | $48

River North | 400 N. Wells St. (Kinzie St.) | 312-822-0191 |
www.kinziechophouse.com

Champions cheer a "quality" "Chicago steak without the steak-house arrogance" at this River North "unsung hero" with a "cozy" if "typical chophouse atmosphere", where you can "sit outside in the summer overlooking the [Merchandise] Mart and the el" tracks; while a few feeders can't find anything that "stands out about it", fans deem it "friendly" and "well priced."

Kith & Kin *American*   - | - | - | E

Lincoln Park | 1119 W. Webster Ave. (bet. Clifton & Seminary Aves.) |
773-472-7070 | www.kithandkinchicago.com

Cognoscenti concur this Lincoln Park New American "neighborhood find" "is going to go far" thanks to "outstanding" cuisine that's "reasonably priced" given the "high quality"; "attentive" "servers are quite knowledgeable", and the space has a clean, "casual" feel with a tin ceiling and a working fireplace in winter.

Kit Kat Lounge &   16 | 19 | 19 | $32
Supper Club ◐ *Eclectic*

Lakeview | 3700 N. Halsted St. (Waveland Ave.) | 773-525-1111 |
www.kitkatchicago.com

"Bachelorettes" advise "be prepared for killer drinks" ("it's the martini menu that sets this place apart"), "amazing desserts and men with better legs than you" at this "distinctive, glamorous" Lakeview supper club where you "come for" the "amazing drag show", not the mostly "disappointing" Eclectic dining (and leave the kiddies at home); P.S. it offers seasonal outdoor seating and a prix fixe special on Fridays.

Kitsch'n on Roscoe *Eclectic*   19 | 19 | 18 | $20

Roscoe Village | 2005 W. Roscoe St. (Damen Ave.) | 773-248-7372 |
www.kitschn.com

"Fun, tasty", affordable Eclectic eats like "green eggs and ham" "or chicken and waffles" come "with a '70s twist" at this "cool", "amusing" Roscoe Village "favorite" that's "laid-back in extremis"; while some call the service "excellent" and others say it's "less than ideal", it's hard not to "like any restaurant that has Tang on the menu"; P.S. dinner is served in summer only.

Klay Oven *Indian*   20 | 16 | 17 | $31

River North | 414 N. Orleans St. (Hubbard St.) | 312-527-3999
Oak Park | 734 Lake St. (bet. Euclid & Oak Park Aves.) |
708-386-3999
www.klayovenrestaurant.com

"A lovely mix" of "well-spiced", "classically prepared" Indian dishes with "complex flavors" has diners saluting these River

North and Oak Park offerings as "solid" citizens (including the service); though a few partakers peg it "a little pricey for not dazzling" dining, both locations have an "excellent, cheap and well-attended lunch buffet."

Knew ☒ *American/Eclectic*   - | - | - | E

Logan Square | 2556 W. Fullerton Ave. (Rockwell St.) | 773-772-7721 | www.knewrestaurant.com

In Logan Square, the latest "location for the husband-and-wife" team behind the defunct Think lures a "loyal following" for their hospitality and "innovative" New American and Eclectic menu with "promise"; though doubters dish that the "decor doesn't match" the "expensive prices", the "wow"-ed crowd assures "BYO keeps overall costs down."

Koda Bistro Ⓜ *French*   - | - | - | E

Far South Side | 10352 S. Western Ave. (bet. 103rd & 104th Sts.) | 773-445-5632 | www.kodabistro.com

Still a "neighborhood secret" in Beverly, this contemporary French bistro boasts an "inventive chef" who crafts a menu of "fabulous", "beautifully presented" seasonal fare that's coupled with an "excellent wine list"; the "warm, welcoming" setting with upscale decor and a "business casual dress code" further elevate an experience that's "worth the trip" to the Far South Side ("don't worry, you won't fall off if you cross Pershing").

Koi *Asian*   21 | 20 | 18 | $36

Evanston | 624 Davis St. (bet. Chicago & Orrington Aves.) | 847-866-6969 | www.koievanston.com

Evanston locals find "fancy", "fair-priced" Asian cuisine at this "light and airy", "contemporary Chinese and Japanese" (and Thai) spot with a "fine sushi bar", a "wonderful array of drinks" and an "always helpful" staff; still, despite "lots of options for fussy eaters", a few frown over some "bland renditions", saying they "should focus on one cuisine."

Kroll's *American*   ▽ 19 | 18 | 21 | $20

South Loop | 1736 S. Michigan Ave. (18th St.) | 312-235-1400 | www.krolls-chicago.com

Graded a "great neighborhood sports bar" "for a burger, beer and ballgame", this Wisconsin import qualifies as "an oasis" in its South Loop location, dishing out "decent food, sandwiches, pizza, wings, etc." in an "upscale bar/grill atmosphere"; there are "no drunk twentysomethings" in the "friendly, diverse crowd", which seals it as a "favorite" for folks who "love" it.

☒ Kuma's Corner ◗ *American*   26 | 15 | 17 | $20

Avondale | 2900 W. Belmont Ave. (Francisco Ave.) | 773-604-8769 | www.kumascorner.com

You'll find "about the best" "mind-blowing" burgers in Chicago (and a mac 'n' cheese that some call the real "star") at this Avondale "heavy metal bar – really!" where the staff is "as friendly as it is tattooed" and "body-pierced", and the "rock-star atmosphere" includes "way too loud" music and "crazy", "long lines"; luckily, the "tables turn quickly", and in summer, you can "sit outside" and escape the noise.

Kuni's *Japanese*

24 | 14 | 22 | $44

Evanston | 511-A Main St. (bet. Chicago & Hinman Aves.) | 847-328-2004 | www.kunisushi.com

"Traditional, unpretentious Japanese" lures loyalists to "Kunisan's" "old-fashioned" Evanston shop serving "beautifully cut", "classic" "sushi the way it should be" – "no trendy rolls" – as well as teriyakis, tonkatsu and sukiyaki "for over 20 years"; "reasonable prices" are appreciated, but lingerers warn "the cost can run up" if you stick with the raw fish and sake all night.

La Bocca della Verità *Italian*

22 | 13 | 19 | $31

Lincoln Square | 4618 N. Lincoln Ave. (bet. Lawrence & Wilson Aves.) | 773-784-6222 | www.laboccachicago.com

This Lincoln Square "friendly, neighborhood ristorante" "isn't well known" "but it should be" say fans of its "authentic Italian" cooking combining "old-world tradition" and "new-world" style; although a few are bothered by "slow" service, the comfortable atmosphere and sidewalk seating in summer make lingering pleasant.

La Cantina Chophouse ●🖼 *Italian*

∇ 21 | 22 | 22 | $34

Loop | Italian Vill. | 71 W. Monroe St. (bet. Clark & Dearborn Sts.) | 312-332-7005 | www.lacantina-chicago.com

A "typical" if "not inspiring" Northern Italian menu with a "flair for seafood" and steak, a massive wine list and a lower-level space with "twinkling lights" and "seasoned waiters" satisfy visitors to this Loop location in the vintage Italian Village complex; it's "definitely recommended for a large family" or "a great late-night" outing since the kitchen is open till 11:30 PM daily (later on weekends).

La Cantina Grill *Mexican*

- | - | - | I

South Loop | 1911 S. Michigan Ave. (bet. Cullerton & 18th Sts.) | 312-842-1911 | www.lacantinagrill.com

A welcome addition to the South Loop, this casual, cheap Mexican cantina proffers the usual south-of-the-border suspects along with a smattering of more serious entrees; the small, dimly lit terra-cotta room has black-and-white photos and a hodgepodge of artifacts, which help set a funky mood – as do the fruit-flavored margaritas.

La Casa de Isaac *Mexican*

20 | 11 | 18 | $26

Highland Park | 431 Temple Ave. (Waukegan Ave.) | 847-433-5550 | www.lacasadeisaac.com

NEW La Casa de Isaac & Moishe *Mexican*

Highland Park | 2014 First St. (bet. Green Bay Rd. & St. John's Ave.) | 847-433-7400 | www.isaacandmoisherestaurant.com

NEW Isaac & Moishe DFV *Mexican*

Highland Park | 311 Waukegan Ave. (Temple Ave.) | 847-433-0557

"What do two nice Jewish boys know about tacos?" ask loyalists of this "festive" Temple Avenue Mexican – "apparently enough to turn out good ones" as well as other classic items (chicken in red mole sauce, enchiladas) and breakfast selections; "it's pretty loud" and sticklers snap it's "not really authentic" (no pork or shellfish and it's "closed Friday nights" until "sundown on Saturday"), but the salsa gets "special kudos" and you can "sit outside" guzzling "great margaritas" in summer; P.S. two siblings opened post-Survey, including Isaac & Moishe DFV, a market with food to go.

La Ciudad *Mexican*

```
-|-|-| I
```

Uptown | 4515 N. Sheridan Rd. (bet. Sunnyside & Windsor Aves.) | 773-728-2887 | www.laciudad.com

Serving a mix of Mexican classics and street food, this Uptowner is sleeker than its low prices would suggest, the contemporary storefront setting decorated in the red, white and green of the Mexican flag and sporting moody black-and-white photographs; P.S. it's BYO, and the staff will mix you a margarita in a salt-rimmed glass if you bring the tequila and mixer.

La Cocina de Frida *Mexican*

```
∇ 20 | 18 | 20 | $31
```

Andersonville | 5403 N. Clark St. (Balmoral Ave.) | 773-271-1907

Frida's *Mexican*

Lakeview | 3755 N. Southport Ave. (Grace St.) | 773-935-2330
www.lacocinadefrida.com

"The decor really makes you think of Frida" Kahlo at this colorful "semi-upscale" Andersonville "neighborhood Mexican" and its Lakeview sister featuring affordable "traditional fare with occasional twists" (and the "chips and margaritas are exceptional"); P.S. both serve up "alfresco" patio dining.

La Crêperie 🅼 *Crêpes/French*

```
21 | 17 | 19 | $27
```

Lakeview | 2845 N. Clark St. (bet. Diversey Pkwy. & Surf St.) | 773-528-9050 | www.lacreperieusa.com

A "charming little gem of a restaurant" that "whisks" diners "back to France", this Lakeview "oasis" offers "inexpensive", "amazing" and "authentic" sweet and savory crêpes; the "cozy, candlelit tables" and "surprising outdoor back garden" are "romantic" enough for "anniversaries" and "laid-back" enough for a bite before or "after a movie at the Landmark."

La Fonda del Gusto 🅼 *Mexican*

```
-|-|-| I
```

Wicker Park | 1408 N. Milwaukee Ave. (bet. Evergreen & Wolcott Aves.) | 773-278-6100 | www.lafondadelgusto.com

"Delicious family recipes" become "affordable", "high-quality" fare at this casual, "attentive" Wicker Park Mexican, run by a husband-and-wife team; the red-brick storefront space features an open kitchen, patio and multiple dining rooms with booth seating and lacquered wood tables.

La Fonda Latino Grill 🅼 *Colombian*

```
-|-|-| M
```

Andersonville | 5350 N. Broadway (Balmoral Ave.) | 773-271-3935 | www.lafondalatinogrill.com

"Authentic", affordable Colombian fare in "good-size portions" accompanied by "fabulous margaritas" and served by "friendly, knowledgeable" staffers earn points for this Andersonville eatery; the bi-level space – with its share of Latin tchotchkes – "gets loud" when it's busy, however, so take advantage of sidewalk seating in summer.

☑ La Gondola *Italian*

| - | - | - | M |

NEW **Lakeview** | 1258 W. Belmont St. (Lakewood Ave.) | 773-935-9011
Lakeview | Wellington Plaza | 2914 N. Ashland Ave. (Wellington Ave.) | 773-248-4433
www.lagondolachicago.com

Lakeview favorite La Gondola spins off a second location in the former Joey's Brickhouse space, serving a similar Southern Italian menu of pizza thick and thin and big portions of hearty pasta classics and steaks (it's more entree-focused than the original); redecorated with advertising posters and Rat Pack memorabilia, the exposed-brick setting exudes a warm tavern feel, while the existing bar, open kitchen and outdoor dining are still in place; P.S. it's also open for lunch on weekends.

NEW La Lagartija Taqueria ☒ *Mexican*

| - | - | - | I |

West Loop | 132 S. Ashland Ave. (bet. Adams & Monroe Sts.) | 312-733-7772 | lalagartijataqueria.com

Laura Cid-Perea, tres leches queen and founder of Pilsen's former Bombon Bakery, is co-owner of this West Loop BYO taqueria where the budget-minded menu majors in tacos (including the requisite al pastor, breakfast and build-your-own options) and minors in everything else casual Mex – from burritos and quesadillas to desserts, smoothies and agua frescas; the citrus-colored, terra-cotta-tiled setting includes a *lagartija* (lizard) sculpture, and just down the street is a more casual sib, Bombon Café.

La Madia *Italian/Pizza*

| 23 | 20 | 21 | $31 |

River North | 59 W. Grand Ave. (bet. Clark & Dearborn Sts.) | 312-329-0400 | www.dinelamadia.com

Expect "gourmet", "thin-crust" pies from a wood-burning oven, supported by "strong salads and sandwiches" and "extensive wines by the glass", at this "reasonably priced" River North "find"; equally appropriate for a "business lunch" or a "cozy" date beside the "crackling fireplace", it errs only when it comes to what a few call "slow service."

Landmark ◑Ⓜ *American*

| 20 | 21 | 22 | $42 |

Lincoln Park | 1633 N. Halsted St. (North Ave.) | 312-587-1600 | www.landmarkgrill.net

"They pay attention to detail" at this Lincoln Park "hot spot" known for "comforting" New American noshes and "delicious seasonal cocktails" perfect for "pre-theater dining" or "late-night bar" hopping; the "huge" space still "manages to feel intimate" thanks to its "many rooms", but it gets "clubby after 10 PM", so "dine early if you want to hear your tablemates."

Lan's China Bistro ● *Chinese* | - | - | - | I |

Old Town | 1507 N. Sedgwick St. (bet. Blackhawk St. & North Ave.) | 312-255-9888 | www.lansoldtown.com

Behind grand red doors worthy of Chinatown, this Old Town Chinese "BYO gem" maintains a budget-friendly menu of MSG-free Mandarin, Sichuan and dim sum faves, as well as hot pots steamed at the dining bar; the setting is minimalist Asian.

☑ Lao Beijing *Chinese* | 24 | 10 | 16 | $24 |

Chinatown | Chinatown Mall | 2138 S. Archer Ave. (Cermak Rd.) | 312-881-0168

☑ Lao Shanghai *Chinese*

Chinatown | 2163 S. China Pl. (Princeton Ave.) | 312-808-0830

☑ Lao Sze Chuan *Chinese*

Chinatown | 2172 S. Archer Ave. (Princeton Ave.) | 312-326-5040 ●

Downers Grove | 1331 W. Ogden Ave. (Oakwood Ave.) | 630-663-0303

www.tonygourmetgroup.com

These regional Chinese chow houses serve "long menus" of "genuine", "standard and exotic" dishes in "minimal" "hole-in-the-wall" dining rooms that draw "lines out the door"; the servers "often don't speak English" so you "must be comfortable not knowing for sure what you're eating", but spice-heads believe it's always a good sign when their "mouth is burning two days later"; P.S. the Chinatown Sze Chuan serves beer and wine only.

𝗡𝗘𝗪 Lao You Ju ● *Chinese* | - | - | - | M |

Chinatown | Richmond Ctr. | 2002 S. Wentworth Ave. (bet. Archer Ave. & Cullerton St.) | 312-225-7818 | www.tonygourmetgroup.com

Multiregional, midpriced neo-Chinese small plates, plus pricier 'house signatures' (golden shark's fin, royal lobster), star at this posh member of the Lao Sze Chuan family set in clubby, red-splashed Chinatown digs with funky chandeliers, a central alabaster bar serving sake and exotic cocktails, and dramatic lighting; P.S. diners can opt for a chef's tasting menu with wine pairings.

La Petite Folie ☒ *French* | 24 | 21 | 21 | $49 |

Hyde Park | Hyde Park Shopping Ctr. | 1504 E. 55th St. (Lake Park Blvd.) | 773-493-1394 | www.lapetitefolie.com

"Straightforward, classic French cooking" and a "superb" all-French wine list meet in this "elegant", "civilized" Hyde Parker that locals call a "neighborhood gem"; while some take issue with the "sometimes slow" service, most say "it's so pleasant, one hardly cares."

La Sardine ☒ *French* | 24 | 20 | 23 | $45 |

West Loop | 111 N. Carpenter St. (bet. Randolph St. & Washington Blvd.) | 312-421-2800 | www.lasardine.com

If you like "excellent", "moderately priced", "traditional French bistro" fare served in an "intimate", "romantic" room by a "uniformly friendly staff" that "knows when to leave you alone", then this West Loop "gem" and sister to Le Bouchon "is the real goods"; in fact, there's "not a thing wrong with this place" unless you count the "crowds" of "friendly repeat customers" who make it "noisy" at times; P.S. the "prix fixe on Tuesdays" is the "best deal."

La Scarola *Italian*   24 | 14 | 21 | $35

River West | 721 W. Grand Ave. (bet. Halsted St. & Union Ave.) | 312-243-1740 | www.lascarola.com

"Entrees feed two" at this "old-school" River West "neighborhood" Italian with the "obligatory red-checkered tablecloths" and a staff that "treats you like family"; the setting is "dumpy", but judging from the "crowded atmosphere" (you may have to wait "even with reservations"), it's the "full-flavored", "fairly priced" dishes that everyone cares about.

Las Palmas *Mexican*   21 | 16 | 22 | $27

Bucktown | 1835 W. North Ave. (Honore St.) | 773-289-4991 | www.laspalmaschicago.com

Buffalo Grove | 86 W. Dundee Rd. (Old Buffalo Grove Rd.) | 847-520-8222 | www.laspalmasbuffalogrove.com

These upscale sibs of a more casual local chain serve "interesting", "fairly authentic" Mexican food along with "great cocktails" in a "bright and cheerful environment"; Bucktown has nightly live entertainment and an "outdoor patio" that "can't be beat on a summer day", while Buffalo Grove offers music on weekend nights.

Las Tablas *Colombian/Steak*   20 | 16 | 20 | $29

Lakeview | 2942 N. Lincoln Ave. (Wellington Ave.) | 773-871-2414

Northwest Side | 4920 W. Irving Park Rd. (bet. Lamon & Laporte Aves.) | 773-202-0999

www.lastablas.com

At once "exotic and familiar", these Colombian steakhouse sibs in Lakeview and the Northwest Side feature "fantastic, flavorful" steak and "perfectly seasoned grilled chicken served on a wood plank"; the "fun", "friendly" atmosphere includes live weekend entertainment (weekly at the Irving Park locale, periodically in Lakeview).

NEW La Taberna   - | - | - | I
Tapas on Halsted *Eclectic*

University Village | 1301 S. Halsted St. (W. Maxwell St.) | 312-243-9980 | www.latabernatapas.com

A medley of small plates ranging from Spanish to South American, along with paella, skewers and planked grill fare, can be paired with a flight of craft sangrias or a fruit punch customized with patrons' booze of choice at this University Villager; the vibrant, multicolored setting features tile mosaics, red chandeliers and a marble bar.

La Tasca *Spanish*   24 | 20 | 21 | $34

Arlington Heights | 25 W. Davis St. (Vail Ave.) | 847-398-2400 | www.latascatapas.com

"Right off the train line" in Arlington Heights, this "lively" veteran offers a seemingly "never-ending" choice of "delicious" tapas for "sharing" as well as "great paellas and fish dishes"; "reservations are a must" (on Fridays and Saturdays, they're accepted only for groups of six or more), but "you're never rushed out", plus the "tasty sangria" and periodic "live entertainment" are "worth the trip" alone.

Laurel Mediterranean Grill *Mediterranean* | - | - | - | M |

Naperville | Iroquois Shopping Ctr. | 1163 E. Ogden Ave. (bet. East & E. Iroquois Aves.) | 630-946-6656 | www.laurelgrill.com

Fare from Turkey, Greece and Lebanon mingle on the midpriced menu at this Naperville strip-mall Med, where the small plates and grilled fare are accompanied by a limited wine list and other beverage options like ouzo, Turkish coffee and Moroccan tea; the setting is open and airy, with Aegean blue-and-white walls, bare-wood cafe tables, a fireplace and lots of windows.

Lawry's The Prime Rib *American/Steak* | 24 | 22 | 23 | $53 |

River North | 100 E. Ontario St. (Rush St.) | 312-787-5000 | www.lawrysonline.com

"Slabs of tender prime rib with equally desirable sides" (and that "famous spinning salad") explain the enduring appeal of this Beverly Hills–based steakhouse chain (including the River North outpost), that's also known for its "unique table service" from "rolling carts"; it's a bit "touristy" and "pricey", but committed customers don't mind, calling it a serious "contender for a last meal."

LB Bistro & Patisserie *American/French* | - | - | - | M |

Streeterville | Sheraton Chicago Hotel & Towers | 301 E. North Water St. (Columbus Dr.) | 312-329-5900 | www.sheratonchicago.com

World Pastry Championship winner Laurent Branlard helms this handsome French-American bistro inside the Streeterville Sheraton, where midpriced breakfast and lunch fare – including build-your-own omelets, parfaits, salads, sandwiches, crêpes and sweets – is served in an upscale, modern deco setting with warm wood, a glass-mosaic floor, a water wall and, from some vantage points, a view of the Chicago River.

Le Bouchon ⊠ *French* | 24 | 19 | 21 | $46 |

Bucktown | 1958 N. Damen Ave. (Armitage Ave.) | 773-862-6600 | www.lebouchonofchicago.com

Bucktown bistro-goers are "brought back to Paris" with Jean Claude Poilevey's "wonderful French food at a reasonable price" "served up by focused servers" in a "cozy, fast-paced dining room"; it's "authentic" right down to the occasional "attitude" and "tiny" with a "huge following" (so "be prepared to wait even if you have a reservation because no one wants to leave"); P.S. "the prix fixe menu is a great bargain."

☒ Le Colonial *Vietnamese* | 24 | 25 | 22 | $50 |

Gold Coast | 937 N. Rush St. (bet. Oak & E. Walton Sts.) | 312-255-0088 | www.lecolonialchicago.com

"Terrific" Vietnamese cuisine "with a French hand" enchants enthusiasts of this "exotic-elegant", "pricey", "exquisite oasis" where an "attentive" staff navigates a "sexy" Gold Coast setting that's a "visual snapshot of pre-war Vietnam with ceiling fans and palms, white tablecloths and orchids"; "be prepared to be elbow-to-elbow with self-aware beautiful people" (it's "a little cramped for Chicago, ok for Saigon") or head for the bar area and "sit on the second story balcony overlooking" the "entertaining show" along Rush Street.

Lee Wing Wah *Chinese*

- | - | - | I

Chinatown | 2147 S. China Pl. (bet. Princeton Ave. & Wells St.) | 312-808-1628 | www.leewingwah-chicago-chinese.com

"Consistently fresh, delicious" fare and "fast, efficient service" make this "Chinatown favorite" Cantonese and seafood specialist a "stable bet"; decor that's "nothing to write home about" is also nothing to gripe about as you can "eat like a king but only need a couple of bucks to settle up."

L'Eiffel Bistrot & Crêperie *Crêpes/French*

21 | 22 | 22 | $37

South Barrington | Arboretum Mall | 100 W. Higgins Rd. (Rte. 59) | 847-428-4783 | www.leiffelbistrot.com

South Barrington's "charming", "pleasantly surprising mall" bistro with a bar delivers French fare (including "wonderful crêpes") and "wine for a very reasonable price"; the "warm, friendly" setting's "eye candy" includes Parisian-style "artistic details" and "lovely outdoor dining."

Lem's BBQ ●⊯ *BBQ*

∇ 25 | 8 | 16 | $22

Far South Side | 311 E. 75th St. (bet. Calumet & Prairie Aves.) | 773-994-2428 | www.lemsbarbq.com

"You can smell the smoke blocks away" at this budget-loving Far South Side "staple" where fans of the "outstanding" barbecue chow down on some of the "best ribs anywhere"; "zero decor" and no seating are part of the package, leaving some praising the "quick in-and-out" experience for "carryout"; P.S. open till 2 AM (4 AM weekends) and closed Tuesdays.

Leonardo's Ristorante Ⓜ *Italian*

- | - | - | M

Andersonville | 5657 N. Clark St. (Hollywood Ave.) | 773-561-5028

An Andersonville "neighborhood" "favorite", this "hidden gem" pleases patrons by serving "terrific", "sophisticated" Northern Italian fare "at a good price" and "with enough menu changes to keep repeat diners intrigued"; the "wine selection", "helpful service" and "friendly atmosphere" are additional reasons locals contend it's not "just another" rustic-looking trattoria.

NEW Leopold Ⓜ *Belgian*

- | - | - | M

Noble Square | 1450 W. Chicago Ave. (bet. Bishop St. & Greenview Ave.) | 312-348-1028 | www.leopoldchicago.com

Chef-driven Belgian pub food stars at this Noble Square watering hole where local, seasonal ingredients show up on a concise, moderately priced menu of hearty fare like steak tartare, moules frites and poutine with merguez sausage; the long, narrow space has an elegant, modern feel with soft lighting, subtle artwork and a reclaimed wood bar, and there's a front lounge area accented by stained-glass panels plus sidewalk seating in season.

Leo's Coney Island *Diner/Hot Dogs*

|‒|‒|‒| I |

Wrigleyville | 3455 N. Southport Ave. (Cornelia Ave.) | 773-281-5367 | www.leoschicago.com

Challenging the local dog dynasty, this Detroit import on a Wrigleyville corner impudently heaps grilled franks with no-bean chili, onions and mustard; the menu expands with other affordable fast-food items including burgers and wings, along with an extensive roundup of breakfast fare and American and Greek diner classics, all served in a casual setting with table seating and takeout, ketchup-colored accents and a Chicago skyline mural.

Le P'tit Paris *Continental/French*

| 20 | 19 | 21 | $50 |

Streeterville | 260 E. Chestnut St. (Dewitt Pl.) | 312-787-8260 | www.lepetitparis.net

"Hidden" "out of the way" in Streeterville, this "quaint", "wonderful little restaurant" issues "entirely authentic" French-Continental cuisine that patrons find "reasonably priced for the quality"; though detractors deem the decor "a bit outdated", Francophiles who "love" the "old-school" setting and "knowledgeable, friendly staff" prefer to keep this place their "secret."

⌶ Les Nomades ⌧Ⓜ *French*

| 29 | 27 | 28 | $113 |

Streeterville | 222 E. Ontario St. (bet. Fairbanks Ct. & St. Clair St.) | 312-649-9010 | www.lesnomades.net

"One of the last bastions of haute cuisine", the No. 1 for Food in Chicago is Streeterville's French "crème de la crème" of "very formal" "fine dining", where chef Chris Nugent's "sophisticated", "beautifully prepared and presented" fare "is en pointe" as is the "extremely attentive service" and "remarkable", "francocentric" wine selection; the "quietly elegant", "clubby townhouse" ("once a private dining club") is a "place out of time and space" with "white linens", an "upstairs fireplace" and "gorgeous flowers", and though it's prix fixe and "*très* pricey", it's "perfect for a special, romantic occasion."

⌶ Le Titi de Paris Ⓜ *French*

| 26 | 24 | 25 | $65 |

Arlington Heights | 1015 W. Dundee Rd. (Kennicott Ave.) | 847-506-0222 | www.letitideparis.com

Chef-owners Michael and Susan Maddox's "creative menu" of "superb" "upscale" French fare with global accents is "prepared with the utmost care and savoir faire" at this "elegant" eatery "hidden in" Arlington Heights; "friendly service" and a "romantic" setting evoking "Parisian sophistication" with chandeliers, fresh flowers and "even the china" are reasons it remains a "favorite" for "special occasions" "after all these years."

NEW Letizia's Fiore *Italian*

|‒|‒|‒| M |

Logan Square | 2456 N. California Ave. (Altgeld St.) | 773-342-4400 | www.superyummy.com

A hybrid coffee shop, bakery and lunch cafe in Logan Square, this family-run Italian features flatbread sandwiches, arancini, fresh pastries and rustic Roman pizzas from a wood-burning oven, all made without artificial ingredients and served in warm ochre surroundings with gleaming wood booths and walls adorned with terra-cotta flower pots; P.S. warm weather brings outdoor dining and a roof garden, and a wine bar is planned downstairs.

Le Vichyssois Ⓜ *French*

26 | 22 | 22 | $52

Lakemoor | 220 Rand Rd. (2 mi. west of Rte. 12) | 815-385-8221 | www.levichyssois.com

"It's a journey to another era" at Bernard Cretier's "unexpected wayside inn" in Lakemoor offering "classic country French cuisine" at "reasonable" tabs in an "elegant", "art museum" milieu accented with antiques; smitten surveyors say that "service can be flawless or a little off, but everyone is always kind", making it "well worth" "the hike to the boonies"; P.S. it's closed Mondays and Tuesdays.

⭐NEW Lillie's Q *BBQ/Southern*

- | - | - | I

Bucktown | 1856 W. North Ave. (Wolcott Ave.) | 773-772-5500 | www.lilliesq.com

Chef and third-generation competitive 'cuer Charlie McKenna (ex Avenues and Tru) is behind this beyond-the-basics Southern barbecue house in Bucktown, a sib to his family's Florida Panhandle original; expect slow-smoked meats with sides like sweet potato fries, mac 'n' cheese and fried pickles, all served in a rustic space with reclaimed wood, meat-hook light fixtures and a working copper still churning out moonshine to be imbibed in mason jars.

Little Bucharest Bistro ◐ *European*

- | - | - | M

Northwest Side | 3661 N. Elston Ave. (Addison St.) | 773-604-8500 | www.littlebucharestbistro.com

This Modern European redo of "the original" located in the Northwest Side offers affordable entrees (some with Romanian influences) and shared plates delivered with "friendly service"; the "charming room" attracts an "eclectic clientele", and the "pleasant experience" includes live entertainment Thursday through Sunday.

LM *French*

22 | 21 | 21 | $48

Lincoln Square | 4539 N. Lincoln Ave. (bet. Sunnyside & Wilson Aves.) | 773-942-7585 | www.lmrestaurant.com

⭐NEW LM Café *French/Sandwiches*

West Loop | Ogilvie Transportation Ctr. | 131 N. Clinton St. (bet. Madison St. & Washington Blvd.) | 312-575-0306 | www.frenchmarketchicago.com

Fans call this Lincoln Square spot "special-occasion" dining "at an everyday price" with its "complex, innovative and well-prepared" "contemporary French" fare, "polished service" and "extremely tasteful modern design" – but lack of "stuffiness"; additionally, the "cocktails are tasty and strong", and the wine list offers "some good picks"; P.S. the train station newcomer specializes in sandwiches.

Lobby, The *European/Seafood*

28 | 28 | 28 | $70

River North | Peninsula Hotel | 108 E. Superior St., 5th fl. (bet. Michigan Ave. & Rush St.) | 312-573-6760 | www.peninsula.com

For a "wonderfully civilized" "splurge", raters recommend this River North Euro seafood specialist in an "amazing" Peninsula Hotel space that's "well lit" with 20-ft. floor-to-ceiling windows; "genteel" service and "discreet celebrity-watching" are in the mix, and while early eaters say "breakfasts are the thing to come for" and the "Sunday brunch" "will please everyone", celebrants suggest "for a special occasion, it's the best tea in town."

Lockwood *American*

 19 | 25 | 19 | $47

Loop | Palmer House Hilton | 17 E. Monroe St. (bet. State St. & Wabash Ave.) | 312-917-3404 | www.lockwoodrestaurant.com

Following the "trend of putting a great restaurant in a hotel lobby", this "lovely" Loop "fine-dining" destination in the historic Palmer House Hilton features an "interesting" New American menu, "delicious" "breakfast buffets" and an "outstanding wine selection"; if service can be "disappointing" and some find it "overpriced", the decor is "stunning" and it's "a relaxing place to dine before theater or symphony"; P.S. a more casual meal can be had at the hotel's Potter's Lounge.

Lokal Ⓜ *European*

- | - | - | M

Bucktown | 1904 W. North Ave. (Wolcott St.) | 773-904-8113 | www.lokalchicago.com

At this edgy Bucktown eatery, "Eastern European–inspired" "contemporary creative comfort food" comes at "value" prices with a limited but affordable wine list and a handful of house cocktails; the space's concrete floor, mineral color scheme and massive mesh light fixtures create a cool urban vibe, and there's an intimate lounge area; P.S. the "brunch deal" includes "bottomless mimosas and Bloody Marys."

Longman & Eagle ◑ *American*

- | - | - | M

Logan Square | 2657 N. Kedzie Ave. (Schubert Ave.) | 773-276-7110 | www.longmanandeagle.com

This Logan Square lair with inn aspirations (it added six rooms upstairs) serves a midpriced New American menu loaded with artisanal ingredients, accompanied by specialty cocktails, microbrews and lots of brown booze; the cozy tavern space features distressed brick and reclaimed wood, with a semi-open kitchen, drafting-style barstools, mismatched chairs, a Wurlitzer jukebox and patio seating.

Los Moles Restaurant *Mexican*

 - | - | - | M

Lakeview | 3140 N. Lincoln Ave. (bet. Barry & Belmont Aves.) | 773-935-9620 | www.losmoles.net

Chef Geno "Bahena still works his magic" at this midpriced Lakeview cantina where the "delicious" Mexican food and drink leaves patrons professing "you had me at mole"; there's a "pleasant, relaxed" vibe and optional "tasting menu" that's an "exceptional value"; P.S. "don't miss the lady making fresh tortillas."

☒ Lou Malnati's Pizzeria *Pizza*

24 | 14 | 19 | $21

River North | 439 N. Wells St. (Hubbard St.) | 312-828-9800
Lincoln Park | 958 W. Wrightwood Ave. (Lincoln Ave.) | 773-832-4030
Far South Side | 3859 W. Ogden Ave. (Cermak Rd.) | 773-762-0800
Evanston | 1850 Sherman Ave. (University Pl.) | 847-328-5400

(continued)

Lou Malnati's Pizzeria

Lincolnwood | 6649 N. Lincoln Ave. (bet. Devon & Pratt Aves.) | 847-673-0800
Buffalo Grove | 85 S. Buffalo Grove Rd. (Lake Cook Rd.) | 847-215-7100
Elk Grove Village | 1050 E. Higgins Rd. (bet. Arlington Heights & Busse Rds.) | 847-439-2000
Schaumburg | 1 S. Roselle Rd. (Schaumburg Rd.) | 847-985-1525
Naperville | 131 W. Jefferson Ave. (bet. Main & Webster Sts.) | 630-717-0700
Naperville | 2879 W. 95th St. (Rte. 59) | 630-904-4222
www.loumalnatis.com
Additional locations throughout the Chicago area

Loyalists swear by these "deep-dish joints" where the "authentic", "home-grown" Chicago-style pizzas are built with "the right amount of everything" including a "flaky", "buttery crust" and "quality ingredients"; just know that service and surroundings vary by location, the latter from "classic" to "sports bar" to "minimal", and the pies are "cooked to order" so you may have to "wait"; P.S. for "yearners" who "live far away", "life will never be the same" since most surveyors say the "in-restaurant" version outshines the "frozen", "shipped" option.

Lou Mitchell's *Diner*   23 | 14 | 21 | $17

Loop | 565 W. Jackson Blvd. (Jefferson St.) | 312-939-3111 ⊟
O'Hare Area | O'Hare Int'l Airport | Terminal 5 (I-190) | 773-601-8989 ◐
www.loumitchellsrestaurant.com

The Loop's "breakfast legend" lives on serving "straight American" "diner-style" morning fare through lunch including "fluffy" "omelets steaming in their own skillets and perfectly done pancakes"; the "old-fashioned" "warmth and character" includes "experienced" staffers who "give out" "Milk Duds and doughnut holes" when there's a "line out the door" to this "cholesterol capital" ("no dieters allowed"); P.S. "get there early and bring cash" (the airport quick-serve takes credit cards).

⊠ Lovells of Lake Forest *American*   23 | 25 | 22 | $54

Lake Forest | 915 S. Waukegan Rd. (Everett Rd.) | 847-234-8013 | www.lovellsoflakeforest.com

There's "no hurrying" at this "classy place for a North Suburban business lunch or romantic date" in Lake Forest that does "delicious, creative" New American fare in a "quiet" setting filled with "very interesting" "memorabilia" from Apollo 13 astronaut Jim Lovell, the owner's father; the staff is "helpful" and surveyors sum it up as "rather expensive for routine dining but great for special occasions"; P.S. the "Captain's Quarters" downstairs is more "informal with fun bands on the weekends."

Loving Hut *Asian/Vegan*   - | - | - | I

Edgewater | 5812 N. Broadway (bet. Hollywood & Thorndale Aves.) | 773-275-8797 | www.lovinghut.us/chicago

Edgewater's former Alice & Friends continues under the same team as this quirky, green-minded chain link with a devoted following for

	FOOD	DECOR	SERVICE	COST

its inexpensive Asian-vegan vittles for lunch and dinner; the spartan remodeled setting features expanded seating and theme photography; P.S. there's no alcohol and no BYO.

☒ L2O *Seafood* — | 28 | 27 | $142

Lincoln Park | Belden-Stratford Hotel | 2300 N. Lincoln Park W. (Belden Ave.) | 773-868-0002 | www.l2orestaurant.com

Former chef de cuisine Francis Brennan has taken over for Laurent Gras (the 'L' of the name, who left post-Survey) at this upscale Lincoln Park prix fixe seafooder from the Lettuce Entertain You group; while the jury is still out on the new kitchen regime, when you factor in dramatic presentations, "scrupulous" service and "eye-popping" decor that's "smart and modern without formality" (top rated in Chicago), it can amount to an "escape from everyday life", especially if you "have the wine pairings" and "don't look at the tab"; P.S. it's dinner only and "jackets are preferred" for gents.

Lucky Monk Burger, Pizza & Beer Co. *Pizza/Pub Food* — | - | - | I

South Barrington | 105 Hollywood Blvd. (Studio Dr.) | 847-898-0500 | www.theluckymonk.com

'Hand-stretched' NYC–style pizza, prime beef burgers and house-made beers are the tasty trifecta at this chic, sprawling Northwest Suburban microbrewery whose name is a nod to the monastic Belgian brewing tradition (order brews in bombers, growlers or kegs to-go); the upscale-casual, warmly lit environs include an imposing installation of stone and beer barrels, cushy leather sofas and tastefully scattered TVs, and there's a waterfront terrace with a fire pit.

☒ Lula Cafe *Eclectic* 26 | 19 | 21 | $31

Logan Square | 2537 N. Kedzie Blvd. (bet. Fullerton Ave. & Logan Blvd.) | 773-489-9554 | www.lulacafe.com

Logan Square's "semi-secret" "neighborhood gem" confers "creative, market-driven" Eclectic dishes "with fresh, local organic ingredients" for breakfast, lunch and dinner in an "unpretentious", "arty environment" with a "quirky staff" that "adds to the milieu"; there are no reservations, so you may encounter a "long wait" – though a coming expansion may alleviate the crush.

LuLu's Dim Sum & Then Sum *Asian* 21 | 15 | 19 | $23

Evanston | 804 Davis St. (Sherman Ave.) | 847-869-4343 | www.lulusdimsum.com

"Delicious", "reasonably priced" "dim sum–style dishes" and an "extensive menu" of "well-prepared Asian" specialties including various "all-you-can-eat" specials keep this "fast-food-looking", "longtime Evanston favorite" with "knowledgeable service" "hopping"; P.S. if purists pan it as "inauthentic", the "kids" will find it "exotic."

Lupita's Ⓜ *Mexican* 21 | 16 | 22 | $25

Evanston | 700 Main St. (Custer Ave.) | 847-328-2255 | www.lupitasmexicanrestaurant.com

"Well-prepared", low-priced Mexican meals are "inventive" or "standard" depending on who's dining at this Evanston "local" that flies "under the radar"; but "prompt", "helpful service" and weekend "nights with music" add to "a pleasant experience."

NEW Lure Izakaya ● *Japanese*

- | - | - | M

Chinatown | 2017 S. Wells St. (26th St.) | 312-225-8989 | www.lurechicago.com

From the owner of the now-shuttered Mulan (and located directly downstairs from its former Chinatown Square digs), this hipster haunt lures diners with midpriced Japanese izakaya eats – think seafood-centric small plates from fried squid head to lobster spaghetti, along with noshes like lotus root chips and avocado tempura; the artfully spartan setting features an open kitchen, space-age light fixtures and a concrete bar pouring signature cocktails, and the mood is enhanced by dress-up theme nights and live music.

LuxBar ● *American*

20 | 20 | 21 | $32

Gold Coast | 18 E. Bellevue Pl. (Rush St.) | 312-642-3400 | www.luxbar.com

A "diversified" Traditional American menu that's a "step up" from the "usual bar food" (and a "value for the area") meets a "hipster look" in a "dark atmosphere" with a "dynamic bar scene" of "drinks and eye candy", luring loungers to this often "noisy" Gold Coast "neighborhood spot"; with "efficient service", it also works for a "shopping break", "catching TV sports" or "people-watching", especially in the "outdoor dining area" or at a seat "overlooking Michigan Avenue"; P.S. the "fireplace" adds appeal "in the winter."

L. Woods Tap & Pine Lodge *American*

20 | 18 | 20 | $31

Lincolnwood | 7110 N. Lincoln Ave. (Kostner Ave.) | 847-677-3350 | www.lwoodsrestaurant.com

From Lettuce Entertain You, this "family-friendly" Lincolnwood "take" on a "Wisconsin roadhouse" is "dependable" for a midpriced American "comfort-food" menu "with something for everyone" served in "casual" confines with "comfortable booths" and "service with a smile"; what some call "uninspired" others peg as "unassuming."

NEW Mac & Min's *Southern*

- | - | - | I

West Loop | 1045 W. Madison St. (bet. Aberdeen & Carpenter Sts.) | 312-563-1008 | www.macandmins.com

The owners of Jerry's have Southernized their West Loop location, revamping it as a BYO counter-service New Orleans spot – think 20-some choices of po' boys (available in small, medium and large), along with muffalettas, salads and assorted sides; the bayou-casual setting is decorated with mounted fish and nautical kitsch, Mardi Gras beads and music posters – including Dr. John, the honorary 'Mac' in the name – and there's also free WiFi and outdoor seating.

Macello *Italian*

- | - | - | M

West Loop | 1235 W. Lake St. (bet. Elizabeth St. & Racine Ave.) | 312-850-9870 | www.macellochicago.com

Fans who admired the "meat-cooler" chic look and "broad, well-priced menu" at this Market District Italian are no doubt glad that it's back in business after having closed for a year after a fire; set in a former

| | FOOD | DECOR | SERVICE | COST |

butchery, it still has "great glass globes hanging from the ceiling" and is serving "tasty pizzas" and other "neighborhood"-friendly fare.

Macku Sushi *Japanese* `- | - | - | M`

Lincoln Park | 2239 N. Clybourn Ave. (bet. Greenview & Webster Aves.) | 773-880-8012 | www.mackusushi.com

Chefs from the defunct Kaze are back at this Lincoln Parker, serving a similar midpriced menu of creative sushi and contemporary Japanese cuisine along with full bar offerings; the spiffed-up storefront setting offers a wall-length banquette and a sushi bar.

☒ Maggiano's Little Italy *Italian* `20 | 19 | 21 | $32`

River North | 516 N. Clark St. (bet. Grand Ave. & Illinois St.) | 312-644-7700
Skokie | Westfield Shoppingtown | 4999 Old Orchard Ctr. (Skokie Blvd.) | 847-933-9555
Schaumburg | 1901 E. Woodfield Rd. (Rte. 53) | 847-240-5600
Naperville | 1847 Freedom Dr. (E. Diehl Rd.) | 630-536-2270
Oak Brook | Oakbrook Center Mall | 240 Oakbrook Ctr. (Rte. 83) | 630-368-0300
www.maggianos.com

"Giant", "family-style" feeds of "Americanized" "comfort food" are the attraction at this ever-expanding, Chicago-bred "franchise" of "Italian-themed" eateries where "kid-friendly" quarters with red-checkered tablecloths are home to generally "timely" service; naysayers nag they're too "noisy" and "generic", but *amici* insist they're "predictably good" and there are "always leftovers", concluding you "can't beat the value, especially for larger groups and families."

Magnolia Cafe Ⓜ *American* `22 | 17 | 22 | $38`

Uptown | 1224 W. Wilson Ave. (Magnolia Ave.) | 773-728-8785 | www.magnoliacafeuptown.com

A "small, refined menu" of "wonderful" New American cuisine that's "fresh and attractively" plated with "seasonal selections" calls to fans of this "conversation-friendly", midpriced Uptown "hidden gem" where they "don't try to do too much, but what they do, they do well"; though the brick-walled, candlelit room is "small", diners "don't feel hemmed in", with the service adding to their "delight" as does a bar that's a "great place to meet."

Maijean Ⓜ *French* `▽ 28 | 24 | 26 | $47`

Clarendon Hills | 30 S. Prospect Ave. (Park Ave.) | 630-794-8900 | www.maijean.com

"You may be transported to Paris" – or "certainly out of the 'burbs" – at this "lovely" Clarendon Hills bistro that's a "consistent" conveyor of "excellent" "French-inspired cuisine" and "wines by the glass" plus an "unusual selection of cheeses", all at "good prices"; "top-flight service", an "art deco" vibe and "outdoor tables" complete the scene.

Main Street Smokehouse ☒ *BBQ* `- | - | - | I`

Libertyville | 536 N. Milwaukee Ave. (School St.) | 847-247-4330 | www.mainstreetsmokehouse.com

Regional American barbecue from a smoker – babybacks, brisket, pulled pork and chicken, all with a choice of sauces – lures the 'cue crowd to this casual, dine-in and take-out Libertyville BYO lair; other options on the budget-friendly menu include sandwiches and traditional sides like cornbread and baked beans.

Maiz Ⓜ *Mexican* ▽ 23 | 15 | 21 | $25

Humboldt Park | 1041 N. California Ave. (Cortez St.) | 773-276-3149 | www.maizchicago.com

Humboldt Parkers looking for a "change from your average taqueria" head for this cantina specializing in "inexpensive, homey" Mexican fare with a focus on "fascinating" corn-based "little dishes, any of which you are likely to enjoy" in the space decked out in pastel colors and terra-cotta; P.S. "be sure to get the [signature] guacamole."

Makisu Sushi Lounge & Grill *Japanese* - | - | - | M

NEW **West Town** | 1725 W. Division St. (Hermitage Ave.) | 773-697-9535

Skokie | Village Crossing Shopping Ctr. | 7150 Carpenter Rd. (Touhy Ave.) | 847-677-9030

www.makisu-sushi.com

Aha Sushi *Japanese*

NEW **Gurnee** | 5101 Washington St. (Milwaukee Ave.) | 847-263-2222 | www.ahabistro.com

A "beautiful" Asian milieu awash with jazzy music belies the Skokie strip-mall setting of this "amazing sushi oasis" where "super-fresh" modern maki, small plates and grilled fare (including steaks) round out the creative midpriced Japanese menu bolstered by "bento box lunch specials", sake and specialty martinis; seating includes a swanky lounge and a sushi bar in a setting featuring dark wood, giant bamboo and panorama windows; P.S. two other outposts opened post-Survey.

Mana Food Bar *Eclectic/Vegetarian* 27 | 21 | 22 | $28

Wicker Park | 1742 W. Division St. (bet. Paulina & Wood Sts.) | 773-342-1742 | www.manafoodbar.com

"Fantastic" "feats of creativity with vegetables" attract a "loving" following to this "cute little" Wicker Park Eclectic-vegetarian small plates specialist with a "no-fake-meat policy" and "cocktail options" to boot; it's "very reasonable for the quality" and in season you can "sit outside and watch the world go by on Division Street" – now if they'd just "accept reservations" or "expand."

Mandarin Kitchen *Chinese* - | - | - | M

Chinatown | 2143 S. Archer Ave. (bet. Princeton & Wentworth Aves.) | 312-328-0228

Those hankering for "hot pots" "highly recommend" this Chinatown midpriced "alternative" for what they call some of "the best" "savory soups" in Chicago, along with noodle "dishes that hold their own" against the competition; P.S. beer is available, but no reservations.

Manghal *Kosher/Mediterranean* - | - | - | M

Evanston | 1805 Howard St. (bet. California & Washtenawa Aves.) | 847-859-2681 | www.manghalgrill.com

Evanston locals keep it kosher at this midpriced Med featuring rotisseried fare on massive skewers and other fresh eats including falafel, shawarma and salads, all served in a simple setting with polished wood tables and chairs, a ceramic tile floor and a fire pit for baking flatbreads; P.S. in keeping with tradition, it's closed Friday and Saturday, and if you opt to BYO, make sure it's kosher.

Manny's Cafeteria & Delicatessen *Deli*   23 | 7 | 14 | $18

South Loop | 1141 S. Jefferson St. (bet. Grenshaw St. & Roosevelt Rd.) | 312-939-2855 图
Southwest Side | Midway Int'l Airport | 5700 S. Cicero Ave. (55th St.) | 773-948-6300
www.mannysdeli.com

For "attitude" with a side of "cardiac arrest", this "no-frills", affordable South Loop deli "icon" delivers "patter on the cafeteria line" to rival the "big-as-your-head sandwiches" and "incredible variety" of "choices from the steam table"; "everybody is right out of central casting", from the "loudmouthed", "old-style Chicago countermen" to the "sociological panorama" of patrons; as for ambiance, acolytes ask "you want decor – the corned beef isn't enough?"; P.S. insiders say the separately owned Midway outpost is a "mere shadow of the main restaurant."

☑ Margie's Candies *American*   22 | 13 | 16 | $11

Bucktown | 1960 N. Western Ave. (Armitage Ave.) | 773-384-1035 ◗
Ravenswood | 1813 W. Montrose Ave. (Ravenswood Ave.) | 773-348-0400
www.margiescandies.nv.switchboard.com

"Go for" the "outrageously colored ice creams" and "big creamy sundaes" "served in plastic clamshells" with both "hot fudge sauce" and "nostalgia on the side" say surveyors who tend to "take a pass on the rest" of the Traditional American fare at these affordable "classic old-time" "ice cream and candy" "emporiums"; the 1921 Bucktown "original" has all the "kitschy" decor but you "can often get into" the "more modern" Ravenswood repeat without the long "wait."

Marigold ☑ *Indian*   23 | 19 | 22 | $38

Uptown | 4832 N. Broadway (bet. Ainslie St. & Lawrence Ave.) | 773-293-4653 | www.marigoldrestaurant.com

"Truly innovative", "upscale" Indian "fusion cooking" with "nuanced flavors" plus "great cocktails" draw devotees to this "hip", "fairly affordable" Uptowner with "friendly, understated" service; the sleek, warm-colored setting is "elegant" yet "comfortable" and suitable for a romantic meal as "you can even hear to talk."

Market *American*   18 | 19 | 12 | $28

West Loop | 1113 W. Randolph St. (bet. Aberdeen & May Sts.) | 312-929-4787 | www.marketbarchicago.com

Cheerleaders champion this West Looper's "creative menu" of moderately priced Traditional American fare that's "surprisingly" "tasty" for an "upscale" "sports bar" and served with an "ample cocktail list" in a "hip" "open room with multiple levels" featuring "lots of TVs"; "outdoor spaces" including a "beer garden" and recently redesigned "rooftop lounge" win favor, though not "slow", "inattentive" service that's just "not up to speed."

	FOOD	DECOR	SERVICE	COST

Markethouse *American*
▽ 21 | 15 | 18 | $41

Streeterville | Doubletree Magnificent Mile | 611 N. Fairbanks Ct. (bet. Ohio & Ontario Sts.) | 312-224-2200 | www.markethousechicago.com

Regulars are rooting for this "hidden" Streeterville "gem" in the Doubletree where the "carefully prepared" New American menu is built on a "theme of market-fresh, seasonal" and organic ingredients and also features a "wonderful cheese selection"; "service is attentive" and "attention to detail" is evident throughout – though some are less thrilled by an atmosphere that understandably "feels like a hotel"; N.B. they serve an all-you-can-eat breakfast buffet daily.

NEW Mastro's Steakhouse ◐ *Steak*
– | – | – | E

River North | 520 N. Dearborn St. (Grand Ave.) | 312-521-5100 | www.mastrosrestaurants.com

This glitzy, Arizona-bred chain has moved into the River North meat market, offering pricey prime steaks and chops backed by create-your-own seafood towers, a massive selection of classic sides and a 500-bottle wine list; the luxe, bi-level environs feature chandeliers, white linens and creamy leather chairs, plus a piano bar open till 1 AM nightly.

NEW Maude's Liquor Bar ◐☒Ⓜ *French*
– | – | – | M

West Loop | 840 W. Randolph St. (bet. Green & Peoria Sts.) | 312-243-9712 | www.maudesliquorbar.com

At this West Loop French boîte from the Gilt Bar gang (headed by Brendan Sodikoff), an open kitchen issues housemade charcuterie, raw-bar fare and bistro classics, accompanied by wines, draft brews and craft cocktails; the cozy setting has a been-here-for-eons feel with low lighting, distressed surfaces (brick, subway tiles, wood tables), antique furniture and tunes from an old record player, plus there's a seductive candlelit lounge upstairs.

Maya Del Sol *Nuevo Latino*
23 | 22 | 24 | $33

Oak Park | 144 S. Oak Park Ave. (bet. Pleasant St. & South Blvd.) | 708-358-9800 | www.mayadelsol.com

"Appealing to all ages", this Oak Park "high-end" Nuevo Latino offers a "broad range of menu items from modest snacks to a full meal" (including Sunday brunch) at "reasonable prices"; there's "an excellent drink menu" with a "crazy selection of 'ritas and specialty tequilas", and the "friendly atmosphere" features an "outdoor garden you won't want to leave."

Maza *Mideastern*
21 | 15 | 21 | $32

Lincoln Park | 2415 N. Ashland Ave. (Fullerton Ave.) | 773-929-9600

"Authentic", "innovative" Lebanese small plates made with "uncommon finesse" come with a "welcoming" vibe and prices fans consider a "bargain" at this Lincoln Park Middle Eastern that's a "solid neighborhood" "standby"; "helpful service" adds to the attraction; P.S. it moved to Ashland Avenue post-Survey, with plans to reopen its former Lincoln Avenue site in the future.

	FOOD	DECOR	SERVICE	COST

M Burger *Burgers*

| - | - | - | I |

NEW **River North** | 5 W. Ontario St. (State St.) | 312-428-3548
Streeterville | 161 E. Huron St. (bet. Michigan Ave. & St. Clair St.) |
312-254-8500 | www.mburgerchicago.com

The Lettuce Entertain You team is behind this tiny Streeterville counter-serve offering inexpensive, made-fresh burgers, skin-on fries, shakes and a few sandwiches; the über-simple, white-tiled space features just a handful of seats, a few of them outdoors, and a window in the wall provides a view of LEYE's Tru next door; P.S. there's now a River North location too.

NEW MC Bistro ⓜ *French/Vietnamese*

| - | - | - | I |

Wicker Park | 1401 N. Ashland Ave. (Blackhawk St.) | 773-489-5600 |
www.mcrestaurantandlounge.com

Julie Mai (of the former Julie Mai's Le Bistro) is behind this intimate, wallet-friendly Wicker Park entry serving French-influenced Vietnamese bites, plus a burger and basic sandwich offerings for the less adventurous (not to mention a dozen bubble-smoothie options); the brightly decorated corner space boasts walls of windows, with artwork and food-market photography adding cultural accents.

McCormick & Schmick's *Seafood*

| 21 | 20 | 21 | $48 |

Loop | 1 E. Wacker Dr. (bet. State St. & Wabash Ave.) | 312-923-7226
Gold Coast | 41 E. Chestnut St. (Rush St.) | 312-397-9500
Rosemont | 5320 N. River Rd. (bet. Foster Ave. & Technology Blvd.) |
847-233-3776
Skokie | Westfield Shoppingtown | 4999 Old Orchard Ctr. (Skokie Blvd.) |
847-763-9811
Schaumburg | 1140 E. Higgins Rd. (bet. Del Lago Dr. & National Pkwy.) |
847-517-1616
Oak Brook | 3001 Butterfield Rd. (Meyers Rd.) | 630-571-3700
www.mccormickandschmicks.com

An "enjoyable" choice for "business and pleasure", this "upscale" seafood chain offers a "daily changing" menu of "freshly caught" fare (plus pastas, steaks and more) in an "upbeat" atmosphere; though it feels too "stamped-out-of-a-mold" for some, its "professional" service is a plus and the "happy-hour bar menu" wins over the after-work crowd.

NEW Meatyballs

| - | - | - | I |

Mobile �" ⓜ *American/Eclectic*
Location varies | 312-315-6127 | www.meatyballsmobile.com

Enterprising chef Phillip Foss (recently of Lockwood) has taken to the streets five to seven days a week in a truck serving Eclectic sandwiches composed of meat, poultry, seafood or veggie 'balls' on baguettes; look for it in the Loop during lunch and varying routes at dinner that can be tracked on Twitter or Facebook.

Medici on 57th *American*

| 17 | 13 | 16 | $19 |

Hyde Park | 1327 E. 57th St. (bet. Kenwood & Kimbark Aves.) |
773-667-7394 | www.medici57.com

Hyde Park's "funky, retro" BYO "local hangout" offers "something for every taste" on its affordable American menu including "great burgers", "breakfasts" and "thin-crust" and "pan pizzas" – plus a "bakery next door"; "nostalgia" reigns in the "scribbles on the walls and tables (including Malia Obama's)", helping make it a "University of Chicago" "fixture", though antis dub it "average" fare for a "captive clientele."

Meiji 🅱 *Japanese*
25 | 22 | 23 | $52

West Loop | 623 W. Randolph St. (bet. Desplaines & Jefferson Sts.) | 312-887-9999 | www.meijirestaurant.com

"Sleek, spare" and "stylish", this "hipster" West Loop Japanese sushi source supplies a selection of "fresh", "imaginative" maki (traditionalists "avoid the rolls and just ask for the best fish") plus a "list of sake" and "attentive" service; meal tickets are "expensive" but mostly considered "worth the splurge."

Melanthios Greek
Char House *Greek/Steak*
- | - | - | M

Lakeview | 3114 N. Broadway (bet. Barry Ave. & Briar Pl.) | 773-360-8572 | www.melanthiosgreekcharhouse.com

Greek classics, steaks and chops and a fair number of vegetarian dishes pair with Greek wines and ouzo at this Lakeview spot; the cozy interior features an open kitchen, fireplace, low-lit iron chandeliers and banquettes, while the white brick and rustic wood facade looks transported from the homeland.

Melting Pot *Fondue*
19 | 18 | 19 | $44

River North | Millennium Center Towers | 609 N. Dearborn St. (bet. Ohio & Ontario Sts.) | 312-573-0011 ◑

Buffalo Grove | 1205 W. Dundee Rd. (Arlington Heights Rd.) | 847-342-6022

Schaumburg | 255 W. Golf Rd. (bet. Higgins & Roselle Rds.) | 847-843-8970 ◑

Downers Grove | 1205 Butterfield Rd. (bet. Finley Rd. & Highland Ave.) | 630-737-0810

Naperville | 4931 S. Rte. 59 (111th St.) | 630-717-8301 www.meltingpot.com

"It's all about sharing" and "cooking your own food" at this chain serving "every kind of fondue", including "delicious" chocolate pots; while it's a "romantic" "treat" for "younger couples" and "fun to do with a group", critics contend it's "overpriced" and "pretentious", and would prefer a "more casual" setup; P.S. go with a large party if you want "two burners."

Mercadito ◑ *Mexican*
22 | 22 | 17 | $38

River North | 108 W. Kinzie St. (bet. Clark & LaSalle Sts.) | 312-329-9555 | www.mercaditorestaurants.com

Enlivening "the competitive River North neighborhood", this mid-priced Mexican Manhattan import issues a "terrific" "upscale take on tacos" and "street-food" small plates plus "eclectic, amazing margaritas"; despite "inconsistent food and service", the "cool feel" and "funky decor" create an atmosphere that's "perfect for happy hour", "girl groups" and "dudes who want a little eye candy"; P.S. seating options include a communal table and sidewalk dining.

	FOOD	DECOR	SERVICE	COST

☒ Mercat a la Planxa *Spanish* | 26 | 24 | 22 | $53 |

South Loop | Blackstone Hotel | 638 S. Michigan Ave. (Balbo Ave.) | 312-765-0524 | www.mercatchicago.com

"Upbeat and swank", this "soaring space" "reminiscent of Barcelona" revitalizes the "former ballroom" of the South Loop's historic Blackstone Hotel, where Jose Garces' "dizzying array" of "adventurous" Catalan tapas (a "cut above the usual" in both "selection and price") and entrees including "roast pig for a large group" is the top-rated Spanish cuisine in this Survey; "gracious service", "outstanding" wines and "unusual sangrias" please patrons who praise the "beautiful", "Gaudí"-esque setting with a "busy bar scene" and an "amazing view" of Grant Park.

Merle's Barbecue *BBQ* | 19 | 16 | 18 | $29 |

Evanston | 1727 Benson Ave. (bet. Church & Clark Sts.) | 847-475-7766 | www.merlesbbq.com

"Bargain prices" and "big portions" of "tasty" "barbecue of any kind" plus "interesting sides" draw crowds at this Evanston "rib joint" with a "'50s Texas" vibe complete with "Elvis memorabilia"; while a few complain about "consistency" and "spotty service", most "leave happy."

Merlo la Salumeria Ⓜ *Italian* | 24 | 21 | 22 | $57 |

Lincoln Park | 2638 N. Lincoln Ave. (Wrightwood Ave.) | 773-529-0747

Merlo on Maple *Italian*

Gold Coast | 16 W. Maple St. (bet. Dearborn & State Sts.) | 312-335-8200 www.merlochicago.com

The Maple Street Merlo remains an "upscale" purveyor of "exquisite", "beautifully prepared" "Italian cuisine with some of the best" "fresh pasta" around, a "wonderful wine list" and "professional service" in a "quaint", "quiet" "converted" Gold Coast "brownstone"; "prices are quite high" but suitable for a "special evening"; P.S. the Salumeria (in the location of the original ristorante) doesn't inspire as much praise.

Mesón Sabika *Spanish* | 23 | 22 | 21 | $37 |

Naperville | 1025 Aurora Ave. (bet. River Rd. & West St.) | 630-983-3000 | www.mesonsabika.com

Tapas Valencia *Spanish*

South Loop | 1530 S. State St. (bet. 15th & 16th Sts.) | 312-842-4444 | www.tapasvalencia.com

Tapas aficionados tout the "huge selection" – from "killer" bacon-wrapped dates to an "extensive" Spanish wine list – at these city and suburban sibs that are popular for "celebrations" and "every other day"; the (sometimes "noisy") original, set in a "historic" "mansion" with a "beautiful patio" in Naperville, is a destination for Sunday brunch, while the "spacious" South Loop hot spot with Miro-esque tile details offers "great value", especially when you "go with a group."

Mexique Ⓜ *Mexican* | 25 | 20 | 23 | $46 |

Noble Square | 1529 W. Chicago Ave. (bet. Armour St. & Ashland Ave.) | 312-850-0288 | www.mexiquechicago.com

"Masterful" and "stunning" are surveyors' superlatives for the "French twist on Mexican" cuisine, "uniquely appetizing and imaginative" menu and "exceptional sauces" at this "hidden gem" "off the beaten path" in Noble Square; add in "friendly, knowledgeable service" and "sophisticated decor" and those for whom it's a "favorite" (including the weekend brunch) warrant it's "worth the price"; P.S. it serves beer, wine, sangria, tequila and digestifs but no cocktails.

Mezé ●☒Ⓜ *Eclectic* — — — M

West Loop | 205 N. Peoria St. (Lake St.) | 312-666-6625 | www.mezerestaurant.com

A midpriced menu of Eclectic small plates is served with red, white and seasonal sangrias, wines by the glass and more than a dozen brews at this West Loop tapas lounge; the sexy setting gets a warm glow from polished wood and backlit panels of thin-sliced marble, while seating options include plush banquettes, dining tables and a central bar.

M Henry Ⓜ *American* 25 18 20 $19

Andersonville | 5707 N. Clark St. (Hollywood Ave.) | 773-561-1600 | www.mhenry.net

NEW M Henrietta Ⓜ *American*

Edgewater | 1133 W. Granville Ave. (Broadway) | 773-761-9700 | www.mhenrietta.com

Fans are "willing to stand in line outside in the cold" for the "original", "delicious" daytime-only dining featuring "seasonal offerings and local products" at this "adorable" and affordable Andersonville BYO American, which post-Survey gained an Edgewater sister that does serve dinner; it's "very popular" – in fact, there's "nothing not to love" except the no-reserving policy and "weekend crowds" (it helps that "summer offers an outdoor patio" at M Henry); P.S. don't forget to "take home some of their great breads and pastries."

NEW Mia Figlia *Italian* — — — I

Northwest Side | 5304 W. Devon Ave. (Spokane Ave.) | 773-792-8300

A team of Tizi Melloul and Mia Francesca alums is behind this Northwest Sider serving well-priced Italian cooking both classic and modern, including a generous selection of antipasti, salads and pizzas, along with a very affordable all-Italian wine list; the upscale-casual space includes a bar, and boasts a clean design mixing wood, tomato-red accents, soft lighting and black-and-white photos.

◪ Mia Francesca *Italian* 26 20 22 $35

Lakeview | 3311 N. Clark St. (School St.) | 773-281-3310 | www.miafrancesca.com

The Lakeview matriarch of the Francesca's family is an "absolute staple" offering "remarkably consistent", "robust" and "always changing" Italian dishes that are "decently priced" and "neither too fancy nor too plain"; the "fast" and "personable" service works well given the "crowded" setting, but the "decibel level can be frightening" so "make reservations" for this "classic" and "leave your conversation at home."

	FOOD	DECOR	SERVICE	COST

☑ Michael ☒ *French* — 28 | 23 | 27 | $67

Winnetka | 64 Green Bay Rd. (Winnetka Ave.) | 847-441-3100 |
www.restaurantmichael.com

Namesake chef and "personality" Michael Lachowicz is "always there,
interacting with his guests" at this Winnetka "winner" where his "exceptional", "delicate and flavorful" New French fare with "spot-on
wine pairings" is served in an "elegant but casual", "conversation-
friendly" room by a staff that "works well together"; it's "pricey", but
"worthwhile for celebrating, relaxing or rewarding a good client."

Milk & Honey *American* — 23 | 14 | 15 | $17

Wicker Park | 1920 W. Division St. (bet. Damen & Wolcott Aves.) |
773-395-9434 | www.milkandhoneycafe.com

Enthusiasts are enamored of this "casual", "counter-service" New
American, saying "every neighborhood" should have a place for
such "delicious" breakfasts and lunches featuring "artisan ingredients" and "amazing baked goods"; the "casual", "cozy" atmosphere
includes "hip" Wicker Park "people-watching" and "lines out the
door" "during hopping weekend brunch", but "they do a nice job of
moving people through"; P.S. if you find the "decor colder than the
old location" "try the patio."

Miller's Pub *American* — 17 | 16 | 19 | $27

Loop | 134 S. Wabash Ave. (bet. Adams & Monroe Sts.) |
312-263-4988 ◑
Southwest Side | Midway Int'l Airport | 5700 S. Cicero Ave. (55th St.) |
773-948-6300
www.millerspub.com

Though it's "close to the Art Institute, symphony" and theater,
there's "nothing arty" about this Loop "legend" that's "classic
Chicago all the way", from the "old warrior surroundings" that include "signed celebrity photos on the walls" to the "ol'-fashioned
American food" (steaks, ribs, sandwiches, burgers); "you can't beat
the prices" or the "long bar for cocktails until 4 AM", but don't expect more than "adequate service"; P.S. there's also a small outpost
at Midway airport.

NEW MingHin ◑ *Chinese* — – | – | – | I

Chinatown | 2168 S. Archer Ave. (Cermak Rd.) | 312-808-1999 |
www.minghincuisine.com

This modern Chinatown Square Chinese breaks the genre's usual
mold with its stylish setting, full bar, long hours (9 AM–2 AM) and
hipster following; the lengthy, ambitious menu features dim sum,
hot pots and dishes made with exotic ingredients, and it all comes at
affordable prices in a bi-level space dressed up with red hanging
lanterns and gold metalwork.

Mirabell *American/German* — ▽ 21 | 20 | 20 | $32

Northwest Side | 3454 W. Addison St. (bet. Kimball & St. Louis Aves.) |
773-463-1962 | www.mirabellrestaurant.com

A "neighborhood" "holdout" on the Northwest Side, this German-
American "just off the Kennedy Expressway" pulls in savorers of

schnitzel, goulash and bratwurst; the setting includes "murals of Salzburg", a beer stein display and servers in traditional garb, but service can be inconsistent.

Mirai Sushi *Japanese* | 25 | 19 | 21 | $52 |

Wicker Park | 2020 W. Division St. (bet. Damen & Hoyne Aves.) | 773-862-8500 | www.miraisushi.com

Surveyors praise this "high-end" Wicker Park sushi "hipster" for its "incredibly fresh fish" and "masterfully prepared" "special rolls that really *are* special"; whether you "go upstairs" to the sake bar "for a darker, more loungey feel" or "downstairs for an open, well-lit" space, the offerings are presented with "flair" by servers who "know their stuff"; P.S. it "can get a bit expensive", but for the quality, "it's what you expect."

Miramar Bistro *French* | 17 | 19 | 19 | $43 |

Highwood | 301 Waukegan Ave. (Highwood Ave.) | 847-433-1078 | www.miramarbistro.com

North Shoreites hike to Highwood for "classic French" bistro fare "with Cuban drinks" ("odd, but it works") at Gabriel Viti's "casual", often "crowded" eatery manned by a "professional staff"; a "racy weekend reputation" appeals to some, but less dazzled diners dis the "loud conditions", "overpriced" fare and "limited menu"; P.S. chef Roland Liccioni departed post-Survey.

Mitchell's Fish Market *Seafood* | 21 | 18 | 19 | $37 |

Glenview | Glenview Town Ctr. | 2601 Navy Blvd. (Patriot Blvd.) | 847-729-3663 | www.mitchellsfishmarket.com

With "reasonably priced", "dependable" "fresh fish" from a daily changing catch, along with "consistent" service, this Glenview dinner-only seafood chain link with a nautical theme is "better than expected"; even if the dishes "lack creativity", "they do their best" with "simple" preparations and there are "so many options" to choose from.

Mity Nice *American* | 17 | 15 | 18 | $29 |

Streeterville | Water Tower Pl. | 835 N. Michigan Ave., Mezzanine level (bet. Chestnut & Pearson Sts.) | 312-335-4745 | www.leye.com

Lettuce Entertain You's "casual" "oasis of calm" in "the wilds" of Streeterville's Water Tower Place, long a suitable stop for American "comfort food and a stiff martini", revamped its menu and look post-Survey (not reflected in the ratings), but it retained favorites like meatloaf and turkey and you can still expect "moderate" prices and "friendly" service, making it a "reliable", "convenient" shopping "respite", if "not a destination."

Mixteco Grill Ⓜ *Mexican* | 25 | 14 | 22 | $30 |

Lakeview | 1601 W. Montrose Ave. (Ashland Ave.) | 773-868-1601

"Wonderfully creative", "vibrant" "haute Mexican" impresses proponents who "want to mainline the moles" at this Lakeview BYO "gem"; the "basic space" is "always crowded" and "noisy", but the "fantastic" fare and "accommodating" service "make up for it."

Mizu Yakitori & Sushi Lounge *Japanese* | 24 | 16 | 21 | $31

Old Town | 315 W. North Ave. (North Park Ave.) | 312-951-8880 |
www.mizurestaurant.com

Regulars "keep coming back" to this "reasonably priced" Old Town
Japanese for "creative", "well-executed" dishes including "inventive
yakitori" and "high-quality" sushi ("they always have cool new
rolls"), plus "flights of sake" and "good mixed drinks"; while it "lacks
the trendy scene of many others", "it more than makes up for it"
with "helpful service" and "consistent" fare.

☒ MK *American* | 27 | 24 | 26 | $72

Near North | 868 N. Franklin St. (bet. Chestnut & Locust Sts.) |
312-482-9179 | www.mkchicago.com

It's continuing "kudos" for Michael Kornick's "classy", "happening"
Near North haunt that's "stood the test of time" and still "shines"
with "honest", "outstanding", "seasonal" New American cuisine
"minus the fussiness"; expect "knockout desserts", a "stellar wine
list" and "excellent service all around" in the "spare", "urban-cool",
"renovated warehouse" space – in other words, it "meets high expectations" "from start to finish."

Mon Ami Gabi *French* | 22 | 21 | 22 | $42

Lincoln Park | Belden-Stratford Hotel | 2300 N. Lincoln Park W.
(Belden Ave.) | 773-348-8886
Oak Brook | Oakbrook Center Mall | 260 Oakbrook Ctr. (Rte. 83) |
630-472-1900
www.monamigabi.com

The "terrific" French bistro bites include a "fantastic variety of steak
frites" and the "best onion soup ever", plus "wines by the glass" "on
a rolling cart" at these "delightful" Lincoln Park and Oak Brook spots
from the Lettuce Entertain You chain; "you can't beat the prices" and
"service is smooth" in the "traditionally" decorated spaces, but a
few call them "cramped" and "predictable"; P.S. Oak Brook serves
lunch as well as dinner, and both sites offer outdoor dining.

Montarra Ⓜ *American* | ▽ 24 | 23 | 24 | $44

Algonquin | 1491 S. Randall Rd. (County Line Rd.) | 847-458-0505 |
www.montarra.com

Diners don't expect this kind of "hidden gem" "all the way out in
Algonquin", where a "talented chef" tempts touters with his "inter-
nationally influenced" New American steakhouse cuisine paired
with an "excellent wine list"; the modern setting with "Chihuly-
inspired fixtures" is surprising in a "small, strip-mall" location, but a
couple of critics found the service less impressive.

Moody's Pub ●◗⊐ *Pub Food* | 19 | 11 | 15 | $19

Edgewater | 5910 N. Broadway (Thorndale Ave.) | 773-275-2696 |
www.moodyspub.com

A "local crowd" "brings cash" ("no credit cards") to this longtime
(since 1959) Traditional American Edgewater "joint" for "reliable",
"inexpensive" burgers, "great onion rings", "potent cocktails", sangria and pitchers of beer beside a "warm fire" in winter or in the

FOOD | DECOR | SERVICE | COST

"wonderful" beer garden with silver maple trees in summer; the "dark", "grubby" interior and "irregular" service, however, can't hold a candle to the fare.

Moon Palace *Chinese*

22 | 15 | 20 | $22

Chinatown | 216 W. Cermak Rd. (Wentworth Ave.) | 312-225-4081 | www.moonpalacerestaurant.com

This "longtime Chinatown favorite" continues to be a "reliable" resource for Chinese chow with "flavors right on the mark", particularly in its "Shanghai specialties" and "fabulous black mushroom soup"; a fairly recent "face-lift" "really spruced up the place", and the "pleasant atmosphere" is buttressed by a "fast", "wonderful" staff.

☒ Morton's The Steakhouse *Steak*

26 | 22 | 25 | $70

Loop | 65 E. Wacker Pl. (bet. Michigan & Wabash Aves.) | 312-201-0410
Gold Coast | Newberry Plaza | 1050 N. State St. (Maple St.) | 312-266-4820
Rosemont | 9525 Bryn Mawr Ave. (River Rd.) | 847-678-5155
Northbrook | 699 Skokie Blvd. (Dundee Rd.) | 847-205-5111
Schaumburg | 1470 McConnor Pkwy. (bet. Golf & Meacham Rds.) | 847-413-8771
Naperville | 1751 Freedom Dr. (Diehl Rd.) | 630-577-1372
www.mortons.com

Carnivores who crown the late Arnie Morton's "old-school" "class act" the "king of the national steakhouse chains" say they're "incredibly consistent" for "fabulous", "prime" "aged beef Chicago-style"; the "ridiculous prices" are offset by "insane amounts of food", a solid wine cellar and "elaborately staged demonstrations" from a staff that "knows how to read the customer", plus the "masculine" spaces – especially at the "original", "clubby" State Street basement – are "classic" "business" settings.

☒ Moto ☒☒ *Eclectic*

27 | 23 | 27 | $142

West Loop | 945 W. Fulton Mkt. (Sangamon St.) | 312-491-0058 | www.motorestaurant.com

Simultaneously "serious and fun", Homaro Cantu's "amazing" West Loop Eclectic is ground zero for "molecular gastronomy", where "nothing looks like what it tastes like" when it comes to the "playful", "cutting-edge" creations; the "expensive" experience includes 10-course tasting menus, "phenomenal service", a "choice wine list" and "stark interiors" that "put the whole focus on the food", so even if a handful find that some of the "gimmicky" dishes "don't quite work", the "mind-bending" "originality" always makes up for it; P.S. it opened Ing in place of its more casual outpost, Otom.

☒ Mr. Beef ☒☒ *Sandwiches*

24 | 7 | 16 | $11

River North | 666 N. Orleans St. (bet. Erie & Huron Sts.) | 312-337-8500

Meat eaters "bite, drip, wipe, sigh, repeat" at River North's "historic", quick-dining "dump", still the sandwich "champ" for its "wonderfully messy", "best beef" sammie "bar none"; "service and decor couldn't get much worse" – the dining room is a "bunch of picnic tables pushed together" and "you order by yelling at" the "guy behind the counter" – but you come here until the wee hours for "a mouthful of bliss, Chicago-style"; P.S. it's cash only, and the kitchen is open until 5 AM Friday and Saturday nights from April–December.

Mrs. Murphy & Sons
Irish Bistro *Pub Food*   22 | 21 | 23 | $31

North Center/St. Ben's | 3905 N. Lincoln Ave. (bet. Byron St. & Larchmont Ave.) | 773-248-3905 | www.irishbistro.com
"Gourmet Irish food? somehow they do it" admit admirers of this "friendly" North Center pub serving an "awesome" brunch and an updated, "traditional" menu (shepherd's pie, corned beef and cabbage, beef and Guinness stew); the setting "in an ex-funeral home" boasts "beautiful stained-glass windows" and an "imposing center bar" "imported from Ireland" that features an "impressive selection of craft, micro and imported beers" plus lots of whiskey choices.

Mt. Everest Restaurant *Indian/Nepalese*   22 | 16 | 19 | $28

Evanston | 630 Church St. (bet. Chicago & Orrington Aves.) | 847-491-1069 | www.mteverestrestaurant.com
"Surprisingly tasty Nepalese options" (including the signature goat dish) back up the "top-notch" Indian fare at this "Evanston standby", deemed "dependable" for "neighborhood" dining "without the hassle of parking on Devon"; the "terrific lunch buffet" where "everything is labeled" is a "great value", but the "outdated" dining room scales no heights.

Mundial Cocina Mestiza Ⓜ *Eclectic*   – | – | – | M

Pilsen | 1640 W. 18th St. (bet. Marshfield Ave. & Paulina St.) | 312-491-9908 | www.mundialcocinamestiza.com
Morphed from its Mexican origins, this casual, inexpensive Pilsen spot serves "creative" Eclectic cuisine based on seasonal ingredients for brunch, lunch and dinner; set in "an unlikely storefront" with colorful tiled decor that seems to go well with the neighborhood, it's a "real find" "if you can find it"; P.S. it no longer offers live entertainment.

Myron & Phil
Steakhouse Ⓜ *Steak*   21 | 14 | 23 | $43

Lincolnwood | 3900 W. Devon Ave. (Springfield Ave.) | 847-677-6663 | www.myronandphil.com
Lincolnwood's "longtime standby" is a "throwback to another era" serving "tasty", "traditional" steakhouse fare with a "free chopped liver" "relish tray" and a "dose of nostalgia" ("nothing has changed in 40 years"); even if the "decor is nothing to write home about", the "well-trained" staff is "caring" and the once mostly "geriatric crowd" "seems to be getting younger"; P.S. there's a "piano bar" on Saturdays.

Mythos Ⓜ *Greek*   23 | 16 | 20 | $28

Lakeview | 2030-32 W. Montrose Ave. (Seeley Ave.) | 773-334-2000
While Lakeview seems like an "unusual location" for Greek, locals feel "lucky" that this "team effort" by two "lovely" sisters is "in the neighborhood" given its "authentic", "homestyle" Hellenic cooking considered "a cut above" Greektown; "wonderful service" and a

"congenial atmosphere", along with a BYO policy that "holds tabs down", are further pluses.

NEW Nabuki *Japanese* — | — | — | E

Hinsdale | 18 E. First St. (bet. Garfield Ave. & Washington St.) | 630-654-8880 | www.nabukihinsdale.com

Sushi, sashimi and other Japanese fare is enlivened with Latin accents at this upscale but kid-friendly Hinsdale addition co-owned by an Il Poggiolo partner; mango and green-tea hues, curvaceous banquettes and funky partitions lend a sleek, contemporary feel to the compact space, which has a small sushi bar in back and high tables built for people-watching up front.

Z Nacional 27 🅰 *Nuevo Latino* 23 | 22 | 21 | $44

River North | 325 W. Huron St. (Orleans St.) | 312-664-2727 | www.n27chicago.com

Loyalists have "lots of fun" at this "neat" River North restaurant-cum-"nightclub" where "delicious and inventive" Nuevo Latino flavors (the name refers to the 27 nations in Latin America) are coupled with a multitude of "mojito and sangria options"; even though some reviewers find the "food and service irregular" and the tapas "expensive", especially given the "casual" vibe, many others flag it their "favorite date night" with "dancing too" (it turns into a "salsa club on weekend nights").

Nagoya Japanese Seafood Buffet *Japanese* — | — | — | M

Naperville | 804 S. Rte. 59 (bet. Aurora & La Fox Aves.) | 630-637-8881 | www.nagoyausa.com

A spin-off of a Baton Rouge original, this sprawling West Suburban sushi castle boasts a midpriced, Japanese smorgasbord of all-you-can-eat fish and shellfish – in raw, hibachi and teriyaki preparations – plus dim sum and a variety of other dishes, accompanied by smoothies and full-bar service; the modern setting is decorated in soothing colors with well-spaced tables and TVs playing sports.

Z Naha 🅰 *American* 27 | 24 | 25 | $64

River North | 500 N. Clark St. (Illinois St.) | 312-321-6242 | www.naha-chicago.com

Locals find "the total package" at this "upscale" River North New American where chef/co-owner Carrie Nahabedian serves up "perfection on a plate" with a "world-class" yet "accessible" fusion of "contemporary styling" and "organic produce" at its "absolute peak"; beyond that, there's a staff that "anticipates your needs" and a "refined atmosphere" in a "cool, modern" space, so even those bothered by the "noise" "get over it" given the "spectacular" value.

Nana *American/Mexican* — | — | — | I

Far South Side | 3267 S. Halsted St. (33rd St.) | 312-929-2486 | www.nanaorganic.com

A charming, family-owned storefront, this Bridgeport American with a Mexican twist features organic and sustainably raised eats along with seasonal cocktails and fresh desserts from the pastry chef mom; exposed brick, retro-industrial copper light fixtures and beautiful woodwork lend a modern farmhouse feel to the space, which also boasts an open kitchen, take-out counter and coffee bar; N.B. reservations for large parties only.

NEW Nano Sushi *Japanese/Thai*

| - | - | - | M |

Northwest Side | 4256 N. Western Ave. (Cullom Ave.) | 773-588-6266 | www.nanosushichicago.com

Sushi and other Asian fare – everything from egg rolls to pad Thai to crab Rangoon – shine on the midpriced menu at this Northwest Sider, where lunch bargains and a BYO policy add extra neighborhood appeal; the urban black-brick setting (inside and out) includes a sushi bar, with red furnishings and lighting adding a devilish glow.

Natalino's Ⓜ *Italian*

| 23 | 19 | 22 | $42 |

Noble Square | 1523 W. Chicago Ave. (Armour St.) | 312-997-3700 | www.natalinoschicago.com

"Don't tell anyone" about this "worth-the-trip" Noble Square "jewel" whisper loyalists or "you'll spoil it for the regulars" who relish the "wonderful", "reasonably priced" Italian fare, "attentive" hospitality and clubby, "warm" setting; budget-watchers love the "daily specials", and night owls can "people-watch" until 2 AM.

NEW Next Ⓜ *Eclectic*

| - | - | - | VE |

West Loop | 953 W. Fulton Mkt. (bet. Morgan & Sangamon Sts.) | 312-226-0858 | www.nextrestaurant.com

This highly anticipated follow-up to Alinea from über-chef Grant Achatz is built around a daring concept, offering themed tasting menus that change quarterly to reflect a different global cuisine and time frame – and equally unusual is the booking system, with diners buying 'tickets' priced on a sliding scale according to day and time; the high-style, modern West Loop setting includes a chef's table and a secluded VIP 'speakeasy', while the adjacent Aviary bar, with upholstered banquettes and torchère lighting, serves crafty cocktails and edgy bar bites.

Next Door Bistro Ⓜ *American/Italian*

| 23 | 13 | 22 | $33 |

Northbrook | 250 Skokie Blvd. (Lake Cook Rd.) | 847-272-1491 | www.nextdoorbistro.com

"Next door to", but no longer affiliated with, Francesco's Hole in the Wall, this "always crowded", "reasonably priced" Northbrooker serves a mix of solid Traditional American and Italian eats and rotating daily specials; just "go early" or make reservations; P.S. they "take credit cards now."

Nia *Mediterranean*

| - | - | - | M |

West Loop | 803 W. Randolph St. (Halsted St.) | 312-226-3110 | www.niarestaurant.com

An extensive menu of seasonal small plates, from grilled octopus to bacon-wrapped dates, is accompanied by signature cocktails and sangria at this "low-key", midpriced West Loop Med; "get a seat by the window and watch the world go by" say fans who find it "worth a visit"; P.S. lunch is now served year-round.

	FOOD	DECOR	SERVICE	COST

Niche ⑤Ⓜ *American*
28 | 27 | 29 | $63

Geneva | 14 S. Third St. (bet. James & State Sts.) | 630-262-1000 | www.nichegeneva.com

"Go west!" urge proponents of this "intimate" Geneva "favorite", "located adjacent to farm country", where the "outstanding" New American fare is filled with "quality" "local and sustainable" ingredients and the service is "top-notch"; add in a "well-thought-out", "affordable" wine list and it's "comfortable and refined at the same time"; P.S. the Food score doesn't reflect a post-Survey chef change.

Nick's Fishmarket ⑤ *Seafood*
23 | 21 | 22 | $62

Rosemont | O'Hare International Ctr. | 10275 W. Higgins Rd. (Mannheim Rd.) | 847-298-8200

NEW Nick's Fishmarket Grill & Bar ⑤ *Seafood*

River North | 222 W. Merchandise Mart Plaza (bet. Franklin & Wells Sts.) | 312-621-0200
www.nicksfishmarketchicago.com

While bereft boosters were "sorry to see the Downtown [location] close", the Rosemont branch offers the same "excellent seafood", including "fresh fish flown in daily"; the "old-fashioned" room "designed for Vegas" strikes some as the perfect "special-occasion" spot, but those who knock "fair" service and "bloated prices" tolerable only when "someone else is buying" sigh maybe it worked "30 years ago, but not now"; P.S. a River North outpost opened post-Survey.

Nickson's Eatery ⑤ *American*
- | - | - | M

La Grange | 30 S. La Grange Rd. (Calendar Ave.) | 708-354-4995 | www.nicksonseatery.com

Regional, local and seasonal ingredients inform the moderately priced Southern-tinged menu at this pastoral-chic La Grange American with a pressed tin ceiling and rough-hewn wood details; the crowd is heavy on the stroller set, but there's a small back-room bar perfect for unwinding over fruity martinis and craft brews.

Nightwood *American*
23 | 21 | 21 | $47

Pilsen | 2119 S. Halsted St. (21st St.) | 312-526-3385 | www.nightwoodrestaurant.com

"Unique, trendy" and "friendly", Lula's Pilsen sib proffers a "funky" and "ever-changing" New American menu of "inventively presented" local and organic ingredients and a "well-chosen, value-oriented wine list"; the "welcoming" space, with a "great patio" in summer and a "fireplace in winter", is "a bit on the loud side", but most rank it worthy of "a repeat" visit; P.S. they've added Sunday brunch.

❷ Nine Steakhouse ⑤ *Seafood/Steak*
24 | 25 | 22 | $63

Loop | 440 W. Randolph St. (Canal St.) | 312-575-9900 | www.n9ne.com

"Yeah baby" exclaims the "lively", "arm candy"–filled crowd at this "flashy" Loop steakhouse where the "inventive" offerings and "creative presentations" include "marvelous seafood" dishes coupled with a "fantastic wine list that won't break the bank"; the service is "fine, but not the reason you come", while the "slick", "disco" decor

	FOOD	DECOR	SERVICE	COST

leaves some surveyors "cold", but the majority finds it "stunning" "for business and romance."

90 Miles Cuban Cafe *Cuban*

22	16	21	$13

Lakeview | 3101 N. Clybourn Ave. (Barry Ave.) | 773-248-2822
Logan Square | 2540 W. Armitage Ave. (Rockwell St.) |
773-227-2822
www.90milescubancafe.com

Diners curb cravings for "authentic, tasty" "Cuban sandwiches", "empanadas, tostones and ropa vieja" at this "friendly", "funky", "no-frills" duo offering a "very casual", "quick, cheap bite" with "cafe cubano" that packs an "unmatchable jolt"; if "parking" and (especially at Lakeview) "seating are at a minimum", outdoor tables provide additional dining space at both locations; P.S. "don't forget it's BYO."

Niu Japanese Fusion Lounge *Asian*

19	20	18	$37

Streeterville | 332 E. Illinois St. (bet. Columbus Dr. & McClurg Ct.) |
312-527-2888 | www.niusushi.com

With "huge portions" of "interesting, modern" Japanese fusion that includes "adventurous" and "classic" sushi presented "like edible works of art", this "crowded" Streeterville "neighborhood" "hot spot" is showing "no [signs of a] recession"; even if diners disagree on whether the dishes are "more style than substance", they concur the service is usually "prompt."

⚡ Nomi Kitchen *French*

-	-	-	E

Gold Coast | Park Hyatt Chicago | 800 N. Michigan Ave. (Chicago Ave.) |
312-239-4030 | www.nomirestaurant.com

Closed for renovation at press time, this acclaimed destination in the Gold Coast's Park Hyatt is slated to reemerge soon with a more relaxed style and fresh new look (white tablecloths are out, an open kitchen is in) as well as a new chef, who will offer an expanded New French menu; expected to remain: the sushi station, "cool" rooftop deck and the "million-dollar" Mag Mile view that helped make it a "memorable", "romantic" "splurge."

Nookies *Diner*

20	12	20	$17

Old Town | 1746 N. Wells St. (bet. Lincoln & North Aves.) |
312-337-2454

Nookies Too *Diner*

Lincoln Park | 2114 N. Halsted St. (bet. Dickens & Webster Aves.) |
773-327-1400

Nookies Tree ☾ *Diner*

Lakeview | 3334 N. Halsted St. (Buckingham Pl) | 773-248-9888
www.nookiesrestaurants.net

For "solid", "affordable" Traditional American "mom food" in "massive portions" "at all hours of the day" (including 24-hour weekend breakfast at Too and Tree, and all-day eats at the Old Town original), this BYO trio of "busy", "convenient" "neighborhood" diner "hangouts" with "just-right" service fills the bill; families who can't "handle the wait" come "with kids before 9."

	FOOD	DECOR	SERVICE	COST

Noon-O-Kabab *Persian* 25 | 18 | 21 | $24

Albany Park | 4661 N. Kedzie Ave. (Leland Ave.) | 773-279-8899 |
www.noonokabab.com

"This place has everything" praise proponents whose "mouths start
watering just thinking" about the "fantastic", "reasonably priced"
Persian fare ("awesome kebabs", "addicting" basmati rice) served
at this "welcoming" Albany Park Middle Eastern; it's "easy to access" by CTA and even by car since there's pain-free parking.

☑ North Pond Ⓜ *American* 25 | 26 | 23 | $65

Lincoln Park | 2610 N. Cannon Dr. (bet. Diversey & Fullerton Pkwys.) |
773-477-5845 | www.northpondrestaurant.com

Loyalists "love" to "sup on the season's freshest ingredients" from
"excellent" chef Bruce Sherman's "dynamic" New American menu
at this "romantic" Arts and Crafts "cabin in the woods" set in an old
field house on Lincoln Park's North Pond; it's "kind of hard to find,
but worth the trouble", though reviewers agree more on the
"unparalleled setting" than on the "precious portions" and hit-or-
miss service since a few detect "attitude" that "needs to be
addressed"; P.S. it serves a prix fixe Sunday brunch as well as lunch
on summer weekdays.

Nosh *Eclectic* ▽ 24 | 16 | 23 | $21

Geneva | 211 James St. (3rd St.) | 630-845-1570 |
www.experiencenosh.com

"The best West Suburban breakfast/lunch" spot "for foodies", this
Geneva daytime destination is "definitely not cookie-cutter" thanks
to its "creative, Eclectic" sweet and savory eats fashioned from
"high-quality ingredients" and delivered in "beautiful plate presentations"; there's a short wine list and patio dining as well, so it's
small wonder that most "wish it were open for dinner."

Nozumi Asian Cuisine *Japanese* - | - | - | M

South Barrington | Arboretum of South Barrington | 100 W. Higgins Rd.
(Rte. 59) | 847-783-0001 | www.nozumiasiancuisine.com

This Northwest Suburban Japanese serves sushi, small plates and
sake at moderate prices; the sprawling, sophisticated space features multiple seating areas (full-service bar, marble sushi bar, tables and semiprivate banquettes) amid exposed ductwork, clubby
music and soft pendant lighting.

Oak Tree
Bakery and Restaurant *American* 17 | 17 | 16 | $25

Gold Coast | Bloomingdale's Bldg. | 900 N. Michigan Ave., 6th fl.
(bet. Delaware & Walton Pls.) | 312-751-1988 | www.oaktreechicago.com

Traditional American eats including "great breakfast", "sandwiches
and salads" along with "terrific views of Michigan Avenue" make
this Gold Coast restaurant/bakery in the Bloomie's building a popular "pit stop" for both "business" folks and the "ladies who lunch" (it
closes at 5 PM daily); although "service can be great or poor" and
dollar-watchers deem it "expensive" for "upscale mall food", the
"decor is lovely."

Oba Contemporary
Japanese ⊠ *Japanese*

| - | - | - | M |

Des Plaines | 1285 Elmhurst Rd. (Algonquin Rd.) | 847-228-8810 |
www.obasushi.net

A tiny Northwest Suburban strip mall houses this contemporary sushi spot serving elaborately presented hot and cold signature maki, nigiri and sashimi, classic rolls and cooked Japanese fare (plus bargain lunches under $10); the clean, modern space includes banquette and table seating, semi-private booths with blinds and a bar serving beer, wine and sake only.

☒ Oceanique ⊠ *French/Seafood*

| 27 | 22 | 27 | $63 |

Evanston | 505 Main St. (bet. Chicago & Hinman Aves.) | 847-864-3435 |
www.oceanique.com

Mark Grosz's "memorable", "magnifique" Evanston eatery offers some of the "best seafood in the city", serving "superb new fusion and old-school dishes" with "unique" "combinations of French and Asian flavors" along with a "fantastic wine list"; the "fancy", "formal" setting and "top-notch service" further elevate the experience (and the prices), but "you get what you pay for" here.

Old Jerusalem Restaurant *Mideastern*

| 19 | 9 | 15 | $20 |

Old Town | 1411 N. Wells St. (bet. North Ave. & Schiller St.) |
312-944-0459 | www.oldjerusalemrestaurant.com

Old Town's "no-frills", BYO "neighborhood" "mom-and-pop" proffers "simple", "affordable" Middle Eastern eats like "homemade hummus", tabbouleh, grape leaves and falafel; the "friendly staff" can't do anything about the "basic decor", so "carry out" or sit "outdoors, weather permitting."

Old Oak Tap ❶ *Pub Food*

| 20 | 23 | 19 | $21 |

Ukrainian Village | 2109 W. Chicago Ave. (Hoyne Ave.) |
773-772-0406 | www.theoldoaktap.com

"Pretend your corner bar got hip and had a sense of humor" and it'd be much like this Ukrainian Village "neighborhood" "hangout" where the New American pub fare "goes above and beyond" ("delicious" homemade pretzels with cheddar stout fondue) and the "solid" international beer selection features a dozen types on tap; with a "modern" space that includes "high ceilings", two fireplaces and a "terrific" partially enclosed year-round patio, as well as service that "clicks", it's a "worthy destination."

Old Town Social *American*

| ▽ 18 | 18 | 16 | $32 |

Old Town | 455 W. North Ave. (Cleveland Ave.) | 312-266-2277 |
www.oldtownsocial.com

While this "hip" Old Town "meat market" "for the social crowd" "seems to want to be several different things", most maintain "it pulls that off nicely"; an "interesting" New American menu of "items meant to be shared", including "delicious cheeses" and charcuterie, plus "personable bartenders", make it "a welcome addition"; P.S. at press time the owners were at work on a new concept in the old Marché space.

	FOOD	DECOR	SERVICE	COST

Olive or Twist 🅼 American
- | - | - | M

Berwyn | 6906 Windsor Ave. (bet. Clinton & Grove Aves.) | 708-484-1808

Robert Nava (The Depot American Diner, ex The Signature Room) flexes his culinary prowess at this loungelike American, a wood-trimmed expansion of a Berwyn martini bar; classic sandwiches, chops and steaks, plus a menu of upscale bar bites (potato-wrapped prawns, a ceviche 'cocktail'), are served in a low-lit, date-appropriate storefront with framed black-and-white photography and muted salmon-hued walls.

One North 🅱 American
15 | 17 | 18 | $41

Loop | UBS Bldg. | 1 N. Wacker Dr. (Madison St.) | 312-750-9700 | www.restaurants-america.com

"Location" may be it's strong suit propose pre-theater diners and "power"-lunchers at this New American in a Loop office building, since the "average" menu "needs a refresh" and the "noise levels are higher than on stage at the opera across the street"; luckily, you can eke out a conversation during the warmer months, when "pleasant" outdoor dining is available; P.S. it's open Saturdays in opera season only.

NEW One.Six One 🅼 Eclectic
- | - | - | M

Little Italy/University Village | 1251-59 W. Taylor St. (Lytle St.) | 312-226-1611 | www.1pointsix1.com

Pronounced 'one point six one' (the mathematical 'golden ratio'), this Little Italy Eclectic offers a mix of midpriced global fare enhanced by sophisticated presentations and a compact international wine list; the spiffy, modern storefront houses an urban-casual setting with a fireplace, funky artwork and free WiFi, with the kitchen dividing the dining area from The Bar 10 Doors.

🆉 One Sixtyblue 🅱 American
26 | 24 | 25 | $66

West Loop | 1400 W. Randolph St. (Ogden Ave.) | 312-850-0303 | www.onesixtyblue.com

Fans of this "first-class" West Loop "favorite", owned in part by former basketball star Michael Jordan, cite chef Michael McDonald's "exceptional" and "unique" New American dishes, the "expansive wine list" and the "helpful, but not intrusive, service", deeming it "modern-chic but warm", "gourmet but comfortable" and "tucked-away but accessible"; sure, it's also "pricey", so look for "bargains on various nights"; P.S. perfect for "dinner on the way to United Center."

Opa! Estiatorio Greek
25 | 22 | 25 | $33

Vernon Hills | 950 Lakeview Pkwy. (Hawthorn Pkwy.) | 847-968-4300 | www.oparestaurant.com

For "a little bit of Greece in Vernon Hills", try this "relaxing" outpost with "large portions" of "authentic Greek cuisine" including "excellent seafood dishes", like "fantastic octopus", and a solid Hellenic wine selection; it's all served in a "light, whitewashed, airy room" or on a "delightful patio" overlooking Bear Lake.

	FOOD	DECOR	SERVICE	COST

Orange *Eclectic*

20	14	17	$19

River North | 738 N. Clark St. (bet. Chicago Ave. & Superior St.) | 312-202-0600

Lincoln Park | 2413 N. Clark St. (Fullerton Pkwy.) | 773-549-7833

Roscoe Village | 2011 W. Roscoe St. (Damen Ave.) | 773-248-0999

Near West | 730 W. Grand Ave. (bet. Halsted St. & Union Ave.) | 312-942-0300

Glenview | 1834 Glenview Rd. (bet. Church & Pine Sts.) | 847-832-1901
www.orangerestaurantchicago.com

Those for whom there's "always something original to try" at this fruitful family of "funky" breakfast-brunch joints don't mind paying "modestly premium prices" for "green eggs and ham", "pancake flights" and "fruit sushi" washed down with "create-your-own" fresh juices and "orange-infused coffee" (alcohol service varies by location); "service is friendly, if occasionally harried", but grumpy graders who grumble over the "gimmicky" grub wonder "why is everybody waiting to get in?"; P.S. they've added several new locations post-Survey, including in Near West, River North and North Suburban Glenview.

🆕 Original Five BBQ 🖾 *BBQ*

-	-	-	I

University Village | 1030 W. Taylor St. (Miller St.) | 312-929-2084 | www.theoriginalfivebbq.com

Wood-smoked 'cue in the five main regional styles (Carolina, Memphis, St. Louis, Kansas City and Texas) and classic sides come calling at this counter-service, paper plate–casual University Villager; open early lunch to late dinner, its digs feature a meaty red-and-brown color scheme, rustic wood tables and counter seating, food photography and free WiFi – but no alcohol and no BYO.

🆉 Original Gino's East *Pizza*

22	15	17	$22

River North | 633 N. Wells St. (Ontario St.) | 312-943-1124 | www.ginoseast.com

Streeterville | 162 E. Superior St. (Michigan Ave.) | 312-266-3337 | www.ginoseast.com

Lincoln Park | 2801 N. Lincoln Ave. (Diversey Pkwy.) | 773-327-3737 | www.ginoseast.com

O'Hare Area | 8725 W. Higgins Rd. (bet. Cumberland & East River Rds.) | 773-444-2244 | www.ginoshiggins.com

Deerfield | Embassy Suites Hotel | 1445 Lake Cook Rd. (Kenmore Ave.) | 847-945-4300 | www.ginoseastdeerfield.com

Libertyville | 820 S. Milwaukee Ave. (bet. Condell & Valley Park Drs.) | 847-362-1300 | www.ginoseast.com

🆕 **Barrington** | 352 Kelsey Rd. (Main St.) | 847-381-8300 | www.ginoseast.com

Rolling Meadows | 1321 W. Golf Rd. (Algonquin Rd.) | 847-364-6644 | www.ginosrollingmeadows.com

St. Charles | Tin Cup Pass Shopping Ctr. | 1590 E. Main St. (Tyler Rd.) | 630-513-1311 | www.ginoseast.com

Wheaton | 315 W. Front St. (West St.) | 630-588-1010 | www.ginoseast.com

Additional locations throughout the Chicago area

Regulars reckon "there's a reason for the multiple locations and rep" of this "relaxed" longtime, Chicago-style deep-dish pizza chain –

namely the "ooey-gooey layers of pure indulgence" over "cornmeal crusts to die for"; just be forewarned: "service is what you'd expect at a big feeder", the "non-pie menu items are weak" and the "out-of-town" "crowds" make them feel a bit like "tourist traps"; P.S. "don't forget a marker" for "writing on the walls, tables, floors, chairs, bathrooms – and even the servers if you ask nicely."

Z Original Pancake House, The *American* 24 | 16 | 20 | $17

Gold Coast | 22 E. Bellevue Pl. (bet. Michigan Ave. & Rush St.) | 312-642-7917

Lincoln Park | 2020 N. Lincoln Park W. (Clark St.) | 773-929-8130

Hyde Park | Village Ctr. | 1517 E. Hyde Park Blvd. (bet. 51st St. & Lake Park Blvd.) | 773-288-2322

Oak Forest | 5148 W. 159th St. (bet. Laramie & Le Claire Aves.) | 708-687-8282

Orland Park | 15256 S. LaGrange Rd. (bet. 151st & 153rd Sts.) | 708-349-0600

Forest Park | 7255 W. Madison St. (bet. Elgin & Marengo Aves.) | 708-771-5411

www.originalpancakehouse.com

Z Walker Bros. Original Pancake House *American*

Lincolnshire | 200 Marriott Dr. (Milwaukee Ave.) | 847-634-2220

Glenview | 1615 Waukegan Rd. (bet. Chestnut & Lake Aves.) | 847-724-0220

Highland Park | 620 Central Ave. (2nd St.) | 847-432-0660

Wilmette | 153 Green Bay Rd. (Isabella St.) | 847-251-6000

Arlington Heights | 825 W. Dundee Rd. (bet. Arlington Heights Rd. & Rte. 53) | 847-392-6600

Lake Zurich | Lake Zurich Theatre Development | 767 S. Rand Rd. (June Terr.) | 847-550-0006

www.walkerbros.net

Additional locations throughout the Chicago area

"Well-prepared, hearty breakfasts" earn this "always-packed", "old family favorite" American chain status as a "shrine" to carbs – especially pancakes, including a "Dutch Baby to live for" and a flapjack that's "the reason apples were invented"; while naysayers "don't understand the attraction" of "long waits" and "screaming children", patrons point out "attentive service" and "low-cost" "belly-busting of the highest order"; P.S. not all locations are open for dinner.

Osteria Via Stato *Italian* 23 | 20 | 22 | $39

River North | 620 N. State St. (Ontario St.) | 312-642-8450

Pizzeria Via Stato *Italian*

River North | 620 N. State St. (Ontario St.) | 312-337-6634

www.osteriaviastato.com

It's "not just a red-sauce menu" at Lettuce Entertain You's "affordable" River North Italian osteria where you can "stuff yourself silly" if you order the prix fixe "cavalcade" of "hearty" dishes to share or go à la carte with options like slow-roasted pork shank; the "homey", Tuscan-style room works for "groups" as well as "romance", and the "family-friendly" adjoining pizzeria fires up "terrific thin-crust" pies.

FOOD | DECOR | SERVICE | COST

Over Easy Café ☑ *American*   27 | 21 | 23 | $17

Ravenswood | 4943 N. Damen Ave. (bet. Ainslie & Argyle Sts.) | 773-506-2605 | www.overeasycafechicago.com

"Resolve to wake up earlier" and "kick-start your day" at this "cute" Ravenswood BYO breakfast, brunch and luncher, where the "creative" choices range from "decadent stuffed French toast" and "outrageous" apple pancakes to grilled Brie-cheese-and-apple sandwiches; the waits can be "long and tedious", however, so it's a good thing the "welcoming" staff pours "free coffee outside on weekends."

🆕 Owen & Engine *British*   - | - | - | M

Logan Square | 2700 N. Western Ave. (Schubert Ave.) | 773-235-2930 | www.owenengine.com

English gastropub eats made with artisanal ingredients (meat pies, Welsh rarebit, bubble and squeak) partner with a rotating selection of cask-conditioned and craft brews, along with signature cocktails, at this Logan Square Victorian lair; the cozy srroundings feature warm wood, area rugs and medallion wall coverings – plus an upstairs 'parlor' with leather club chairs and a fireplace; P.S. it's open until 2 AM most nights, with a pub menu served after dinner hours.

Oysy *Japanese*   20 | 18 | 19 | $33

River North | 50 E. Grand Ave. (bet. Rush St. & Wabash Ave.) | 312-670-6750

South Loop | 888 S. Michigan Ave. (9th St.) | 312-922-1127 www.oysysushi.com

The name of this "stylish" Japanese duo means "delicious" – and the majority of reviewers says it applies to the "tasty", "reasonably priced" sushi offerings, "complex rolls" and small plates brought to table by the "eye-candy waitresses"; but finicky fin-atics point to "dull combinations" and "inconsistent" service that make them "nothing special"; P.S. the South Loop locale offers "brilliant outdoor dining" "opposite Grant Park" in the summer and music on weekends.

Palette Bistro ☑ *American*   - | - | - | M

Lakeview | 2834 N. Southport Ave. (Wolfram St.) | 773-477-2565 | www.paletteonsouthport.com

"A bit off the beaten path", this "little" "gem" in Lakeview is "especially appropriate" for an "intimate, romantic" dinner or weekend brunch; the "gorgeous corner space" features "numerous windows and French doors", "warm woods" and a "showpiece carved bar", and both the "delicious" American menu and the wine list are "as low-key or upscale" "as you want"; P.S. there's summer sidewalk seating.

Palm, The *Steak*   24 | 21 | 23 | $67

Loop | Swissôtel | 323 E. Wacker Dr. (bet. Lake Shore Dr. & Michigan Ave.) | 312-616-1000 | www.thepalm.com

"Perfect" lobster, "superb" steaks and "hefty" cocktails are the signatures of this "bustling", "special-occasion" chophouse chain in the Loop with a "dark men's-club" look and "wonderful atmosphere" enhanced by "caricatures of celebs" (and "locals") covering the walls; "impeccable", "old-school" service seals the deal, so while it's "not cheap", most conclude it's "worth it."

Pane Caldo *Italian* | 23 | 21 | 21 | $62 |

Gold Coast | 72 E. Walton St. (bet. Michigan Ave. & Rush St.) | 312-649-0055 | www.pane-caldo.com

"Superb" Italian fare, a solid wine list and generally "knowledgeable" service are on offer at this "quaint", "romantic" Gold Coast "gem" that "feels like Milan" with its amber-hued walls and dark-blue ceilings; but the "intimate" setting strikes some as "cramped", while others feel their wallet's pain from "overpricing."

ⓩ Pappadeaux Seafood Kitchen *Seafood* | 21 | 19 | 19 | $35 |

Westmont | 921 Pasquinelli Dr. (Oakmont Ln.) | 630-455-9846 | www.pappas.com

Suburbanites who swim to this "buzzing", "casual" Westmont sea-fooder with a Cajun-Creole "flair" are content with the "huge portions", "wide variety of sauces" and "piquant flavors"; dissenters who won't make a return lap, however, cite "mixed service", a "semi-industrial setting" and "unimaginative", "middling" fare that's "more fried than fish."

Paramount Room *American* | ∇ 24 | 17 | 23 | $22 |

River West | 415 N. Milwaukee Ave. (bet. Hubbard & Kinzie Sts.) | 312-829-6300 | www.paramountroom.com

Its sign is "a beacon" along a "dark stretch of Milwaukee Avenue" say denizens drawn to this bi-level River West "neighborhood" noshery set in a former speakeasy, where the "surprisingly diverse menu" of "simple", "delicious" New American pub fare includes Kobe burgers that drip juice "down your arm" and a Reuben with house-cooked and -cured corned beef; the "bartenders know their stuff" too, mixing "excellent drinks" in a tavern space with distressed floors and lofted ceilings.

NEW Paris Club ● *French* | - | - | - | M |

River North | 59 W. Hubbard St. (bet. Clark & Dearborn Sts.) | 312-595-0800 | www.parisclubchicago.com

The Melman brothers (Hub 51) have transformed the former Brasserie Jo into this midpriced Francophile serving small plates designed by Jean Joho (Everest) and Tim Graham (Tru), plus caviar by the ounce and wine on tap; the rustic River North setting is done up with mirrored walls, reclaimed wood tables and Parisian landscape photography, and there's also seasonal sidewalk seating and an upstairs lounge.

Parkers' Restaurant & Bar *American* | 23 | 22 | 24 | $43 |

Downers Grove | 1000 31st St. (Highland Ave.) | 630-960-5701 | www.parkersamerican.com

A post-Survey name change and menu retool (not reflected in the Food score) shifted the emphasis from seafood to New American fare, including wood-fired pizzas, at this Western Suburbs spot, but it retains its "comfortable", "corporate" atmosphere and "accom-

FOOD | DECOR | SERVICE | COST

modating staff"; the "well-spaced tables" work for "business" or "romance", so while some admit the "common man might find the prices a bit steep", admirers believe its assets "make up for it."

Park 52 *American*

19 | 21 | 21 | $46

Hyde Park | 5201 S. Harper Ave. (52nd St.) | 773-241-5200 | www.park52chicago.com

While the American menu (with a touch of Southern flair) may "not be adventurous", seasonal "specials are usually more interesting" at this Hyde Park spot decorated in "vibrant colors" and "elaborate furnishings"; supporters say the neighborhood "needs more places like this", but judging from complaints over "food that could be better" and service that merely "tries hard", this eatery's still "not quite good enough"; P.S. it serves Sunday brunch.

Park Grill *American*

20 | 21 | 19 | $37

Loop | Millennium Park | 11 N. Michigan Ave. (bet. Madison & Washington Sts.) | 312-521-7275 | www.parkgrillchicago.com

With a "wonderful setting" "under 'the bean'" in Millennium Park, this "friendly", "stylish restaurant" serves up a "view of the ice skaters in winter" and a "delightful" "patio scene in summer"; but while some park here for "tasty" New American fare, including "the best burgers", spoilsports who skewer "inconsistent", "good-to-pedestrian" eats and a staff that "can't handle the lunch crowds" label it "for tourists."

Parrot Cage ☒ *American*

- | - | - | M

Far South Side | South Shore Cultural Ctr. | 7059 S. South Shore Dr. (71st St.) | 773-602-5333

What a "find on the [Far] South Side" say gourmands of this "creative" New American that's part of the Washburne Culinary Institute and manned by student-cooks who produce "excellent", "reasonably priced" steak, lamb and fish and "interesting vegetarian options", all accompanied by a "bargain wine list" (and a low-corkage BYO policy); the colorful space has outdoor seating, a "gorgeous" view of the lake and is surrounded by parrots' nests, but it's too bad the "pleasant" service "can be spotty"; P.S. cognoscenti concur the Wednesday–Thursday "three-course meal is a real deal."

Parthenon ● *Greek*

21 | 17 | 21 | $30

Greektown | 314 S. Halsted St. (bet. Jackson Blvd. & Van Buren St.) | 312-726-2407 | www.theparthenon.com

"A consistent favorite" for more than 40 years, this Greektown "staple" has a "triple-A" Grecian formula: "huge portions" of "authentic, affordable, appetizing" eats served "family-style" from 11 AM to midnight, service with a "sense of humor" and a "fun", "casual" space "broken up into smaller rooms"; however, critics advise "don't focus on the surroundings", which are "somewhat campy."

Pasha ☒ *Spanish*

- | - | - | M

West Loop | 802 W. Randolph St. (Halsted St.) | 312-243-4442 | www.pashachicago.com

Creative Spanish small and main plates using local and organic ingredients, specialty libations and a predominantly Spanish wine list mark this Market District haunt; the cozy, low-lit lair features candlelight and a bar with backlit booze bottles, and the Latin band Bandoleros (who are also co-owners) perform on Thursdays and Saturdays.

Pasta Palazzo *Italian*
▽ 22 | 15 | 19 | $19

Lincoln Park | 1966 N. Halsted St. (Armitage Ave.) | 773-248-1400 | www.pastapalazzo.com

Lincoln Park locals "love" this "cozy" Italian with "attentive service" and "reasonable prices" for "pasta and more pasta" (try the jalapeño gnocchi), "great salads" and "excellent apps"; the "casual" spot can be "loud", but most say it's an "enjoyable stop for a neighborhood" meal; P.S. no reservations, but they now accept credit cards.

Pegasus ● *Greek*
20 | 17 | 18 | $28

Greektown | 130 S. Halsted St. (bet. Adams & Monroe Sts.) | 312-226-4666 | www.pegasuschicago.com

Pegasus on the Fly ● *Greek*

Southwest Side | Midway Int'l Airport | 5700 S. Cicero Ave. (55th St.) | 773-581-1522 | www.pegasusonthefly.com

"In the heart of Greektown", this "favorite" features a "wide range" of "terrific dishes" including "classic" spanakopita, broiled whole fish and "yummy" Greek tapas brought to table by "accommodating" servers; a "bright", "cozy" interior "with painted Mykonos windmills" and a summertime rooftop with "views of the Chicago skyline" elevate this one "a step above other restaurants in the area"; P.S. the Midway fly-by is open 24/7.

Pelago Ristorante *Italian*
▽ 26 | 24 | 27 | $53

Streeterville | Raffaello Hotel | 201 E. Delaware Pl. (Mies van der Rohe Way) | 312-280-0700 | www.pelagorestaurant.com

Chef-owner Mauro Mafrici "knows how to cook" pronounce proponents of the "superb", "creative" Italian at his Streeterville dining room serving lunch and dinner; it's "worth seeking out" in a "hidden hotel" off Michigan Avenue, given the "winning" dishes, "outstanding service" and "tastefully decorated" space with porcelain chandeliers, white leather chairs and a mother of pearl fireplace; P.S. there's seasonal patio seating.

Penny's Noodle Shop *Asian*
20 | 12 | 17 | $15

Lakeview | 3400 N. Sheffield Ave. (Roscoe St.) | 773-281-8222 Ⓜ
Lincoln Park | 950 W. Diversey Pkwy. (Sheffield Ave.) | 773-281-8448
Wicker Park | 1542 N. Damen Ave. (North Ave.) | 773-394-0100 Ⓜ
Northfield | 320 S. Happ Rd. (Mt. Pleasant St.) | 847-446-4747
Oak Park | 1130 Chicago Ave. (Harlem Ave.) | 708-660-1300
www.pennysnoodleshop.com

Champions of "cheap", "palate-pleasing", "predictable" Asian dishes defer to this "casual", "quick-service", "no-frills" string of noodle shops for a "wide variety" of "simple dishes" with "fresh ingredients" and "lots of vegetarian options"; some sophisticated palates pooh-pooh "bland", "faux" fare, but penny-savers praise the "plentiful" portions that are "perfect for recessionary times"; P.S. Lakeview and Northfield are BYO, the others offer beer and wine.

🆕 Pensiero Ristorante Ⓜ *Italian* — | — | — | E

Evanston | Margarita Inn | 1566 Oak Ave. (Davis St.) | 847-475-7779 | www.pensieroitalian.com

After the temporary closure of Evanston's 20-plus-year-old Va Pensiero, the owner of the Margarita Inn (where it's located) opted to reopen it as Pensiero Ristorante, which boasts a new chef, a similar but updated menu of seasonal, artisanal Italian fare (including the signature salt-crusted whole fish and chocolate budino), most of the same staff, a Boot-heavy wine list and specialty cocktails; the refreshed space retains the original's old-world charm.

🆕 Perennial Virant *American* — | — | — | M

Lincoln Park | Park View Hotel | 1800 N. Lincoln Ave. (Clark St.) | 312-981-7070 | www.perennialchicago.com

Infusing the former Perennial with the vision of Vie's Paul Virant (he'll split his time between the two), this revamped Lincoln Parker, set to open at press time, will take full advantage of its proximity to Green City Market by offering farm-to-table New American fare, including prix fixe options, sharing plates and brunch; the prime Park View Hotel location has been given a chic rehab complete with a concrete bar and outdoor seating sure to draw see-and-be-seen types.

Perry's Deli Ⓩ *Deli* 26 | 12 | 17 | $11

Loop | 174 N. Franklin St. (bet. Lake & Randolph Sts.) | 312-372-7557 | www.perrysdeli.com

"One of the best delis in town", this Loop favorite gets so crowded you may have to "fight for a table" after you order one of its "huge", "tasty" sandwiches "piled high" with house-cooked meats; you're not going for the decor (takeout may be better) or the quirky service ("leave your cell phone outside" cause if you use it "Perry himself will yell at you"), but "it's worth it" for sammies "so big you can only eat half."

Pete Miller's Seafood & 22 | 21 | 21 | $51
Prime Steak *Seafood/Steak*

Evanston | 1557 Sherman Ave. (bet. Davis & Grove Sts.) | 847-328-0399 ◖

Wheeling | 412 N. Milwaukee Ave. (bet. Dundee & Lake Cook Rds.) | 847-243-3700

www.petemillers.com

These "suburban steakhouses" are considered "friendly", "clubby" connections for a "basic menu" of "high-quality" "prime" steaks and "even better seafood" in a "dark" setting reminiscent of "the mid '40s"; while most agree the service is usually "reliable", scorers are split over whether the "live jazz" (Tuesday through Saturday) is "great" or so "loud" it's "difficult to tolerate"; P.S. Evanston is dinner-only, while Wheeling serves lunch weekdays.

Petterino's *American* 19 | 19 | 21 | $42

Loop | Goodman Theatre Bldg. | 150 N. Dearborn St. (Randolph St.) | 312-422-0150 | www.petterinos.com

"Theatergoers" and the "business crowd" fill this Lettuce Entertain You Loop American in the Goodman Theatre building, where "snappy" service (both in speed and, sometimes, "attitude") keeps the "clubby", "bustling" room under control; the straightforward fare is generally "dependable" – and the "after-7 prix fixe" (Monday through Thursday) is a "bargain" – but tougher critics suspect something's "missing in the kitchen" given the "lackluster" offerings.

P.F. Chang's China Bistro *Chinese* | 20 | 19 | 19 | $31 |

River North | 530 N. Wabash Ave. (Grand Ave.) | 312-828-9977
Northbrook | Northbrook Court Shopping Ctr. | 1819 Lake Cook Rd. (Northburg Court Dr.) | 847-509-8844
Schaumburg | Woodfield Mall | 5 Woodfield Mall (Frontage & Golf Rds.) | 847-610-8000
Orland Park | Orland Park Crossing | 14135 S. La Grange Rd. (Southwest Hwy.) | 708-675-3970
Lombard | 2361 Fountain Square Dr. (bet. Butterfield & Meyers Rds.) | 630-652-9977
www.pfchangs.com

"Light, delicious", "Americanized" Chinese food keeps fans "coming back" – especially for the "standout" lettuce wraps – to this "trendy", "stylish" chain; though not everyone is convinced ("overpriced", "ordinary", "loud"), the "consistent" service is a plus, as is the "smart" menu "catering to people with allergies" and other needs.

Philly G's *Italian* | 21 | 22 | 23 | $37 |

Vernon Hills | 1252 Rte. 45 E. (Rte. 21) | 847-634-1811 | www.phillygs.com

"People of all ages enjoy" this "welcoming" Vernon Hills Italian where "you feel like you're at someone's home" dining on "authentic", old-school fare like "veal francese", chicken cacciatore and pasta carbonara; the "reliable service" gets it right in the "sprawling", "old-mansion" space with an "enclosed outdoor porch" and live weekend entertainment.

Phil Stefani's 437 Rush 🛇 *Italian/Steak* | 24 | 21 | 24 | $48 |

River North | 437 N. Rush St. (Hubbard St.) | 312-222-0101 | www.stefanirestaurants.com

Traditionalists tout the "upper-end", "Chicago-style fine-dining" experience at Phil Stefani's "classic white-tablecloth Italian steakhouse" that works well for "business" folks "sealing a deal" and "titled ladies comparing vacation plans"; the food "doesn't blow away" everyone, but the "cheerful and knowledgeable service", including a "roving maitre d'/tenor who takes requests", certainly creates an "inviting" vibe in a River North location that's "convenient to many hotels."

Pho & I *Thai/Vietnamese* | - | - | - | I |

Lakeview | 2932 N. Broadway (Oakdale Ave.) | 773-549-5700 | www.phoandichicago.com

A hybrid Vietnamese-Thai, this budget-friendly Lakeview BYO serves apps, buns, curries, noodles and rice dishes in addition to the namesake soup; the upscale-casual storefront boasts spare, modern design with bare white tables, warm wood, recessed lighting and a red accent wall.

	FOOD	DECOR	SERVICE	COST

☑ Phoenix *Chinese* `23` `12` `17` `$26`

Chinatown | 2131 S. Archer Ave., 2nd fl. (Wentworth Ave.) | 312-328-0848 | www.chinatownphoenix.com

While "best known for" its "large variety" of "daily dim sum" "from the commonplace to the weird", this "huge" moderately priced Chinatowner is also sought out for "gourmet Chinese dinners" (the "Peking duck is always available"); service swings from a "paragon of efficiency" to "hit-and-miss", "fluent English is at a premium" and the surroundings are "drab", yet it remains "extremely popular", so just remember to "come early" or "be prepared for a wait" "on weekends."

Phở 777 *Vietnamese* `21` `8` `15` `$15`

Uptown | 1065 W. Argyle St. (bet. Kenmore & Winthrop Aves.) | 773-561-9909

Whether it's "delicious" or merely "decent", surveyors suggest the "authentic", "tasty Vietnamese" fare – including an "amazing number of phos" plus noodles, "fresh spring rolls and shrimp paste on sugar cane" – at this Uptown BYO is "hot", "satisfying" and "maybe one of the best values in all of Chicago", even if decor and service are "no-frills"; P.S. the menu is offered mid-morning through late evening.

Phò Xe Tǎng *Vietnamese* `26` `8` `13` `$13`

Uptown | 4953-55 N. Broadway (Argyle St.) | 773-878-2253 | www.tank-noodle.com

"In the land of pho", "this is one of the best" say satisfied slurpers at this "always-busy" budget Uptown BYO (aka Tank Noodle) that's a "reliable" source for "excellent", "fresh" Vietnamese fare delivered with "quick service"; there's "zero atmosphere" at communal round tables, but devotees declare the "constant wait is a testament" to "broad appeal"; P.S. it's closed Wednesdays.

Piazza Bella *Italian* `21` `17` `19` `$30`

Roscoe Village | 2116 W. Roscoe St. (bet. Damen & Western Aves.) | 773-477-7330 | www.piazzabellachicago.net

"Delicious" midpriced Italian cooking in a "comfortable", "casual" setting with "cute", "authentic" atmosphere draws Roscoe Villagers to this "neighborhood" trattoria for a "date" or "family" outing; nit-pickers note that "service could use some improvement", but an expansion a while back "alleviated the crowding" and there's also an "outdoor dining area"; P.S. "don't miss the Sunday brunch with unlimited mimosas."

Piccolo Sogno *Italian* `24` `23` `22` `$50`

Near West | 464 N. Halsted St. (Grand Ave.) | 312-421-0077 | www.piccolosognorestaurant.com

Even the most "avid" fans of Northern Italian cuisine say chef Tony Priolo (ex Coco Pazzo) "pushes the boundaries" "of quality and authenticity" at this "visually beautiful" Near West "treasure" with "wine choices" so vast and "reasonably priced" they make "an oenophile weep for joy"; "in summertime" a "glorious" garden is "heaven" to habitués, so if "service is inconsistent" and it can be "a bit noisy", most still insist it's "truly a little dream."

	FOOD	DECOR	SERVICE	COST

Piece *Pizza*   23 | 14 | 19 | $20

Wicker Park | 1927 W. North Ave. (Damen Ave.) | 773-772-4422 |
www.piecechicago.com

"New Haven thin-crust pizza in a stuffed-crust town" scores with
surveyors at this "cavernous" Wicker Park "sports bar" serving "customized" pies (choose your "sauce" and "top your 'za with everything from clams to mashed potatoes") and "interesting" "fresh"
microbrews, all at "decent prices"; "service is serviceable" but the
setting has "screens all over tuned to various" games, and if it's
"crowded" and "loud" (like during the "live-band karaoke" on
Saturday nights), Piece Out does delivery and takeout next door.

Pierrot Gourmet *French*   20 | 20 | 18 | $35

River North | Peninsula Hotel | 108 E. Superior St. (bet. Michigan Ave. &
Rush St.) | 312-573-6749 | www.peninsula.com

"It costs more than other places to have a coffee, croissant, lunch"
or early dinner, but not as much as a "trip abroad" at this "serene"
River North "oasis" featuring "flatbreads, sandwiches, salads,
quiches" and other French bistro fare crafted from "high-quality ingredients" and proffered by generally "professional service" in an
"upscale" "Continental cafe" space that's "part of the Peninsula
Hotel"; P.S. they have a seasonal patio.

Piggery, The *American/BBQ*   - | - | - | I

Lakeview | 1625 W. Irving Park Rd. (Marshfield Ave.) | 773-281-7447 |
www.thepiggerychicago.com

This little piggy comes to Lakeview with a passel of budget-loving
porcine profferings; ribs are a mainstay, and there's pork in every
conceivable comfort-food dish (and replacing other proteins in
items like pot roast, salad, poppers and nachos), all served with
craft beers on tap in an upscale sports-bar setting with reclaimed
wood floors and lighting that still flatters at 2 AM (nightly closing
time, though the kitchen closes earlier).

Pine Yard *Chinese*   18 | 11 | 16 | $23

Evanston | 1033 Davis St. (Oak St.) | 847-475-4940 |
www.pineyardrestaurant.com

"Spicy Sichuan" and Mandarin dishes secure supporters for this enduring Evanston Chinese where the "hot, fresh" fare comes at "reasonable prices" in a simple, contemporary setting; while naysayers
lament it's a "shadow of its old self", fans favor the prix fixe "lunch
specials" (available Monday–Saturday) and note that service is so
"prompt" you're "served practically before you've read the menu."

Pingpong ● *Asian*   20 | 17 | 17 | $28

Lakeview | 3322 N. Broadway (bet. Aldine Ave. & Buckingham Pl.) |
773-281-7575 | www.pingpongrestaurant.com

"Cute" and compact, this "local" Boys Town "scene" "keeps it interesting" with a mix of "delicious", "above-average" Asian eats
("i.e. Japanese, Korean, Thai", Chinese) plus cocktails in a "lively" atmosphere with "loud music"; the "stark white", "fashionista" setting
includes a seasonal patio; it was temporarily closed at press time.

| | FOOD | DECOR | SERVICE | COST |

Pinstripes *American/Italian* | 17 | 18 | 17 | $28 |

Northbrook | 1150 Willow Rd. (bet. Patriot Blvd. & Waukegan Rd.) | 847-480-2323
Barrington | 100 W. Higgins Rd. (Rte. 59) | 847-844-9300
www.pinstripes.com

Some regulars roll into these "classy", "comfortable" suburban "bowling-alley restaurants" for their "reasonably priced", "tasty" traditional American-Italian bistro fare and "Sunday buffet brunch" with special children's stations, while sporty types call them a "blast" for "bowling, bocce, booze" and "birthday parties"; P.S. seating options include "leather sofas" and "inviting patios."

Z Pita Inn *Mediterranean/Mideastern* | 24 | 9 | 17 | $12 |

Glenview | 9854 N. Milwaukee Ave. (bet. Central & Golf Rds.) | 847-759-9990
Skokie | 3910 Dempster St. (Crawford St.) | 847-677-0211
Wheeling | 122 S. Elmhurst Rd. (Dundee Rd.) | 847-808-7733
www.pita-inn.com

Offering "healthy" fare "as delicious as it is cheap", this trio of "dependable" Med and Middle Eastern "self-service standbys" earns accolades as "one of the best deals around" for an "alternative to fast food"; "frenzied but efficient" "counter" service controls "crowds" of "loyal pita, hummus" and falafel fans, and while there's "zero atmosphere", the "decor is simple and functional"; P.S. the prix fixe "businessperson's lunch" "is hard to beat."

Pitchfork Food & Saloon *BBQ* | - | - | - | I |

North Center/St. Ben's | 2922 W. Irving Park Rd. (Richmond St.) | 773-866-2010 | www.pitchforkchicago.com

This low-cost North Center arrival slings barbecue essentials plus sandwiches, salads, wings and chili mac to accompany its big whiskey selection and rotating chalkboard menu of over 35 bourbons; the stylishly casual brick-and-wood space is outfitted with a tin ceiling, taxidermy, framed stained glass and antique gaslights, plus multiple plasmas and dartboards for entertainment.

Pizza Capri *Pizza* | 20 | 12 | 16 | $22 |

Lincoln Park | 1733 N. Halsted St. (Willow St.) | 312-280-5700
Hyde Park | 1501 E. 53rd St. (Harper Ave.) | 773-324-7777
www.pizzacapri.com

"Unique and delicious" "crispy, thin pizza" and a "variety" of "creative salads and pasta dishes" add up to a "tasty meal at a fair price" at these "atypical Italian" eateries where the "decor is institutional" but "friendly" "service makes it a pleasant dining experience"; P.S. Lincoln Park is BYO, Hyde Park offers beer and wine.

Pizza D.O.C. *Pizza/Italian* | 23 | 15 | 20 | $25 |

Lincoln Square | 2251 W. Lawrence Ave. (bet. Bell & Oakley Aves.) | 773-784-8777 | www.mypizzadoc.com

"One of the pioneers in the wood-fired pizza revolution", this "happening" Lincoln Square Italian woos with "wonderful" "Neapolitan" "thin pizza with a wide variety of toppings" including "egg" and "potato" ("but don't overlook the rest of the menu", like "excellent spaghetti carbonara"); the "family-friendly" "bistro atmosphere" can be "noisy", and while the "excellent pies" are "not cheap", they're "always satisfying"; P.S. it serves all-you-can-eat Sunday brunch.

Pizza Rustica *Pizza* - | - | - | M

Wrigleyville | 3913 N. Sheridan Ave. (Sheffield Ave.) | 773-404-8955 | www.pizzarusticachicago.com

Veterans of the 'za wars will want to check out the Venetian-style version (thin and flaky) at this small Wrigleyville BYO 'pizza kitchen', which also serves other affordable Italian dishes made from family recipes; you can create your own toppings or personalize a pasta dish by choosing among noodles and sauces, and it's all served in a warmly lit room with rotating local art; P.S. there's a sidewalk cafe.

Pizzeria Serio Ⓜ *Pizza* - | - | - | M

Lakeview | 1708 W. Belmont Ave. (bet. Paulina St. & Ravenswood Ave.) | 773-525-0600 | www.pizzeriaserio.com

Lakeview residents now have a NY-style pizza option in the form of this spiffy midpriced storefront specializing in chewy thinnish crust (but not skinny) pies made from hand-stretched dough in an 800-degree brick oven; the brick theme extends to the facade and walls, with the loftlike feel enhanced by wood floors and exposed ductwork.

Pizzeria Uno ❶ *Pizza* 22 | 14 | 16 | $23

River North | 29 E. Ohio St. (Wabash Ave.) | 312-321-1000

Pizzeria Due ❶ *Pizza*

River North | 619 N. Wabash Ave. (bet. Ohio & Ontario Sts.) | 312-943-2400
www.unos.com

Among "Chicago's top tourist destinations", this "historic" River North duo of "deep-dish" "icons" ("not the chain Uno, the original") is beloved for its "buttery, crunchy crust" and "generous portions of meat, cheese and sauce" ("prepare for a reptilian stupor" that's "worth every groan"); "servers struggle to do their best" at the "crowded" and perhaps "shopworn" sire, so some head to the "quieter" (at least sometimes) sequel for the "same pizza", and while loyalists insist they've "upheld the tradition", others lament they've "lost a little pizzazz over the years."

P.J. Clarke's *American* 17 | 14 | 17 | $27

Streeterville | Embassy Suites Hotel | 302 E. Illinois St. (Columbus Dr.) | 312-670-7500

Gold Coast | 1204 N. State Pkwy. (Division St.) | 312-664-1650
www.pjclarkeschicago.com

No relation to New York, these "old-school" Gold Coast and Streeterville "watering holes" with "lively bar scenes" and a "neighborhood hangout feel" boast the American "comfort-food" "basics", including "classic burgers", meatloaf, "big salads" and "nice sandwiches" at "reasonable prices" in pleasantly "pubby" setting (with patios).

	FOOD	DECOR	SERVICE	COST

NEW PL8 ⓜ *Chinese/Japanese* — | - | - | - | M

Barrington | 736 W. Northwest Hwy. (Hart Rd.) | 847-382-1988 |
www.pl8simplyasian.com

Aficionados of Asian cuisine can find midpriced modern Chinese,
Japanese and sushi (including multiple maki) in one go at this super-
chic Barrington hybrid that also hosts a bar scene fueled by fusion
cocktails; highlights of the black-white-and-red setting include upholstered booths, exotic lanterns, corrugated railcar siding and
petrified wood booths.

Pomegranate *Mediterranean/Mideastern* ▽ 18 | 11 | 15 | $13

Evanston | 1633 Orrington Ave. (bet. Church & Davis Sts.) |
847-475-6002 | www.eatpom.com

"Fresh, fast Middle Eastern" meals including "salads, pitas and entrees" "at a good price" have raters "returning again and again" to
this red-walled Evanston order-at-the-counter BYO for a "quick
bite" – and "they deliver, a big bonus."

Pompei Pizza *Italian* 19 | 14 | 16 | $16

Streeterville | 212 E. Ohio St. (bet. Fairbanks Ct. & St. Clair St.) |
312-482-9900
Lakeview | 2955 N. Sheffield Ave. (bet. Oakdale & Wellington Aves.) |
773-325-1900
Little Italy/University Village | 1531 W. Taylor St. (bet. Ashland Ave. &
Laflin St.) | 312-421-5179
Schaumburg | 1261 E. Higgins Rd. (bet. Meacham Rd. & National Pkwy.) |
847-619-5001
Oakbrook Terrace | 17 W. 744 22nd St. (bet. Butterfield Rd. &
Summit Ave.) | 630-620-0600
www.pompeipizza.com

A "wide selection" of "solid", "quick-service Italian specialties" like
"strudel pizza", "pasta in good-size portions and tasty salad specials" are a "value for a quick lunch or dinner" at this "cafeteria-
style" series; service varies and it's "not fine dining, but you can
bring the whole family and not break the bank", so most are "glad
it's in the neighborhood."

NEW Pork Shoppe ⓜ *BBQ* — | - | - | - | I

Avondale | 2755 W. Belmont Ave. (California Ave.) | 773-961-7654 |
www.porkshoppechicago.com

This funky-casual Avondale storefront showcases local pork and
beef barbecue (offered in different portion sizes with three sauce
choices) along with classic sides like cornbread, mac 'n' cheese and
'burnt end' baked beans, with bourbon and beer to boot; the rustic
dining room mixes regular tables with butcher block communal
seating amid industrial lighting and ductwork, mirrors and the
occasional farm/pig artifact.

NEW Portage, The ⓜ *American* — | - | - | - | M

Northwest Side | 3938 N. Central Ave. (bet. Dakin St. & Irving Park Rd.) |
773-853-0779 | www.theportagechicago.com

Folks from the former Tizi Melloul are behind this casual neighborhood Portage Park gastropub, home to creative, midpriced

American comfort food with gourmet leanings (duck-fat fries, mac 'n' cheese, Kobe burger) for dinner and Sunday brunch, and classic desserts including housemade ice creams and apple pie; the modernized pub setting features a wood and granite bar, modern light fixtures and seasonal outdoor dining (rare in the 'hood).

Port Edward Ⓜ *American*

- | - | - | E

Algonquin | 20 W. Algonquin Rd. (Harrison St.) | 847-658-5441 | www.portedward.com

This long-standing Suburban Northwest bastion of straightforward seafood and Sunday champagne brunch buffets serves a Traditional American menu full of steak and surf 'n' turf combos (some rather pricey) plus regular specials, e.g. clambakes, crab nights, prime rib dinners; overlooking the Fox River, the sprawling, multiple-room space features cozy booths, a table in a boat (on an indoor koi pond) and a gift shop, and there's regular live entertainment.

Ⓩ Potbelly Sandwich Shop *Sandwiches*

19 | 13 | 17 | $10

Loop | One Illinois Ctr. | 111 E. Wacker Dr. (Michigan Ave.) | 312-861-0013 Ⓢ
Loop | Insurance Exchange | 175 W. Jackson Blvd. (bet. Financial Pl. & Wells Sts.) | 312-588-1150 Ⓢ
Loop | 190 N. State St. (Lake St.) | 312-683-1234
Loop | 303 W. Madison St. (Franklin St.) | 312-346-1234 Ⓢ
Loop | 55 W. Monroe St. (bet. Clark & Dearborn Sts.) | 312-577-0070 Ⓢ
River North | 508 N. Clark St. (bet. Grand Ave. & Illinois St.) | 312-644-9131
River North | Shops at North Bridge | 520 N. Michigan Ave., 4th fl. (Grand Ave.) | 312-644-1008
Lakeview | 3424 N. Southport Ave. (bet. Newport Ave. & Roscoe St.) | 773-289-1807
Lincoln Park | 1422 W. Webster Ave. (Clybourn Ave.) | 773-755-1234
Lincoln Park | 2264 N. Lincoln Ave. (bet. Belden & Webster Aves.) | 773-528-1405
www.potbelly.com
Additional locations throughout the Chicago area

"For a quick, economical lunch", they keep the "cattle line" "moving" at this "multitude" of "reliable" relatives serving "unique" "toasted sandwiches" that Dagwoods deem "better than fast-food burgers" "at a very competitive price" (it's Milwaukee's Best Buy); "location doesn't matter", the goods "are always hot and fresh" and noshers note "live music adds to the experience" (it varies by location) so that even those who name it "nothing special" concede it's "better than other chains."

Praga Ⓜ *American/Eclectic*

- | - | - | M

Lombard | 229 W. St. Charles Rd. (bet. Elizabeth & Lincoln Sts.) | 630-495-0470 | www.pragabonton.com

Lombard locals laud this NewAmerican–Eclectic "gem" "for an enjoyable evening" over "tasty, authentic" dishes combined with a "diverse wine list" "that would cost much more in the city"; "helpful service" and "outdoor summer seating" "under umbrellas" add to the reasons "you can't beat it for the price."

	FOOD	DECOR	SERVICE	COST

Prairie Fire *American* | - | - | - | M |

West Loop | 215 N. Clinton St. (bet. Fulton & Lake Sts.) | 312-382-8300 |
www.prairiefirechicago.com

The power team behind North Suburban Prairie Grass Cafe migrates back downtown (chef-owners Sarah Stegner and George Bumbaris starred for years at the late, great Ritz-Carlton Dining Room), bringing its New American comfort food to the West Loop (some PGC signatures, some new dishes); the landmark building, formerly Powerhouse, is warmly lit and handsomely appointed in dark wood and earth tones with a modernized Prairie School vibe, plus there's weekend brunch, seasonal outdoor seating and a dine-at bar with house cocktails, a separate, lighter menu and plasma TVs.

Prairie Grass Cafe *American* | 22 | 19 | 21 | $37 |

Northbrook | 601 Skokie Blvd. (bet. Dundee & Lake Cook Rds.) |
847-205-4433 | www.prairiegrasscafe.com

"Celebrity chefs" Sarah Stegner and George Bumbaris "come down to earth" in Northbrook by serving "straightforward" New American comfort food "with élan" and the "best local ingredients" – including "homestyle desserts" and weekend brunch – supported by a "fine list of beers, wines and specialty drinks" in a "casual", "modern Arts and Crafts dining room"; some say "service could improve", but given the "accessible prices" and "downtown quality", most give a thumbs-up for "lunch or dinner, family or date night."

Prasino *American/Vegetarian* | - | - | - | M |

La Grange | 93 S. La Grange Rd. (Cossitt Ave.) | 708-469-7058
NEW **St. Charles** | 51 S. First St. (bet. Illinois & Main Sts.) |
630-908-5200
www.prasino.com

Green-minded, gourmet fare finds a home at these La Grange and St. Charles New Americans offering midpriced, all-day menus with plenty of vegetarian and vegan options, plus organic drink lists; the contemporary, eco-chic settings are rendered in reclaimed materials, from the bare wood tables to the light fixtures, and a third location is planned for the Bucktown/Wicker Park area.

NEW Pret A Manger 🗷 *Sandwiches* | - | - | - | I |

Loop | 100 N. LaSalle St. (bet. Randolph & Washington Sts.) | 312-660-9494
Loop | 211 W. Adams St. (Wells St.) | 312-546-8270
www.pret.com

This London-based sandwich chain arrives in the Loop to tempt weekday office workers with a changing array of quality, ready-made sammies, salads and wraps, displayed in a gleaming refrigerated case and grabbed to-go or enjoyed in digs with floor-to-ceiling windows; P.S. the day's leftovers are donated to charity.

NEW Prince Creperie Ⓜ *Crêpes/French* | - | - | - | I |

Albany Park | 4645 N. Kedzie Ave. (bet. Eastwood & Leland Aves.) |
773-681-6563 | www.princecreperie.com

A massive lunch and dinner menu of affordable, authentic Parisian crêpes (sweet and savory), salads, smoothies and exotic tea drinks is the draw at this Albany Park BYO; the tiny storefront by the El stop is warmed by a friendly proprietor, cozy booths, traditional Middle Eastern rugs and background music.

NEW Prix Fixe 🛇Ⓜ *French/Italian* | - | - | - | M |

Lincoln Square | 4835 N. Western Ave. (bet. Gunnison St. & Lawrence Ave.) | 773-681-0651 | www.dineprixfixe.com

A compact space with an open kitchen, local art and warm, low lighting is home to this casual Lincoln Square arrival that, true to its name, offers frequently changing prix fixe menus featuring French- and Italian-inflected fare fashioned from local, seasonal ingredients; both the chef and GM have worked as culinary instructors, hence the staff includes Le Cordon Bleu students gaining hands-on experience; P.S. it serves beer and wine but you can also BYO ($5 corkage).

Prosecco 🛇 *Italian* | 24 | 23 | 23 | $57 |

River North | 710 N. Wells St. (bet. Huron & Superior Sts.) | 312-951-9500 | www.ristoranteprosecco.com

Bubbly boosters say this "sophisticated" River Norther cooks up regional dishes "with a little twist" while pouring from an "extensive" exclusively Italian wine list, all delivered by an "accommodating", "professional" staff in a "warm, comfortable, Venetian-style" setting that includes a "huge bar"; it's "not cheap", but the fare is "satisfying" and "reliable", and most agree it's an "enjoyable" "experience overall" for a "romantic" "date" or "dinner with friends."

Province 🛇 *American* | 23 | 22 | 22 | $48 |

West Loop | 161 N. Jefferson St. (bet. Lake & Randolph Sts.) | 312-669-9900 | www.provincerestaurant.com

Chef Randy Zweiban's "great instincts" combine with "locally sourced ingredients" for a "lovely", "inventive" "seasonal" New American menu with Latin and Spanish "accents" offered in "various plate sizes" at this "green" West Looper in a LEED-certified building; the "smart, sleek" dining room is decorated with "natural branches", the "cocktails are fabulous" and there's an "interesting wine list", and though a faction of faultfinders say there's "more style than substance", most find the staff "knowledgeable."

🗷 Publican, The *American* | 25 | 20 | 22 | $47 |

West Loop | 837 W. Fulton Mkt. (Green St.) | 312-733-9555 | www.thepublicanrestaurant.com

Those who "do swine and brew totally dig" this "unique" West Loop "pork paradise" "from the team that brought us Avec and Blackbird", an "offal good place" that "caters to the well-heeled hipster" willing to "get out of the comfort zone and try something new" from a "wonderfully innovative" New American pub menu paired with an "extensive" "beer selection like no other"; be prepared for a "loud atmosphere" with "European flair" in the farmhouse-style setting with "communal tables" (or "swinging-door pens" "for more privacy"), and know that the "knowledgeable staff" is "overwhelmed at times"; P.S. the owners were working on their nearby butcher/bakery at press time.

	FOOD	DECOR	SERVICE	COST

NEW Public House *Pub Food*

	-	-	-	M

River North | 400 N. State St. (Kinzie St.) | 312-265-1240 |
www.publichousechicago.com

A handwritten menu of American gastropub eats (bowls of mussels three ways, mac 'n' cheese with numerous filling options, lobster pot pie, flatbreads and smokehouse meats) pairs with cocktails and a cicerone's lengthy beer list at this sprawling River North tavern; some of the booths feature pour-it-yourself table taps (issuing beer and booze), and there's also DJ entertainment, 20-plus plasmas and massive windows that open to the street in warmer weather.

Puck's at the MCA ☒ *American*   20 | 21 | 18 | $33

Streeterville | Museum of Contemporary Art | 220 E. Chicago Ave. (Mies van der Rohe Way) | 312-397-4034 | www.mcachicago.org

"For lunch when mind and feet give out" in Streeterville's Museum of Contemporary Art, Wolfgang Puck's "informal" "respite" delivers "better-than-average" midpriced New American fare ("there's nothing like the Chinois chicken salad") and a Sunday "brunch buffet" that's "over the top" in a "pretty" space with a "delightful outdoor terrace" showcasing "beautiful city and lake views"; P.S. museum admission is not required to dine.

Purple Pig, The ◐ *Mediterranean*   - | - | - | M

River North | 500 N. Michigan Ave. (Illinois St.) | 312-464-1744 | www.thepurplepigchicago.com

Talent from Heaven on Seven and Mia Francesca have teamed up for this River North Med offering midpriced sharing plates heavy on the pig parts, plus a wine list with numerous selections by the glass, quartino or half-bottle; the sleek space features communal hightops, a white marble bar and outdoor seating overlooking the Mag Mile, while design highlights include reclaimed wood floors, wine barrels and illuminated menu descriptions; P.S. food is served until midnight (1 AM on weekends).

Quartino ◐ *Italian*   21 | 18 | 21 | $32

River North | 626 N. State St. (Ontario St.) | 312-698-5000 | www.quartinochicago.com

"A lovely assortment" of "small-plate Italian dishes", "authentic pizzas" and "addictive housemade salumi" for "sharing" are served up at this "loud, happening", moderately priced River North trattoria that's usually "packed solid"; tables "are very close, so be prepared to get friendly" and when it's "mayhem" service gives some "agita", but "outstanding" "cheap" "wine by the carafe" helps as does "outdoor seating" – plus it's one of the "best late-night options" in the area (1 AM most nights, midnight Sundays); P.S. "definitely try the housemade limoncello."

Quince ☒ *American*   23 | 23 | 24 | $53

Evanston | Homestead Hotel | 1625 Hinman Ave. (Davis St.) | 847-570-8400 | www.quincerestaurant.net

Despite "chef turnovers", this "exceptionally pleasant" New American "hidden in a residential" Evanston hotel issues "innovative preparations" of pricey New American cuisine "with flair" and an "admirable wine list" ferried by an "accommodating staff" (that's earned a boost in scores); the "warm, relaxing" setting includes a "handsome porch", and while a few left "disappointed", most want to "go back."

Raj Darbar *Indian*

▽ 18 | 13 | 18 | $29

Lincoln Park | 2660 N. Halsted St. (Wrightwood Ave.) | 773-348-1010 | www.rajdarbar.com

Lincoln Park's "go-to" for "decent Indian food" at a "decent value" including "delicious tikka masala" and "biryani" (plus an "excellent Sunday lunch buffet"), this subcontinental longtimer also offers "attentive" service from a "well-meaning" staff and is a "favorite" "for delivery" with a wide geographic range.

NEW Raj Palace *Indian*

- | - | - | I

Schaumburg | 855-57 E. Schaumburg Rd. (bet. Pleasant Dr. & Roselle Rd.) | 847-524-3007 | www.rajpalace.net

A big menu of classic Indian fare is washed down with lassi drinks or concoctions from the full bar at this Suburban Northwest standby; plush booths, colorful lighting and white tablecloths give the shopping-center space an upscale feel, but prices are affordable – and deal-hunters will appreciate the daily bargain lunch buffet.

Ras Dashen *Ethiopian*

▽ 23 | 18 | 22 | $30

Edgewater | 5846 N. Broadway (bet. Ardmore & Rosedale Aves.) | 773-506-9601 | www.rasdashenchicago.com

Ethiopian fare including "terrific fish" "ranges from very mild to quite spicy", so there's "something for everyone" at this flatware-free, "lovely, authentic-feeling" Edgewater eatery; "service can be hit-or-miss on a crowded night", but it's "friendly" and the Friday "live music" is "not too loud for conversation"; P.S. a beer list includes some regional selections, and there's also outdoor seating.

RA Sushi *Japanese*

19 | 18 | 16 | $35

Gold Coast | 1139 N. State St. (Elm St.) | 312-274-0011
Glenview | 2601 Aviator Ln. (Patriot Blvd.) | 847-510-1100
Lombard | Shops on Butterfield | 310 Yorktown Ctr. (Highland Ave.) | 630-627-6800
www.rasushi.com

"Decent sushi" in "creative combos" and a selection of Japanese hot dishes are the draw at this midpriced city and suburban chain; surveyors call out the "happy-hour deals", "sake selection" and other drinks, though "service is spotty", and those who mark it "mediocre" maintain it's "not bad, but you won't hear a 'ra' from me either."

RB Grille *Seafood/Steak*

- | - | - | M

River North | Rock Bottom Brewery | 1 W. Grand Ave. (State St.) | 312-755-0890 | www.rbgrille.com

The River North location of the Rock Bottom Brewery chain grows a 'grille' with this more upscale (but still affordable) steak-and-seafood concept set in a refined, warm-brown space done up with wood paneling, shimmering drapery and candles; P.S. the brewery's beer list is offered on tap, along with a large wine list with plenty of by-the-glass options.

Real Tenochtitlán ⓜ *Mexican*

▽ 20 | 15 | 19 | $36

Logan Square | 2451 N. Milwaukee Ave. (bet. Richmond St. & Sacramento Ave.) | 773-227-1050 | www.realtenochtitlan.com

Supporters say "if you can swallow the name, you'll love" the "luscious moles and other Mexican specialties" at Geno Bahena's "high-end" yet moderately priced "out-of-the-way" Logan Square BYO where "service aims to please" in a colorful, rustic setting; what some call "pedestrian" fare "with a few sophisticated exceptions", others dub "tasty and satisfying."

NEW Real Urban Barbecue *BBQ*

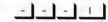

Highland Park | Port Clinton Square Shopping Ctr. | 610 Central Ave., Ste. 177 (2nd St.) | 224-770-4227 | www.realurbanbbq.com

A 'cue master who spent time on the competition circuit is smoking and saucing the meats at this citified North Suburban BYO where the budget-friendly menu includes babybacks and St. Louis–style ribs (wet, dry or rubbed), sandwiches (available in mini sizes) and unexpected sides such as cranberry bread pudding, flame-roasted Fuji apples and sweet potato soufflé; the funky counter-service setting sports corrugated metal counters and wall treatments, retro advertising signs and a ceramic animal and cookie jar collection

Red Brick *Eclectic/Mediterranean*

Lakeview | 1938 W. Irving Park Rd. (bet. Damen & Wolcott Aves.) | 773-904-8540 | www.redbrickchicago.com

Casual Mediterranean and Eclectic comfort foods feed Lakeview locals at this low-cost neighborhood spot serving everything from falafel to meatball sandwiches to chili to steaks; the low-key environs are done up with yellow brick walls adorned with framed photos and vintage ads, and seating options include red leather banquettes and a fireplace-equipped front lounge; P.S. the bar boasts 10 plasma screens tuned to the games.

NEW Redd Herring *American*

- | - | - | M

Clarendon Hills | 31 S. Prospect Ave. (bet. Ann St. & Park Ave.) | 630-908-7295 | www.redd-herring.com

Socca chef-owner Roger Herring is the namesake behind this casual, wood-and-brick-trimmed Clarendon Hills American bistro, whose moderately priced, contemporary comfort fare (including a rotating selection of pizzettes) is injected with French and Italian flavors; catering to a neighborhood crowd, its charms include a beyond-the-basics kids' menu plus a smart selection of wines and craft brews dispensed from a small copper-top bar.

NEW Redflame ⓜ *Pizza*

- | - | - | M

Lincoln Park | 2417 N. Clybourn Ave. (Marshfield Ave.) | 312-462-0486 | www.redflamepizza.com

Proud of its 'two step, two flame process' (first grilling, then cooking under a flame), this Clybourn Corridor pizza purveyor puts out 15-plus pies made with locally sourced ingredients; the wood-filled, tavernlike space features a mural of the Chicago skyline and an original century-old mahogany bar, and there's also seasonal outdoor seating.

Reel Club *Seafood*
23 | 21 | 22 | $42

Oak Brook | Oakbrook Center Mall | 272 Oakbrook Ctr. (Rte. 83) | 630-368-9400 | www.leye.com

Higher food and service scores support surveyors who say LEYE's Oak Brook mall fishery "has improved so much since it opened", with a "professional" staff delivering a variety of "delicious" "options for seafood lovers" (though "nothing too fancy") and an "interesting wine list" in contemporary digs; some say tabs are "reasonable", others "a bit overpriced", but most are reeled in for a "date", "weekend afternoon" or "after a day of shopping"; P.S. "in summer the outdoor seating" adds to the "happy" experience.

Retro Bistro Ⓜ *French*
23 | 18 | 23 | $41

Mt. Prospect | Mount Prospect Commons | 1746 W. Golf Rd. (Busse Rd.) | 847-439-2424 | www.retrobistro.com

Conjuring "memories of eating in France", this "friendly", "low-key" "shining star" in a "dumpy" Mount Prospect "strip mall" is "always reliable" for "excellent bistro" fare at a "wonderful value" (the prix fixe deals "cannot be beat"); fans "love the wine selection" and the "friendly, cozy bar" – plus "they're glad to have you as a customer."

Revolution Brewing ❶ *Pub Food*
- | - | - | M

Logan Square | 2323 N. Milwaukee Ave. (bet. California & Fullerton Aves.) | 773-227-2739 | www.revbrew.com

This hip Logan Square brewpub brings midpriced beer-friendly fare (burgers, salads, pizza) to a striking rehabbed historic building with tin ceilings, repurposed wood and vintage bourbon barrels (with light fixtures fashioned from the rusted hoops), a fireplace and an open kitchen; the big bar boasts 16 handles (10 house), 50-plus bottled beers and more than 25 American bourbons.

🆕 Rewster's Café Ⓜ *American*
- | - | - | I

Logan Square | 3152 W. Diversey Ave. (Kedzie Ave.) | 773-647-3432 | www.rewsterscafe.com

At this Logan Square arrival, expect an affordable counter-service menu of creative American cooking with French influences for breakfast and 'lunch' (served through the early dinner hour) along with baked goods, coffee drinks and fine teas (no alcohol); true to its name, roosters can be found through the casual neighborhood setting, which also includes colorful walls and tabletops, as well as WiFi access.

Reza's *Mediterranean/Mideastern*
18 | 14 | 18 | $28

River North | 432 W. Ontario St. (Orleans St.) | 312-664-4500
Andersonville | 5255 N. Clark St. (Berwyn Ave.) | 773-561-1898 ❶
Oak Brook | 40 N. Tower Rd. (Butterfield Rd.) | 630-424-9900
www.rezasrestaurant.com

"Plentiful" (some say "gigantic") portions and "huge" brunch and lunch buffets – not to mention "tasty, authentic Persian" options –

keep this Middle Eastern–Med trio "busy"; though most pundits appreciate the "laid-back" setting and "bountiful" choices – regulars advise for such an "affordable" tab "do not expect ambiance or pampered service" and you might even "bring your meat tenderizer."

Rhapsody *American*

| 20 | 21 | 21 | $50 |

Loop | Symphony Ctr. | 65 E. Adams St. (bet. Michigan & Wabash Aves.) | 312-786-9911 | www.rhapsodychicago.com

With its "emphasis on local ingredients", this "quiet" "pre-concert" "find" is favored for "creative" New American fare, a "convenient" Loop location adjacent to Symphony Center and "pleasant service"; while many "meaningful conversations" are sparked over the "fabulous" wine selection plus there's a "friendly bar" and "garden" patio that "doubles your enjoyment", thrifty types figure "it would be overpriced somewhere else."

Ria ⧄Ⓜ *American*

| - | - | - | E |

Gold Coast | The Elysian | 11 E. Walton St. (bet. Rush & State Sts.) | 312-880-4400 | www.riarestaurantchicago.com

The Gold Coast's Elysian is home to this opulent white-tablecloth destination offering visually striking American culinary creations with an emphasis on seafood and global flavors; there's also an encyclopedic wine list, and a champagne cart that rolls through the posh, sparkling space decorated with cushy banquettes, silk walls, silver leather chairs and a modern wall sculpture representing a school of fish.

Ribs 'n' Bibs ❶ *BBQ*

| 21 | 7 | 17 | $22 |

Hyde Park | 5300 S. Dorchester Ave. (53rd St.) | 773-493-0400

Dishing out "authentic" barbecue, this rustic Hyde Park carryout with limited indoor and outdoor seating sidesteps "pizzazz" to concentrate on its "great sauce" and "tender", "meaty ribs and tips"; it's considered "a must" for "U of C students after an evening of study", though regulars recommend leaving extra time, given "how lo-o-o-ng it takes" to get the goods.

Ⓩ Riccardo Trattoria *Italian*

| 27 | 19 | 23 | $46 |

Lincoln Park | 2119 N. Clark St. (bet. Dickens & Webster Aves.) | 773-549-0038 | www.riccardotrattoria.com

Dining at this "understated" Lincoln Park trattoria – the top-rated Italian in this Survey – "truly and genuinely" "brings back trips to Italy" say insiders, who prefer to steer the "masses" away from their "tiny gem" offering "fantastic" "classic" and "seasonal" dishes delivered by a "personable", "on-point staff"; a "delightful", simple setting with wood tables further evokes the "unpretentious" "spirit of Tuscany" for a "bargain" of a "special" experience that fans long to repeat "again and again."

NEW Rice Bistro Ⓜ *Thai*

| - | - | - | I |

Lakeview | 2964 N. Lincoln Ave. (bet. George St. & Wellington Ave.) | 773-880-9522 | www.ricebistrochicago.com

This charming, family-friendly neighborhood Thai 'bistro' in Lakeview offers inexpensive, classic cookery for lunch and dinner, with no-corkage BYO an added bonus; the serene, modern environs feature natural light streaming in from French doors and banquette seating, plus a sun-dappled outdoor patio in season.

Ringo *Japanese* - | - | - | M

Lincoln Park | 2507 N. Lincoln Ave. (bet. Fullerton Pkwy. & Wrightwood Ave.) | 773-248-5788 | www.ringosushi.com

"Don't tell anybody about the [frequent] all-you-can-eat sushi" promotion beg those hooked on this "dependable", "friendly" Japanese, a "more-affordable option in Lincoln Park" where the decor may be "lacking" but the "cheap" rolls – especially the signature "firecracker" – are "particularly tasty"; though the place is "unmemorable" to a few, any shortcomings can be remedied by "ordering out more often than dining in."

Rise *Japanese* 21 | 20 | 17 | $39

Wrigleyville | 3401 N. Southport Ave. (Roscoe St.) | 773-525-3535 | www.risesushi.com

Adherents "look for every excuse to return" to this midpriced Wrigleyville sib to Shine Morida and Sushi Taiyo that serves "creative sushi" in a "modern" setting with "floor-to-ceiling windows"; the Japanese fare "rises to the occasion" when dining with "girlfriends or for a date night" with "beautiful rolls and people" adding visual appeal, and though service swings from "friendly" to "snarky", it all "fits" the Southport "scene."

Risqué Café *BBQ* - | - | - | M

Lakeview | 3419 N. Clark St. (bet. Newport Ave. & Roscoe St.) | 773-525-7711 | www.risquechicago.com

Though it's "not for families", this "entertaining" "tongue-in-cheek" Lakeview "joint" – from the owner of the late Fixture and Meritage – is a "good-ol' barbecue" place say smoke-seekers who troll the "impressive" "binder full" of beer, single-malt scotch and whiskey amid "blood-red walls" "covered with pinups"; whether considered a perk or deterrent, edgy B-movies and vintage "soft-core porn" on the TV help pass time while waiting for the grub, which gets mixed reviews.

Ristorante al Teatro Ⓜ *Italian/Mediterranean* - | - | - | M

Pilsen | Thalia Hall | 1227 W. 18th St. (Allport St.) | 312-784-9100 | www.alteatro.us

"Trying hard and succeeding", this "simply addictive" Italian-Med set in Pilsen's historic Thalia Hall is a "pleasant surprise" with a midpriced menu that includes 20 kinds of pizza, "delicious" housemade gelato and coffee roasted on-site; the "lovely space" features columns, murals and vintage photos, plus a downstairs wine cellar with a water wall, and the "friendly staff" contributes to the "neighborhood feel"; P.S. Sunday brunch is an "amazing value."

Riva *Seafood* 20 | 22 | 20 | $54

Streeterville | Navy Pier | 700 E. Grand Ave. (Lake Shore Dr.) | 312-644-7482 | www.rivanavypier.com

"Request a table by the window" at this "elegant" Streeterville seafooder to best appreciate the "beautiful" "skyline" and "shimmering" "lake views"; though it's "expensive" and perhaps not for the "typical Navy Pier tourist", it's an oasis of "calm" for those heading to the "Shakespeare Theater" or attending a "business conference", though service is sometimes "not up to par."

R.J. Grunts *American*   19 | 16 | 19 | $23

Lincoln Park | 2056 N. Lincoln Park W. (bet. Armitage & Dickens Aves.) | 773-929-5363 | www.rjgruntschicago.com

"Melman's original" "Lettuce" restaurant in Lincoln Park "still serves up the '70s in warmth and style" along with American "cheap eats" delivered by a "friendly staff" in a "down-to-earth" "dive" setting – albeit a "packed" one – adorned with photos of employees; those who "need a fix" hit the "salad bar" ("it was the first in Chicago and remains one of the best") or order it alongside burgers or Sunday brunch and chow down to a "throwback soundtrack" while "loving that things never change here."

⚡ RL *American*   23 | 26 | 23 | $53

Gold Coast | 115 E. Chicago Ave. (Michigan Ave.) | 312-475-1100 | www.rlrestaurant.com

Shoppers "doing the Mag Mile" pepper the "elegant clientele" at this "classy" Gold Coaster that exudes a "members-only" feel with its "chichi" crowd and "graciously served" – if "exorbitantly" priced – "classic" American fare; located "next to his flagship store", it's just "what you would expect from Ralph Lauren" with a setting "decked out in leather" and a "fireplace in the bar" that appeals whether "you're a millionaire or just want to feel like one"; P.S. a seat in the "sidewalk cafe is a must in the summer."

Robinson's No. 1 Ribs *BBQ*   21 | 8 | 14 | $22

Loop | Union Station | 225 S. Canal St. (bet. Adams St. & Jackson Blvd.) | 312-258-8477 | www.rib1.com
Lincoln Park | 655 W. Armitage Ave. (Orchard St.) | 312-337-1399 | www.rib1.com
Oak Park | 940 W. Madison St. (Clinton St.) | 708-383-8452 | www.rib1.com

"Distinctive sauce" slathers "lip-smackingly delicious", "meaty" ribs at this affordable city and suburban "Chicago tradition" for "top-notch barbecue"; since "the atmosphere isn't much" and service "could be better", many prefer "takeout", but always come "back for more" – including "peach cobbler"; P.S. there's a dog-friendly patio in Lincoln Park.

Rockit Bar & Grill ◐ *American*   19 | 17 | 17 | $29

River North | 22 W. Hubbard St. (bet. Dearborn & State Sts.) | 312-645-6000
Wrigleyville | 3700 N. Clark St. (Waveland Ave.) | 773-645-4400 | www.rockitbarandgrill.com

A "young, hip crowd" chows down on "high-end" "bar food" from a menu printed on "dollar-bin vintage vinyl" at this "trendy" mid-priced River North American with a Wrigleyville sib; while the signature "Kobe burger" and "truffle fries" are "all that", the atmosphere is "laid-back" and the service "prompt", the less-impressed simply "focus on the drinks"; P.S. there's a build-your-own "Bloody Mary cart" during weekend brunch.

Roditys ● *Greek*

21 | 16 | 19 | $30

Greektown | 222 S. Halsted St. (bet. Adams St. & Jackson Blvd.) | 312-454-0800 | www.roditys.com

"Close the menu" and "trust" the waiters, who are "part of the ambiance" at this "family"-friendly Greektown "standard" dispensing "saganaki", "moussaka", "lamb in alternate preparations" and other "well-done" Hellenic fare; the "comfortable" setting might not be "quite as polished" as at higher-end spots, but the "convenient" location and "reasonable prices" make up for that.

Rolis Restaurant *Mexican*

- | - | - | I

Uptown | 5004 N. Sheridan Rd. (Argyle St.) | 773-728-6200

The new owners of Uptown's former Riques may have changed the name, but they've kept the same fresh, affordable BYO Mexican concept – think classic entrees and combination plates, tortas (sandwiches), seafood, omelets and other egg dishes; the colorful, casual setting offers well-spaced tables on a painted concrete floor with deep-blue and sunny-yellow walls.

Rollapalooza *Japanese*

- | - | - | I

Lakeview | 3344 N. Halsted St. (bet. Buckingham Pl. & Roscoe St.) | 773-281-6400 | www.rollapaloozachicago.com

Cravings for "creative rolls" are satisfied at this colorful Boystown neighborhood sushi spot, where the "variety" of "offerings" "won't disappoint"; coupled with service by "nice people", it's determined a "value" for both dining in and "takeout."

Rootstock Wine & Beer Bar ●◐ *American*

∇ 24 | 22 | 23 | $29

Humboldt Park | 954 N. California Ave. (Augusta Blvd.) | 773-292-1616 | www.rootstockbar.com

"Way cool" if "out of the way", this Humboldt Park "neighborhood joint" from Webster's Wine Bar vets offers "craft beers", a compact but "well-done wine list" and "excellent" midpriced New American small plates, charcuterie and cheeses; the funky digs include secondhand furniture, and when it comes to "pairing recommendations", the "welcoming, attentive" "hipster" staff is "spot on"; P.S. seasonal patio seating and late-night hours are a "real treat" too.

Ropa Restaurant & Wine Bar Ⓜ *Mediterranean*

- | - | - | M

Rogers Park | 1146 W. Pratt Blvd. (Sheridan Rd.) | 773-508-0002 | www.roparestaurant.com

Named for the Rogers Park neighborhood where it resides, this midpriced Mediterranean charmer with "high ceilings" and "big windows" in a "lovely" wood-and-tile dining room fills a "dire need" say option-strapped locals, serving "surprisingly good" salads, pasta, seafood and steaks; when service is "a bit slow", ordering a wine flight can pass the time; P.S. there's live piano on Wednesdays.

Rosal's Italian Kitchen ⬧ *Italian*   26 | 18 | 23 | $32

Little Italy/University Village | 1154 W. Taylor St. (Racine Ave.) | 312-243-2357 | www.rosals.com

Go ahead – "use the loaf of bread" to "chase the sauce" at this "simple" but "phenomenal" Little Italy Sicilian where "personable" servers and "authentic", "reasonably priced" "homemade Italian favorites" in "huge portions" make up for the "no-frills" setting; just keep in mind that it's akin to "eating at a friend's house", meaning the kitchen's delivery may be "slow"; P.S. there's a *"Big Night"*-themed menu the last Tuesday of the month.

Rosded Ⓜ *Thai*   - | - | - | I

Lincoln Square | 2308 W. Leland Ave. (Lincoln Ave.) | 773-334-9055

A massive lunch and dinner menu of old-guard, budget-friendly Thai fare lures Lincoln Square date-nighters and families to this long-running (since 1976) neighborhood BYO; the cozy wood-paneled space has a handful of tables, and takeout is an option too.

Rose Angelis Ⓜ *Italian*   24 | 20 | 22 | $32

Lincoln Park | 1314 W. Wrightwood Ave. (bet. Racine & Southport Aves.) | 773-296-0081 | www.roseangelis.com

Ravenous regulars "go hungry" to this "quaint", "financially affordable" Italian "institution" in Lincoln Park that's a popular pick for "first dates" and dinner with "friends" or "family"; "its strengths" – including "giant portions" of "rustic" fare and the "best patio imaginable" – are enough to keep tables in "high demand", especially with its no-reservations policy, though disheartened diners are "still not sure why people wait hours on weekends."

☑ Rosebud, The *Italian*   22 | 19 | 20 | $41

Little Italy/University Village | 1500 W. Taylor St. (Laflin St.) | 312-942-1117

☑ Rosebud Italian Specialties & Pizzeria *Italian*
(fka Rosebud Burger & Comfort Foods)

Naperville | 22 E. Chicago Ave. (bet. State St. and Wabash Ave.) | 630-548-9800

☑ Rosebud of Highland Park *Italian*

Highland Park | 1850 Second St. (Central Ave.) | 847-926-4800

☑ Rosebud of Schaumburg *Italian*

Schaumburg | 1370 Bank Dr. (Meacham Rd.) | 847-240-1414

☑ Rosebud on Rush *Italian*

Streeterville | 720 N. Rush St. (Superior St.) | 312-266-6444

☑ Rosebud Theater District ⬧ *Italian*

Loop | 3 First National Plaza | 70 W. Madison St. (bet. Clark & Dearborn Sts.) | 312-332-9500
www.rosebudrestaurants.com

Red sauce–seekers head for the "original" Taylor Street "cornerstone" and its "old-school" Italian cousins in the city and suburbs for "classics" in "large portions" at "reasonable prices"; though dissenters claim "incredibly loud" confines, "bland", "generic" preparations and "surly" service, fans still say they "can't eat there enough."

Rosebud Prime *Steak*   25 | 22 | 24 | $57

Loop | 1 S. Dearborn St. (Madison St.) | 312-384-1900

Rosebud Steakhouse *Steak*

Streeterville | 192 E. Walton St. (Mies van der Rohe Way) | 312-397-1000
www.rosebudrestaurants.com

Loop and Streeterville "movers and shakers" are "packed like sardines" into these "classy", "energetic" "business-lunch" and "pre-theater" beef "fixtures" that are rated the "best of the 'Buds'" by surveyors; an "impeccable" staff knows the "expensive" "steak and chop–driven menu" inside out; P.S. you might need "earplugs on weekends."

Rosebud Trattoria *Italian*   22 | 17 | 22 | $42

River North | 445 N. Dearborn St. (Illinois St.) | 312-832-7700 |
www.rosebudrestaurants.com

Part of the Rosebud *famiglia*, this "casual" River North offshoot serves "hearty" Italian classics such as meatballs "like mama used to make" as well as Roman-style thin-crust pies, daily fish selections and regional specialties on a seasonally changing menu; a "decent wine list", soft-colored decor with wood accents and "cheerful" service help keep things pleasant, even when it's "packed cheek to jowl."

Roti Mediterranean Grill *Mediterranean*   21 | 13 | 17 | $14

Loop | 310 W. Adams St. (bet. Franklin St. & Lower Wacker Dr.) |
312-236-3500 | www.rotiusa.com Ⓢ

NEW Loop | 33 N. Dearborn St. (bet. Calhoun Pl. & Washington St.) |
312-263-9000 | www.roti.com Ⓢ

River West | 10 S. Riverside Plaza (bet. Madison & Monroe Sts.) |
312-775-7000 | www.rotiusa.com Ⓢ

Northbrook | 984 Willow Rd. (Three Lakes Dr.) | 847-418-2400 |
www.rotiusa.com

Vernon Hills | 1240 Rte. 45 E. (bet. Hickory Ave. & Shady Ln.) |
847-883-8800 | www.rotiusa.com

"Healthy", "delicious choices" of "quick", "counter-service" Mediterranean fare is served "cafeteria-style" at this chain catering to Loop lunch-breakers and their suburban counterparts; considering the "good value" and "quality", surveyors warn "expect to compete for a chair" for a payoff that's "refreshingly enjoyable."

Roy's *Hawaiian*   25 | 23 | 23 | $53

River North | 720 N. State St. (Superior St.) | 312-787-7599 |
www.roysrestaurant.com

"Visit the islands" without leaving town at this "transcendent" River North catch, a "stylish", tropically decorated link in the Hawaiian chain where the "fusion" fare – including "butterfish that melts in your mouth" – hooks its share of fanatics; it's just "like every other Roy's" down to an "attentive yet unobtrusive staff", and if cost-crunchers carp that it's "expensive", the "prix fixe is a deal."

NEW Rub BBQ Company Ⓜ *BBQ*   - | - | - | I

West Rogers Park | 2407 W. Lunt Ave. (Western Ave.) | 773-675-1410 |
www.rubbbqcompany.com

This family-owned West Rogers Park 'cue shack focuses on a handful of meaty faves including St. Louis–style ribs, brisket and pulled pork or chicken, all hand-rubbed in 14 spices, slow-smoked in hickory and accompanied by fresh sides like a 'spiral staircase of cheese' (rotini with five cheeses) and custard-filled cornbread; the super-casual counter-service setting is dotted with padded booths, and there's a wall of reclaimed barn wood sporting a handful of country-themed signs.

Ruby of Siam *Thai* | 23 | 14 | 20 | $18

Loop | 170 W. Washington St. (bet. LaSalle Blvd. & Wells St.) | 312-609-0000 🈂

Skokie | Skokie Fashion Sq. | 9420 Skokie Blvd. (Gross Point Rd.) | 847-675-7008

www.rubyofsiam.com

Siam Splendour *Thai*

Evanston | 1125 Emerson St. (Ridge Ave.) | 847-492-1008 | www.siamsplendour.com

With possibly the "biggest Thai menu in town", these Skokie (BYO) and Evanston (now with a new name and managment) outposts turn out "outstanding" Siamese "standards" – plus "dishes not often seen" – for patrons who don't mind less-than-stellar decor and service considering the "affordable", "high-quality" fare; fans say the "lunch buffet is a buy" and a convenient "way to introduce novices to the pleasures" of the cuisine; P.S. there's also a Loop BYO locale.

NEW Rudy's Bar & Grille ◐ *American* | - | - | - | M

Loop | 69 E. Madison St. (State St.) | 312-332-8111 | www.rudysbarandgrillechicago.com

A scion of the Malnati pizza clan is behind this casual prime burger boîte in the Loop that also dishes up American comfort foods along with cocktails, craft beers, shakes and even 'milkshake martinis'; the bustling tavern setting boasts funky light fixtures and vintage photos, and night owls will like that the bar is open late on Saturdays.

Rumba 🈂Ⓜ *Nuevo Latino* | ▽ 23 | 24 | 25 | $48

River North | 351 W. Hubbard St. (bet. N. Kingsbury & N. Orleans Sts.) | 312-222-1226 | www.chicagorumba.com

Salsa "dancing on the weekends" (the "floor gets packed") and "people-watching" add to the "lively" vibe at this River North supper club that also dishes up Nuevo Latino plates; the setting – floor-to-ceiling red velvet curtains, overstuffed booths – is as "excellent" as the drinks, which include a signature punch and classic mojito, but the initiated warn that "service goes downhill" when the decibels rise.

Russell's Barbecue *BBQ* | 19 | 9 | 14 | $16

Rolling Meadows | 2885 Algonquin Rd. (bet. Carriageway & Newport Drs.) | 847-259-5710

Elmwood Park | 1621 N. Thatcher Ave. (North Ave.) | 708-453-7065

www.russellsbarbecue.com

Opened in 1930, this Elmwood Park "landmark" dishes out barbecue "for the ages" say devotees who chow down on the beef and "pork sandwiches" and other "low-cost", "family-friendly" fare served on "paper plates"; though it "never changes" (including the "simple decor") and doubters are "bewildered by all the fuss", nostalgists contend the original "classic" and its Rolling Meadows mate remain "venerable" choices for "ribs and a beer."

Russian Tea Time *Russian*　　　22 | 22 | 22 | $40

Loop | 77 E. Adams St. (bet. Michigan & Wabash Aves.) | 312-360-0000 | www.russianteatime.com

"Borscht" boosters flock to this "atmospheric" (some say "weird, dark") mahogany-paneled Loop spot serving "authentic", "filling" Russian cuisine, afternoon tea and "vodka flights" that "sneak up on you"; naysayers think it needs "new energy" and is "a little over-priced", but pluses include its "convenient location near the Art Institute" and "pleasant service" that adds to the "civility."

☑ Ruth's Chris Steak House *Steak*　　25 | 20 | 23 | $62

River North | 431 N. Dearborn St. (Hubbard St.) | 312-321-2725
Northbrook | Renaissance North Shore Hotel | 933 Skokie Blvd. (Dundee Rd.) | 847-498-6889
South Barrington | Arboretum Mall | 100 W. Higgins Rd. (Rte. 59) | 847-551-3730
www.ruthschris.com

"Prime steaks sizzling in butter" keep herds of carnivores coming to this "big-box" chophouse chain (born in the bayou) with River North and suburban locations, where the "delicious, unique" beef presen-tion includes a "hot platter"; the "men's club atmosphere" and ser-vice that's "their trademark" make it suitable for a special "occasion", with the tabs to match.

NEW Ruxbin **Ⓜ** *Eclectic*　　　- | - | - | M

Noble Square | 851 N. Ashland Ave. (Pearson St.) | 312-624-8509 | www.ruxbinchicago.com

There's an enthusiastic, youthful team behind this funky, urban Noble Square BYO where the Eclectic menu from Edward Kim, who externed at Per Se, melds Asian, Euro and American influences; the cozy, low-lit setting is rife with raw and industrial elements like re-claimed wood, fruit-shipping crates and pages torn from old cook-books, plus seating options that make use of seat belts, old theater chairs, church pews and used leather jackets; P.S. no reserving.

Sabatino's **●** *Italian*　　　24 | 17 | 24 | $33

Northwest Side | 4441 W. Irving Park Rd. (bet. Cicero & Pulaski Aves.) | 773-283-8331 | www.sabatinoschicago.com

"You keep waiting for the Rat Pack to stroll in" at this "cavernous" Northwest Side "flashback" decked out in dimly lit "'70s decor" and serving "large portions" of "flaming" "tableside" dishes along with its "old-fashioned", "red-gravy Italian" fare (plus "value"-minded "specials"); though it isn't "hard on the pocketbook", the "Midwest-style service" is "wonderful" and "it's impossible to leave hungry."

Sable Kitchen & Bar **●** *American*　　- | - | - | M

River North | Hotel Palomar | 505 N. State St. (Illinois St.) | 312-755-9704 | www.sablechicago.com

At this swanky gastro-lounge in River North's Kimpton boutique ho-tel, chef Heather Terhune (ex Atwood Cafe) crafts small, medium and large plates of midpriced, locavore-friendly New American fare, plus brick-oven flatbreads, accompanied by an ambitious cocktail program; the updated 'supper club' setting features cushy leather booths, a big bar, a fireplace and a seasonal patio.

Sabor Saveur Ⓜ *French/Mexican* — | — | — | M

Ukrainian Village | 2013 W. Division St. (Damen Ave.) | 773-235-7310 | www.saborsaveur.com

"Adventuresome" French-Mexican cuisine is on the menu "full of treats" (including "delicious" hazelnut-sauced lobster enchiladas) cooked up in the open kitchen of this midpriced Ukrainian Village hybrid; the painted white-brick dining room features "white table-cloths", candles in ornate holders and a gallerylike feel, while in the rear a curvaceous "more casual" communal area accommodates "larger parties"; P.S. it's "BYO at the moment."

Sai Café *Japanese* 25 | 16 | 20 | $41

Lincoln Park | 2010 N. Sheffield Ave. (Armitage Ave.) | 773-472-8080 | www.saicafe.com

"Solid sushi" from "friendly", "skilled chefs" draws devotees to this "reliable" Lincoln Park Japanese "neighborhood place" where "portions are large" and diners feel "welcome"; though some find it a little "expensive" with a "limited" wine and sake list, three differently decorated rooms lure everyone from "singles" to "seniors" to "families."

NEW Saigon Grill Ⓢ *Chinese/Vietnamese* — | — | — | I

Jefferson Park | 5736 N. Elston Ave. (bet. Major & Parkside Aves.) | 773-628-7156

A no-frills counter-service BYO, this Jefferson Parker serves a small menu of inexpensive Vietnamese and Chinese fare (egg rolls, fried rice, skewers and noodles), cooked to order for lunch and dinner; the salmon-colored storefront exterior gives way to a spare, mint-green interior with two dining rooms and a cut-out that provides a peek into the kitchen.

NEW Saigon Sisters Ⓢ *Vietnamese* — | — | — | I

West Loop | 567 W. Lake St. (bet. Clinton & Jefferson Sts.) | 312-496-0090 | www.saigonsisters.com

This casual West Loop sib to the French Market food stand of the same name serves a changing menu of affordable Vietnamese street food faves – pho, banh mi and spring rolls – plus creative modern dishes such as caramel chicken wings with lemongrass, ginger and chiles; lunch and dinner are offered daily.

NEW Sakura *Japanese* — | — | — | M

Logan Square | 2507 W. Fullerton Ave. (Campbell Ave.) | 773-772-4412 | www.satkura.com

Signature maki with elaborate presentations and unusual names (Gnome, Nightelf) plus a handful of Mexican fusion items and a full complement of classic sushi, starters and entrees fill the lunch, dinner and light-night menus at this modern Japanese BYO in Logan Square; warm lighting reflects off of orange walls in a cozy dining room with elegant tablecloths, a sushi bar and, in a nod to the name, a faux cherry blossom installation.

NEW Salatino's & Doughboys *Italian*   - | - | - | M

Little Italy/University Village | 626 S. Racine Ave. (Harrison St.) | 312-226-9300

At this double-duty Little Italy dining concept from Francesca's father Scott Harris, family recipes revived from the onetime neighborhood favorite Gennaro's make up the midpriced menu at Salatino's, a warm trattoria setting with red-checkered tablecloths, a tin ceiling and '50s-era photography; next door in a quaint brick row house, Doughboys dishes out pizzas (including a gargantuan nine-ft. version), salads and sandwiches.

Saloon Steakhouse *Steak*   23 | 20 | 22 | $56

Streeterville | Seneca Hotel | 200 E. Chestnut St.
(Mies van der Rohe Way) | 312-280-5454 | www.saloonsteakhouse.com
An "alternative to the see-and-be-seen" options, this "busy" Streeterville steakhouse "well-hidden" in the Seneca Hotel serves "great food without the 'tude", "tourists" or "uptightness"; the "neighborhood" clientele calls it a "value" for its "jumbo martinis", "insanely sized portions" and "outstanding rib-eyes" as much as the "retro"-meets-"metro" setting, "attentive, knowledgeable" service and the ability to "hear your own conversation."

Salpicón *Mexican*   26 | 20 | 23 | $49

Old Town | 1252 N. Wells St. (bet. Goethe & Scott Sts.) | 312-988-7811 | www.salpicon.com
Amigos attest this "smolderingly sublime", "upscale" Old Towner offers "genius" "modern Mexican creations" (such as "finger-licking-good quail") from Priscila Satkoff along with an "outstanding" tequila selection and a wine list that's "one of the best around"; while a "lively" colorful space that's "relatively small and challenged" leaves some "begging for more comfortable seating", "super-personal service" adds incentive to "look for excuses to return"; a post-Survey remodeling is not reflected in the Decor score.

Salsa 17 *Mexican*   22 | 21 | 21 | $29

Arlington Heights | 17 W. Campbell St. (bet. Dunton & Vail Aves.) | 847-590-1122 | www.salsa17.com
"Upscale compared to most" "neighborhood Mexican" cantinas, this renamed Arlington Heights spot offers an "extensive menu" of moderately priced "inventive dishes" ("don't miss the moles"), "guacamole made fresh tableside" and "great margaritas"; it's "fun" "for couples or family" but even amigos find the "noise level" "overwhelming" on "mariachi band nights."

Sam & Harry's Steakhouse *Steak*   - | - | - | E

Schaumburg | Renaissance Schaumburg Hotel & Convention Ctr. | 1551 N. Thoreau Dr. (Meacham Rd.) | 847-303-4050 | www.samandharrys.com
"Sweet", "succulent" crab legs and aged prime Delmonico and other steaks net regulars and conventioneers at this national chain link

	FOOD	DECOR	SERVICE	COST

that's "a bit hidden" in the Renaissance Schaumburg Hotel; generally "attentive service" and "impressive decor" are pluses, though some call the "quality"-to-"money" ratio "just ok."

San Gabriel Mexican Cafe   *Mexican* | 17 | 15 | 14 | $31 |

Bannockburn | Bannockburn Green Shopping Ctr. | 2535 Waukegan Rd. (Half Day Rd.) | 847-940-0200 | www.sangabcafe.com

"Excellent" "tableside-made guacamole", an extensive tequila selection and "margaritas with fresh-squeezed lime juice" attract spice-lovers to this upscale, midpriced Bannockburn hacienda in a "strip mall" – one of the few options for "Mexican in Lake County"; though a few shrug there's "nothing memorable" about the menu, the decor is "authentic" and there's "outdoor seating in the summer too."

Sanook   *Japanese/Thai* | - | - | - | M |

North Center/St. Ben's | 2845 W. Irving Park Rd. (Mozart St.) | 773-463-7299 | www.sanookchicago.com

There's a clubby vibe to this contemporary, midpriced Pan-Asian BYO in North Center, where faraway landscapes are projected on walls and a large menu of "competently prepared Thai dishes" and inventive sushi reel in a crowd; those who are "unimpressed" find the blue-and-white setting "sterile" and the service "lacking."

San Soo Gab San ● *Korean* | ∇ 21 | 12 | 14 | $31 |

Lincoln Square | 5247 N. Western Ave. (Foster Ave.) | 773-334-1589

When late-night kalbi cravings hit, surveyors navigate to the Northwest Side and this midpriced "Korean barbecue joint" in Lincoln Square, where the tables are filled with "little [side] dishes"; sure, it helps to "know Korean" and the "smoky" scent leaves diners ready to "shower afterwards", but that's a small price to pay for such "consistently" "delicious" grub – even "at 2 AM."

Santorini ● *Greek/Seafood* | 21 | 20 | 20 | $37 |

Greektown | 800 W. Adams St. (Halsted St.) | 312-829-8820 | www.santorinichicago.com

Shouts of "*opa!*" punctuate this "inviting" Halsted Street "taverna" that "excels at seafood" – including "terrific chargrilled octopus" – and other "reasonably priced" fare offered with "gracious service"; loyalists swear it was "transplanted straight from the Aegean" and is "a cut above most Greektown places", particularly when in the "cozy bar" or by the "warm fireplace in winter", plus it's a "hit with a group"; P.S. "valet parking" is complimentary.

Sapore di Napoli Ⓜ *Pizza* | ∇ 20 | 9 | 16 | $23 |

Lakeview | 1406 W. Belmont Ave. (Southport Ave.) | 773-935-1212 | www.saporedinapoli.net

"An alternative to Chicago deep-dish", the "Neapolitan pizzas" at this kid-friendly Lakeview BYO – "thin-crust", "wood-fired" pies topped with the "freshest of ingredients" – are a "great getaway" from their heftier competitors, whether dining in or doing takeout; a "selection of gelato", an open kitchen and thrifty tabs are added reasons to frequent the small, casual, earth-toned storefront; P.S. no reserving.

	FOOD	DECOR	SERVICE	COST

Sapori Trattoria *Italian*

| | 23 | 18 | 23 | $36 |

Lincoln Park | 2701 N. Halsted St. (Schubert Ave.) | 773-832-9999 | www.saporitrattoria.net

"Families" and other locals flock to this Lincoln Park "neighborhood trattoria" where the "simple", "consistent" midpriced Italian fare includes handmade pasta and desserts that "shine"; regulars know to "make a reservation" and request "outdoor seating in summer", as it's sometimes "impossible to talk" in the "cozy interior" with "warm brick and low lighting"; a "helpful staff", "reasonably priced wines" and "frequent diner's discounts" sweeten the deal.

Sarkis Cafe ⊯ *Diner*

| | ∇ 15 | 5 | 13 | $14 |

Evanston | 2632 Gross Point Rd. (Crawford St.) | 847-328-9703

"Colorful local characters" and "Northwestern kids" "with hangovers" wolf down breakfasts (especially omelets) and other cheap diner fare – including a famed, cheesy sausage sandwich dubbed the "disaster" – from Evanston's quintessential, if "small", "greasy spoon" with a name that pays homage to its "unique" original owner; though detractors assure the "fixture" is "stuck in '70s mode", cognoscenti concur if you're willing to "accept this place for what it is", it's generally "enjoyable."

Sarks in the Park *Sandwiches*

| | - | - | - | I |

Lincoln Park | 444 W. Fullerton Pkwy. (Clark St.) | 773-404-9000 | www.sarksinthepark.com

Lincoln Parkers "no longer have to drive to the suburbs", heading instead to this "popular" nook (a sibling of the Evanston original) for AM eats; it's a "knockout location for outdoor eating", though the "tiny" space and "complacent service" strike some as "nothing to write home about"; P.S. hours are expanded in summer.

NEW Sawtooth Restaurant & Lounge *Vietnamese*

| | - | - | - | M |

West Loop | 1350 W. Randolph St. (Ada St.) | 312-526-3320 | www.sawtoothrestaurant.com

Not your Little Vietnam staple, this ultramod Market District Vietnamese stands out from the pack with Eames chairs, a communal table and outdoor seating, as well as a second-floor lounge and semi-private dining; swanksters sup on midpriced fare both classic and modern – from spring rolls and chicken curry to lotus stem salad and stuffed roasted quail – paired with a serious choice of boutique and organic booze, craft brews and a sommelier-selected wine list.

Sayat Nova *Armenian*

| | 23 | 19 | 21 | $28 |

Streeterville | 157 E. Ohio St. (bet. Michigan Ave. & St. Clair St.) | 312-644-9159 | www.sayatnovachicago.com

"Wonderful aromas" greet devotees of this "friendly", "decades"-old Streeterville Armenian adorned with cut-out lanterns and "hidden" just "steps off Michigan Avenue"; even the "outstanding lamb" dishes "won't break the bank" – although a "parking space" may cost "twice the price" of a meal; P.S. a DJ spins Saturday nights.

	FOOD	DECOR	SERVICE	COST

☑ Schwa 🅢🅜 *American*

| | 29 | 15 | 25 | $105 |

Wicker Park | 1466 N. Ashland Ave. (Le Moyne St.) | 773-252-1466 | www.schwarestaurant.com

Zealots call Michael Carlson a "god among men" for his "fascinating" New American cuisine with "bright, surprising flavors" and a "side of wit"; the prix fixe menu is "served by the chefs", adding to an "unforgettable" experience that unfolds in a "relaxed", "small" Wicker Park BYO storefront; though it's "not inexpensive", fans contend it offers a "wonderful value", and if a few gripe that this "quirky" place comes off as "too complicated" for its own good, the fact that you must "persevere" to "secure a reservation" proves they're outvoted.

Scoozi! *Italian*

| | 19 | 20 | 20 | $36 |

River North | 410 W. Huron St. (bet. Kingsbury & Orleans Sts.) | 312-943-5900 | www.leye.com

"After all these years", this "consistent" River North Lettuce Entertain You Italian "standby" is still "buzzing with laughter" and crowds – complete with "squirmy kids" – in its art deco setting; service is "enthusiastic" and the thin-crust, brick-oven pizza and homemade gnocchi have fans, though dissenters suggest the midpriced "Americanized" fare and scene aren't "intended to be taken seriously."

🆕 Seadog Sushi Bar ➊ *Japanese*

| | - | - | - | M |

Noble Square | 1500 W. Division St. (Greenview Ave.) | 773-235-8100 | www.seadogsushibar.com

Creative contemporary Japanese fare at moderate prices is the draw at this neighborhood BYO in Noble Square; the funky storefront space features exposed brick, elaborate stone tile flooring and a sushi bar; P.S. dinner only.

☑ Seasons *American*

| | 27 | 25 | 27 | $83 |

Gold Coast | Four Seasons Hotel | 120 E. Delaware Pl., 7th fl. (bet. Michigan Ave. & Rush St.) | 312-649-2349 | www.fourseasons.com

Acolytes aver the "formal" experience "never fails" at this "swellegant" Gold Coast hotel eatery, where "fabulous" dining on chef Kevin Hickey's "innovative" seasonal New American cuisine merits the "big splurge"; even if the "room looks like every other Four Seasons", the view from the seventh floor combined with a "comfortable", "quiet" setting and "phenomenal" service make for a "perfect evening"; P.S. Sunday "brunch is wonderful."

Seasons 52 *American*

| | - | - | - | M |

Schaumburg | 1770 E. Higgins Rd. (bet. Mall Dr. & Martingale Rd.) | 847-517-5252 | www.seasons52.com

A national 'fresh grill' chain with a calorie-counting concept – no dish over 475 calories, including custom flatbreads and mini desserts – comes to Northwest Suburban Schaumburg serving midpriced New American lunch and dinner crafted with local ingredients, with 60 wines by the glass and specialty martinis from the bar; the handsome, upscale environment with warm wood and rustic stone elements features a fireplace and piano bar.

	FOOD	DECOR	SERVICE	COST

Semiramis ⊠ *Lebanese*
- | - | - | I

Albany Park | 4639 N. Kedzie Ave. (bet. Eastwood & Leland Aves.) | 773-279-8900 | www.semiramisrestaurant.com

Fresh, authentic Lebanese fare including a variety of vegetarian mezes (e.g. hummus, dolmas, tabbouleh) is offered at this intimate, inexpensive Albany Park outpost decorated with native textiles, elegant drapery and stained-glass pendant lighting; if you don't BYO, try their fresh lemonade or Arabic coffee with cardamom.

Sepia *American*
24 | 24 | 24 | $56

West Loop | 123 N. Jefferson St. (bet. Randolph & Washington Sts.) | 312-441-1920 | www.sepiachicago.com

"Interesting", "not too-clever" New American fare by NoMI vet Andrew Zimmerman – much of it "locavore" "riffs on classic dishes" – plus "fantastic" cocktails draw devotees to this "pricey", "beautiful", "modern" yet "warm" "Michelle Obama favorite" in the West Loop; "muted lighting" sparks "tête-à-têtes" (when it's not "monstrously noisy") and the "cordial" service can get "harried at times", but mostly it's "wonderful in every possible way."

1776 ⊠ *American*
22 | 18 | 22 | $40

Crystal Lake | 397 W. Virginia St./Rte. 14 (bet. Dole & McHenry Aves.) | 815-356-1776 | www.1776restaurant.com

Loyalists proclaim they're "treated like family" by the "informed staff" – starting with "owner Andy [Andresky], a font of wine advice" for the 600-bottle list – at this "reliable" "favorite in Crystal Lake" that dishes out "fair portions" of "inventive" New American cuisine including "wonderful game"; the setting is "comfortable", but the resistance reckons it's "getting old" and the sometimes "pricey" fare is not all "it should be"; still, "way out" in the Northwest Suburbs, "it's the best you'll find."

☑ Shanghai Terrace ⊠ *Asian*
25 | 28 | 27 | $66

River North | Peninsula Hotel | 108 E. Superior St., 5th fl. (bet. Michigan Ave. & Rush St.) | 312-573-6744 | www.chicago.peninsula.com

A "stunning", '30s-style Asian supper club setting sets the stage at this expensive, "elegant" and "tranquil" respite in the Peninsula Hotel in River North, where acolytes claim they've had some of the "best Chinese meals outside of China"; "wonderful" Michigan Avenue views from the "outdoor terrace" in summer add to the appeal, as does "knowledgeable" service, though the less-smitten are "disappointed" that the former "chef is gone"; P.S. lunch hours vary by season.

☑ Shaw's Crab House *Seafood*
24 | 21 | 23 | $50

River North | 21 E. Hubbard St. (bet. State St. & Wabash Ave.) | 312-527-2722

Schaumburg | 1900 E. Higgins Rd. (Rte. 53) | 847-517-2722
www.shawscrabhouse.com

"Like an old friend", this "justly crowded" River North "fish house" "favorite" (with a Schaumburg sibling) from Lettuce Entertain You

	FOOD	DECOR	SERVICE	COST

"always delivers" a "dependable" experience featuring "hand-shucked" bivalves, "huge king crab legs" and global, sustainably focused seafood served in the oyster bar and "throwback-chic" dining room; the "service can't be beat", but this "trip to the oceanside" "ain't cheap" – unless you just come for a "designer martini" and "great jazz" (Tuesdays, Thursdays and Sundays); P.S. both offer a popular Sunday brunch buffet.

Shine *Chinese/Japanese*
-	-	-	M

Lincoln Park | 756 W. Webster Ave. (Halsted St.) | 773-296-0101 | www.shinerestaurant.com

In Lincoln Park down the street from its original digs, this "dependable" Chinese–Japanese "combo" with two dining rooms – one dim and relaxed, the other a brighter sushi bar – remains a "cut above" your average "neighborhood" spot; it suits "any occasion" by appealing to "raw-fish-fearing friends" and fin fans alike thanks to its varied menu, "welcoming" staff and "hot" entrees in "huge portions for the price."

Shui Wah *Chinese*
∇ 24	4	13	$18

Chinatown | 2162 S. Archer Ave. (Cermak Rd.) | 312-225-8811

"Everyone knows how good it is" confirm cognoscenti of this budget-loving Chinatowner and its "excellent selection" of "no-frills dim sum" offered from breakfast through lunchtime (it's open for dinner too); salt-and-pepper squid, Hong Kong–style dumplings and such are ordered "off a list" rather than "carted around" the small, carpeted room – just "be prepared to wait" for a table.

Shula's Steakhouse *Steak*
21	20	20	$62

Streeterville | Sheraton Chicago Hotel & Towers | 301 E. North Water St. (Columbus Dr.) | 312-670-0788
Itasca | Westin Chicago NW | 400 Park Blvd. (Thorndale Ave.) | 630-775-1499
www.donshula.com

Cheerleaders of this "memorabilia"-laden steak chain promise "even Bears fans" feel at home at the Streeterville (dinner only) and Itasca outposts decorated in an undefeated 1972 Dolphins theme; diners who'd opt to "read a football rather than throw one" (the menu's printed on a pigskin) praise "large" cuts of beef, "comfortable booths" "roomy" enough for a "lineman" and service with "great humor", though some feel they "drop the ball" with the price.

Siboney Cuban Cuisine *Cuban*
-	-	-	I

Bucktown | 2165 N. Western Ave. (bet. Palmer St. & Shakespeare Ave.) | 773-276-8776 | www.siboneychicago.com

"Intensely flavorful" ropa vieja lures surveyors to Bucktown's "pretty" Cuban storefront with its bright, mural-decorated exterior; once inside the casual-chic, wood-trimmed dining room with moody lighting, vintage tin ceiling and slow-spinning tropical fans, expect "outstanding" service and "reasonable prices", with Latin jazz Friday and Saturday helping smooth out any missteps; P.S. an adjacent cafeteria has been added.

⚡ Signature Room *American*

FOOD 18 | DECOR 26 | SERVICE 19 | COST $54

Streeterville | John Hancock Ctr. | 875 N. Michigan Ave., 95th fl. (bet. Chestnut St. & Delaware Pl.) | 312-787-9596 | www.signatureroom.com

"When out-of-towners are in tow", surveyors "skip the Hancock Observatory" and head for this 95th-floor Streeterville American where the "view on a clear day" is so "priceless" that "marriage proposals arrive daily"; an "impressive" Sunday brunch and Saturday lunch buffet (an "unbelievable deal") are further incentives to overlook sometimes "erratic service", "dated" decor and "unpredictable" fare; P.S. don't forget to "check out" the vista "from the ladies' room."

Sikia Ⓜ *African*

– | – | – | M

Far South Side | Washburne Culinary Institute | 740 W. 63rd St. (Halsted St.) | 773-602-5200 | www.ccc.edu/sikia

This on-campus African restaurant is a "diamond in the rough", operated for dinner Thursday through Saturday by "students" at Englewood's Washburne Culinary Institute; the "vibrant" BYO – adorned with "interesting artwork" and "artifacts" – leaves most diners "surprised" by fare such as "wonderful tagines" delivered by a "hospitable staff" at moderate prices; P.S. Sunday brunch and live entertainment on weekends are added incentives.

🆕 Silom 12 *Thai*

– | – | – | M

Bucktown | 1846-48 N. Milwaukee Ave. (bet. Bloomington & Oakley Aves.) | 773-489-1212 | www.silom12chicago.com

Spicy, authentic Thai fare, vegetarian options and chef specialties like osso buco and crispy soft-shell crab meet on the menu at this midpriced Bucktown BYO situated in the former Cafe Matou digs; fresh flowers and a candle installation warm an otherwise minimalist, industrial black-and-white setting, complete with metal barstools and space-age molded chairs, a communal table and bare globe lighting.

Silver Seafood ❶ *Chinese/Seafood*

23 | 10 | 16 | $23

Uptown | 4829 N. Broadway (Lawrence Ave.) | 773-784-0668 | www.silverseafoodrestaurant.com

For "excellent" Cantonese "north of Chinatown", surveyors stop by this affordable Uptown "family-style" storefront with a "large", "varied" menu emphasizing "fresh", "first-rate" seafood; adventure-seekers recommend "jumping off the deep end" to order from the more "authentic" specialties but warn "language can be an issue", as can the lack of service and "shabby surroundings"; P.S. only beer, wine and sake are served.

Simply It *Vietnamese*

22 | 11 | 18 | $22

Lincoln Park | 2269 N. Lincoln Ave. (Belden Ave.) | 773-248-0884 | www.simplyitrestaurant.com

"The name says it all" at this "super-hospitable" Vietnamese "gem" in Lincoln Park from a former owner of the "late, lamented Pasteur", where the "killer value" at lunch and "BYO policy" help make for an "easy-on-the-wallet" "best-kept secret"; "outstanding" pho and "clay pot preparations" are some of the reasons greedy types say it "deserves some attention" but "not too much."

☑ Sixteen *American*

| 22 | 27 | 22 | $100 |

River North | Trump International Hotel & Tower | 401 N. Wabash Ave. (Kinzie St.) | 312-588-8030 | www.trumpchicagohotel.com

A "voyeur's view of the city" distinguishes Trump International Hotel & Tower's "stunning" River Norther, where 30-ft. "floor-to-ceiling windows" and a "striking" Swarovski-crystal chandelier are a backdrop for "delicious" New American fare that's "creative" but not "gimmicky"; "polite", "professional service" and a deep wine list complete an "over-the-top" package enjoyed "best on an expense account"; P.S. dining outside on the terrace affords a sweeping open-air view.

Smak-Tak *Polish*

| - | - | - | I |

Northwest Side | 5961 N. Elston Ave. (bet. Austin & Mason Aves.) | 773-763-1123 | www.smaktak.com

Cravings for hearty Polish sustenance are fed at this casual, wood-beamed Jefferson Park chalet (complete with small fireplace), a go-to for cheap, pan-fried pierogi drenched in butter, comforting soups and starchy, meaty main courses – not to mention a gut-busting, goulash-filled potato pancake; true gluttons can cap off meals with fruit-filled dumplings and blintzes.

🆕 Smashburger *Burgers*

| - | - | - | I |

Batavia | Trader Joe's Shopping Ctr. | 842 N. Randall Rd. (Fabyan Pkwy.) | 630-593-5030 | www.smashburger.com

Gussied-up burgers (with customized toppings), fried chicken sammies and rosemary-garlic fries lure fast-food fans to this Batavia strip-mall outpost of a Denver-based chain; the track-lit, counter-service digs feature gleaming mosaic tiles, a labyrinth of burgundy-backed booths and exposed ductwork; P.S. more locations are in the works.

Smith & Wollensky *Steak*

| 23 | 22 | 23 | $63 |

River North | 318 N. State St. (Upper Wacker Dr.) | 312-670-9900 | www.smithandwollensky.com

Steakhouse stalwarts recommend bringing "an extra stomach", "your wallet and someone else's" plus "your cardiologist on speed dial" to this "nostalgic", clubby River Norther with a "riverside" location offering "fantastic views" – especially from the "patio"; while some detractors assert it "isn't as memorable" as the NYC original, the majority of the "well-heeled crowd" (including businessmen) appreciates the "knowledgeable staff" and "fine cuts of beef."

☑ Smoke Daddy *BBQ*

| 24 | 14 | 18 | $25 |

Wicker Park | 1804 W. Division St. (Wood St.) | 773-772-6656 | www.thesmokedaddy.com

"Real-deal Q", "slow-grilled and oh-so-smoky" attracts "neighborhood" ribs lovers to this "crowded" Wicker Park "joint" with a retro vibe – and on most nights, "live music" to "keep you entertained" during the "wait time"; with an "offbeat staff" and "funky setting" featuring jazz and other "memorabilia" plus "interesting beers" and "cheap" tabs, cravers ask "how can you go wrong?"

NEW Smokey Bears Barbeque House *BBQ*

| - | - | - | I |

Albany Park | 3314 W. Foster Ave. (bet. Christiana & Spaulding Aves.) | 773-583-2327 | www.smokeybearsbbq.webs.com

Hickory-smoked barbecue classics (think brisket, ribs, tips, pulled pork and turkey legs) are the draw at this super-casual counter-service Albany Parker owned by two brothers, with their pastry chef sister doing the homey desserts and their mom's baked beans among the side dishes; the laid-back, funky space is decorated with bears and musicians, and note that there's no alcohol service or BYO.

☑ Smoque BBQ Ⓜ *BBQ*

| 26 | 10 | 18 | $19 |

Northwest Side | 3800 N. Pulaski Rd. (Grace St.) | 773-545-7427 | www.smoquebbq.com

An "unexpected gem in an unexpected spot", this Northwest Side BYO is where "brisket lovers" "don't wear good clothes" to dive into "messy" but "terrific" barbecue ribs and other "beyond belief" smoked meat; despite "efficient" "counter service", fans "rub elbows with neighbors" at "cramped" tables when lucky – and endure "lines out the door" when not – but most agree this "decently priced" "real thing" is "worth it"; P.S. "save room for the sides" including "amazing mac 'n' cheese."

NEW Snarf's *Sandwiches*

| - | - | - | I |

River North | 600 W. Chicago Ave. (Larrabee St.) | 312-644-1500 | www.eatsnarfs.com

At this River North outpost of a Colorado-based sub shop, toasted sandwiches ranging from deli classics to house specialties (including some veggie options) come in three sizes, and are accompanied by salads and soda-fountain favorites; the industrial, counter-serve setting has red diner-style tables and booths and is decorated with crayon colors, plus the chain's eccentric cartoon imagery.

Socca *French/Italian*

| 22 | 18 | 20 | $42 |

Lakeview | 3301 N. Clark St. (Aldine Ave.) | 773-248-1155 | www.soccachicago.com

"Fools" can go on "waiting an eternity" "down the street" say regulars of this "little gem" in Lakeview dishing up "reasonably priced", "upper-end" Italian-French "must tries" in "laid-back", bistro-style surroundings; service is "attentive", and when the dining room gets "conversationally challenged", the "lovely outdoor seating" is a "delightful" fair-weather alternative.

Sola *American*

| 25 | 21 | 22 | $45 |

Lakeview | 3868 N. Lincoln Ave. (Byron St.) | 773-327-3868 | www.sola-restaurant.com

Chef-owner Carol Wallack turns out "consistently" "wonderful" New American dishes with a "seasonal" "Hawaiian-Asian" influence in "surprisingly casual" Lakeview digs; the "innovative" fish dishes

FOOD | DECOR | SERVICE | COST

"amaze" (you'd "trade your firstborn" for a taste), but this "refined" "neighborhood" "heavyweight" also serves a "superb" weekend brunch loaded with "twists" on "breakfast classics"; though most find the service "solid", some admit "if the place is busy", it "can be slow."

Sol de Mexico *Mexican*

25 | 19 | 23 | $34

Northwest Side | 3018 N. Cicero Ave. (bet. Nelson St. & Wellington Ave.) | 773-282-4119 | www.soldemexicochicago.com

Experience "mole to the max" urge compadres of this "cozy" mid-priced regional Mexican "joint" on the Northwest Side that fans reckon would be "booked solid" if not for its "location" along a "desolate stretch of Cicero"; those deeming it "worth the drive" to the colorful digs are "still talking about" the "glorious" lamb in Oaxacan black mole, "impressive" tequila list and "charming staff."

NEW Sono Wood Fired *Pizza*

- | - | - | M

Lincoln Park | 1582 N. Clybourn Ave. (bet. Dayton & Halsted Sts.) | 312-255-1122 | www.sonowoodfired.com

This pizza counterpart to Lincoln Park's Burger Bar (with a separate entrance) serves more than a dozen varieties of crunchy-chewy thin-crust pies along with a smattering of Italian starters, salads and pastas for dinner daily; the cozy wine-bar setting with exposed brick and an elaborately tiled wood-burning oven also features a bar issuing a compact list of affordable Italian, Spanish and South American wines.

NEW South Branch
Tavern Grille Ⓢ *Pub Food*

- | - | - | M

Loop | 100 S. Wacker Dr. (Monroe St.) | 312-546-6177 | www.southbranchchicago.com

Hungry high-financiers and other Loop denizens can diversify their pub portfolios at this sweeping, swanky watering hole on the Chicago River where the upscale bar-food menu (duck wings, Waldorf wrap, fish tacos, four-cheese mac) pairs with beefy lists of beers and brown spirits for lunch or dinner; its handsome digs feature bare trees, limestone, plush upholstered seating (including communal tables) and waterside alfresco dining with a dedicated bar in warm weather.

Southern, The ◐Ⓜ *Southern*

- | - | - | M

Bucktown | 1840 W. North Ave. (bet. Honore St. & Wolcott Ave.) | 773-342-1840 | www.thesouthernchicago.com

Southern Mac Ⓢ *Southern*
NEW Location varies | www.thesouthernmac.com

The former Chaise Lounge is reborn as this more casual, late-night Bucktown Southerner with creative and classic bar food, plates and sides accompanied by beers and specialty cocktails with a drawl; high-tops with steel stools, reclaimed wood banquettes and safety lighting lend a raw, stylized look to the first floor, while the second-floor roof deck houses two cozy draped cabanas along with lounge-style seating; P.S. it launched a rolling mac (and cheese) truck.

	FOOD	DECOR	SERVICE	COST

South Gate Cafe *American* | 20 | 18 | 21 | $38 |

Lake Forest | 655 Forest Ave. (Deerpath Rd.) | 847-234-8800 |
www.southgatecafe.com

"You won't find a better" patio "in summertime" promise patrons who remain "delighted" by this "longtime" Lake Forest midpriced American set in a century-old building; though service may sometimes be "slow", enthusiasts enjoy the "constantly changing" seasonal "eclectic" menu, especially for "lunch in the garden room."

Southport Grocery & Café *American* | 22 | 14 | 17 | $18 |

Lakeview | 3552 N. Southport Ave. (bet. Addison & Eddy Sts.) |
773-665-0100 | www.southportgrocery.com

The "wait" "on weekends" for brunch is "brutal" but "worth it" vouch veterans of this "crowded" Lakeview grocer and affordable New American cafe that "satisfies your sweet tooth" with "cupcake pancakes" and mascarpone- and preserve-filled "adult pop tarts"; the "fresh and healthy" lunch options and sandwiches are "awesome" too, so that complaints that it's "too small" and service can be "slow" are drowned out by fans' "stomach growling."

South Water Kitchen *American* | 16 | 16 | 18 | $33 |

Loop | Hotel Monaco | 225 N. Wabash Ave. (Lake St.) | 312-236-9300 |
www.southwaterkitchen.com

Feeling like a "hideaway" "surrounded" by "tourist-laden joints", this "solid" Loop American adjacent to the Hotel Monaco dishes up "varied" regional "home cooking" that's "priced right"; the "cozy, casual" setting is "welcoming on cold winter days and nights", and while snipers snip that "nothing stands out", proponents note that it's "convenient" to theaters and works for "Downtown lunch or after-work drinks."

Spacca Napoli Pizzeria Ⓜ *Pizza* | 23 | 18 | 21 | $27 |

Ravenswood | 1769 W. Sunnyside Ave. (bet. Hermitage &
Ravenswood Aves.) | 773-878-2420 | www.spaccanapolipizzeria.com

Groupies of this "authentic" Neapolitan pizzeria in Ravenswood gush about its "'scary great" pies with "heavenly crusts" that are "never overwhelmed" by their "supporting cast" of "fresh ingredients" – provided "you don't mind waiting" "for a table"; the "convivial" atmosphere adds to the appeal for most with "friendly service" that's "like visiting your Italian grandma", though a few find the fare "a bit pricey"; N.B. the Decor score does not reflect a post-Survey expansion.

🄯 Spiaggia *Italian* | 27 | 27 | 27 | $93 |

Gold Coast | One Magnificent Mile Bldg. | 980 N. Michigan Ave., 2nd fl.
(Oak St.) | 312-280-2750 | www.spiaggiarestaurant.com

"It may be cheaper to fly to Rome" than to dine at Tony Mantuano's Gold Coast "destination", but surveyors succumb to the "breathtaking" cheese selection, "delicate, handmade pastas", "velvety sauces" and entrees that "sing your name" matched by a "superb", "extensive Italian wine list"; the "quiet", "elegant", "multilevel" dining room offering "exquisite views of the lake" – alone "an experience" – has "attentive" yet "unobtrusive" service, but "as as-tounding as it is", some favor the less "formal" "cafe next door"; P.S. jackets are required.

Spoon Thai *Thai*   23 | 14 | 19 | $21

Lincoln Square | 4608 N. Western Ave. (Wilson Ave.) | 773-769-1173 | www.spoonthai.com

Fanatics call this budget-friendly "authentic" Lincoln Square BYO "not your average Thai" – especially if you're "adventurous" enough to "order off" the translated "no-longer-secret" menu ("try the Isaan sausage"); while some "stick to the specials and authentic items", others go for the "usual choices"; still, the "simple" setting and service aren't quite as "lovely" as the "delicious" fare.

Spring World *Chinese*   - | - | - | M

Chinatown | 2109 S. China Pl. (Wells St.) | 312-326-9966

"One of the hidden" Chinatown "gems", this Yunnan "quiet storefront" preps "wonderful", spicy dishes (anything with "special mushrooms" is "to die for"); though it may be "a bit pricier" than its neighbors, the "unusual" fare helps justify the expense, earning it cult status.

Sprout 🅜 *American/French*   28 | 22 | 24 | $82

Lincoln Park | 1417 W. Fullerton Ave. (bet. Janssen & Southport Aves.) | 773-348-0706 | www.sproutrestaurant.com

Dale Levitski's "mysterious", "cryptic" prix fixe menu "surprises", delivering "real excitement" and "complex flavors" at this "in-spired", "high-end" "seasonal" French-American bistro in Lincoln Park; low lighting, red-velvet banquettes and French doors that open to an enclosed patio lend the "attractive" space a "welcoming" feel-ing; wines, beers and libations – like the earthy name – lean organic; P.S. it now serves Sunday brunch.

Stained Glass Wine Bar Bistro *American*   23 | 19 | 22 | $46

Evanston | 1735 Benson Ave. (bet. Church & Clark Sts.) | 847-864-8600 | www.thestainedglass.com

"Ever-changing" flights and a "strong" wine list lend credibility to this "intimate" exposed-brick "Evanston staple" with a "serious", slightly pricey American menu that samplers deem built for "grazing" (but there are entrees too); while often "crowded", this storefront remains a "favorite" among "novices and wine snobs" alike, though service ranges from "spotty" to "friendly" and "knowledgeable."

Stanley's Kitchen & Tap *American*   18 | 15 | 14 | $19

Lincoln Park | 1970 N. Lincoln Ave. (Armitage Ave.) | 312-642-0007 | www.stanleyskitchenandtap.com

"Down-home" and "laid-back", this American Lincoln Parker dishes up "quality" "comfort food" that's "the next-best thing" to "carbo-loading" at "grandma's house" – providing granny enjoys "a little hair of the dog"; the "cheap" regular menu includes "un-beatable fried chicken and mac 'n' cheese", and "weekend brunch" is a guaranteed "hangover cure", just don't be in a rush because the "staff is slow."

	FOOD	DECOR	SERVICE	COST

Star of Siam *Thai*
`20` `17` `19` `$21`

River North | 11 E. Illinois St. (State St.) | 312-670-0100 |
www.starofsiamchicago.com

Among the most "established" Thai eateries in town (opened in
1984), this "inexpensive" mainstay with "faux floor seating" plus
"regular tables" "never disappoints" its followers, who find it a
"cozy", "dependable" spot for "big servings" in River North; purists
opine "it's probably not very authentic", but with "quick", "friendly
service", it's a viable "lunch option."

State and Lake *American*
`21` `20` `22` `$38`

Loop | theWit Hotel | 201 N. State St. (Lake St.) | 312-239-9400 |
www.stateandlakechicago.com

Named after its location, theWit hotel's ground-floor "hot spot" in the
Loop is a "delight" with its "cool", curvaceous bar lined with seltzer
bottles and "pleasant" earthy-hued dining room for "creative" "reasonably priced" New American fare; cognoscenti call it "convenient"
and "quick" for lunch or dinner with a staff that's "eager to please."

NEW Stax Café *American*
`-` `-` `-` `I`

Little Italy/University Village | 1401 W. Taylor St. (Loomis St.) |
312-733-9871 | www.staxcafe.com

It's daylight dining only at this corner cafe in University Village focusing on breakfast faves like stacks of creative pancakes, French
toast and waffles along with egg dishes and some lunch salads,
wraps and sandwich staples; the casual-chic space is done in toasty
shades of brown with an open kitchen, juice bar (fruit and veg), coffee drinks and free WiFi.

Steve's Deli *Deli*
`17` `13` `16` `$18`

River North | 354 W. Hubbard St. (bet. Kingsbury & Orleans Sts.) |
312-467-6868 | www.stevesdeli.com

"Delicious" deli fare hits River North by way of this casually decorated
Michigan transplant that serves "huge" sandwiches (corned beef,
brisket, chopped liver), salads and hearty soups; those with quibbles
find it "a bit overpriced" and "cannot understand the popularity."

Sticky Rice *Thai*
`-` `-` `-` `I`

North Center/St. Ben's | 4018 N. Western Ave. (bet. Cuyler Ave. &
Irving Park Rd.) | 773-588-0120 | www.stickyricethai.com

Vibrant yellow, red and orange hues set the tone at this affordable North Center BYO, where the Northern Thai menu offers a
chance to try some out-of-the-ordinary fare (fried caterpillars,
omelets peppered with ant eggs); those looking for something a little more familiar can opt for the wide selection of soups, curries
and noodle dishes.

Stir Crazy *Asian*
`19` `17` `18` `$24`

Northbrook | Northbrook Court Shopping Ctr. | 1186 Northbrook Ct.
(Lake Cook Rd.) | 847-562-4800

Schaumburg | Woodfield Mall | 5 Woodfield Mall (Frontage & Golf Rds.) |
847-330-1200

(continued)

(continued)

Stir Crazy

Oak Brook | Oakbrook Center Mall | 105 Oakbrook Ctr. (Rte. 83) | 630-575-0155
Warrenville | 28252 Diehl Rd. (Windfield Rd.) | 630-393-4700
www.stircrazy.com

"If your meal isn't good, you have yourself to blame" given that most choose to "assemble ingredients" for their stir-fries at these eco-nomical, "ever popular" Asian woks that "cater to families" with "suburban palates"; those who accept it "for what it is" and are will-ing to get "creative" or order off the menu find it "worthwhile."

Sugartoad *American*

19 | 19 | 19 | $53

Naperville | Hotel Arista | 2139 CityGate Ln. (bet. Ferry Rd. & I-88) | 630-778-8623 | www.sugartoad.com

In a dining room designed by Dirk Lohan, grandson of Mies van der Rohe, this New American "hidden in" Naperville's Hotel Arista serves farm-focused regional cuisine; though fans call it a "rare jewel", others come with "high expectations", only to have them "dashed" by "overpriced" meals and iffy service.

Sullivan's Steakhouse *Steak*

22 | 21 | 20 | $57

River North | 415 N. Dearborn St. (Hubbard St.) | 312-527-3510
Lincolnshire | 250 Marriott Dr. (Milwaukee Ave.) | 847-883-0311
Naperville | 244 S. Main St. (bet. Jackson & Jefferson Aves.) | 630-305-0230
www.sullivansteakhouse.com

Beef eaters declare this "clubby" 1940s-inspired threesome ("part of a national chain") "worth the price" of admission for a "faithful steakhouse experience"; though some think others "in town are bet-ter" and decry spotty service, a "bustling bar", signature martinis and live jazz "add value."

Sunda *Asian*

23 | 24 | 20 | $55

River North | 110 W. Illinois St. (bet. Clark & LaSalle Sts.) | 312-644-0500 | www.sundachicago.com

The "prettiest people" "fight the crowds" for a table at this "hip", "happening" River North "knockout" from the Rockit Bar & Grill team with a "contemporary" setting and a "unique take" on Asian fusion fare that's "long on style"; the initiated urge bring "friends so you can try everything" including the "amazing duck buns", "inter-esting sushi" and "handcrafted cocktails"; add in a "courteous", "knowledgeable staff" and "what's not to like" – except perhaps the "high" prices.

Sun Wah BBQ *Chinese*

- | - | - | I

Uptown | 5039 N. Broadway (bet. Argyle & Winona Sts.) | 773-769-1254 | www.sunwahbbq.com

Relocated to Uptown digs after 25 years, this cheap Chinese churns out a big menu of seafood dishes, lo meins, rice congees and noodle soups, but the meats hanging in the front window clue you in to the main focus: house-roasted Hong Kong–style BBQ, including duck served from a tableside cart; there's a bustling carry-out area as well as a brightly lit dining room, and you can BYO ($5 corkage fee) or choose from the beer, wine and limited liquor selection.

Z Superdawg Drive-In ⊄ *Burgers/Hot Dogs*   21 | 15 | 18 | $11

Northwest Side | 6363 N. Milwaukee Ave. (Devon Ave.) | 773-763-0660 ●

Wheeling | 333 S. Milwaukee Ave. (Mors Ave.) | 847-459-1900
www.superdawg.com

"Return to your adolescent years" at Chicago's No. 1 Bang for the Buck, a "kitschy" "car-hopping" Northwest Side "drive-in" "icon" (with a Wheeling outpost) where the "dawgs" come "stuffed" into a "cute box" and deliver an "elevated" "spin" on the Chicago hot dog (even if the "relish is a little too green"); though "cravers" concede "the car steers itself here" for "easy-on-the-budget" "burgers, fries" and "thick shakes" too, the "freaky blinking-eyed mascots" on the roof "are reason enough to go"; P.S. cash-only.

Sura ● *Thai*   ∇ 20 | 19 | 16 | $24

Lakeview | 3124 N. Broadway (Briar Pl.) | 773-248-7872 |
www.surachicago.com

"It's like eating inside of an iPod" declare fans of this "hip", futuristic Lakeview Thai with clear, hemispheric seats hanging from the ceiling; popular with the after-work crowd, it features a menu that's built "for sharing", so everyone can "try several items"; insiders also note that everything is "value"-minded befitting a "local" crowd.

Sushi Ai *Japanese*   - | - | - | M

Palatine | 710 W. Euclid Ave. (Parkside Dr.) | 847-221-5100 |
www.sushi-ai.com

"Downtown caliber sushi" lures fish fanciers to this Japanese in a Palatine "strip mall", where "fresh", "artfully prepared" signature rolls (e.g. the Dirty Old Man) offer "unexpected pleasure" at moderate prices; "comfortable booths and tables" and "attentive" but "not overbearing" service are enhanced by conversation starters on walls adorned with '50s-era records and bold, modern art.

Sushi Naniwa *Japanese*   23 | 15 | 23 | $38

River North | 607 N. Wells St. (bet. Ohio & Ontario Sts.) |
312-255-8555 | www.sushinaniwa.com

Supporters call this "fantastic" River North Japanese a "low-key version" of its sibling, Bob San, minus the "frills, bells, whistles" and "long waits"; fortunately, the "reasonably priced" selection of "high-quality", "super-fresh" "slabs of sushi" and "solid" "cooked" dishes make up for the "unassuming" "straightforward" setting, as does service that's taken a ratings jump; P.S. the "patio is great for summer."

Sushi Para *Japanese*   - | - | - | M

Palatine | 1268 E. Dundee Rd. (Baldwin Ln.) | 847-202-9922
Sushi Para D *Japanese*

Lincoln Park | 543 W. Diversey Pkwy. (bet. Lampden & Lehmann Cts.) |
773-248-1808

(continued)

(continued)

Sushi Para II *Japanese*
Lincoln Park | 2256 N. Clark St. (bet. Belden Ave. & Grant Pl.) | 773-477-3219

NEW Sushi Para M *Japanese*
Bucktown | 1633 N. Milwaukee Ave. (bet. Damen & North Aves.) | 773-252-6828
www.sushiparachicago.com

Sushi Sai *Japanese*
Loop | 123 N. Wacker Dr. (bet. Franklin St. & Wacker Dr.) | 312-332-8822 | www.sushisaionline.com

This sushi chain originated in Palatine and has since spread to Lincoln Park, the Loop and Bucktown; expect all the Japanese basics plus all-you-can-eat sushi at moderate prices in varying settings; P.S. the Bucktown and Lincoln Park branches are BYO.

Sushisamba Rio ● *Japanese/S American*   21 | 24 | 19 | $51
River North | 504 N. Wells St. (bet. Grand Ave. & Illinois St.) | 312-595-2300 | www.sushisamba.com

"Hold on to your hats" for an "East meets South" experience at River North's "sexy", "clubby" hub for Brazilian-Peruvian-Japanese cuisine; the "attractive", "over-the-top" dining room lures "celebs" and others who "go to be seen" and are willing to "pay for" the "ambiance", which comes complete with an "aural assault" and "peppy servers"; P.S. the "cool" year-round rooftop deck is a "killer" perch for cocktails.

Sushi Taiyo *Japanese*   - | - | - | M
River North | Sheraton Four Points Hotel | 58 E. Ontario St. (bet. Rush St. & Wabash Ave.) | 312-440-1717 | www.taiyochicago.com

"Fabulous" sushi and Pan-Asian creations via the Rise and Shine crew are served in a "small", "cool space" featuring funky bamboo ceiling art at this midpriced River North Japanese "just off Michigan Avenue"; though some suggest there's nothing "to rave about", the few surveyors who've sampled it promise "guaranteed quality" and a menu "similar" to its siblings; P.S. second-floor Izakaya Hapa serves Asian bar bites and sake-infused cocktails Friday and Saturday.

Z Sushi Wabi *Japanese*   27 | 18 | 20 | $44
West Loop | 842 W. Randolph St. (bet. Green & Peoria Sts.) | 312-563-1224 | www.sushiwabi.com

"Sushi snobs" regard this modern West Loop Japanese as "one of the best" spots to "belly up" for "inventive" maki ("it's like buttah"); just "plan to spend a few bucks", and keep in mind that "service lacks often" and tables in the "industrial"-looking setting afford little "privacy from your neighbors" – most notably during "prime time" when it's "crowded" and "high-energy (translate: loud)."

Sushi X *Japanese*   21 | 13 | 18 | $33
River West | 1136 W. Chicago Ave. (bet. May St. & Racine Ave.) | 312-491-9232 | www.rollingatsushix.com

Stark, modern details give way to "inventive" rolls at this "consistent", moderately priced River West sushi bar where fin fanatics find the BYO policy a "huge bonus"; some deem the "dining room" "pretty dreadful", but "takeout and delivery are terrific" and portions are "generous."

Swordfish *Japanese* ▽ 27 | 21 | 24 | $44

Batavia | 207 N. Randall Rd. (McKee St.) | 630-406-6463 | www.swordfishsushi.com

"Put on your blinders" and "you'll never know" you're in "the boonies" attest admirers of the "outstanding" "fresh" sushi served at this contemporary far West Suburban Japanese (a sibling to Wildfish) that's "nestled in a strip mall"; trendy rolls, creative hot dishes and "excellent drinks" add to the "downtown" feel, as does the service and slightly pricey tabs.

Szechwan North *Chinese* 19 | 12 | 16 | $25

Glenview | 2857 Pfingsten Rd. (Willow Rd.) | 847-272-0007 | www.szechwannorth.com

Glenview locals look to this "master of Sichuan cooking" for affordable "traditional dishes" made with "quality ingredients" and "care", contending it's "one of the better" "in the 'burbs"; those who had "forgotten" about it are "pleasantly surprised" when they go back, saying they "wish" it were "closer."

Table Fifty-two *American/Southern* 24 | 23 | 23 | $60

Gold Coast | 52 W. Elm St. (bet. Clark & Dearborn Sts.) | 312-573-4000 | www.tablefifty-two.com

For "knockout" "soul food north of the Mason-Dixon line", surveyors jump aboard the "biscuit bandwagon" at this "upscale" Gold Coast American belonging to Oprah's onetime chef, Art Smith; enthusiasts dub the "beautiful" "homestyle" setting – plus "hummingbird cake" and "fried chicken" that leave you "feeling fat" – an "interesting take" on the Southern experience, and though a few say it's "overhyped and overpriced", most find the service "lovely."

Taco Fuego ● *Mexican* – | – | – | I

Lakeview | 1648 W. Belmont Ave. (bet. Ashland Ave. & Paulina St.) | 773-935-9472 | www.tacofuego.com

Quick, casual, el cheapo Mexican comestibles – including lots of tacos, quesadillas and burritos (watch out for the foot-long 'monster') – plus classic plates like fajitas and even breakfast fare are on offer at this little, no-frills Lakeview taqueria; dishes come liberally laced with über-hot habanero peppers, and there are seven fresh salsa varieties to choose from, so you'll likely want some liquid relief in the form of horchata, jamaica and sodas.

NEW Taco Joint
Urban Taqueria & Cantina *Mexican* – | – | – | I

Lincoln Park | 1969 N. Halsted St. (bet. Armitage Ave. & Willow St.) | 312-951-2457 | www.tacojoint.com

Regional Mexican street fare – tacos, tortas, huaraches and guacamoles – is served lunch through late night (and from a walk-up window that serves even later) at this Lincoln Park cantina where Mexican beers and 50 tequilas available in flights and cocktails (or by the bottle, with storage lockers if you don't finish) accompany the meal; the funky-casual setting features an ultradistressed bar and flooring, dangling lightbulbs and boozy wall murals.

☒ Takashi Ⓜ *American/French*   26 | 20 | 23 | $62

Bucktown | 1952 N. Damen Ave. (Armitage Ave.) | 773-772-6170 | www.takashichicago.com

"Vibrant" flavors launch seemingly "simple" dishes to "culinary stardom" at Ambria vet Takashi Yagihashi's Japanese-tinged French-American "gem" in Bucktown that's akin to "eating in someone's" "understated, classy" house, albeit one with an "interesting" wine and sake list; service, generally viewed as "attentive" "without being intrusive", and "less than astronomical prices" result in near "uniformly positive experiences"; P.S. "check out the hip upstairs dining room" "if there's a table available" or try his upcoming casual concept in River North, Slurping Turtle.

☒ Tallgrass Ⓜ *French*   28 | 23 | 24 | $74

Lockport | 1006 S. State St. (10th St.) | 815-838-5566 | www.tallgrassrestaurant.com

It's "well worth the drive from Downtown" gush groupies of this "relaxed", "romantic" French in a "beautiful" vintage building, where "decades of culinary experience" "shows" in the modern prix fixe-only menu; it's "still a value" after all these years, with a "knowledgeable" staff and "fantastic" wine list that's "extremely fairly" priced sealing its status as a "special night out" in the Southwest Suburbs; P.S. jackets are suggested.

Tamales *Mexican*   20 | 16 | 21 | $27

Highland Park | 493 Central Ave. (St. Johns Ave.) | 847-433-4070 | www.tamalesrestaurant.com

"Unique" dishes "make it hard to choose" when dining at this brightly colored North Shore Mexican that's known for its "unconventional tamales" and "phenomenal duck tacos" plus "personalized service"; fans of the "small", "crowded" setting promise it's "worth the wait" – "especially in summer" when outdoor seating becomes available and even more so when you have an "amazing margarita" in hand.

Tamarind *Asian*   23 | 19 | 20 | $28

South Loop | 614 S. Wabash Ave. (Harrison St.) | 312-379-0970 | www.tamarindsushi.com

An "extensive" selection of midpriced Pan-Asian dishes from "solid" sushi to design-"your-own stir-fry" plus "lots of" noodle dishes means this bamboo-walled South Looper has something for "almost everyone"; service is generally "efficient", and there's a summer patio; P.S. Wednesday nights cater to singles ('come alone, dine together') from 7:30 to 10 PM.

Tango *Argentinean*   ▽ 22 | 16 | 20 | $33

Naperville | 5 W. Jackson Ave. (Washington St.) | 630-848-1818 | www.tangogrill.com

You'll want to dollop the "chimichurri" "on anything" plus "sop it up with the bread" say habitués of this "enjoyable" midpriced

Argentinean in Downtown Naperville where you can "go the tapas route" and "share everything" or try the signature 26-inch steak; it's a "regular stop" for some, who cite "value" and "solid service" as draws.

Tango Sur *Argentinean/Steak*
24	16	19	$32

Lakeview | 3763 N. Southport Ave. (Grace St.) | 773-477-5466
Meat mavens meet at this "beloved" BYO Argentine that serves "wonderfully" prepared, "quality beef" to "expats" and "Lakeview twentysomethings"; a "loud" setting and "ridiculously long waits" that "do not abate late" can be "frustrating", but "eye-candy waiters" and "huge" portions offering "incredible value" "are worth it"; P.S. its newer, more romantic sib, Folklore, is a relatively mellower late-night alternative.

Tank Sushi *Japanese*
23	19	18	$39

Lincoln Square | 4514 N. Lincoln Ave. (Sunnyside Ave.) | 773-769-2600 | www.tanksushi.com
Zealots assure the sushi and rolls really are "all that" at this midpriced Lincoln Square Japanese that offers "creative" "combinations" in a "lively", contemporary setting complete with a "thwump-thwump soundtrack"; "friendly" service adds to the allure, and penny-pinchers applaud the "best-kept secret in town" – "half price" maki during lunch Monday–Friday and on weekends from 1-6 PM.

Tanoshii *Japanese*
-	-	-	E

Andersonville | 5547 N. Clark St. (Gregory St.) | 773-878-6886
Loyalists laud this "one-of-a-kind" Japanese "neighborhood institution" located "off the beaten path" in Andersonville as an "excellent" option for sushi including "some winners you can't find anywhere else"; "regulars" "go with friends" to try as many "concoctions as possible" or ask the chef to "custom design" maki to suit their "cravings", assuring that "dinner will surely please, even if the check doesn't."

Tapas Barcelona *Spanish*
21	18	18	$29

Evanston | Northshore Hotel Retirement Home | 1615 Chicago Ave. (bet. Church & Davis Sts.) | 847-866-9900 | www.tapasbarcelona.com
"Delicious" tapas lure an "amiable crowd" of "families, couples and Northwestern students" to this "casual" Evanston Spaniard that has been a "favorite" "for years" and delivers "super value"; though service "can be slow", sangria and a "selection of sherries" help to pass the time, and while the "colorful" indoors can get "noisy", sitting on the "pleasant" patio affords a "wonderful" "alfresco" experience.

Tapas Gitana *Spanish*
24	18	22	$34

NEW **Lakeview** | 3445 N. Halsted St. (bet. Cornelia & Newport Aves.) | 773-296-6046 **M**
Northfield | Northfield Village Ctr. | 310 Happ Rd. (bet. Willow Rd. & Winnetka Ave.) | 847-784-9300
www.tapasgitana.com
For a "fine" "variety of cold and hot" tapas plus "killer paella", patrons "keep coming back" to this romantic "gem" "tucked away" in

the North Shore where a "cordial", "attentive" staff, occasional "live music", a "lovely", "large patio" and "reasonable prices" help "take it over the top"; P.S. a Lakeview outpost was added post-Survey.

Tapas Las Ramblas Ⓜ *Spanish*   ▽ 23 | 20 | 19 | $28

Andersonville | 5101 N. Clark St. (Carmen Ave.) | 773-769-9700 | www.tapaslasramblas.com

Andersonvillers grab a "group of friends" for a "slice of sunny Barcelona" at this "convivial" "better-than-neighborhood" "tapas joint" with a "bright, colorful", lantern-lit dining room and windows that swing open on breezy days; most find the "broad selection" of "reasonably priced" "small plates" a "pleasant surprise" and the service "fair" but "friendly."

Tarantino's Ⓜ *Italian*   22 | 20 | 22 | $39

Lincoln Park | 1112 W. Armitage Ave. (Seminary Ave.) | 773-871-2929 | www.tarantinos.com

There may not be "a lot of hype" surrounding this midpriced Lincoln Park trattoria, but it's nonetheless a "favorite" cozy "comfort zone" for "neighborhood Italian" including "solid pasta"; admirers warn "you'll be tempted to order" "three times more than you can eat" because dishes "never fail to satisfy", while a "friendly staff" helps to keep it "consistently enjoyable."

Tasting Room ◑ 🗷 *American*   20 | 21 | 21 | $34

West Loop | 1415 W. Randolph St. (Ogden Ave.) | 312-942-1313 | www.thetastingroomchicago.com

"Wine and cheese lovers" rendezvous over "interesting", "smaller-sized" New American dishes and entrees at this "quiet" West Loop "date spot" with some of the "best views of Chicago" from its "second-floor" lounge; cohorts concur there's "plenty to keep you interested" – starting with the "extensive" vino selection explained by a "knowledgeable staff" – and moderate tabs won't break the bank.

Tavern at the Park 🗷 *American*   20 | 19 | 20 | $42

Loop | 130 E. Randolph St. (Michigan Ave.) | 312-552-0070 | www.tavernatthepark.com

Its "choice location" overlooking Millennium Park lends a "lovely setting" to this bi-level New American, while its "convenient" Loop address and "varied menu" make it popular with a mix of "tourists", "business" types and theatergoers; adventurers admit there's "nothing exotic" in the mix, and adversaries note "spotty service" adding "you pay for the view whether you get it or not"; luckily, there's seasonal patio seating; P.S. rooftop dining was in the works at press time.

Tavern on Rush ◑ *Steak*   21 | 20 | 20 | $49

Gold Coast | 1031 N. Rush St. (Bellevue Pl.) | 312-664-9600 | www.tavernonrush.com

"People-watching" from a "second-floor window" is highly recommended at this "Viagra triangle" steakhouse that's "always jammed" with "politicos", "pretty people" and "pickup" artists

| | FOOD | DECOR | SERVICE | COST |

working the "happening" Gold Coast "scene"; "perfect drinks" and solid meat dishes are additional come-ons, even though some "suspect expense accounts abound" and there's "too much attitude" from the staff; still, "nothing's better than a patio seat in summer."

Taxim *Greek*
22 | 17 | 20 | $45

Wicker Park | 1558 N. Milwaukee Ave. (Damen Ave.) | 773-252-1558 | www.taximchicago.com

"Don't expect broken plates and *'opas!'*" at this Wicker Park Greek where "lovely", "modern" fare is delivered with "helpful service" in an "elegant" setting with copper-top tables, hanging lanterns and exposed brick; the "interesting" "seasonal offerings" made with "fresh ingredients" are a "unique" alternative to "flaming cheese", yet are "not absurdly expensive"; P.S. there's also a sidewalk cafe and deck with city view.

Tempo ●⊄ *Diner*
20 | 13 | 17 | $20

Gold Coast | 6 E. Chestnut St. (State St.) | 312-943-4373 | www.tempocafechicago.com

"Honest breakfasts" (some say "late-night lifesavers") and other diner fare is dished out 24/7 at this "pretense"-free, "cash-only" Gold Coast spot offering "delicious omelets" so big they "spill" off the plate; the "old-fashioned"-meets-contemporary setting isn't "long on ambiance" but service is "efficient" and "easygoing", and though "the wait on weekends is a drag" most contend it's "worth it" P.S. it's BYO inside but no alcohol is allowed in the outdoor cafe.

Terragusto *Italian*
25 | 16 | 20 | $48

Roscoe Village | 1851 W. Addison St. (bet. Ravenswood & Wolcott Aves.) | 773-248-2777 | www.terragustocafe.com Ⓜ

"Focus on the fresh, housemade pastas" to enter "carb-loading paradise" promise patrons of this "cozy" BYO Roscoe Villager that dishes out "simple", "organic" Italian fare including "extraordinary", "robust" sauces; "friendly, informed" service takes the edge off "pricey" tabs; P.S. at press time, its Lincoln Park sibling (at 340 West Armitage Avenue) was reportedly being remade into Pastaterra, a casual, counter-service pasta spot.

Terzo Piano *Italian*
21 | 23 | 20 | $36

Loop | Art Institute of Chicago | 159 E. Monroe St. (bet. Columbus Dr. & Michigan Ave.) | 312-443-8650 | www.terzopianochicago.com

"Giant windows" look out from a "spectacular", "minimalist" "white" setting "worthy" of its location in the Modern Wing of the Art Institute at Tony Mantuano's "artful" Spiaggia sibling serving "high-end" Italian dishes by day (and dinner Thursday only); while some find it "a bit pricey for lunch" and dub the decor the "most luxurious high-school cafeteria ever", service is "fine" enough and the "views of Millennium Park" (especially from the terrace) are "stunning" – plus you can dine without paying museum admission if you enter via the park's bridge; P.S. the Terzo team also runs the more casual Caffè Moderno on the second floor.

	FOOD	DECOR	SERVICE	COST

Texas de Brazil Churrascaria *Brazilian*   22 | 21 | 22 | $55

River North | 51 E. Ohio St. (bet. N. Rush St. & N. Wabash Ave.) | 312-670-1006

Schaumburg | Woodfield Mall | 5 Woodfield Mall (Frontage & Golf Rds.) | 847-413-1600

www.texasdebrazil.com

Sages suggest avoiding the "exceptional" salad bars to focus on "meat and more meat" at these "Brazilian-style" "all-you-can-eat" churrascarias in River North and Schaumburg where it's "socially acceptable" to "stuff yourself"; gaucho waiters "could double as a NASCAR pit crew" as they round the "gorgeous rooms", leading "über-meat" fans to say it's "worth" the "splurge"; P.S. the city site features aerial "wine angels", who fetch bottles from a showy, two-story cellar.

Thai Classic *Thai*   23 | 16 | 20 | $22

Lakeview | 3332 N. Clark St. (Buckingham St.) | 773-404-2000 | www.thaiclassicrestaurant.com

"Flavorful and aromatic traditional dishes" are the hallmark of this affordable, casual Lakeview "favorite", a long-standing Thai BYO with a "quiet", "lovely" setting and service that's "right on"; the "generous" buffet, offered at lunchtime on Saturdays and Sundays, gets accolades for its "many options" that "all taste fresh"; P.S. the kitchen is "not afraid to crank up the spice level" when asked.

Thai Pastry *Thai*   23 | 10 | 16 | $21

Uptown | 4925 N. Broadway (bet. Ainslie & Argyle Sts.) | 773-784-5399

Harwood Heights | 7350 W. Lawrence Ave. (Odell Ave.) | 708-867-8840

www.thaipastry.com

Devotees say this "funky little coffee shop–style" Uptown Thai (with a Suburban Northwest sibling) has "awesome" "authentic" fare plus a "notable" bakery; the "beautifully presented" dishes – including some "unusual" alternatives to "standard-issue" options – come with usually "rapid-fire service" and a "check so small you'll shake your head"; P.S. the "lunch specials are a steal."

Thai Urban Kitchen 🖾 *Asian*   16 | 14 | 15 | $26

Loop | Ogilvie Transportation Ctr. | 500 W. Madison St. (Canal St.) | 312-575-0266 | www.thaiurbankitchen.com

Ogilvie train station's "tasty little oasis", this midpriced Sura sibling seduces more than commuters with a Pan-Asian–Japanese "mix" served in "chic" "modern" quarters with oversize windows and "attractive" globe lighting; for "lunch"-time Loop workers and the "pre-opera" crowd, the waterfall thankfully soothes when service gets "confused."

Thalia Spice *Asian*   19 | 16 | 18 | $36

River West | 833 W. Chicago Ave. (Green St.) | 312-226-6020 | www.thaliaspice.com

Simply Thalia *Thai*

NEW **Loop** | Block 37 | 108 N. State St. (bet. Randolph & Washington Sts.) | 312-750-9098 | www.simplythalias.com

"Surprisingly" "eclectic" and "original" Pan-Asian fare in an "inviting", "out-of-the-way" River West setting runs the gamut from Thai to "sushi, curry" and "attractive" "fusion" plates – all in "small servings" at moderate prices; the "friendly" "helpful" staff adds to the "warm atmosphere" in which surveyors note you can "have a conversation with your date"; P.S. a Loop outpost opened post-Survey.

33 Club *American*　　　　　20 | 25 | 20 | $45

Old Town | 1419 N. Wells St. (bet. Burton Pl. & Schiller St.) | 312-664-1419 | www.33clubchicago.com

"Stunning" decor dazzles at this "cavernous", "noisy" Old Town New American "'it' place" from Jerry Kleiner (Carnivale, Gioco) that boasts "beautiful" "velvet touches", "plenty of color" and a "sweeping staircase" recalling "the Titanic"; if the "decent" service is not quite as "impressive" and the "standard" fare is somewhat "expensive" (though "portions are enormous"), admirers advise you "come for the vibe" and "people-watching" – plus the "lively bar and outdoor cafe"; P.S. the Food score does not reflect a recent chef change.

NEW Three Aces ● *Italian/Pub Food*　　— | — | — | M

Little Italy/University Village | 1321 W. Taylor St. (Ada St.) | 312-243-1577 | www.threeaceschicago.com

This hip neighborhood joint in Little Italy pairs seasonal-artisanal gastropub plates (many Italian-influenced) with regional craft brews and specialty cocktails; exposed brick, black leather seating, reclaimed light fixtures from Joliet Prison and rockin'-literati artwork (think Tom Waits and Nelson Algren) lend a denizens-of-the-night vibe, as do a photo booth, a billiard table and late-night service till 3 AM on Saturdays.

Three Happiness ● *Chinese*　　　21 | 11 | 14 | $22

Chinatown | 209 W. Cermak Rd. (Wentworth Ave.) | 312-842-1964

You've "got to love those carts" say fans of this "popular" Chinatowner for affordable dim sum and "don't-miss egg rolls" plus dishes "never shown to tourists"; though it's open 24 hours on weekends and almost around-the-clock on weekdays, there are still waits (they're "worth it"); P.S. there's no connection to nearby New Three Happiness.

312 Chicago *Italian*　　　　　21 | 21 | 21 | $42

Loop | Hotel Allegro | 136 N. LaSalle St. (Randolph St.) | 312-696-2420 | www.312chicago.com

Dialed in as a "solid choice" for a "classy" "business breakfast or lunch" and an "upscale after-work" and "pre-theater" stop (the "efficient" staff helps diners "make the curtain"), this Loop lair adjacent to the Hotel Allegro serves "fresh, seasonally focused" Italian fare; a renovation of the "comfortable, clubby" space boosted the Decor score, but "it gets noisy", so for some the "convenient location" is the main draw; P.S. the "prix fixe is quite a bargain."

Tiffin *Indian*　　　　　　　21 | 18 | 21 | $29

West Rogers Park | 2536 W. Devon Ave. (Maplewood Ave.) | 773-338-2143

"More upscale than" its "surrounding Devon Avenue" neighbors, this midpriced Indian in West Rogers Park gets props for "delicious" mainstays such as "tikka" and "tandoori" plus "amazingly complex vegetarian dishes"; hotheads note even "their mild is impressively spicy" and are sure to ask the "hovering" staff for extra "tasty naan" to "soak up the sauce"; P.S. the "lunch buffet" offers lots of "variety" at a "good price."

Tin Fish *Seafood*   23 | 18 | 20 | $40

Tinley Park | Cornerstone Ctr. | 18201 S. Harlem Ave. (183rd St.) | 708-532-0200 | www.tinfishrestaurant.com

"Pick your fish", "your preparation" and "accompaniment" and enjoy the "unique" experience offered at this "solid" midpriced Tinley Park seafooder where tin finned creatures hang from the ceiling; the "beautifully prepared" "fresh" fare, "good" "selection of wines" and helpful staff add to a "visit" surveyors call "worth the drive."

Toast *American*   22 | 16 | 19 | $19

Lincoln Park | 746 W. Webster Ave. (Halsted St.) | 773-935-5600
Bucktown | 2046 N. Damen Ave. (bet. Dickens & McLean Aves.) | 773-772-5600
www.toast-chicago.com

"Original breakfast creations" fanatics call "so good they cause hallucinations" are on the menu at this "funky" Bucktown and Lincoln Park pair where diners brave "daunting lines" to indulge; lunch items are also available, prices are "pretty reasonable" and the "efficient" but "not necessarily friendly" service gets the job done, even during the madcap "weekend brunch"; P.S. closed at dinner.

Tocco Ⓜ *Italian*   12 | 15 | 10 | $33

Bucktown | 1266 N. Milwaukee Ave. (bet. Ashland Ave. & Paulina St.) | 773-687-8895 | www.toccochicago.com

"Impress your date" at this "upscale" but "cozy" midpriced Bucktown wine bar, an ultramod hot-pink, black-and-white sibling to the former Follia that serves "robust" fare including pizzas and "basic" pastas; service ranges from "attentive" to a "helping of attitude", and though some aren't "running back" others say it's "worth a visit."

Todai *Asian*   - | - | - | M

Schaumburg | Woodfield Mall | E-109 Woodfield Mall (Golf Rd.) | 847-619-1088 | www.todaichicago.com

Woodfield Mall is home to this international chain's first Chicago outpost, which focuses on Asian fusion fare and offers a 160-ft. 'international seafood and sushi buffet' plus other dishes made to order; the massive, ultramodern space draws shoppers, families and seniors and is open for both lunch (cheaper) and dinner (which features some higher-end ingredients).

Topaz Café *American*   ▽ 23 | 22 | 23 | $41

Burr Ridge | 780 Village Center Dr. (County Line Rd.) | 630-654-1616 | www.topazcafe.com

Southwest Suburbanites are "thrilled" to have this "sleek", slightly pricey Burr Ridge sibling to Westmont's Amber Cafe around as a "regular" haunt for "impressive" New American fare "perfectly prepared" with "many seasonal" ingredients; the urban space – with an open kitchen, stylish lounge and patio – is "inviting" once you get past the "not particularly exciting" mall-centered address, and the experience is enhanced by "professional service."

Topo Gigio Ristorante *Italian*   23 | 18 | 20 | $38

Old Town | 1516 N. Wells St. (North Ave.) | 312-266-9355 | www.topogigiochicago.com

"Charming" and "accommodating", this midpriced Old Town "neighborhood standby" turns out "traditional" Italian fare that's "consistently respectable if not exciting" with "something for everyone" from "kids" to "cougars" (though some just "go for the bar scene"); its "outside patio" is a prime summer perch for "people-watching" adding to the reasons regulars say it's on the "topo my list."

☑ Topolobampo ⌧Ⓜ *Mexican*   28 | 24 | 26 | $68

River North | 445 N. Clark St. (bet. Hubbard & Illinois Sts.) | 312-661-1434 | www.rickbayless.com

"Converts" call Rick Bayless' "modern", "refined" River North standout "the best" "gourmet Mexican" "in the country", declaring the "remarkable" "regional" flavors "expensive but worth it"; the art-adorned, "white-tablecloth" setting – plus the "fine wine service" and a "skilled", "professional" staff – makes patrons "forget" preconceptions about "south-of-the-border" cuisine (just be sure to reserve "long in advance"); P.S. "value"-hunters might try the chef's "casual Frontera Grill" next door or grab a torta from nearby Xoco.

Trader Vic's *Polynesian*   17 | 21 | 19 | $46

Gold Coast | Newberry Plaza | 1030 N. State St. (Maple St.) | 312-642-6500 | www.tradervicschicago.com

"Nostalgic kitsch" "beyond belief" attracts "tourists" and locals to this spendy Gold Coast link in the Polynesian chain with "decent" pupu platters, "umbrella drinks" (including the original "mai tai") and endless "campy" tiki trappings; while not everyone "writes home about" the fare or service, and some say it's a "shadow of its former, grander days", few argue it's anything but a "genuine good time."

Tramonto's
Steak & Seafood *Seafood/Steak*   24 | 25 | 22 | $63

Wheeling | Westin Chicago North Shore | 601 N. Milwaukee Ave. (Lake Cook Rd.) | 847-777-6575 | www.westinnorthshore.com

Namesake chef Rick Tramonto has departed these North Shore digs now owned by Westin hotels, but the steak and seafood menu and extensive wine cellar holding "some wonderful bargains" remain, delivered with "professional service" in a "stylish dining room" with a waterfall wall; however, "for the price", some diners squawk that the "choppy" "concept" "doesn't live up to expectations."

Trattoria D.O.C. *Italian/Pizza*   19 | 16 | 19 | $33

Evanston | 706 Main St. (Custer Ave.) | 847-475-1111 | www.trattoria-doc.com

"City folks" meet their "North Suburban friends" at this "solid", "family-friendly" Neapolitan pizza place in Evanston that offers "fantastic" "wood-fired" pies along with pasta and other Italian fare plus wine at "everyday affordable" prices; despite a few grumbles about "inconsistent" service, most agree it's "fine if you're in the area."

Trattoria Gianni Ⓜ *Italian*
▽ 26 | 19 | 24 | $38

Lincoln Park | 1711 N. Halsted St. (bet. North Ave. & Willow St.) | 312-266-1976 | www.trattoriagianni.com

"Convenient" "before or after a show at the Steppenwolf or Royal George" theaters, this fireplace-lit Lincoln Parker is a fixture for "fresh", "authentic" Italian favorites plus "always accommodating" service and a "wonderfully edited selection of wines"; partisans promise it's "worth" visiting; P.S. try the patio when it's warm.

Trattoria Isabella *Italian*
▽ 26 | 26 | 24 | $35

West Loop | 217 N. Jefferson St. (bet. Fulton & Lake Sts.) | 312-207-1900 | www.trattoriaisabellachicago.com

"Generous" portions of red-sauce Italian "standards" (housemade pasta, "brick-oven pizza") bring "bliss" to *amici* of this "affordable" West Looper in a "comfortable", wood-trimmed setting; service that's "on the mark" helps make it "recommended for families too"; P.S. the "outdoor patio and bar with a flat-screen TV is a gem."

Trattoria No. 10 Ⓢ *Italian*
24 | 21 | 23 | $43

Loop | 10 N. Dearborn St. (bet. Madison & Washington Sts.) | 312-984-1718 | www.trattoriaten.com

Subterranean digs belie the "wonderful" experience at this "quiet", "consistent" Loop "Italiano" known for its "winning" "homemade ravioli" and "attentive" service in a "charming atmosphere" complete with arches and murals; a "must for theatergoers", "business lunches" and "romantic dates", it offers "good value" for something so "refined"; P.S. the "after-work buffet is spectacular."

Trattoria Roma *Italian*
21 | 13 | 19 | $38

Old Town | 1535 N. Wells St. (bet. North Ave. & Schiller St.) | 312-664-7907 | www.trattoriaroma.com

There's a reason this "neighborhoody" Old Town Italian is "packed with locals" – the "no-nonsense" moderately priced menu of pasta, pizza, fish and other dishes offers a "can't-miss" meal; though it's "compact" and "service is sometimes slow when it's busy", "people don't mind" as it's "warm" and "user-friendly"; P.S. the Decor score doesn't reflect the post-Survey expansion of the bar.

Trattoria Trullo *Italian*
23 | 19 | 21 | $44

Lincoln Square | 4767 N. Lincoln Ave. (Lawrence Ave.) | 773-506-0093

"Puglian" fare is "truly a treat" at this Lincoln Square kitchen where "real Italians" go in search of "quality" cooking from the "convivial" chef-owner; a "neighborhood feel", "value" prices and a "friendly", "informed staff" help "make the experience."

Trattoria 225 *Italian*
- | - | - | M

Oak Park | 225 Harrison St. (Harvey Ave.) | 708-358-8555 | www.trattoria225.com

Situated in Oak Park's Arts District, this spacious, "family-friendly" "neighborhood place" with exposed-brick walls, local artwork and a concrete bar supplies moderately priced "creative", "wood-grilled" seasonal Italian fare ("pizza is the star") delivered by an "earnest" staff; the majority appreciates having a "nice glass of wine" as the younger set looks over the "kids' menu"; P.S. there was a post-Survey change in ownership.

Tre Kronor Scandinavian

23	17	22	$23

Albany Park | 3258 W. Foster Ave. (bet. Sawyer & Spaulding Aves.) | 773-267-9888 | www.trekronorestaurant.com

Expats are in "herring heaven" at this "spare" Albany Park Scandinavian serving "excellent renditions" of "affordable" "comfort food" "all day" including "outstanding fish" – "especially anything with salmon"; a "Sunday brunch tradition", the "homey" "storefront" BYO is also a "winner" come Christmas when the "amazing" "julbord" smorgasbord makes "memories" that last "all year."

ⓩ Tru Ⓑ French

28	27	28	$130

Streeterville | 676 N. St. Clair St. (bet. Erie & Huron Sts.) | 312-202-0001 | www.trurestaurant.com

Streeterville's jacket-required, "world-class" New French stays "true to its reputation" with "flawless" "super-luxury" tastings and famed, "expense account"–required "crystal steps of caviar"; while perhaps "a little stuffy", this "adult-only" go-to for "anniversaries" and "special occasions" is capped by a "wonderful wine selection", "serene", art-adorned dining room and "extraordinary" service that resembles "heaven on earth."

Tub Tim Thai Ⓑ Thai

▽	24	14	20	$21

Skokie | 4927 Oakton St. (Niles Ave.) | 847-675-8424 | www.tubtimthai.com

They "do everything a little bit better" than their peers say fans of this Downtown Skokie storefront Thai that impresses even those who take multiple "trips to Thailand"; praise goes to the "complex", "reasonably priced" menu of both "unique" and familiar offerings, "beautiful presentations", "gracious hospitality" and "rotating, original" local artwork in the "cozy" surroundings; but a fickle few find it's "not worth all the acclaim it gets."

Tufano's Vernon Park Tap Ⓜ⇄ Italian

20	13	20	$26

Little Italy/University Village | 1073 W. Vernon Park Pl. (Carpenter St.) | 312-733-3393

You'll think you've "walked straight into a mob movie" at this "down-to-earth" University Village Italian, where the "blackboard menu" features "honest", "family-style" dishes with "huge flavors" (go for the "lemon chicken to die for"); but the "charismatic" staff and generous portions at this 1930s vintage "standby" don't sway the handful of detractors put off by the "long waits"; P.S. cash only.

Turquoise Turkish

23	18	21	$34

Roscoe Village | 2147 W. Roscoe St. (bet. Hamilton Ave. & Leavitt St.) | 773-549-3523 | www.turquoisedining.com

For "unbelievable", "authentic" Turkish fare with "flair", boosters beat a path to this "inviting", moderately priced Roscoe Village "treasure" serving "gorgeous home-baked bread" and "outstanding" lamb in an "elegant but not ornate" white-tablecloth setting (there's sidewalk seating also); just "be patient in summer during the busy weekend crush."

Tuscany *Italian*
22 | 19 | 21 | $39

Little Italy/University Village | 1014 W. Taylor St. (Morgan St.) | 312-829-1990
Wheeling | 550 S. Milwaukee Ave. (Manchester Dr.) | 847-465-9988
Oak Brook | 1415 W. 22nd St. (Rte. 83) | 630-990-1993 ⓢ
www.tuscanychicago.com

Wake up and "smell the garlic" at Phil Stefani's Tuscan offspring, where the "classics" "do not fail", the service "never feels rushed" and the "old-world ambiance", though varied from one location to the next, seems "intimate"; go-to spots for "business meals", dates and "family events", they generally afford a "tasty" trip, unless you're among the minority that regards this "carb" extravaganza as an "uninspired" "chain operation."

Tweet ⌷ *American*
22 | 18 | 20 | $18

Uptown | 5020 N. Sheridan Rd. (Argyle St.) | 773-728-5576 | www.tweet.biz

"Locals" can't get enough of Uptown's "fun, bright", inexpensive neighborhood New American that serves "one of the best" brunches in Chicago, plus "caloric" breakfasts and daytime eats, including a "terrific Reuben" sandwich, crab cakes and organic burgers "worth" the "forever wait"; "smile your way through" by ordering a Bloody Mary from the "charming" staff – they're "welcoming to all"; P.S. "be sure to bring cash."

Twin Anchors *BBQ*
23 | 14 | 20 | $29

Old Town | 1655 N. Sedgwick St. (bet. Eugenie St. & North Ave.) | 312-266-1616 | www.twinanchorsribs.com

This "pure Chicago" "institution" in Old Town has achieved "landmark status" for its "dripping, sock-it-to-me ribs" ("gotta get 'em 'zesty'"), its "funky", "old-school" digs and its "jeans and a T-shirt" crowd that, at one time, included Sinatra; still, notwithstanding this restaurant's role "in the movie *Return to Me*", a contingent of 'cue cravers complains about "waits" and "perfunctory service", crying it "rests on its laurels"; P.S. reservations aren't taken so "go early" or carry out.

Twist *Eclectic*
21 | 17 | 21 | $30

Lakeview | 3412 N. Sheffield Ave. (bet. Newport Ave. & Roscoe St.) | 773-388-2727 | www.twistinchicago.com

Its "creative" small plates may suffer from an "identity crisis" ("not really Spanish, not really Latin"), but this Eclectic spot is "a good alternative" to the "bar scene" "around Wrigleyville"; those who deem the "inventive" bites, like the "bacon-wrapped dates", "outstanding" believe the "lively", "close quarters" are "so worth the squeeze", but others say the "average dishes" push them toward "better places for tapas in Chicago"; P.S. no reservations.

	FOOD	DECOR	SERVICE	COST

Twisted Spoke ● *Pub Food* | 18 | 16 | 16 | $20 |

Noble Square | 501 N. Ogden Ave. (Grand Ave.) | 312-666-1500 |
www.twistedspoke.com

Regulars "get revved up" over this "funky", "family-friendly" Noble
Square pseudo "biker bar" with one of the "best outdoor" patios "in
the city" and decor of "metal tables" and motorcycle parts; the "hospitable", "heavily tattooed servers" appear to "care" about the
"solid" "American bar food", "delicious" burgers, "killer Bloody
Marys" and "wide beer and liquor selection" they sling, but "despite
attempts to be edgy" – every Saturday post-midnight they turn on the
"old-school porn" for a 'Smut and Eggs' event – it's all "pretty tame."

Udupi Palace *Indian* | 23 | 11 | 16 | $19 |

West Rogers Park | 2543 W. Devon Ave. (bet. Maplewood Ave. &
Rockwell St.) | 773-338-2152
Schaumburg | Market Sq. | 730 E. Schaumburg Rd. (Plum Grove Rd.) |
847-884-9510
www.udupipalace.com

The "wide selection" of "painfully spicy", primarily Southern Indian
dishes "clears sinus passages" at this "simple" Rogers Park BYO with a
"reliable" Schaumburg sibling; "adventurous" diners tout the "pip-
ing hot" preps, including "to-die-for" dosas and "consistently exceptional" "for the dollar" vegetarian fare, though hotheads gripe about
"bland" eats and servers who seem to do little more than "try."

NEW Ukai Japanese | - | - | - | M |
Restaurant *Japanese*

Lakeview | 1059 W. Belmont Ave. (Seminary Ave.) | 773-868-9900 |
www.ukaichicago.com

This stylish Lakeview BYO turns out funky specialty maki, classic
cooked fare and some contemporary twists on dishes like caprese
salad and crab rangoon, all served in an industrial-meets-Asian setting with plush banquettes, box lanterns and a sushi bar backed by
a glowing red lattice; P.S. it gets its name from the Japanese practice
of using cormorants for fishing.

Uncle Bub's *BBQ* | - | - | - | I |

Westmont | 132 S. Cass Ave. (bet. Dallas & Richmond Sts.) |
630-493-9000 | www.unclebubs.com

BBQ-slathered porcine and poultry parts are among the draws at
this hickory-and-applewood-scented, counter-service smoke shack
in Westmont, where farm tools and a wall of hot sauce are among
the rough-hewn, roadhouse-inspired trappings; a popular weekly
pig roast, bustling catering biz and kid-friendly confines (spacious,
high-backed booths, complimentary soft-serve) add to its charm.

Uncle John's BBQ ⌧� *BBQ* | - | - | - | I |

Far South Side | 337 E. 69th St. (Calumet Ave.) | 773-892-1233
Finger-lickers fawn over this no-frills South Side cash and "carryout-
only" BBQ "winner", pronouncing the "heavenly" "hot links" and
"terrific" "tips" – bestowed from behind a glass-enclosed counter –
"truly authentic"; the "deeply smoky" "goodness" extends to sauce

	FOOD	DECOR	SERVICE	COST

you'll want to "sip through a straw", so dress the part because it "almost never lasts the car ride home."

Uncle Julio's Hacienda *Tex-Mex*   18 | 16 | 17 | $25

Old Town | 855 W. North Ave. (Clybourn Ave.) | 312-266-4222 | www.unclejulios.com

Fajita fans go *loco* over the "fresh-made tortillas" and other "tasty" Tex-Mex – accompanied by "swirled" libations – at this Old Town hub that's a "solid" choice for families, "friends and parties"; even if faultfinders say the "Americanized" fare in a "big box", "cheesy", "warehouse" setting "isn't the best on the block", others "love it."

Uncommon Ground *Eclectic/Coffeehouse*   22 | 19 | 20 | $27

Edgewater | 1401 W. Devon Ave. (Glenwood Ave.) | 773-465-9801

Lakeview | 3800 N. Clark St. (Grace St.) | 773-929-3680
www.uncommonground.com

"Down-to-earth diners" dig the "earthy" Eclectic "comfort" fare featuring "locally sourced ingredients" (some from the "rooftop garden") at this "laid-back" Lakeview coffee shop, bar and performance venue with an Edgewater counterpart in a former speakeasy; popular for brunch, it's a "great place to meet friends anytime", but tightwads "avoid it for dinner" saying it's too "costly" then.

Union Pizzeria *Pizza*   23 | 19 | 19 | $26

Evanston | 1245 Chicago Ave. (bet. Dempster & Hamilton Sts.) | 847-475-2400 | www.unionevanston.com

A "young, hip crowd" that includes lots of "Northwestern students" converges over "crisp" "wood-fired pies", "fabulous small-bite appetizers" and large, affordable beer and wine lists at this Evanston pizzeria from the folks behind Campagnola; though the "cool scene", "family-friendly" vibe and "funky", "modern decor", including wood-beam-and-ductwork ceilings, are pluses, potential pitfalls include what some call "small portions", "high prices" and "lackadaisical" service; P.S. it also houses the performance venue Space.

NEW Uptowner Café *American/Burgers*   - | - | - | I

Lincoln Park | 2233 N. Lincoln Ave. (bet. Belden & Webster Aves.) | 773-661-2299 | www.theuptownercafe.com

At this inexpensive Lincoln Parker with a St. Paul sibling, the classic American fare includes eggs and omelets, burgers, sandwiches and a kids' menu, all served in a simple diner setting with white walls, tile floors and high-backed private booths; in a clever twist, it reopens for wee-hour dining starting at 10 PM Thursday–Saturday.

Urbanbelly Ⓜ *Asian*   24 | 14 | 15 | $23

Logan Square | 3053 N. California Ave. (bet. Barry Ave. & Nelson St.) | 773-583-0500 | www.urbanbellychicago.com

Bill Kim's "stunning" "labor of love" in a Logan Square "strip mall" achieves cult status courtesy of "quirky", "operatic" Asian fusion noodles and dumplings that "defy traditional logic"; the "hip" counter-only service, the "communal seating" in a space "with all the panache of a shed" and the BYO policy only leave surveyors more "smitten" with this "real bargain"; the main problems are "crowds" and not knowing "what to order" when "everything looks fabulous."

Veerasway ☒ Indian
21 | 20 | 19 | $41

West Loop | 844 W. Randolph St. (bet. Green & Peoria Sts.) | 312-491-0844 | www.veerasway.com

Offering a "moderately priced", "creatively reimagined" "twist on Indian" street food, with small plates and staples that "beat the sari off" Devon Street competitors, this West Loop storefront with a communal table and an on-display tandoor oven attracts a "lively", trendy crowd; thankfully, "warm" service helps soften the blow for the few who order one of the "complete misses" from a menu that also has plenty of "big hits"; P.S. watch out for the "inventive" and "delicious" – but "deceptively alcoholic" – cocktails.

Venus Greek-Cypriot Cuisine Greek
– | – | – | M

Greektown | 820 W. Jackson Blvd. (bet. Green & Halsted Sts.) | 312-714-1001 | www.venuschicago.com

Diners in the mood for something "a little different from [traditional] Greek" head to this well-priced Cypriot "gem" in Greektown where the "wonderful" menu includes both typical Hellenic fare and some "unusual" dishes (the meze is an "outstanding way to sample a full array"); the staff is "attentive" and "friendly", plus there's live piano on Fridays and Greek music on Saturdays.

Vermilion Indian/Nuevo Latino
22 | 22 | 21 | $50

River North | 10 W. Hubbard St. (bet. Dearborn & State Sts.) | 312-527-4060 | www.thevermilionrestaurant.com

"New taste sensations" abound at this "inventive", "Indian-meets-Latin" "hybrid" in River North, where the expensive, high "sensory" "thrill" takes place in a "sexy", "vibrant" dining room punctuated with images from hot fashion photog Farrokh Chothia; while service generally is "spot-on", a handful of "frustrated" diners dis the "odd" combos and "weird" flavors; P.S. there's an offshoot, At Vermilion, in NYC.

Via Carducci Italian
23 | 18 | 21 | $36

Lincoln Park | 1419 W. Fullerton Ave. (bet. Janssen & Southport Aves.) | 773-665-1981

Via Carducci La Sorella Italian

Wicker Park | 1928 W. Division St. (Winchester Ave.) | 773-252-2246 www.viacarducci-lasorella.com

"Loyal customers" champion this reasonably priced Lincoln Park Southern Italian – and its Wicker Park mate – for "never failing to deliver" "homey" if "ubiquitous" "favorites", including "outstanding" thin-crust pizza and "out-of-this-world" gnocchi in a "quaint", "romantic" "cafe" setting; "personal" service aside, however, a few bellyachers balk over what they call a "lack of flavor."

Viand Bar & Kitchen American
22 | 18 | 23 | $33

Streeterville | 155 E. Ontario St. (Michigan Ave.) | 312-255-8505 | www.viandchicago.com

Chef Steve Chiappetti knows how to do "simple food" right say proponents of this moderately priced Streeterville New American with an "attentive", "friendly staff" in a setting with art deco touches adjacent to the Marriott Courtyard; though the comfort food is "interesting" but "a bit heavy" to some, the "awesome French toast" strikes a note at breakfast, and the quarters are "cozy in winter and delightful outside in summer."

Viceroy of India *Indian*
21 | 18 | 18 | $26

Northwest Side | 2520 W. Devon Ave. (bet. Campbell & Maplewood Aves.) | 773-743-4100
Lombard | 233 E. Roosevelt Rd. (Highland Ave.) | 630-627-4411
www.viceroyofindia.com

A "wide selection" of moderately priced, "authentic" Indian dishes, including "consistently excellent" curries, is the hallmark of this "upscale" "pioneer" with locations on the Northwest Side and in Lombard; while the "great lunch buffet" pleases bargain-hunters and vegetarians, detractors say the "drab interior" makes you "feel like you're eating in a self-serve cafeteria."

Victory's Banner *Eclectic/Vegetarian*
∇ 24 | 16 | 22 | $17

Roscoe Village | 2100 W. Roscoe St. (Hoyne Ave.) | 773-665-0227 | www.victorysbanner.com

"Sensational" vegetarian and vegan fare lures tree-huggers to this "small", "bright", affordable Roscoe Village breakfast, lunch and brunch "find" that's "packed" on weekends; the "who-needs-meat-anyway" vibe and "sweet, attentive service" – not to mention the "recommended" French toast – attract legions of disciples, but others say the "spiritual", even "cult"-like, atmosphere can be "kind [of] creepy."

🅩 Vie Ⓧ *American*
27 | 25 | 28 | $68

Western Springs | 4471 Lawn Ave. (Burlington Ave.) | 708-246-2082 | www.vierestaurant.com

Locavores "drive from the city" and beyond to Paul Virant's "deservedly respected" New American "haven" in Western Springs, where "magical" dishes are crafted using "simple", "sustainable" ingredients (including house-"pickled garnishes" and "great charcuterie"); the "lovely" 1940s-era, French-inspired interior, the "wonderful" service and the high prices – though "lower than Downtown" – place it in the "special-occasion category", but admirers could "eat [here] every day"; P.S. Virant will divide his time between this flagship and Lincoln Park's Perennial Virant.

Village, The ◑ *Italian*
21 | 21 | 20 | $36

Loop | Italian Vill. | 71 W. Monroe St., 2nd fl. (bet. Clark & Dearborn Sts.) | 312-332-7005 | www.italianvillage-chicago.com

This "romantic" 83-year-old Loop "standby" – one of the Capitanini family's Italian Village trio at the same location – "looks the same" as ever with its twinkly "little lights" and "private booths"; a "favorite" with "pre-theater"-goers and "tourists" who find "familiar" comfort in the "reasonably priced", "reliable" pastas, extensive wine list and "professional" staff, it's merely "mediocre" to modernists, who quip it "tastes like" it's been around since 1927.

	FOOD	DECOR	SERVICE	COST

NEW Vincent M *American/Dutch*   - | - | - | M

Andersonville | 1475 W. Balmoral Ave. (bet. Clark St. & Glenwood Ave.) | 773-334-7168 | www.vincentchicago.com

HB Home Bistro chef-owner Joncarl Lachman goes American with a 'strong Dutch accent' at this Andersonville charmer in the former La Tache space, named in a nod to Van Gogh and showcasing cuisine of the Netherlands – think pickled herring, various moules frites and haddock on snert (a thick pea soup); the quaint environs feature black-and-white photography of Amsterdam, seasonal outdoor seating and a zinc bar where Adam Seger concocts craft cocktails with a focus on gin and genever.

Vinci M *Italian*   21 | 19 | 23 | $43

Lincoln Park | 1732 N. Halsted St. (Willow St.) | 312-266-1199 | www.vincichicago.com

Those who "stumble upon" Paul LoDuca's "unparalleled" Lincoln Park *"cucina"* – located "across from [the] Steppenwolf" Theatre – "linger" in a "relaxed atmosphere" over "amazing", "homemade" Tuscan cuisine, including "delicate" pasta and a "do-not-miss" grilled portobello and polenta appetizer; because the "respectable" classics are brought to table by "friendly servers" at "more than reasonable prices", the majority considers it a "winner."

Vintage 338 ◐⊠ *European*   - | - | - | M

Lincoln Park | 338 W. Armitage Ave. (bet. Clark St. & Lincoln Ave.) | 773-525-0521 | www.vintage338.com

A compact Euro wine list and tapas-style 'Southern European' small-plates selection of cheese and charcuterie, plus spreads, salads and sandwiches with artisanal ingredients lure Lincoln Parkers to this comfortably elegant, midpriced wine bar done in neutrals and dark wood with sparkling light fixtures, vintage mirrors and seasonal patio.

Vito & Nick's ⊅ *Pizza*   25 | 12 | 18 | $17

Far South Side | 8433 S. Pulaski Rd. (84th Pl.) | 773-735-2050 | www.vitoandnick.com

This "respected" South Side pizzeria has tossed out cracker-"thin crust" "at its best" amid carpeted walls and "sultry" blue lighting for more than 30 years; the "personable" staff "runs on no one's schedule but their own", so you may have to "flag your waitress down" to get your pie – luckily "it's worth the wait"; P.S. the "army who eat here daily can't be wrong."

Vivere ⊠ *Italian*   22 | 21 | 22 | $53

Loop | Italian Vill. | 71 W. Monroe St. (bet. Clark & Dearborn Sts.) | 312-332-4040 | www.vivere-chicago.com

Christened "the best" of the Italian Village trio, this "romantic-yet-bustling", "modern" Italian with a "fabulous" wine list and "super-cool" "Jordan Mozer eye-candy" room is a "convenient" "pre-theater choice" in the Loop; while "formal and costly" compared to its kin, it "deserves a bit more respect" say its fans, but foes frown over "spotty" service that leads to waits so long "your clothes might go out of style"; P.S. be sure to "make reservations."

Vivo *Italian*

24 | 20 | 20 | $39

West Loop | 838 W. Randolph St. (bet. Green & Peoria Sts.) | 312-733-3379 | www.vivo-chicago.com

A "cozy but luxurious" "date spot" for Southern Italian fare along Randolph Street's Restaurant Row, this longtime West Loop trattoria inspires the pasta-loving populace with both "inventive" and traditional preparations; while claustrophobes cringe over "crammed together" tables, the "nice wine list" and "sizable portions" make up for it; P.S. "for a special occasion", ask for the "adorable" "elevator shaft table" perched "above the main floor."

Volare *Italian*

24 | 17 | 21 | $40

Streeterville | 201 E. Grand Ave. (St. Clair St.) | 312-410-9900
Oakbrook Terrace | 1919 S. Meyers Rd. (22nd St.) | 630-495-0200
www.volarerestaurant.com

You'll feel like "*la famiglia*" at this "quaint" Streeterville Venetian with an equally "lively", wood-trimmed Oakbrook Terrace sib, where the "fairly priced", "hearty portions" of "real Italian" fare (try the osso buco) are "incredible" and the staff "bends over backwards"; the close, "crowded" tables and bad acoustics, however, mean the "fracas" reaches "deafening" levels.

Volo Restaurant & Wine Bar 🗷 *American*

- | - | - | M

Roscoe Village | 2008 W. Roscoe St. (Damen Ave.) | 773-348-4600 | www.volorestaurant.com

Oenophiles wish this New American "taste of California" in Roscoe Village would stay "undiscovered", but the "outstanding" small plates and "excellent" wines keep it buzzing; what's more, the "exceptional" patio and "romantic booths" are "perfect for a date."

Wakamono *Japanese*

22 | 19 | 15 | $32

Lakeview | 3317 N. Broadway (Buckingham Pl.) | 773-296-6800 | www.wakamonosushi.com

"Amazing" fish at "value prices" hooks "happy campers" at this Lakeview Japanese with "inventive" rolls, "delicious" sashimi and plenty of cooked selections; you can BYO or order one of the "excellent drinks" – both a consolation for the "painfully slow service" that leads to "long waits on weekends"; P.S. there's sidewalk seating.

🆕 Wasabi Ⓜ *Japanese*

- | - | - | M

Logan Square | 2539 N. Milwaukee Ave. (bet. Logan Blvd. & Sacramento Ave.) | 773-227-8180 | www.wasabichicago.com

Beyond basic and signature sushi, this Logan Square BYO boasts an extensive, midpriced menu of Japanese dinner and brunch fare; behind the quaint storefront exterior, the minimal, modern setting features exposed brick, low lighting and a sushi bar.

Wave *Mediterranean*

∇ 13 | 21 | 13 | $58

Streeterville | W Chicago Lakeshore | 644 N. Lake Shore Dr. (Ontario St.) | 312-255-4460 | www.waverestaurant.com

"Beautiful decor" and a "great view of the lake" set the tone at this "trendy" Mediterranean small-plates concept off the lobby of

Streeterville's W Hotel; fans find the "pretty" fare is exactly what "you'd expect", yet grouches grump that the "quality" and "attitude" is enough to make them "wave goodbye"; P.S. desserts are a "steal", and a "long, interesting drink menu" adds happy-hour appeal.

Weber Grill *BBQ*
20 | 18 | 19 | $36

River North | Hilton Garden Inn | 539 N. State St. (Grand Ave.) | 312-467-9696
Schaumburg | 1010 N. Meacham Rd. (American Ln.) | 847-413-0800
Lombard | 2331 Fountain Square Dr. (Meyers Rd.) | 630-953-8880
www.webergrillrestaurant.com

It's like a "year-round barbecue" in your backyard say sizzle-seekers of this trio of midpriced "meat-lovers' paradises" in River North and the 'burbs, where "industrial-size" Webers fire up the burgers, pork ribs, beef brisket and Parmesan-crusted tilapia; while the "decor won't win you over" and it can get "overrun with tourists", "convention attendees" and those who "can tolerate long waits", it "beats standing outside to grill in winter."

Webster Wine Bar ● *Eclectic*
20 | 18 | 20 | $30

Lincoln Park | 1480 W. Webster Ave. (bet. Ashland Ave. & Clybourn St.) | 773-868-0608 | www.websterwinebar.com

Whether "you're an expert or not", the "oddball" but "amazing" vinos – many poured "by the glass" – at this "candlelit" Lincoln Park wine bar "boggle the mind", especially when teamed with "terrific cheeses" and Eclectic small plates; though "off the beaten track", it's a prime perch for "dates", "pre-movie drinks" or powwows with colleagues, and all benefit from the "ridiculously knowledgeable", "friendly" staff and "fair prices."

West Town Tavern 🗷 *American*
24 | 21 | 21 | $43

Noble Square | 1329 W. Chicago Ave. (Throop St.) | 312-666-6175 | www.westtowntavern.com

"So cozy [you'll] want to bring your blankie", this "consistent" New American charmer located in Noble Square gets "accolades" for "delicious comfort food", including "traditional" ("but not boring") fried chicken and "exceptional" pot roast; "whether you graze" or "order a full meal", it's a "standout" thanks to "reasonable" prices, a "simple" yet "amazing" wine list and "darn nice", "knowledgeable" service.

White Fence Farm Ⓜ *American*
22 | 18 | 21 | $22

Romeoville | 1376 Joliet Rd. (Bolingbrook Dr.) | 630-739-1720 | www.whitefencefarm-il.com

The "mouthwatering" Traditional American fare from this "South Suburban icon" is "as good as it ever was" attest fanatics of the "fantastic", "juicy" fried chicken, "really special" corn fritters and "great hushpuppies"; with seating in "lots of different" "old-fashioned" rooms filled with "kitschy decor", it's all "worth the drive" to "the boonies"; P.S. check out the "auto museum and farm animals" at the on-site petting zoo.

	FOOD	DECOR	SERVICE	COST

☒ Wiener's Circle ●⌿ Hot Dogs   21 | 5 | 14 | $9

Lincoln Park | 2622 N. Clark St. (Wrightwood Ave.) | 773-477-7444 | www.wienercircle.net

"Go after the bars close", "yell out your order" and add "a couple of expletives" for "the full experience" at Lincoln Park's "sassy" "side show" where the "staff commentary is almost as good" as the char-dogs (some of the "best" in the city); the "wild scene" "never gets old" say its "foul-mouthed fans", but sober sorts bristle at the service and decor, saying "go somewhere else if you aren't completely inebriated."

☒ Wildfire Steak   23 | 21 | 21 | $43

River North | 159 W. Erie St. (bet. LaSalle Blvd. & Wells St.) | 312-787-9000
Lincolnshire | 235 Parkway Dr. (Milwaukee Ave.) | 847-279-7900
Glenview | 1300 Patriot Blvd. (Lake Ave.) | 847-657-6363
Schaumburg | 1250 E. Higgins Rd. (National Pkwy.) | 847-995-0100
Oak Brook | Oakbrook Center Mall | 232 Oakbrook Ctr. (Rte. 83) | 630-586-9000
www.wildfirerestaurant.com

"Consistent" from "location to location", these "always packed" River North and suburban steakhouses from the Lettuce Entertain You group have a "broad", if pricey, menu of "superb" wood-grilled meat ("love the trio of filets"), "solid sides" and "excellent seafood" – all in "huge portions"; still, the sometimes "mediocre service", "unpleasantly noisy" environs and "clubby", "1940s"-ish decor make it feel a bit "like a chain" for some; P.S. "reservations are a must."

Wildfish Japanese   21 | 17 | 17 | $37

Deerfield | Deerfield Commons Shopping Ctr. | 730 Waukegan Rd. (bet. Deerfield Rd. & Osterman Ave.) | 847-317-9453
Arlington Heights | Arlington Town Sq. | 60 S. Arlington Heights Rd. (bet. Northwest Hwy. & Sigwalt St.) | 847-870-8260
www.wildfishsushi.com

Sushi fans are "impressed" with the "innovative", "artistically presented" "specialty rolls" and "wide selection of sake" at this loungey Deerfield and Arlington Heights Japanese duo where "Chicago quality" begets "Chicago prices"; still, a minority is brought down by service that ranges from "enthusiastic" to "comically bad."

Wishbone Southern   21 | 16 | 20 | $21

Roscoe Village | 3300 N. Lincoln Ave. (School St.) | 773-549-2663
West Loop | 1001 W. Washington Blvd. (Morgan St.) | 312-850-2663
Berwyn | 6611 Roosevelt Rd. (bet. Clarence & East Aves.) | 708-749-1295 Ⓜ
www.wishbonechicago.com

Find "inexpensive" Southern "comfort" at this "down-home" threesome where the meals (including some Cajun choices) are "nothing fancy" but are nonetheless a "slice of heaven" – especially the grits, biscuits and other "classic" breakfast selections; they "don't miss a beat on the plate", but the "bustling" dining rooms can get "crowded", so "come early" and don't be put off by the "laid-back", "perfunctory" service.

NEW Wolcott's ◐ *American*

FOOD	DECOR	SERVICE	COST
-	-	-	I

Ravenswood | 1843 W. Montrose Ave. (Honore St.) | 773-334-4848 |
www.wolcottschicago.com

This Ravenswood sports bar dishes up affordable American eats ranging from bar-food faves to vegetarian options, paired with 10 tap brews and signature cocktails, all served till late nightly; the casual modern pub setting is outfitted with a half-dozen TVs and wall of windows (plus outdoor seats in warm weather).

Woo Lae Oak *Korean*

FOOD	DECOR	SERVICE	COST
20	21	17	$39

Rolling Meadows | 3201 Algonquin Rd. (Newport Dr.) |
847-870-9910 | www.woolaeoakchicago.com

Kimchi cravers are "shocked" to find "such a large, high-end" Korean barbecue in Rolling Meadows, "highly recommending" this "formal" eatery with "wonderful" decor and "solid" grill-your-own grub; those not on an "expense account" opt for the weekday "lunch special" – and don't be "in a rush" because service "can be slow."

Xni-Pec *Mexican*

FOOD	DECOR	SERVICE	COST
-	-	-	M

Brookfield | 3755 Grand Blvd. (Brookfield Ave.) | 708-290-0082 |
www.xnipec.us

Foodies head off the beaten path to this family-run Yucatecan nestled in a triangular Brookfield storefront; the warmly lit space hosts diners enjoying affordable homespun dishes, augmented by rustic, *abuela*-style specials, fruity cocktails and imported brews.

Xoco ⊠Ⓜ *Mexican*

FOOD	DECOR	SERVICE	COST
25	16	18	$20

River North | 449 N. Clark St. (Illinois St.) | 312-334-3688 |
www.xocochicago.com

Master chef Rick Bayless' LEED-certified "counter-service"-meets-"haute"-style River North Mexican cultivates *pasión* among "street-food" enthusiasts, who brave the "cosmic" waits for "outstanding" tortas ("especially any with pork"), "giant bowls of caldos", "addictive churros" and cacao bean–to-cup hot chocolate; "what it lacks in comfort" – an "odd" ordering protocol, "cramped", communal seating – is forgiven once the "awe-inspiring" eats arrive.

Yard House *American*

FOOD	DECOR	SERVICE	COST
18	17	18	$28

Glenview | The Glen | 1880 Tower Dr. (Patriot Blvd.) | 847-729-9273 |
www.yardhouse.com

"It's all about the beer" (over 130 by draft) at this family-friendly North Suburban outpost of a national chain; fans say it sometimes "transcends the typical" with its "modernized" American pub grub, famed suds by the half-"yard" and "perfect" setting "for happy hours or to watch a game", but "don't go there if you want to talk" because the "noise level is horrendous"; P.S. there's a gluten-free menu.

NEW Yindee *Japanese/Thai*

FOOD	DECOR	SERVICE	COST
-	-	-	I

Lakeview | 1824 W. Addison St. (Wolcott Ave.) | 773-525-4040 |
www.yindeechicago.com

Under the El tracks, this little Lakeview BYO doubles up with a menu of budget-friendly Thai and Japanese eats (including sushi), plus daily lunch deals from both cuisines; handmade bamboo tables populate a colorful room with pendant lighting and good-luck symbols like a painting of Asian carp and a kitschy collection of cat figurines.

Yolk *American* | 22 | 17 | 20 | $17 |

River North | 747 N. Wells St. (bet. Chicago Ave. & Superior St.) | 312-787-2277
Streeterville | 355 E. Ohio St. (bet. Fairbanks & McClurg Cts.) | 312-822-9655
South Loop | 1120 S. Michigan Ave. (11th St.) | 312-789-9655
www.yolk-online.com

The South Loop original "is so good that they opened another" outpost of this "yolk"-hued, "phenomenal breakfast" (and BYO lunch) nook in River North, where the same "alluring aroma" of "bacon waffles", pancakes and omelets prompts you to order a "gigantic portion"; the lines can seem "endless" and the acoustics "terrible", but the majority finds the affordable offerings "worth the wait"; P.S. there's also a location in Streeterville.

Yoshi's Café Ⓜ *French/Japanese* | 25 | 19 | 25 | $51 |

Lakeview | 3257 N. Halsted St. (Aldine Ave.) | 773-248-6160 | www.yoshiscafe.com

Yoshi Katsumura's "quaint little" Lakeview haunt is "still good after many, many years" insists the "eclectic crowd" that appreciates its "warm" "welcome", "elegantly remodeled" space and "no-shortcuts" approach to "unpretentious" and "unique" Japanese/French–influenced fare; just remember, "you get what you pay for" here, so "be prepared to spend."

⅂⅂⅂ Yuca Café *Eclectic* | - | - | - | I |

Wicker Park | 2257 W. North Ave. (Oakley Blvd.) | 773-227-6600

Hearty, affordable breakfast and lunch fare – from American classics to more globally inspired eats like Dutch crêpes – whets Wicker Park appetites at this BYO cafe in Pannenkoeken's former home; the modern space has funky art and an outdoor dining area in season.

Zak's Place Ⓩ *American* | - | - | - | E |

Hinsdale | 112 S. Washington St. (bet. 1st & 2nd Sts.) | 630-323-9257 | www.zaksplace.com

"Comfortable" and "down-to-earth", this Hinsdale "gem" named for a beloved pet offers "serious", "seasonal" New American fare and a 300-bottle wine list in a setting with exposed brick, cherry wood and copper trim; proponents tell of bar bites that are "uniformly delicious" and servers who "could sell ice to Eskimos", though the downer is prices that can be "astounding."

Zaleski & Horvath MarketCafe *Deli* | - | - | - | I |

⅀ℲℲ Hyde Park | 1323 E. 57th St. (bet. Kenwood & Kimbark Aves.) | 773-363-0070 Ⓩ Ⓜ
Kenwood | 1126 E. 47th St. (Greenwood Ave.) | 773-538-7372
www.zhmarketcafe.com

Luxe cheeses, salads and playfully named panini – detailed on a chalkboard behind the glass counter – entice at this quaint Kenwood deli with a more frenetic Hyde Park sib; locals get a jolt from the espresso bar, the better for browsing metal shelves brimming with imported ingredients like olive oil, organic grain and pasta.

Zapatista *Mexican*

20 | 20 | 17 | $30

NEW **Lincoln Park** | 444 W. Fullerton Pkwy. (Clark St.) | 773-525-4100
South Loop | 1307 S. Wabash Ave. (13th St.) | 312-435-1307
Northbrook | 992 Willow Rd. (Old Willow Rd.) | 847-559-0939
www.zapatistamexicangrill.com

"Holy guacamole" effuse amigos over this "airy", "upscale" South Loop Mexican (with newer Northbrook and Lincoln Park sibs) that caters to a "young crowd" "jonesing for a 'rita", "Americanized" fajita, tableside guac and "anything with pork" ("these guys know how to treat a pig"); though the service is "erratic" and the noise level will leave you "conversationally challenged", at least you can head for the "fabulous" sidewalk patio in warm weather.

Zealous ⊠Ⓜ *American*

25 | 24 | 22 | $67

River North | 419 W. Superior St. (Sedgwick St.) | 312-475-9112 | www.zealousrestaurant.com

"Genius" chef-owner Michael Taus remains "at the top of his game", creating "inventive flavor combinations" that "blow you away" at his "plush" New American in River North; fans like the "soothing", "bamboo"-trimmed setting and "well-stocked wine cellar", but fault-finders point to the "high price point" and "inconsistent service."

Zed 451 *Eclectic*

21 | 24 | 22 | $54

River North | 739 N. Clark St. (Superior St.) | 312-266-6691 | www.zed451.com

"Gorge yourself" at this Eclectic River North "churrascaria with a twist" – it's the "hippest" "all-you-can-eat ever" and "not for the weak of appetite"; an "imaginative", seasonal salad bar, "wonderful service", "beautiful", "high-style" dining room and "stellar rooftop" terrace draw the "young and trendy", but wallet-watchers warn that you pay a high price for the "scene", so it's a good thing you won't have to "eat for a week after."

Zhivago Ⓜ *Continental*

16 | 16 | 17 | $31

Skokie | 9925 Gross Point Rd. (bet. Kedvale & Keeler Aves.) | 847-982-1400 | www.zhivagochicago.com

Surveyors seesaw on this "serviceable" North Shore Continental that offers up Russian and Eastern European "favorites"; while those with an "affinity" for goulash, beef stroganoff and schnitzel appreciate the hearty cooking and find the kitted-out "banquet hall setting" with dramatic gilding, murals and drapery "unique", others call it "mediocre" overall, noting that "crowds around 5:30" "tell you a lot"; P.S. live music heats up the dance floor on Fridays and Saturdays.

Zia's Trattoria *Italian*

24 | 18 | 21 | $35

Edison Park | 6699 N. Northwest Hwy. (Oliphant Ave.) | 773-775-0808 | www.ziaschicago.com

"Dressed-up" "soccer moms" and families endure the "long waits" and "cramped surroundings" of this "accessible" Edison Park "discovery" in order to enjoy "deftly executed", "huge portions" of "hearty" Italian fare, from the "better-than-expected appetizers" to the "delicious" carb-heavy entrees coupled with a "serviceable wine list"; but a few fusspots frown that the "friendly" staff delivers "spotty" service and the room gets pretty "noisy."

Zocalo *Mexican*

20 | 18 | 19 | $34

River North | 358 W. Ontario St. (Orleans St.) | 312-302-9977 | www.zocalochicago.com

"Upscale" "modern" Mexican fare delivered by "solid" servers at "reasonable prices" draws diners to this "loftlike" River Norther where you've "gotta have the trio of guacamole", guajillo-tinged barbacoa and a margarita; presuming you "order right", "you won't be disappointed" say scribes, who further recommend "sipping tequila" in the "exposed-brick space" or on the sidewalk in summer; P.S. Sunday and Tuesday prix fixe dinners further cajole the chile-charmed.

Zodiac Room ☒ *American*

- | - | - | M

Streeterville | Neiman Marcus | 737 N. Michigan Ave., 4th fl. (Chicago Ave.) | 312-243-8908 | www.neimanmarcus.com

Ladies who lunch frequent this hushed, fourth-floor Neiman Marcus respite overlooking Michigan Avenue, where meals begin with a complimentary cup of chicken consommé, popovers and strawberry butter; befitting its upscale Magnificent Mile address, the contemporary space is hung with art, while the menu emphasizes figure-flattering salads and sandwiches, with a handful of heftier options thrown in – presumably for the suits who occasionally show up.

CHICAGO
INDEXES

LOCATION MAPS

Cuisines

Includes names, locations and Food ratings.

AFRICAN

Bolat | **Lakeview**	-॒
Icosium Kafe | **multi.**	19॒
Sikia | **Far S Side**	-॒

AMERICAN

Abigail's | **Highland Pk**	24॒
NEW A 'Cappella | **S Loop**	-॒
NEW Acre | **Andersonville**	-॒
NEW Act One Pub | **Rogers Pk**	-॒
Adelle's | **Wheaton**	25॒
Z Alinea | **Lincoln Pk**	29॒
Amber Cafe | **Westmont**	22॒
American Girl | **Streeterville**	16॒
Ann Sather | **multi.**	21॒
NEW Aquitaine | **Lincoln Pk**	-॒
Atwater's | **Geneva**	20॒
Atwood Cafe | **Loop**	22॒
Z Avenues | **River N**	26॒
Bad Apple | **North Ctr/St. Ben's**	-॒
Bakin' & Eggs | **Lakeview**	19॒
Bandera | **Streeterville**	22॒
Bank Lane | **Lake Forest**	23॒
Bar Louie | **multi.**	16॒
NEW Bedford | **Wicker Pk**	-॒
Bijan's | **River N**	19॒
Billy Goat | **multi.**	17॒
Bin | **multi.**	21॒
NEW Bistro One West | **St. Charles**	-॒
Bite Cafe | **Ukrainian Vill**	-॒
Z Blackbird | **W Loop**	27॒
Bluebird | **Bucktown**	20॒
Blue 13 | **River N**	24॒
Boka | **Lincoln Pk**	25॒
Bongo Room | **multi.**	24॒
Z Bonsoirée | **Logan Sq**	26॒
Boston Blackies | **multi.**	19॒
Branch 27 | **Noble Sq**	17॒
Breakfast Club | **Near W**	20॒
Briejo | **Oak Pk**	14॒
Bristol | **Bucktown**	23॒
Broadway Cellars | **Edgewater**	21॒
Browntrout | **North Ctr/St. Ben's**	24॒
Cab's Wine Bar | **Glen Ellyn**	24॒
Café Absinthe | **Bucktown**	23॒
Café 103 | **Far S Side**	-॒
Café Selmarie | **Lincoln Sq**	23॒
Ceres' Table | **Uptown**	-॒
Chalkboard | **Lakeview**	22॒
Z Charlie Trotter's | **Lincoln Pk**	27॒

Z Cheesecake Factory | **multi.**	19॒
NEW Chef Amaury's | **Aurora**	-॒
Chef's Station | **Evanston**	24॒
NEW Chez Violette | **Rogers Pk**	-॒
Chicago Firehouse | **S Loop**	20॒
Cité | **Streeterville**	20॒
CityGate | **Naperville**	-॒
Clubhouse | **Oak Brook**	21॒
Corner 41 | **North Ctr/St. Ben's**	-॒
Courtright's | **Willow Spgs**	25॒
Z Crofton on Wells | **River N**	26॒
NEW Currents/River | **Loop**	-॒
Custom House | **Printer's Row**	25॒
Dan McGee | **Frankfort**	-॒
Z David Burke Prime | **River N**	25॒
Deleece Grill | **Lakeview**	20॒
Depot/Diner | **Far W**	-॒
Distinctive Cork | **Naperville**	21॒
Ditka's | **multi.**	22॒
DMK Burger | **Lakeview**	22॒
NEW D'Noche/Café Con Leche | **Logan Sq**	-॒
Drake Bros.' | **Gold Coast**	-॒
Drawing Room | **Gold Coast**	23॒
Duchamp | **Bucktown**	17॒
Duckfat | **Forest Pk**	-॒
NEW Eatt | **River N**	-॒
Ed Debevic's | **River N**	15॒
Eggsperience Café | **multi.**	-॒
Elate | **River N**	21॒
Epic | **River N**	-॒
Erwin | **Lakeview**	23॒
Feast | **multi.**	19॒
Fifty/50 | **Wicker Pk**	21॒
545 North | **Libertyville**	20॒
Flo | **Noble Sq**	22॒
NEW Fork | **Lincoln Sq**	-॒
Fred's | **Gold Coast**	19॒
NEW Frontier | **Noble Sq**	-॒
Z Gage | **Loop**	22॒
Gale St. Inn | **multi.**	22॒
Gemini Bistro | **Lincoln Pk**	21॒
NEW George St. Pub | **Lakeview**	-॒
Gilt Bar | **River N**	-॒
NEW Girl/The Goat | **W Loop**	-॒
Z Glenn's Diner | **Ravenswood**	24॒
Glen Prairie | **Glen Ellyn**	23॒
Goose Island | **multi.**	17॒
Gordon Biersch | **Bolingbrook**	16॒
Graham Elliot | **River N**	24॒

Grill on Alley | **Streeterville**	21
Hackney's | **multi.**	18
Hamburger Mary's | **Andersonville**	17
Happ Inn | **Northfield**	17
Hard Rock | **River N**	12
HB Home Bistro | **Lakeview**	25
Hearty | **Lakeview**	-
Hemmingway's | **Oak Pk**	21
NEW Henri | **S Loop**	-
Hot Chocolate | **Bucktown**	24
NEW Hoyt's | **Loop**	-
NEW Hubbard Inn | **River N**	-
Hub 51 | **River N**	21
Ina's | **W Loop**	23
NEW Ing | **W Loop**	-
Inovasi | **Lake Bluff**	-
NEW IPO | **Loop**	-
Jack's/Halsted | **Lakeview**	21
J. Alexander's | **multi.**	20
Jam | **Ukrainian Vill**	21
Jane's | **Bucktown**	22
Jilly's Cafe | **Evanston**	21
John's Pl. | **multi.**	18
NEW Kanela | **Lakeview**	-
Karyn's/Green | **Greektown**	-
Z Keefer's | **River N**	25
NEW Kinderhook Tap | **Oak Pk**	-
NEW Kingfisher | **Andersonville**	-
Kith/Kin | **Lincoln Pk**	-
Knew | **Logan Sq**	-
Kroll's | **S Loop**	19
Z Kuma's | **Avondale**	26
Landmark | **Lincoln Pk**	20
Lawry's | **River N**	24
LB Bistro/Patisserie | **Streeterville**	-
Lockwood | **Loop**	19
Longman/Eagle | **Logan Sq**	-
Lou Mitchell's | **multi.**	23
Z Lovells | **Lake Forest**	23
Luxbar | **Gold Coast**	20
L. Woods Tap | **Lincolnwood**	20
Magnolia Cafe | **Uptown**	22
Z Margie's Candies | **multi.**	22
Market | **W Loop**	18
Markethouse | **Streeterville**	21
NEW Meatyballs | **Location Varies**	-
Medici/57th | **Hyde Pk**	17
M Henry/Henrietta | **multi.**	25
Milk/Honey | **Wicker Pk**	23
Miller's Pub | **multi.**	17
Mirabell | **NW Side**	21
Mity Nice | **Streeterville**	17

Z MK | **Near North**	27
Montarra | **Algonquin**	24
Moody's Pub | **Edgewater**	19
Z Naha | **River N**	27
Nana | **Far S Side**	-
Next Door | **Northbrook**	23
Niche | **Geneva**	28
Nickson's Eatery | **La Grange**	-
Nightwood | **Pilsen**	23
Nookies | **multi.**	20
Z North Pond | **Lincoln Pk**	25
Oak Tree Bakery and Restaurant | **Gold Coast**	17
Old Oak Tap | **Ukrainian Vill**	20
Old Town Social | **Old Town**	18
Olive or Twist | **Berwyn**	-
One North | **Loop**	15
Z One Sixtyblue | **W Loop**	26
Z Original/Walker Pancake | **multi.**	24
Over Easy | **Ravenswood**	27
Palette Bistro | **Lakeview**	-
Paramount Room | **River W**	24
Parkers' | **Downers Grove**	23
Park 52 | **Hyde Pk**	19
Park Grill | **Loop**	20
Parrot Cage | **Far S Side**	-
NEW Perennial Virant | **Lincoln Pk**	-
Petterino's | **Loop**	19
Piggery | **Lakeview**	-
Pinstripes | **multi.**	17
Pitchfork | **North Ctr/St. Ben's**	-
P.J. Clarke's | **multi.**	17
NEW Portage | **NW Side**	-
Port Edward | **Algonquin**	-
Praga | **Lombard**	-
Prairie Fire | **W Loop**	-
Prairie Grass | **Northbrook**	22
Prasino | **multi.**	-
Province | **W Loop**	23
Z Publican | **W Loop**	25
NEW Public House | **River N**	-
Puck's/MCA | **Streeterville**	20
Quince | **Evanston**	23
NEW Redd Herring | **Clarendon Hills**	-
Rhapsody | **Loop**	20
Ria | **Gold Coast**	-
R.J. Grunts | **Lincoln Pk**	19
Z RL | **Gold Coast**	23
Rockit B&G | **multi.**	19
Rootstock | **Humboldt Pk**	24
NEW Rudy's B&G | **Loop**	-
Sable | **River N**	-

Sarkis Cafe | **Evanston**	15
Sarks/Park | **Lincoln Pk**	−
🖪 Schwa | **Wicker Pk**	29
🖪 Seasons | **Gold Coast**	27
Seasons 52 | **Schaumburg**	−
Sepia | **W Loop**	24
1776 | **Crystal Lake**	22
🖪 Signature Room | **Streeterville**	18
🖪 Sixteen | **River N**	22
NEW Smashburger | **Batavia**	−
Sola | **Lakeview**	25
NEW South Branch | **Loop**	−
South Gate | **Lake Forest**	20
Southport | **Lakeview**	22
South Water | **Loop**	16
Sprout | **Lincoln Pk**	28
Stained Glass | **Evanston**	23
Stanley's | **Lincoln Pk**	18
State/Lake | **Loop**	21
NEW Stax Café | **Little Italy/University Vill**	−
Sugartoad | **Naperville**	19
Table Fifty-two | **Gold Coast**	24
🖪 Takashi | **Bucktown**	26
Tasting Room | **W Loop**	20
Tavern/Park | **Loop**	20
Tavern/Rush | **Gold Coast**	21
33 Club | **Old Town**	20
Toast | **multi.**	22
Topaz Café | **Burr Ridge**	23
Tweet | **Uptown**	22
Twisted Spoke | **Noble Sq**	18
NEW Uptowner | **Lincoln Pk**	−
Viand Bar | **Streeterville**	22
🖪 Vie | **W Springs**	27
NEW Vincent | **Andersonville**	−
Volo | **Roscoe Vill**	−
Weber Grill | **multi.**	20
West Town | **Noble Sq**	24
White Fence | **Romeoville**	22
🖪 Wildfire | **multi.**	23
NEW Wolcott's | **Ravenswood**	−
Yard House | **Glenview**	18
Yolk | **multi.**	22
Zak's Place | **Hinsdale**	−
Zealous | **River N**	25
Zhivago | **Skokie**	16
Zodiac Room | **Streeterville**	−

ARGENTINEAN

NEW Caminito | **Lincoln Pk**	−
Folklore | **Ukrainian Vill**	−
Tango | **Naperville**	22
Tango Sur | **Lakeview**	24

ARMENIAN

Sayat Nova | **Streeterville**	23

ASIAN

aja | **River N**	−
Belly Shack | **Humboldt Pk**	23
NEW Bento Box | **Bucktown**	−
Big Bowl | **multi.**	20
Bonsai Café | **Evanston**	−
China Grill | **Loop**	22
Flat Top | **multi.**	20
Han 202 | **Bridgeport**	25
Hot Woks | **multi.**	23
ItaliAsia | **River N**	−
Karma | **Mundelein**	23
Koi | **Evanston**	21
Loving Hut | **Edgewater**	−
Pingpong | **Lakeview**	20
🖪 Shanghai Terrace | **River N**	25
Stir Crazy | **multi.**	19
Sunda | **River N**	23
Simply/Thalia | **River W**	19
Trader Vic's | **Gold Coast**	17

AUSTRIAN

Julius Meinl | **multi.**	21

BARBECUE

Carson's | **multi.**	22
NEW Chicago Q | **Gold Coast**	−
Fat Willy's | **Logan Sq**	23
Hecky's | **Evanston**	20
Honey 1 BBQ | **Bucktown**	20
Lem's BBQ | **Far S Side**	25
NEW Lillie's Q | **Bucktown**	−
L. Woods Tap | **Lincolnwood**	20
Main St. Smoke | **Libertyville**	−
Merle's BBQ | **Evanston**	19
NEW Original Five | **University Vill**	−
Piggery | **Lakeview**	−
Pitchfork | **North Ctr/St. Ben's**	−
NEW Pork Shoppe | **Avondale**	−
NEW Real Urban BBQ | **Highland Pk**	−
Ribs 'n' Bibs | **Hyde Pk**	21
Risqué Café | **Lakeview**	−
Robinson's Ribs | **multi.**	21
NEW Rub BBQ | **W Rogers Pk**	−
Russell's BBQ | **multi.**	19
🖪 Smoke Daddy | **Wicker Pk**	24
NEW Smokey Bears BBQ | **Albany Pk**	−
🖪 Smoque BBQ | **NW Side**	26
Twin Anchors | **Old Town**	23

Vote at ZAGAT.com

Uncle Bub's | **Westmont**	–
Uncle John's BBQ | **Far S Side**	–
Weber Grill | **multi.**	20

BELGIAN

Hopleaf | **Andersonville**	23
NEW Leopold | **Noble Sq**	–

BRAZILIAN

Al Primo Canto | **multi.**	24
Chama Gaucha | **Downers Grove**	–
Fogo de Chão | **River N**	24
Texas de Brazil | **multi.**	22

BRITISH

NEW Blokes/Birds | **Lakeview**	–
NEW Owen/Engine | **Logan Sq**	–

BURGERS

NEW Ace Bar | **Lincoln Pk**	–
Billy Goat | **multi.**	17
Boston Blackies | **multi.**	19
NEW Burger Bar | **Lincoln Pk**	–
NEW Burger Boss | **Elmwood Pk**	–
Chicago Burgerwurks | **Brookfield**	–
Choppers | **Wicker Pk**	–
Counter | **Lincoln Pk**	20
DMK Burger | **Lakeview**	22
Ed Debevic's | **River N**	15
Edzo's | **Evanston**	–
Epic Burger | **Loop**	22
NEW Everest Burger | **Glencoe**	–
Five Guys | **multi.**	20
Hackney's | **multi.**	18
Hamburger Mary's | **Andersonville**	17
Hop Häus | **multi.**	19
J. Wellington's | **Wicker Pk**	–
Z Kuma's | **Avondale**	26
Lucky Monk | **S Barrington**	–
M Burger | **multi.**	–
P.J. Clarke's | **multi.**	17
NEW Rudy's B&G | **Loop**	–
NEW Smashburger | **Batavia**	–
Z Superdawg | **multi.**	21
Twisted Spoke | **Noble Sq**	18
NEW Uptowner | **Lincoln Pk**	–
Z Wiener's Circle | **Lincoln Pk**	21

CAJUN

Dixie Kitchen | **multi.**	19
Z Heaven/Seven | **multi.**	23
Z Pappadeaux | **Westmont**	21
Wishbone | **multi.**	21

CENTRAL AMERICAN

Conoce/Panama | **Logan Sq**	–

CHINESE

(* dim sum specialist)

Ben Pao | **River N**	21
Cantonesia | **Chinatown**	–
Chens | **Wrigleyville**	22
Dee's | **Lincoln Pk**	19
Double Li | **Chinatown**	–
Emperor's Choice | **Chinatown**	23
Evergreen | **Chinatown**	23
Fornetto Mei | **Gold Coast**	20
Hai Yen | **multi.**	21
House/Fortune | **Chinatown**	23
Katy's Dumpling | **multi.**	–
Lan's Bistro | **Old Town**	–
Z Lao | **multi.**	24
NEW Lao You Ju | **Chinatown**	–
Lee Wing Wah | **Chinatown**	–
LuLu's* | **Evanston**	21
Mandarin Kitchen | **Chinatown**	–
NEW MingHin | **Chinatown**	–
Moon Palace | **Chinatown**	22
P.F. Chang's | **multi.**	20
Z Phoenix* | **Chinatown**	23
Pine Yard | **Evanston**	18
NEW PL8 | **Barrington**	–
NEW Saigon Grill | **Jefferson Pk**	–
Shine | **Lincoln Pk**	–
Shui Wah* | **Chinatown**	24
Silver Seafood | **Uptown**	23
Spring World | **Chinatown**	–
Sun Wah BBQ | **Uptown**	–
Szechwan North | **Glenview**	19
Three Happiness* | **Chinatown**	21

COFFEEHOUSES

Bourgeois Pig | **Lincoln Pk**	–
Café Selmarie | **Lincoln Sq**	23
Julius Meinl | **multi.**	21
Uncommon Ground | **multi.**	22

COFFEE SHOPS/ DINERS

Bakin' & Eggs | **Lakeview**	19
Chicago Diner | **Lakeview**	22
Depot/Diner | **Far W**	–
Ed Debevic's | **River N**	15
Eleven City | **S Loop**	19
Z Glenn's Diner | **Ravenswood**	24
Leo's Coney Island | **Wrigleyville**	–
Lou Mitchell's | **multi.**	23
Manny's | **multi.**	23
Milk/Honey | **Wicker Pk**	23

Nookies	**multi.**	20
Orange	**multi.**	20
🅉 Original/Walker Pancake	**multi.**	24
Sarkis Cafe	**Evanston**	15
Tempo	**Gold Coast**	20

COLOMBIAN

La Fonda/Grill	**Andersonville**	-
Las Tablas	**multi.**	20

CONTINENTAL

Le P'tit Paris	**Streeterville**	20
Zhivago	**Skokie**	16

COSTA RICAN

Irazu	**Bucktown**	22

CREOLE

🅉 Heaven/Seven	**multi.**	23
🅉 Pappadeaux	**Westmont**	21

CRÊPES

Crêpe Crave	**Wicker Pk**	-
Crêpe Town	**Lakeview**	-
L'Eiffel Bistrot	**S Barrington**	21
NEW Prince Crepe	**Albany Pk**	-

CUBAN

Cafe 28	**North Ctr/St. Ben's**	26
Habana Libre	**Noble Sq**	22
90 Miles	**multi.**	22
Siboney	**Bucktown**	-

CZECH

Czech Plaza	**Berwyn**	22

DELIS

Bagel	**multi.**	19
NEW City Provisions	**Ravenswood**	-
Eleven City	**S Loop**	19
Frances' Deli	**Lincoln Pk**	-
Manny's	**multi.**	23
Perry's Deli	**Loop**	26
Steve's Deli	**River N**	17
Zaleski/Horvath	**multi.**	-

DUTCH

NEW Vincent	**Andersonville**	-

ECLECTIC

NEW Aviary, The	**W Loop**	-
Briejo	**Oak Pk**	14
Café 103	**Far S Side**	-
Cellar/Stained Glass	**Evanston**	21
Deleece	**Lakeview**	19
Flight	**Glenview**	17
Foodlife	**Streeterville**	19

NEW Gaztro-Wagon	**Edgewater**	-
Grand Lux	**River N**	20
Han 202	**Bridgeport**	25
Heartland Cafe	**Rogers Pk**	16
Hub 51	**River N**	21
Jacky's/Prairie	**Evanston**	21
Jane's	**Bucktown**	22
Kit Kat	**Lakeview**	16
Kitsch'n/K-Cafe	**Roscoe Vill**	19
Knew	**Logan Sq**	-
NEW La Taberna	**University Vill**	-
🅉 Lula Cafe	**Logan Sq**	26
Mana	**Wicker Pk**	27
NEW Meatyballs	**Location Varies**	-
Mezé	**W Loop**	-
🅉 Moto	**W Loop**	27
Mundial	**Pilsen**	-
NEW Next	**W Loop**	-
Nosh	**Geneva**	24
NEW One.Six One	**Little Italy/University Vill**	-
Orange	**multi.**	20
Praga	**Lombard**	-
Red Brick	**Lakeview**	-
NEW Ruxbin	**Noble Sq**	-
Twist	**Lakeview**	21
Uncommon Ground	**Lakeview**	22
Victory's Banner	**Roscoe Vill**	24
Webster Wine	**Lincoln Pk**	20
NEW Yuca Café	**Wicker Pk**	-
Zed 451	**River N**	21

ETHIOPIAN

NEW Awash	**Edgewater**	-
Demera	**Uptown**	-
🅉 Ethiopian Diamond	**multi.**	23
Ras Dashen	**Edgewater**	23

EUROPEAN

Balsan	**Gold Coast**	-
Little Bucharest	**NW Side**	-
Lokal	**Bucktown**	-
Vintage 338	**Lincoln Pk**	-

FILIPINO

Coobah	**Lakeview**	17
Isla Filipino	**Lincoln Sq**	-

FONDUE

Geja's Cafe	**Lincoln Pk**	21
Melting Pot	**multi.**	19

FRENCH

NEW Aquitaine	**Lincoln Pk**	-
Atwater's	**Geneva**	20

NEW Bistronomic | **Gold Coast**	‑
NEW Bluette | **Wilmette**	‑
Z Bonsoirée | **Logan Sq**	26
Café Absinthe | **Bucktown**	23
Café/Architectes | **Gold Coast**	24
Z Carlos' | **Highland Pk**	27
Dining Room/Kendall | **Near W**	23
Dorado | **Lincoln Sq**	23
Z Everest | **Loop**	27
Froggy's | **Highwood**	22
Z Gabriel's | **Highwood**	25
Jilly's Cafe | **Evanston**	21
La Petite Folie | **Hyde Pk**	24
Le P'tit Paris | **Streeterville**	20
Z Les Nomades | **Streeterville**	29
Z Le Titi/Paris | **Arlington Hts**	26
Le Vichyssois | **Lakemoor**	26
LM | **multi.**	22
NEW Maude's Liquor | **W Loop**	‑
NEW MC Bistro | **Wicker Pk**	‑
Mexique | **Noble Sq**	25
Z Michael | **Winnetka**	28
Z Nomi Kitchen | **Gold Coast**	‑
Z Oceanique | **Evanston**	27
NEW Paris Club | **River N**	‑
NEW Prince Crepe | **Albany Pk**	‑
NEW Prix Fixe | **Lincoln Sq**	‑
NEW Rewster's Café | **Logan Sq**	‑
Sabor Saveur | **Ukrainian Vill**	‑
Sprout | **Lincoln Pk**	28
Z Takashi | **Bucktown**	26
Z Tallgrass | **Lockport**	28
Z Tru | **Streeterville**	28
Yoshi's Café | **Lakeview**	25

FRENCH (BISTRO)

Z Barrington Country | **Barrington**	25
Bistro Bordeaux | **Evanston**	‑
Z Bistro Campagne | **Lincoln Sq**	25
Bistro 110 | **Gold Coast**	21
Bistrot Margot | **Old Town**	20
Bistrot Zinc | **Gold Coast**	21
Café Bernard | **Lincoln Pk**	19
Cafe Central | **Highland Pk**	24
Cafe Pyrenees | **Libertyville**	21
Café Touché | **Edison Pk**	25
Chez Joël | **Little Italy/University Vill**	24
Cyrano's Bistrot | **River N**	22
D & J Bistro | **Lake Zurich**	24
Hemmingway's | **Oak Pk**	21
Kiki's | **Near North**	25
Koda | **Far S Side**	‑

La Crêperie | **Lakeview**	21
La Sardine | **W Loop**	24
LB Bistro/Patisserie | **Streeterville**	‑
Le Bouchon | **Bucktown**	24
L'Eiffel Bistrot | **S Barrington**	21
Maijean | **Clarendon Hills**	28
Miramar Bistro | **Highwood**	17
Mon Ami Gabi | **multi.**	22
Pierrot Gourmet | **River N**	20
Retro Bistro | **Mt. Prospect**	23
Socca | **Lakeview**	22

FRENCH (BRASSERIE)

Deca | **Streeterville**	‑

GERMAN

NEW Bauer's Brauhaus | **Palatine**	‑
Berghoff | **multi.**	18
Edelweiss | **Norridge**	19
Mirabell | **NW Side**	21

GREEK

Artopolis | **Greektown**	22
Athena | **Greektown**	21
Costa's | **Oakbrook Terr**	22
Greek Islands | **multi.**	21
Melanthios | **Lakeview**	‑
Mythos | **Lakeview**	23
Opa! Estiatorio | **Vernon Hills**	25
Parthenon | **Greektown**	21
Pegasus | **multi.**	20
Roditys | **Greektown**	21
Santorini | **Greektown**	21
Taxim | **Wicker Pk**	22
Venus | **Greektown**	‑

HAITIAN

NEW Chez Violette | **Rogers Pk**	‑

HAWAII REGIONAL

Roy's | **River N**	25

HOT DOGS

Z Al's Beef | **multi.**	23
Edzo's | **Evanston**	‑
Felony Franks | **W Loop**	‑
Franks 'N' Dawgs | **Lincoln Pk**	‑
Gene & Jude's | **O'Hare Area**	‑
Gold Coast | **multi.**	19
Z Hot Doug's | **NW Side**	27
Leo's Coney Island | **Wrigleyville**	‑
Z Superdawg | **multi.**	21
Z Wiener's Circle | **Lincoln Pk**	21

INDIAN

Chicago Curry	**S Loop**	25
NEW Cumin	**Wicker Pk**	-
Curry Hut	**Highwood**	20
Essence/India	**Lincoln Sq**	21
Gaylord Indian	**multi.**	22
Hema's Kitchen	**multi.**	22
Z India House	**multi.**	25
Indian Garden	**multi.**	21
Jaipur	**W Loop**	-
Klay Oven	**multi.**	20
Marigold	**Uptown**	23
Mt. Everest	**Evanston**	22
Raj Darbar	**Lincoln Pk**	18
NEW Raj Palace	**Schaumburg**	-
Tiffin	**W Rogers Pk**	21
Udupi Palace	**multi.**	23
Veerasway	**W Loop**	21
Vermilion	**River N**	22
Viceroy/India	**multi.**	21

INDONESIAN

Angin Mamiri	**W Rogers Pk**	-

IRISH

Chief O'Neill's	**NW Side**	18
Irish Oak	**Wrigleyville**	19
Mrs. Murphy	**North Ctr/St. Ben's**	22

ITALIAN

(N=Northern; S=Southern)

Accanto	**Logan Sq**	-
Al Primo Canto	**multi.**	24
Angelina	**S**	**Lakeview**	21
Anna Maria	**Ravenswood**	24
Anteprima	**Andersonville**	25
Antica Pizza	**Andersonville**	23
NEW Antico	**Bucktown**	-
Antico Posto	**Oak Brook**	22
Z A Tavola	**N**	**Ukrainian Vill**	26
Aurelio's Pizza	**multi.**	23
Bacchanalia	**SW Side**	24
Bacino's	**multi.**	22
Basil Leaf	**N**	**Lincoln Pk**	18
Bella Notte	**S**	**Noble Sq**	21
NEW Bia for Mia	**River W**	-
NEW Bivona	**Lincoln Pk**	-
Brio	**Lombard**	22
Bruna's	**SW Side**	26
Buona Terra	**N**	**Logan Sq**	24
Cafe Bionda/To Go	**S Loop**	22
Z Café Spiaggia	**Gold Coast**	25
NEW Calabruzzi's	**Bridgeport**	-
Campagnola	**Evanston**	25
Carlucci	**N**	**Downers Grove**	19

Carlucci	**N**	**Rosemont**	20
Carmine's	**Gold Coast**	22
Ciao Napoli	**Logan Sq**	-
Cibo Matto	**Loop**	24
Club Lucky	**S**	**Bucktown**	19
Z Coco Pazzo	**N**	**River N**	25
Coco Pazzo	**N**	**Streeterville**	22
Cucina Paradiso	**Oak Pk**	20
NEW Davanti	**Little Italy/University Vill**	-
Dave's Italian	**S**	**Evanston**	17
Del Rio	**Highwood**	20
Dinotto	**Old Town**	19
Di Pescara	**Northbrook**	19
NEW DiSotto	**Streeterville**	-
NEW Donatella	**Evanston**	-
NEW Due Lire	**Lincoln Sq**	-
Edwardo's Pizza	**multi.**	20
EJ's Pl.	**N**	**Skokie**	22
Erie Cafe	**River N**	22
Filippo's	**Lincoln Pk**	24
Fiorentino's	**S**	**Lakeview**	22
NEW Florentine	**Loop**	-
Fontana Grill	**Uptown**	-
Fornetto Mei	**Gold Coast**	20
Francesca's	**multi.**	22
Francesco's	**Northbrook**	24
Frankie's Scaloppine	**Gold Coast**	18
Frasca Pizza	**Lakeview**	20
Z Gabriel's	**Highwood**	25
Gaetano's	**Forest Pk**	24
Gioco	**N**	**S Loop**	25
Gruppo/Amici	**N**	**Rogers Pk**	16
Harry Caray's	**multi.**	20
Il Mulino	**Gold Coast**	25
Il Poggiolo	**Hinsdale**	19
Isacco	**N**	**St. Charles**	-
ItaliAsia	**River N**	-
La Bocca/Verità	**Lincoln Sq**	22
La Cantina Chop	**N**	**Loop**	21
Z La Gondola	**Lakeview**	-
La Madia	**River N**	23
La Scarola	**River W**	24
Leonardo's	**N**	**Andersonville**	-
NEW Letizia's Fiore	**Logan Sq**	-
Macello	**W Loop**	-
Z Maggiano's	**multi.**	20
Merlo	**N**	**multi.**	24
NEW Mia Figlia	**NW Side**	-
Z Mia Francesca	**Lakeview**	26
Natalino's	**W Town**	23
Next Door	**Northbrook**	23
Osteria/Pizzeria Via Stato	**S**	**River N**	23

Pane Caldo | N | **Gold Coast**	23	
Pasta Palazzo | **Lincoln Pk**	22	
Pelago | **Streeterville**	26	
NEW Pensiero | **Evanston**	–	
Philly G's | **Vernon Hills**	21	
Phil Stefani's | **River N**	24	
Piazza Bella | **Roscoe Vill**	21	
Piccolo Sogno | **Near W**	24	
Pinstripes | **multi.**	17	
Pizza Capri | **multi.**	20	
Pizza D.O.C. | **Lincoln Sq**	23	
Pizza Rustica | **Wrigleyville**	–	
Pompei Pizza | **multi.**	19	
NEW Prix Fixe | **Lincoln Sq**	–	
Prosecco | **River N**	24	
Quartino | **River N**	21	
Z Riccardo | N | **Lincoln Pk**	27	
Rist. al Teatro | **Pilsen**	–	
Rosal's | S | **Little Italy/University Vill**	26	
Rose Angelis | **Lincoln Pk**	24	
Z Rosebud | **multi.**	22	
Rosebud Trattoria | **River N**	22	
Sabatino's | **NW Side**	24	
NEW Salatino's/Doughboys | **Little Italy/University Vill**	–	
Sapore/Napoli | **Lakeview**	20	
Sapori Trattoria | **Lincoln Pk**	23	
Scoozi! | **River N**	19	
Socca | **Lakeview**	22	
NEW Sono | **Lincoln Pk**	–	
Spacca Napoli | **Ravenswood**	23	
Z Spiaggia | **Gold Coast**	27	
Tarantino's | **Lincoln Pk**	22	
Terragusto | **Roscoe Vill**	25	
Terzo Piano | **Loop**	21	
NEW Three Aces | **Little Italy/University Vill**	–	
312 Chicago | **Loop**	21	
Tocco | **Bucktown**	12	
Topo Gigio | **Old Town**	23	
Trattoria D.O.C. | **Evanston**	19	
Trattoria Gianni | **Lincoln Pk**	26	
Trattoria Isabella | **W Loop**	26	
Trattoria No. 10 | **Loop**	24	
Trattoria Roma | **Old Town**	21	
Trattoria Trullo | S | **Lincoln Sq**	23	
Trattoria 225 | **Oak Pk**	–	
Tufano's Tap | S | **Little Italy/University Vill**	20	
Tuscany | N | **multi.**	22	
Via Carducci | S | **multi.**	23	
Village | **Loop**	21	
Vinci | **Lincoln Pk**	21	
Vito & Nick's | **Far S Side**	25	
Vivere | **Loop**	22	
Vivo | **W Loop**	24	
Volare | **multi.**	24	
Zia's Trattoria | **Edison Pk**	24	

JAMAICAN

Ja' Grill | **Lincoln Pk**	–

JAPANESE

(* sushi specialist)

Agami* | **Uptown**	24
Ai Sushi* | **River N**	24
Akai Hana* | **Wilmette**	21
NEW Arami* | **W Town**	–
NEW Ara On* | **Loop**	–
Aria* | **Loop**	24
Benihana | **multi.**	18
Blue Ocean* | **Ravenswood**	23
Bob San* | **Wicker Pk**	24
Butterfly* | **multi.**	22
Chens* | **Wrigleyville**	22
NEW Chikurin Sushi* | **Wicker Pk**	–
NEW Chizakaya | **Lakeview**	–
Coast Sushi/South Coast* | **multi.**	24
Dee's* | **Lincoln Pk**	19
NEW Fin Sushi | **Ravenswood**	–
NEW Gosu | **Logan Sq**	–
NEW Gyu-Kaku | **Streeterville**	–
Hachi's Kitchen* | **Logan Sq**	–
Hana* | **Rogers Pk**	–
Indie Cafe* | **Edgewater**	24
Itto Sushi* | **Lincoln Pk**	24
Z Japonais* | **River N**	24
NEW Kai Sushi* | **W Town**	–
Kamehachi* | **multi.**	21
Kansaku* | **Evanston**	22
Katakana/Koko* | **Logan Sq**	–
Z Katsu* | **NW Side**	27
Kin* | **Noble Sq**	–
Kuni's* | **Evanston**	24
NEW Lure Izakaya | **Chinatown**	–
Macku Sushi* | **Lincoln Pk**	–
Makisu/Aha Sushi* | **multi.**	–
Meiji* | **W Loop**	25
Mirai Sushi* | **Wicker Pk**	25
Mizu Yakitori* | **Old Town**	24
NEW Nabuki | **Hinsdale**	–
Nagoya | **Naperville**	–
NEW Nano Sushi* | **NW Side**	–
Niu | **Streeterville**	19
Nozumi* | **S Barrington**	–
Oba* | **Des Plaines**	–

CHICAGO

CUISINES

Oysy* | **multi.**	20
NEW PL8 | **Barrington**	-
RA Sushi* | **multi.**	19
Ringo* | **Lincoln Pk**	-
Rise* | **Wrigleyville**	21
Rollapalooza* | **Lakeview**	-
Sai Café* | **Lincoln Pk**	25
NEW Sakura* | **Logan Sq**	-
Sanook | **North Ctr/St. Ben's**	-
NEW Seadog Sushi* | **Noble Sq**	-
Shine* | **Lincoln Pk**	-
Sushi Ai* | **Palatine**	-
Sushi Naniwa* | **River N**	23
Sushi Para/Sai* | **multi.**	-
Sushisamba Rio* | **River N**	21
Sushi Taiyo* | **River N**	-
Z Sushi Wabi* | **W Loop**	27
Sushi X* | **River W**	21
Swordfish* | **Batavia**	27
Tamarind* | **S Loop**	23
Tank Sushi* | **Lincoln Sq**	23
Tanoshii* | **Andersonville**	-
Thai Urban* | **Loop**	16
Todai* | **Schaumburg**	-
NEW Ukai* | **Lakeview**	-
Wakamono* | **Lakeview**	22
NEW Wasabi* | **Logan Sq**	-
Wildfish* | **multi.**	21
NEW Yindee | **Lakeview**	-
Yoshi's Café | **Lakeview**	25

JEWISH

Bagel | **multi.**	19
Manny's | **multi.**	23

KOREAN

(* barbecue specialist)

Amitabul | **NW Side**	21
Cho Sun Ok | **North Ctr/St. Ben's**	-
NEW Del Seoul | **Lakeview**	-
NEW Gosu | **Logan Sq**	-
Jin Ju | **Andersonville**	23
San Soo Gab San* | **Lincoln Sq**	21
Woo Lae Oak* | **Rolling Meadows**	20

KOSHER/
KOSHER-STYLE

Manghal | **Evanston**	-

LEBANESE

Kan Zaman | **River N**	-
Maza | **Lincoln Pk**	21
Semiramis | **Albany Pk**	-

MEDITERRANEAN

Andies | **multi.**	18
Artopolis | **Greektown**	22

Z Avec | **W Loop**	26
CityGate | **Naperville**	-
Corner 41 | **North Ctr/St. Ben's**	-
NEW Donatella | **Evanston**	-
Laurel | **Naperville**	-
Manghal | **Evanston**	-
Nia | **W Loop**	-
Z Pita Inn | **multi.**	24
Pomegranate | **Evanston**	18
Purple Pig | **River N**	-
Red Brick | **Lakeview**	-
Reza's | **multi.**	18
Rist. al Teatro | **Pilsen**	-
Ropa | **Rogers Pk**	-
Roti | **multi.**	21
Semiramis | **Albany Pk**	-
Venus | **Greektown**	-
Wave | **Streeterville**	13

MEXICAN

Adobo | **Old Town**	21
Big Star | **Wicker Pk**	23
Bombon Café | **W Loop**	-
Cafe 28 | **North Ctr/St. Ben's**	26
Chilam Balam | **Lakeview**	25
Co-Si-Na | **Andersonville**	-
De Cero | **W Loop**	21
Decolores | **Pilsen**	-
Don Juan's | **Edison Pk**	20
Dorado | **Lincoln Sq**	23
Dos Diablos | **River N**	-
Estrella Negra | **Logan Sq**	-
NEW Fogón | **Noble Sq**	-
Fonda del Mar | **Logan Sq**	25
Fonda Isabel | **Lombard**	-
La Cocina/Frida | **multi.**	20
Z Frontera Grill | **River N**	27
Fuego | **Logan Sq**	24
La Casa/Isaac | **Highland Pk**	20
La Cantina Grill | **S Loop**	-
La Ciudad | **Uptown**	-
La Fonda/Gusto | **Wicker Pk**	-
NEW La Lagartija | **W Loop**	-
Las Palmas | **multi.**	21
Los Moles | **Lakeview**	-
Lupita's | **Evanston**	21
Maiz | **Humboldt Pk**	23
Mercadito | **River N**	22
Mexique | **Noble Sq**	25
Mixteco Grill | **Lakeview**	25
Nana | **Far S Side**	-
Real Tenochtitlán | **Logan Sq**	20
Rolis | **Uptown**	-
Sabor Saveur | **Ukrainian Vill**	-

Salpicón | **Old Town**	26
Salsa 17 | **Arlington Hts**	22
San Gabriel | **Bannockburn**	17
Sol de Mexico | **NW Side**	25
Taco Fuego | **Lakeview**	-
NEW Taco Joint | **Lincoln Pk**	-
Tamales | **Highland Pk**	20
Z Topolobampo | **River N**	28
Xni-Pec | **Brookfield**	-
Xoco | **River N**	25
Zapatista | **multi.**	20
Zocalo | **River N**	20

MIDDLE EASTERN

Aladdin's Eatery | **Lincoln Pk**	18
Al Bawadi Grill | **Bridgeview**	-
Alhambra | **W Loop**	16
Andies | **multi.**	18
Chickpea | **W Town**	22
Old Jerusalem | **Old Town**	19
Z Pita Inn | **multi.**	24
Pomegranate | **Evanston**	18

MOROCCAN

Andalous | **Lakeview**	22

NEPALESE

Chicago Curry | **S Loop**	25
NEW Cumin | **Wicker Pk**	-
Curry Hut | **Highwood**	20
Mt. Everest | **Evanston**	22

NEW MEXICAN

NEW Abiquiù | **Lakeview**	-

NOODLE SHOPS

Joy Yee | **multi.**	20
Katy's Dumpling | **multi.**	-
Mandarin Kitchen | **Chinatown**	-
Penny's Noodle | **multi.**	20
Urbanbelly | **Logan Sq**	24

NUEVO LATINO

Belly Shack | **Humboldt Pk**	23
Z Carnivale | **Loop**	23
Coobah | **Lakeview**	17
NEW Danzón | **Logan Sq**	-
Depot Nuevo | **Wilmette**	18
Estrella Negra | **Logan Sq**	-
Havana | **River N**	-
Maya Del Sol | **Oak Pk**	23
Z Nacional 27 | **River N**	23
Rumba | **River N**	23
Vermilion | **River N**	22

PERSIAN

Noon-O-Kabab | **Albany Pk**	25
Reza's | **multi.**	18

PIZZA

Antica Pizza | **Andersonville**	23
Art of Pizza | **Lakeview**	22
Aurelio's Pizza | **multi.**	23
Bacino's | **multi.**	22
NEW Big Stuff | **Lincoln Pk**	-
NEW Boiler Room | **Logan Sq**	-
Bricks | **multi.**	22
Chicago Pizza | **Lincoln Pk**	23
Ciao Napoli | **Logan Sq**	-
Coalfire Pizza | **Noble Sq**	23
Crust | **Wicker Pk**	19
Edwardo's Pizza | **multi.**	20
Flo/Santos Pizza | **S Loop**	-
Frankie's Scaloppine | **Gold Coast**	18
Frasca Pizza | **Lakeview**	20
Z Giordano's | **multi.**	23
Great Lake | **Andersonville**	23
Gruppo/Amici | **Rogers Pk**	16
Z La Gondola | **Lakeview**	-
La Madia | **River N**	23
Z Lou Malnati's | **multi.**	24
Lucky Monk | **S Barrington**	-
Z Original Gino's East | **multi.**	22
Parkers' | **Downers Grove**	23
Piece | **Wicker Pk**	23
Pizza Capri | **multi.**	20
Pizza D.O.C. | **Lincoln Sq**	23
Pizza Rustica | **Wrigleyville**	-
Pizzeria Uno/Due | **River N**	22
Pizzeria Serio | **Lakeview**	-
Osteria/Pizzeria Via Stato | **River N**	23
Pompei Pizza | **multi.**	19
NEW Redflame | **Lincoln Pk**	-
NEW Salatino's/Doughboys | **Little Italy/University Vill**	-
Sapore/Napoli | **Lakeview**	20
NEW Sono | **Lincoln Pk**	-
Spacca Napoli | **Ravenswood**	23
Trattoria D.O.C. | **Evanston**	19
Union Pizza | **Evanston**	23
Vito & Nick's | **Far S Side**	25

POLISH

Flo/Santos Pizza | **S Loop**	-
Smak-Tak | **NW Side**	-

POLYNESIAN

Trader Vic's | **Gold Coast**	17

PUB FOOD

NEW Acre | **Andersonville**	-
NEW Act One Pub | **Rogers Pk**	-
Bad Apple | **North Ctr/St. Ben's**	-

NEW Bangers/Lace | **Wicker Pk**	–
Bar Louie | **multi.**	16
Billy Goat | **multi.**	17
NEW Blokes/Birds | **Lakeview**	–
Boston Blackies | **multi.**	19
Chief O'Neill's | **NW Side**	18
Duke/Perth | **Lakeview**	20
Flo/Santos Pizza | **S Loop**	–
NEW Fork | **Lincoln Sq**	–
Fountainhead | **Ravenswood**	–
NEW Frontier | **Noble Sq**	–
NEW George St. Pub | **Lakeview**	–
Goose Island | **multi.**	17
Gordon Biersch | **Bolingbrook**	16
NEW Haymarket Pub | **W Loop**	–
Irish Oak | **Wrigleyville**	19
Jury's | **North Ctr/St. Ben's**	18
NEW Kinderhook Tap | **Oak Pk**	–
NEW Leopold | **Noble Sq**	–
Lucky Monk | **S Barrington**	–
Moody's Pub | **Edgewater**	19
Mrs. Murphy | **North Ctr/St. Ben's**	22
Old Oak Tap | **Ukrainian Vill**	20
NEW Owen/Engine | **Logan Sq**	–
NEW Portage | **NW Side**	–
Z Publican | **W Loop**	25
NEW Public House | **River N**	–
Revolution Brewing | **Logan Sq**	–
NEW Three Aces | **Little Italy/University Vill**	–
Twin Anchors | **Old Town**	23

RUSSIAN

Russian Tea | **Loop**	22

SANDWICHES

Z Al's Beef | **multi.**	23
Bagel | **multi.**	19
Ba Le Sandwich | **Uptown**	–
Berghoff | **multi.**	18
NEW Big Stuff | **Lincoln Pk**	–
Birchwood | **Bucktown**	23
Bourgeois Pig | **Lincoln Pk**	–
NEW Del Seoul | **Lakeview**	–
NEW Gaztro-Wagon | **Edgewater**	–
NEW Grahamwich | **River N**	–
Z Hannah's Bretzel | **Loop**	23
Jerry's | **Wicker Pk**	22
LM | **W Loop**	22
NEW Mac/Min's | **W Loop**	–
Z Mr. Beef | **River N**	24
Z Potbelly Sandwich | **multi.**	19
NEW Pret A Manger | **Loop**	–
NEW Rewster's Café | **Logan Sq**	–

Sarks/Park | **Lincoln Pk**	–
NEW Snarf's | **River N**	–
Southport | **Lakeview**	22

SCANDINAVIAN

Tre Kronor | **Albany Pk**	23

SCOTTISH

Duke/Perth | **Lakeview**	20

SEAFOOD

Big & Little's | **River N**	–
Z Bob Chinn's | **Wheeling**	23
Cape Cod Room | **Streeterville**	22
Z Catch 35 | **multi.**	24
Chinn's Fishery | **Lisle**	25
C-House | **Streeterville**	21
Davis St. Fish | **Evanston**	19
Devon Seafood | **River N**	21
Di Pescara | **Northbrook**	19
Emperor's Choice | **Chinatown**	23
NEW Fish Bar | **Lakeview**	–
Fonda del Mar | **Logan Sq**	25
Fulton's | **River N**	19
Z Glenn's Diner | **Ravenswood**	24
NEW GT Fish/Oyster | **River N**	–
Half Shell | **Lakeview**	24
Holy Mackerel! | **Lombard**	21
Z Hugo's | **multi.**	24
Z Joe's Sea/Steak | **River N**	26
NEW Joey's Shrimp | **Humboldt Pk**	–
Z Keefer's | **River N**	25
NEW Kingfisher | **Andersonville**	–
La Cantina Chop | **Loop**	21
Lee Wing Wah | **Chinatown**	–
Lobby | **River N**	28
Z L2O | **Lincoln Pk**	–
McCormick/Schmick | **multi.**	21
Mitchell's | **Glenview**	21
Nagoya | **Naperville**	–
Nick's Fishmarket | **multi.**	23
Z Nine Steakhouse | **Loop**	24
Z Oceanique | **Evanston**	27
Z Pappadeaux | **Westmont**	21
Pelago | **Streeterville**	26
Pete Miller | **multi.**	22
RB Grille | **River N**	–
Reel Club | **Oak Brook**	23
Riva | **Streeterville**	20
Sam/Harry's Steak | **Schaumburg**	–
Santorini | **Greektown**	21
Z Shaw's Crab | **multi.**	24
Silver Seafood | **Uptown**	23

Tin Fish | **Tinley Park**	23
Tramonto's | **Wheeling**	24

SMALL PLATES

(See also Spanish tapas specialist)

☑ Avec | Med. | **W Loop**	26
Bluebird | Amer. | **Bucktown**	20
Boka | Amer. | **Lincoln Pk**	25
Bolat | Eclectic | **Lakeview**	–
Browntrout | Amer. | **North Ctr/St. Ben's**	24
Cellar/Stained Glass | Eclectic | **Evanston**	21
C-House | Seafood | **Streeterville**	21
NEW Davanti | Italian | **Little Italy/University Vill**	–
NEW DiSotto | Italian | **Streeterville**	–
Distinctive Cork | Amer. | **Naperville**	21
Flight | Eclectic | **Glenview**	17
NEW Girl/The Goat | Amer. | **W Loop**	–
☑ Green Zebra | Veg. | **Noble Sq**	26
NEW IPO | Amer. | **Loop**	–
NEW Lao You Ju | Chinese | **Chinatown**	–
Maza | Lebanese | **Lincoln Pk**	21
Mezé | Eclectic | **W Loop**	–
Nia | Med. | **W Loop**	–
Purple Pig | Med. | **River N**	–
Quartino | Italian | **River N**	21
Rootstock | Amer. | **Humboldt Pk**	24
Sable | Amer. | **River N**	–
Tango | Argent. | **Naperville**	22
Taxim | Greek | **Wicker Pk**	22
NEW Three Aces | Italian | **Little Italy/University Vill**	–
Vintage 338 | Euro. | **Lincoln Pk**	–
Volo | Amer. | **Roscoe Vill**	–
Wave | Med. | **Streeterville**	13
Webster Wine | Eclectic | **Lincoln Pk**	20

SOUL FOOD

Dee's Place | **Wicker Pk**	–

SOUTH AMERICAN

NEW D'Noche/Café Con Leche | **Logan Sq**	–
Sushisamba Rio | **River N**	21

SOUTHERN

Big Jones | **Andersonville**	21
Chicago's/Chicken & Waffles | **multi.**	–

Dee's Place | **Wicker Pk**	–
Dixie Kitchen | **multi.**	19
Fat Willy's | **Logan Sq**	23
NEW Lillie's Q | **Bucktown**	–
NEW Mac/Min's | **W Loop**	–
Nickson's Eatery | **La Grange**	–
Southern/Mac | **multi.**	–
Table Fifty-two | **Gold Coast**	24
Wishbone | **multi.**	21

SOUTHWESTERN

Bandera | **Streeterville**	22
Flo | **Noble Sq**	22

SPANISH

(* tapas specialist)

Azucar* | **Logan Sq**	22
Cafe Ba-Ba-Reeba!* | **Lincoln Pk**	22
Café Iberico* | **River N**	22
Café Marbella* | **Jefferson Pk**	–
☑ Emilio's Tapas* | **multi.**	24
1492* | **River N**	21
NEW La Taberna* | **University Vill**	–
La Tasca* | **Arlington Hts**	24
☑ Mercat | **S Loop**	26
Mesón Sabika* | **multi.**	23
Pasha | **W Loop**	–
Tapas Barcelona* | **Evanston**	21
Tapas Gitana* | **multi.**	24
Tapas Las Ramblas* | **Andersonville**	23
Twist* | **Lakeview**	21

STEAKHOUSES

Benihana | **multi.**	18
Benny's Chop | **River N**	–
☑ Capital Grille | **multi.**	25
Carmichael's | **W Loop**	22
Chama Gaucha | **Downers Grove**	–
☑ Chicago Chop | **River N**	25
NEW Chicago Cut | **River N**	–
☑ David Burke Prime | **River N**	25
Deleece Grill | **Lakeview**	20
Ditka's | **multi.**	22
EJ's Pl. | **Skokie**	22
Erie Cafe | **River N**	22
Fleming's | **multi.**	23
Fogo de Chão | **River N**	24
Folklore | **Ukrainian Vill**	–
Fulton's | **River N**	19
☑ Gene/Georgetti | **River N**	24
☑ Gibsons | **multi.**	26
Grill on Alley | **Streeterville**	21
Grillroom | **Loop**	15

Harry Caray's | **multi.**	20
🄩 Joe's Sea/Steak | **River N**	26
🄩 Keefer's | **River N**	25
Kinzie Chop | **River N**	22
La Cantina Chop | **Loop**	21
Las Tablas | **multi.**	20
Lawry's | **River N**	24
NEW Mastro's Steak | **River N**	-
Melanthios | **Lakeview**	-
Montarra | **Algonquin**	24
🄩 Morton's | **multi.**	26
Myron/Phil Steak | **Lincolnwood**	21
🄩 Nine Steakhouse | **Loop**	24
Palm | **Loop**	24
Pete Miller | **multi.**	22
Phil Stefani's | **River N**	24
RB Grille | **River N**	-
Rosebud Prime/Steak | **multi.**	25
🄩 Ruth's Chris | **multi.**	25
Saloon Steak | **Streeterville**	23
Sam/Harry's Steak | **Schaumburg**	-
Shula's Steak | **multi.**	21
Smith/Wollensky | **River N**	23
Sullivan's Steak | **multi.**	22
Tango | **Naperville**	22
Tango Sur | **Lakeview**	24
Tavern/Rush | **Gold Coast**	21
Texas de Brazil | **Schaumburg**	22
Tramonto's | **Wheeling**	24
🄩 Wildfire | **multi.**	23
Zed 451 | **River N**	21

SWEDISH

Ann Sather | **multi.**	21

TEX-MEX

Dos Diablos | **River N**	-
Uncle Julio's | **Old Town**	18

THAI

Aroy | **Lincoln Sq**	-
🄩 Arun's | **NW Side**	28
Butterfly | **multi.**	22
Chens | **Wrigleyville**	22
Duck Walk | **multi.**	19
NEW Fin Sushi | **Ravenswood**	-
Indie Cafe | **Edgewater**	24
Kin | **Noble Sq**	-
NEW Nano Sushi | **NW Side**	-
Pho & I | **Lakeview**	-
NEW Rice Bistro | **Lakeview**	-

Rosded | **Lincoln Sq**	-
Ruby/Siam | **multi.**	23
Sanook | **North Ctr/St. Ben's**	-
NEW Silom 12 | **Bucktown**	-
Spoon Thai | **Lincoln Sq**	23
Star/Siam | **River N**	20
Sticky Rice | **North Ctr/St. Ben's**	-
Sura | **Lakeview**	20
Thai Classic | **Lakeview**	23
Thai Pastry | **multi.**	23
Thai Urban | **Loop**	16
Tub Tim Thai | **Skokie**	24
NEW Yindee | **Lakeview**	-

TURKISH

A La Turka | **Lakeview**	20
Turquoise | **Roscoe Vill**	23

VEGETARIAN

(* vegan)

Aladdin's Eatery | **Lincoln Pk**	18
Amitabul* | **NW Side**	21
Andies | **multi.**	18
Blind Faith* | **Evanston**	21
Chicago Diner | **Lakeview**	22
🄩 Ethiopian Diamond | **multi.**	23
🄩 Green Zebra | **Noble Sq**	26
Heartland Cafe | **Rogers Pk**	16
Hema's Kitchen | **multi.**	22
Karyn's* | **multi.**	20
Karyn's/Green* | **Greektown**	-
Loving Hut* | **Edgewater**	-
Mana | **Wicker Pk**	27
Mexique* | **Noble Sq**	25
Prasino | **multi.**	-
Tiffin | **W Rogers Pk**	21
Udupi Palace | **multi.**	23
Victory's Banner | **Roscoe Vill**	24

VIETNAMESE

Ba Le Sandwich | **Uptown**	-
Hai Yen | **multi.**	21
🄩 Le Colonial | **Gold Coast**	24
NEW MC Bistro | **Wicker Pk**	-
Pho & I | **Lakeview**	-
Pho 777 | **Uptown**	21
Phò Xe Tång | **Uptown**	26
NEW Saigon Grill | **Jefferson Pk**	-
NEW Saigon Sisters | **W Loop**	-
NEW Sawtooth | **W Loop**	-
Simply It | **Lincoln Pk**	22

Locations

Includes names, cuisines, Food ratings and, for locations that are mapped, top list with map coordinates.

City North

ANDERSONVILLE/ EDGEWATER

NEW Acre	*Pub*	-
Andies	*Med./Mideast*	18
Ann Sather	*Amer./Swedish*	21
Anteprima	*Italian*	25
Antica Pizza	*Pizza*	23
NEW Awash	*Ethiopian*	-
Big Jones	*Southern*	21
Broadway Cellars	*Amer.*	21
Co-Si-Na	*Mex.*	-
Z Ethiopian Diamond	*Ethiopian*	23
Francesca's	*Italian*	22
NEW Gaztro-Wagon	*Eclectic*	-
Great Lake	*Pizza*	23
Hamburger Mary's	*Burgers*	17
Hopleaf	*Belgian*	23
Icosium Kafe	*African*	19
Indie Cafe	*Japanese/Thai*	24
Jin Ju	*Korean*	23
NEW Kingfisher	*Seafood*	-
La Cocina/Frida	*Mex.*	20
La Fonda/Grill	*Colombian*	-
Leonardo's	*Italian*	-
Loving Hut	*Asian/Vegan*	-
M Henry/Henrietta	*Amer.*	25
Moody's Pub	*Pub*	19
Ras Dashen	*Ethiopian*	23
Reza's	*Med./Mideast.*	18
Tanoshii	*Japanese*	-
Tapas Las Ramblas	*Spanish*	23
Uncommon Ground	*Eclectic/Coffee*	22
NEW Vincent	*Amer./Dutch*	-

GOLD COAST

(See map on page 239)

TOP FOOD

Spiaggia	*Italian*	**G4**	27
Seasons	*Amer.*	**H3**	27
Morton's	*Steak*	**G2**	26
Gibsons	*Steak*	**G2**	26
Café Spiaggia	*Italian*	**G4**	25
Il Mulino	*Italian*	**F1**	25
Le Colonial	*Viet.*	**H2**	24
Merlo	*Italian*	**G2**	24
Hugo's	*Seafood*	**G2**	24
Table Fifty-two	*Amer./Southern*	**F1**	24

LISTING

Balsan	*Euro.*	-
Big Bowl	*Asian*	20
NEW Bistronomic	*French*	-
Bistro 110	*French*	21
Bistrot Zinc	*French*	21
Café/Architectes	*French*	24
Z Café Spiaggia	*Italian*	25
Carmine's	*Italian*	22
NEW Chicago Q	*BBQ*	-
Ditka's	*Steak*	22
Drake Bros.'	*American*	-
Drawing Room	*Amer.*	23
Edwardo's Pizza	*Pizza*	20
Feast	*Amer.*	19
Fornetto Mei	*Chinese/Italian*	20
Frankie's Scaloppine	*Italian/Pizza*	18
Fred's	*Amer.*	19
Gaylord Indian	*Indian*	22
Z Gibsons	*Steak*	26
Z Hugo's	*Seafood*	24
Il Mulino	*Italian*	25
Z Le Colonial	*Viet.*	24
Luxbar	*Amer.*	20
McCormick/Schmick	*Seafood*	21
Merlo	*Italian*	24
Z Morton's	*Steak*	26
Z Nomi Kitchen	*French*	-
Oak Tree Bakery and Restaurant	*Amer.*	17
Z Original/Walker Pancake	*Amer.*	24
Pane Caldo	*Italian*	23
P.J. Clarke's	*Amer.*	17
RA Sushi	*Japanese*	19
Ria	*Amer.*	-
Z RL	*Amer.*	23
Z Seasons	*Amer.*	27
Z Spiaggia	*Italian*	27
Table Fifty-two	*Amer./Southern*	24
Tavern/Rush	*Steak*	21
Tempo	*Diner*	20
Trader Vic's	*Polynesian*	17

LAKEVIEW/ WRIGLEYVILLE

NEW Abiquiù	*New Mex.*	-
A La Turka	*Turkish*	20
Z Al's Beef	*Sandwich*	23

Andalous	*Moroccan*	22
Angelina	*Italian*	21
Ann Sather	*Amer./Swedish*	21
Art of Pizza	*Pizza*	22
Bagel	*Deli*	19
Bakin' & Eggs	*Amer.*	19
NEW Blokes/Birds	*British*	-
Bolat	*African*	-
Chalkboard	*Amer.*	22
Chens	*Asian*	22
Chicago Diner	*Diner/Vegetarian*	22
Chilam Balam	*Mex.*	25
NEW Chizakaya	*Japanese*	-
Coobah	*Filipino/Nuevo Latino*	17
Crêpe Town	*Crêpes*	-
Deleece	*Eclectic*	19
Deleece Grill	*Amer.*	20
NEW Del Seoul	*Korean*	-
DMK Burger	*Burgers*	22
Duck Walk	*Thai*	19
Duke/Perth	*Scottish*	20
Erwin	*Amer.*	23
Fiorentino's	*Italian*	22
NEW Fish Bar	*Seafood*	-
Flat Top	*Asian*	20
Frasca Pizza	*Pizza*	20
La Cocina/Frida	*Mex.*	20
NEW George St. Pub	*Pub*	-
Z Giordano's	*Pizza*	23
Goose Island	*Pub*	17
Half Shell	*Seafood*	24
HB Home Bistro	*Amer.*	25
Hearty	*Amer.*	-
Irish Oak	*Pub*	19
Jack's/Halsted	*Amer.*	21
Julius Meinl	*Austrian*	21
NEW Kanela	*Amer.*	-
Kit Kat	*Eclectic*	16
La Crêperie	*Crêpes/French*	21
Z La Gondola	*Italian*	-
Las Tablas	*Colombian/Steak*	20
Leo's Coney Island	*Diner/Hot Dogs*	-
Los Moles	*Mex.*	-
Melanthios	*Greek/Steak*	-
Z Mia Francesca	*Italian*	26
Mixteco Grill	*Mex.*	25
Mythos	*Greek*	23
90 Miles	*Cuban*	22
Nookies	*Diner*	20
Palette Bistro	*Amer.*	-
Penny's Noodle	*Asian*	20
Pho & I	*Thai/Viet.*	-
Piggery	*Amer./BBQ*	-

Pingpong	*Asian*	20
Pizza Rustica	*Pizza*	-
Pizzeria Serio	*Pizza*	-
Pompei Pizza	*Italian*	19
Z Potbelly Sandwich	*Sandwich*	19
Red Brick	*Eclectic/Med.*	-
NEW Rice Bistro	*Thai*	-
Rise	*Japanese*	21
Risqué Café	*BBQ*	-
Rockit B&G	*Amer.*	19
Rollapalooza	*Japanese*	-
Sapore/Napoli	*Pizza*	20
Socca	*French/Italian*	22
Sola	*Amer.*	25
Southport	*Amer.*	22
Sura	*Thai*	20
Taco Fuego	*Mex.*	-
Tango Sur	*Argent./Steak*	24
Tapas Gitana	*Spanish*	24
Thai Classic	*Thai*	23
Twist	*Eclectic*	21
NEW Ukai	*Japanese*	-
Uncommon Ground	*Eclectic/Coffee*	22
Wakamono	*Japanese*	22
NEW Yindee	*Japanese/Thai*	-
Yoshi's Café	*French/Japanese*	25

LINCOLN PARK

(See map on page 240)

TOP FOOD

Alinea	*Amer.*	**I7**	29
Charlie Trotter's	*Amer.*	**G6**	27
Riccardo	*Italian*	**F10**	27
Boka	*Amer.*	**I7**	25
North Pond	*Amer.*	**B10**	25
Sai Café	*Japanese*	**G5**	25
Rose Angelis	*Italian*	**B3**	24
Merlo	*Italian*	**B5**	24
Itto Sushi	*Japanese*	**B6**	24
Lou Malnati's	*Pizza*	**B5**	24
Original/Walker Pancake	*Amer.*	**F10**	24
Chicago Pizza	*Pizza*	**F10**	23
Sapori Trattoria	*Italian*	**A7**	23
Via Carducci	*Italian*	**D2**	23
Hema's Kitchen	*Indian*	**C9**	22

LISTING

NEW Ace Bar	*Burgers*	-
Aladdin's Eatery	*Mideast.*	18
Z Alinea	*Amer.*	29
NEW Aquitaine	*Amer./Fr.*	-
Bacino's	*Italian*	22
Basil Leaf	*Italian*	18
NEW Big Stuff	*Pizza/Sandwich*	-

NEW Bivona | *Italian*	-‌
Boka | *Amer.*	25
Bourgeois Pig | *Coffee/Sandwich*	-‌
Bricks | *Pizza*	22
NEW Burger Bar | *Burgers*	-‌
Cafe Ba-Ba-Reeba! | *Spanish*	22
Café Bernard | *French*	19
NEW Caminito | *Argent.*	-‌
Z Charlie Trotter's | *Amer.*	27
Chicago Pizza | *Pizza*	23
Counter | *Burgers*	20
Dee's | *Asian*	19
Duck Walk | *Thai*	19
Edwardo's Pizza | *Pizza*	20
Filippo's | *Italian*	24
Five Guys | *Burgers*	20
Frances' Deli | *Deli*	-‌
Franks 'N' Dawgs | *Hot Dogs*	-‌
Geja's Cafe | *Fondue*	21
Gemini Bistro | *Amer.*	21
Goose Island | *Pub*	17
Hai Yen | *Chinese/Viet.*	21
Hema's Kitchen | *Indian*	22
Icosium Kafe | *African*	19
Itto Sushi | *Japanese*	24
Ja' Grill | *Jamaican*	-‌
J. Alexander's | *Amer.*	20
John's Pl. | *Amer.*	18
Karyn's | *Vegan/Veg.*	20
Kith/Kin | *Amer.*	-‌
Landmark | *Amer.*	20
Z Lou Malnati's | *Pizza*	24
Z L2O | *Seafood*	-‌
Macku Sushi | *Japanese*	-‌
Maza | *Mideast.*	21
Merlo | *Italian*	24
Mon Ami Gabi | *French*	22
Nookies | *Diner*	20
Z North Pond | *Amer.*	25
Orange | *Eclectic*	20
Z Original Gino's East | *Pizza*	22
Z Original/Walker Pancake | *Amer.*	24
Pasta Palazzo | *Italian*	22
Penny's Noodle | *Asian*	20
NEW Perennial Virant | *Amer.*	-‌
Pizza Capri | *Pizza*	20
Z Potbelly Sandwich | *Sandwich*	19
Raj Darbar | *Indian*	18
NEW Redflame | *Pizza*	-‌
Z Riccardo | *Italian*	27
Ringo | *Japanese*	-‌
R.J. Grunts | *Amer.*	19
Robinson's Ribs | *BBQ*	21

Rose Angelis | *Italian*	24
Sai Café | *Japanese*	25
Sapori Trattoria | *Italian*	23
Sarks/Park | *Sandwiches*	-‌
Shine | *Chinese/Japanese*	-‌
Simply It | *Viet.*	22
NEW Sono | *Pizza*	-‌
Sprout | *Amer./French*	28
Stanley's | *Amer.*	18
Sushi Para/Sai | *Japanese*	-‌
NEW Taco Joint | *Mex.*	-‌
Tarantino's | *Italian*	22
Toast | *Amer.*	22
Trattoria Gianni | *Italian*	26
NEW Uptowner | *Amer./Burgers*	-‌
Via Carducci | *Italian*	23
Vinci | *Italian*	21
Vintage 338 | *Euro.*	-‌
Webster Wine | *Eclectic*	20
Z Wiener's Circle | *Hot Dogs*	21
Zapatista | *Mex.*	20

LINCOLN SQUARE/ UPTOWN

Agami | *Japanese*	24
Aroy | *Thai*	-‌
Ba Le Sandwich | *Sandwich/Viet.*	-‌
Z Bistro Campagne | *French*	25
Café Selmarie | *Amer.*	23
Ceres' Table | *Amer.*	-‌
Demera | *Ethiopian*	-‌
Dorado | *French/Mex.*	23
NEW Due Lire | *Italian*	-‌
Essence/India | *Indian*	21
Fontana Grill | *Italian*	-‌
NEW Fork | *Pub*	-‌
Hai Yen | *Chinese/Viet.*	21
Isla Filipino | *Filipino*	-‌
Julius Meinl | *Austrian*	21
La Bocca/Verità | *Italian*	22
La Ciudad | *Mex.*	-‌
LM | *French*	22
Magnolia Cafe | *Amer.*	22
Marigold | *Indian*	23
Pho 777 | *Viet.*	21
Phò Xe Tǎng | *Viet.*	26
Pizza D.O.C. | *Pizza/Italian*	23
NEW Prix Fixe | *French/Italian*	-‌
Rolis | *Mex.*	-‌
Rosded | *Thai*	-‌
San Soo Gab San | *Korean*	21
Silver Seafood | *Chinese/Seafood*	23
Spoon Thai | *Thai*	23
Sun Wah BBQ | *Chinese*	-‌

Tank Sushi | *Japanese*	23	🆕 Rub BBQ | *BBQ*	-
Thai Pastry | *Thai*	23	Tiffin | *Indian*	21
Trattoria Trullo | *Italian*	23	Udupi Palace | *Indian*	23
Tweet | *Amer.*	22		

NEAR NORTH

Fleming's | *Steak*	23
Kiki's | *French*	25
Ⓩ MK | *Amer.*	27

NORTH CENTER/ ST. BEN'S

Bad Apple | *Pub*	-
Browntrout | *American*	24
Cafe 28 | *Cuban/Mex.*	26
Cho Sun Ok | *Korean*	-
Corner 41 | *Amer.*	-
Jury's | *Pub*	18
Mrs. Murphy | *Pub*	22
Pitchfork | *BBQ*	-
Sanook | *Japanese/Thai*	-
Sticky Rice | *Thai*	-

OLD TOWN

Adobo | *Mex.*	21
Bistrot Margot | *French*	20
Dinotto | *Italian*	19
Flat Top | *Asian*	20
Kamehachi | *Japanese*	21
Lan's Bistro | *Chinese*	-
Mizu Yakitori | *Japanese*	24
Nookies | *Diner*	20
Old Jerusalem | *Mideast.*	19
Old Town Social | *Amer.*	18
Salpicón | *Mex.*	26
33 Club | *Amer.*	20
Topo Gigio | *Italian*	23
Trattoria Roma | *Italian*	21
Twin Anchors | *BBQ*	23
Uncle Julio's | *Tex-Mex*	18

ROGERS PARK/ WEST ROGERS PARK

🆕 Act One Pub | *Amer.*	-
Angin Mamiri | *Indonesian*	-
🆕 Chez Violette | *Haitian*	-
Ⓩ Ethiopian Diamond | *Ethiopian*	23
Five Guys | *Burgers*	20
Gold Coast | *Hot Dogs*	19
Gruppo/Amici | *Italian*	16
Hana | *Japanese*	-
Heartland Cafe | *Eclectic/Veg.*	16
Hema's Kitchen | *Indian*	22
Hop Häus | *Burgers*	19
Indian Garden | *Indian*	21
Ropa | *Med.*	-

Downtown

LOOP

Ⓩ Al's Beef | *Sandwich*	23
🆕 Ara On | *Asian*	-
Aria | *Asian*	24
Atwood Cafe | *Amer.*	22
Aurelio's Pizza | *Pizza*	23
Bacino's | *Italian*	22
Berghoff | *German*	18
Billy Goat | *Amer.*	17
Boston Blackies | *Burgers*	19
Ⓩ Carnivale | *Nuevo Latino*	23
Ⓩ Catch 35 | *Seafood*	24
China Grill | *Asian*	22
Cibo Matto | *Italian*	24
🆕 Currents/River | *Amer.*	-
Epic Burger | *Burgers*	22
Ⓩ Everest | *French*	27
Flat Top | *Asian*	20
🆕 Florentine | *Italian*	-
Ⓩ Gage | *Amer.*	22
Ⓩ Giordano's | *Pizza*	23
Gold Coast | *Hot Dogs*	19
Grillroom | *Steak*	15
Ⓩ Hannah's Bretzel | *Sandwiches*	23
Ⓩ Heaven/Seven | *Cajun/Creole*	23
Hot Woks | *Asian*	23
🆕 Hoyt's | *Amer.*	-
🆕 IPO | *Amer.*	-
Kamehachi | *Japanese*	21
La Cantina Chop | *Italian*	21
Lockwood | *Amer.*	19
Lou Mitchell's | *Diner*	23
McCormick/Schmick | *Seafood*	21
Miller's Pub | *Amer.*	17
Ⓩ Morton's | *Steak*	26
Ⓩ Nine Steakhouse | *Seafood/Steak*	24
One North | *Amer.*	15
Palm | *Steak*	24
Park Grill | *Amer.*	20
Perry's Deli | *Deli*	26
Petterino's | *Amer.*	19
Ⓩ Potbelly Sandwich | *Sandwich*	19
🆕 Pret A Manger | *Sandwich*	-
Rhapsody | *Amer.*	20
Robinson's Ribs | *BBQ*	21
Ⓩ Rosebud | *Italian*	22

Rosebud Prime/Steak	*Steak*	25
Roti	*Med.*	21
Ruby/Siam	*Thai*	23
NEW Rudy's B&G	*Amer.*	-
Russian Tea	*Russian*	22
NEW South Branch	*Pub*	-
South Water	*Amer.*	16
State/Lake	*Amer.*	21
Sushi Para/Sai	*Japanese*	-
Tavern/Park	*Amer.*	20
Terzo Piano	*Italian*	21
Thai Urban	*Asian*	16
Simply/Thalia	*Thai*	19
312 Chicago	*Italian*	21
Trattoria No. 10	*Italian*	24
Village	*Italian*	21
Vivere	*Italian*	22

RIVER NORTH

(See map on page 238)

TOP FOOD

Topolobampo	*Mex.*	**D6**	28
Naha	*Amer.*	**D6**	27
Frontera Grill	*Mex.*	**D6**	27
Joe's Sea/Steak	*Seafood/Steak*	**C8**	26
Avenues	*Amer.*	**A8**	26
Crofton on Wells	*Amer.*	**C5**	26
Zealous	*Amer.*	**A4**	25
Shanghai Terrace	*Asian*	**A8**	25
Xoco	*Mex.*	**D6**	25
Coco Pazzo	*Italian*	**D5**	25
David Burke Prime	*Steak*	**C8**	25
Keefer's	*Amer.*	**D7**	25
Chicago Chop	*Steak*	**B7**	25
Ruth's Chris	*Steak*	**D7**	25
Roy's	*Hawaiian*	**A7**	25

LISTING

Ai Sushi	*Japanese*	24
aja	*Asian*	-
Al Primo Canto	*Brazilian/Italian*	24
Z Al's Beef	*Sandwich*	23
Z Avenues	*Amer.*	26
Benny's Chop	*Steak*	-
Ben Pao	*Chinese*	21
Big & Little's	*Seafood*	-
Big Bowl	*Asian*	20
Bijan's	*Amer.*	19
Billy Goat	*Amer.*	17
Bin	*Amer.*	21
Blue 13	*Amer.*	24
Café Iberico	*Spanish*	22
Carson's	*BBQ*	22
Z Chicago Chop	*Steak*	25

NEW Chicago Cut	*Steak*	-
Chicago's/Chicken & Waffles	*Southern*	-
Z Coco Pazzo	*Italian*	25
Z Crofton on Wells	*Amer.*	26
Cyrano's Bistrot	*French*	22
Z David Burke Prime	*Steak*	25
Devon Seafood	*Seafood*	21
Dos Diablos	*Tex-Mex*	-
NEW Eatt	*Amer.*	-
Ed Debevic's	*Diner*	15
Eggsperience Café	*Amer.*	-
Elate	*Amer.*	21
Epic	*Amer.*	-
Erie Cafe	*Italian/Steak*	22
Fogo de Chão	*Brazilian/Steak*	24
1492	*Spanish*	21
Z Frontera Grill	*Mex.*	27
Fulton's	*Seafood/Steak*	19
Z Gene/Georgetti	*Steak*	24
Gilt Bar	*Amer.*	-
Z Giordano's	*Pizza*	23
Graham Elliot	*Amer.*	24
NEW Grahamwich	*Sandwich*	-
Grand Lux	*Eclectic*	20
NEW GT Fish/Oyster	*Seafood*	-
Hard Rock	*Amer.*	12
Harry Caray's	*Italian/Steak*	20
Havana	*Nuevo Latino*	-
Z Heaven/Seven	*Cajun/Creole*	23
Hop Häus	*Burgers*	19
NEW Hubbard Inn	*Amer.*	-
Hub 51	*Amer./Eclectic*	21
Z India House	*Indian*	25
ItaliAsia	*Asian/Italian*	-
Z Japonais	*Japanese*	24
Z Joe's Sea/Steak	*Seafood/Steak*	26
Kamehachi	*Japanese*	21
Kan Zaman	*Lebanese*	-
Karyn's	*Vegan/Veg.*	20
Z Keefer's	*Amer.*	25
Kinzie Chop	*Steak*	22
Klay Oven	*Indian*	20
La Madia	*Italian/Pizza*	23
Lawry's	*Amer./Steak*	24
Lobby	*Euro./Seafood*	28
Z Lou Malnati's	*Pizza*	24
Z Maggiano's	*Italian*	20
NEW Mastro's Steak	*Steak*	-
M Burger	*Burgers*	-
Melting Pot	*Fondue*	19
Mercadito	*Mex.*	22
Z Mr. Beef	*Sandwiches*	24

☑ Nacional 27 | *Nuevo Latino*	23	Billy Goat | *Amer.*	17
☑ Naha | *Amer.*	27	Cape Cod Room | *Seafood*	22
Nick's Fishmarket | *Seafood*	23	☑ Capital Grille | *Steak*	25
Orange | *Eclectic*	20	☑ Cheesecake Factory | *Amer.*	19
☑ Original Gino's East | *Pizza*	22	C-House | *Seafood*	21
Osteria/Pizzeria Via Stato | *Italian*	23	Cité | *Amer.*	20
		Coco Pazzo | *Italian*	22
Oysy | *Japanese*	20	Deca | *French*	-
NEW Paris Club | *French*	-	NEW DiSotto | *Italian*	-
P.F. Chang's | *Chinese*	20	☑ Emilio's Tapas | *Spanish*	24
Phil Stefani's | *Italian/Steak*	24	Foodlife | *Eclectic*	19
Pierrot Gourmet | *French*	20	Francesca's | *Italian*	22
Pizzeria Uno/Due | *Pizza*	22	Grill on Alley | *Amer.*	21
☑ Potbelly Sandwich | *Sandwich*	19	NEW Gyu-Kaku | *Japanese*	-
Prosecco | *Italian*	24	Indian Garden | *Indian*	21
NEW Public House | *Pub*	-	Kamehachi | *Japanese*	21
Purple Pig | *Med.*	-	LB Bistro/Patisserie | *Amer./French*	-
Quartino | *Italian*	21	Le P'tit Paris | *Continental/French*	20
RB Grille | *Seafood/Steak*	-	☑ Les Nomades | *French*	29
Reza's | *Med./Mideast.*	18	Markethouse | *Amer.*	21
Rockit B&G | *Amer.*	19	M Burger | *Burgers*	-
Rosebud Trattoria | *Italian*	22	Mity Nice | *Amer.*	17
Roy's | *Hawaiian*	25	Niu | *Asian*	19
Rumba | *Nuevo Latino*	23	☑ Original Gino's East | *Pizza*	22
☑ Ruth's Chris | *Steak*	25	Pelago | *Italian*	26
Sable | *Amer.*	-	P.J. Clarke's | *Amer.*	17
Scoozi! | *Italian*	19	Pompei Pizza | *Italian*	19
☑ Shanghai Terrace | *Asian*	25	Puck's/MCA | *Amer.*	20
☑ Shaw's Crab | *Seafood*	24	Riva | *Seafood*	20
☑ Sixteen | *Amer.*	22	☑ Rosebud | *Italian*	22
Smith/Wollensky | *Steak*	23	Rosebud Prime/Steak | *Steak*	25
NEW Snarf's | *Sandwiches*	-	Saloon Steak | *Steak*	23
Star/Siam | *Thai*	20	Sayat Nova | *Armenian*	23
Steve's Deli | *Deli*	17	Shula's Steak | *Steak*	21
Sullivan's Steak | *Steak*	22	☑ Signature Room | *Amer.*	18
Sunda | *Asian*	23	☑ Tru | *French*	28
Sushi Naniwa | *Japanese*	23	Viand Bar | *Amer.*	22
Sushisamba Rio | *Japanese/S Amer.*	21	Volare | *Italian*	24
		Wave | *Med.*	13
Sushi Taiyo | *Japanese*	-	Yolk | *Amer.*	22
Texas de Brazil | *Brazilian*	22	Zodiac Room | *Amer.*	-
☑ Topolobampo | *Mex.*	28		
Vermilion | *Indian/Nuevo Latino*	22		
Weber Grill | *BBQ*	20		
☑ Wildfire | *Steak*	23		
Xoco | *Mex.*	25		
Yolk | *Amer.*	22		
Zealous | *Amer.*	25		
Zed 451 | *Eclectic*	21		
Zocalo | *Mex.*	20		

City Northwest

AVONDALE

☑ Kuma's | *Amer.*	26
NEW Pork Shoppe | *BBQ*	-

BUCKTOWN

(See map on page 242)

TOP FOOD

Takashi | *Amer./French* | **E5**	26
Coast Sushi/South Coast | *Japanese* | **D5**	24

STREETERVILLE

American Girl | *Amer.*	16
Bandera | *Amer.*	22

Hot Chocolate	Amer.	**G5**	24
Le Bouchon	French	**E5**	24
Bristol	Amer.	**C7**	23

LISTING

NEW Antico	Italian	-
NEW Bento Box	Asian	-
Birchwood	Sandwiches	23
Bluebird	Amer.	20
Bricks	Pizza	22
Bristol	Amer.	23
Café Absinthe	Amer./French	23
Club Lucky	Italian	19
Coast Sushi/South Coast	Japanese	24
Duchamp	Amer.	17
Feast	Amer.	19
Honey 1 BBQ	BBQ	20
Hot Chocolate	Amer.	24
Irazu	Costa Rican	22
Jane's	Amer./Eclectic	22
Las Palmas	Mex.	21
Le Bouchon	French	24
NEW Lillie's Q	BBQ/Southern	-
Lokal	Euro.	-
Z Margie's Candies	Amer.	22
Siboney	Cuban	-
NEW Silom 12	Thai	-
Southern/Mac	Southern	-
Sushi Para/Sai	Japanese	-
Z Takashi	Amer./French	26
Toast	Amer.	22
Tocco	Italian	12

EDISON PARK/ O'HARE AREA

Bar Louie	Pub	16
Berghoff	German	18
Big Bowl	Asian	20
Billy Goat	Amer.	17
Café Touché	French	25
Z Capital Grille	Steak	25
Carlucci	Italian	20
Z Cheesecake Factory	Amer.	19
Don Juan's	Mex.	20
Fleming's	Steak	23
Gene & Jude's	Hot Dogs	-
Z Gibsons	Steak	26
Gold Coast	Hot Dogs	19
Harry Caray's	Italian/Steak	20
Lou Mitchell's	Diner	23
McCormick/Schmick	Seafood	21
Z Morton's	Steak	26
Nick's Fishmarket	Seafood	23
Oba	Japanese	-

Z Original Gino's East	Pizza	22
Z Original/Walker Pancake	Amer.	24
Sullivan's Steak	Steak	22
Z Wildfire	Steak	23
Zia's Trattoria	Italian	24

HUMBOLDT PARK

Belly Shack	Asian	23
NEW Joey's Shrimp	Seafood	-
Maiz	Mex.	23
Rootstock	Amer.	24

LOGAN SQUARE

Accanto	Italian	-
Azucar	Spanish	22
NEW Boiler Room	Pizza	-
Z Bonsoirée	Amer./French	26
Buona Terra	Italian	24
Ciao Napoli	Pizza	-
Conoce/Panama	Central Amer.	-
NEW Danzón	Nuevo Latino	-
NEW D'Noche/Café Con Leche	Amer./S. Amer.	-
Estrella Negra	Mex./Nuevo Latino	-
Fat Willy's	BBQ/Southern	23
Fonda del Mar	Mex./Seafood	25
Fuego	Mex.	24
Z Giordano's	Pizza	23
NEW Gosu	Japanese/Korean	-
Hachi's Kitchen	Japanese	-
Katakana/Koko	Japanese	-
Knew	Amer./Eclectic	-
NEW Letizia's Fiore	Italian	-
Longman/Eagle	Amer.	-
Z Lula Cafe	Eclectic	26
90 Miles	Cuban	22
NEW Owen/Engine	British	-
Real Tenochtitlán	Mex.	20
Revolution Brewing	Pub	-
NEW Rewster's Café	Amer.	-
NEW Sakura	Japanese	-
Urbanbelly	Asian	24
NEW Wasabi	Japanese	-

NORTHWEST SIDE/ RAVENSWOOD

Al Primo Canto	Brazilian/Italian	24
Amitabul	Korean	21
Andies	Med./Mideast	18
Anna Maria	Italian	24
Z Arun's	Thai	28
Blue Ocean	Japanese	23
Café Marbella	Spanish	-
Chief O'Neill's	Pub	18

City South

BRIDGEPORT

CHINATOWN

FAR SOUTH SIDE

Café 103 | *Amer./Eclectic* - ⌋
Koda | *French* - ⌋
Lem's BBQ | *BBQ* 25⌋
🅔 Lou Malnati's | *Pizza* 24⌋
Nana | *Amer./Mex.* - ⌋
Parrot Cage | *Amer.* - ⌋
Sikia | *African* - ⌋
Uncle John's BBQ | *BBQ* - ⌋
Vito & Nick's | *Pizza* 25⌋

HYDE PARK/ KENWOOD

Bar Louie | *Pub* 16⌋
Edwardo's Pizza | *Pizza* 20⌋
🅔 Giordano's | *Pizza* 23⌋
La Petite Folie | *French* 24⌋
Medici/57th | *Amer.* 17⌋
🅔 Original/Walker Pancake | *Amer.* 24⌋
Park 52 | *Amer.* 19⌋
Pizza Capri | *Pizza* 20⌋
Ribs 'n' Bibs | *BBQ* 21⌋
Zaleski/Horvath | *Deli* - ⌋

PILSEN

Decolores | *Mex.* - ⌋
Mundial | *Eclectic* - ⌋
Nightwood | *Amer.* 23⌋
Rist. al Teatro | *Italian/Med.* - ⌋

PRINTER'S ROW

Bar Louie | *Pub* 16⌋
Custom House | *Amer.* 25⌋
Hackney's | *Burgers* 18⌋

SOUTH LOOP

🆕 A 'Cappella | *Amer.* - ⌋
Bongo Room | *Amer.* 24⌋
Cafe Bionda/To Go | *Italian* 22⌋
Chicago Curry | *Indian/Nepalese* 25⌋
Chicago Firehouse | *Amer.* 20⌋
Edwardo's Pizza | *Pizza* 20⌋
Eleven City | *Diner* 19⌋
Flo/Santos Pizza | *Pizza/Pub Food* - ⌋
Gioco | *Italian* 25⌋
🆕 Henri | *Amer.* - ⌋
Joy Yee | *Asian* 20⌋
Kroll's | *Amer.* 19⌋
La Cantina Grill | *Mex.* - ⌋
Manny's | *Deli* 23⌋
🅔 Mercat | *Spanish* 26⌋
Mesón Sabika | *Spanish* 23⌋
Oysy | *Japanese* 20⌋
Coast Sushi/South Coast | *Japanese* 24⌋

Tamarind | *Asian* 23⌋
Yolk | *Amer.* 22⌋
Zapatista | *Mex.* 20⌋

SOUTHWEST SIDE

Bacchanalia | *Italian* 24⌋
Bruna's | *Italian* 26⌋
🅔 Giordano's | *Pizza* 23⌋
Gold Coast | *Hot Dogs* 19⌋
Harry Caray's | *Italian/Steak* 20⌋
Manny's | *Deli* 23⌋
Miller's Pub | *Amer.* 17⌋
Pegasus | *Greek* 20⌋

City West

FAR WEST

Depot/Diner | *Diner* - ⌋

GREEKTOWN

Artopolis | *Greek/Med.* 22⌋
Athena | *Greek* 21⌋
🅔 Giordano's | *Pizza* 23⌋
Greek Islands | *Greek* 21⌋
Karyn's/Green | *Amer./Vegan* - ⌋
Parthenon | *Greek* 21⌋
Pegasus | *Greek* 20⌋
Roditys | *Greek* 21⌋
Santorini | *Greek/Seafood* 21⌋
Venus | *Greek* - ⌋

LITTLE ITALY/ UNIVERSITY VILLAGE

🅔 Al's Beef | *Sandwich* 23⌋
Chez Joël | *French* 24⌋
🆕 Davanti | *Italian* - ⌋
Francesca's | *Italian* 22⌋
🆕 La Taberna | *Eclectic* - ⌋
🆕 One.Six One | *Eclectic* - ⌋
🆕 Original Five | *BBQ* - ⌋
Pompei Pizza | *Italian* 19⌋
Rosal's | *Italian* 26⌋
🅔 Rosebud | *Italian* 22⌋
🆕 Salatino's/Doughboys | *Italian* - ⌋
🆕 Stax Café | *Amer.* - ⌋
🆕 Three Aces | *Italian/Pub* - ⌋
Tufano's Tap | *Italian* 20⌋
Tuscany | *Italian* 22⌋

NEAR WEST

Breakfast Club | *Amer.* 20⌋
Dining Room/Kendall | *French* 23⌋
Orange | *Eclectic* 20⌋
Piccolo Sogno | *Italian* 24⌋

CHICAGO

LOCATIONS

NOBLE SQUARE

Bella Notte	*Italian*	21
Branch 27	*Amer.*	17
Butterfly	*Japanese/Thai*	22
Coalfire Pizza	*Pizza*	23
Flo	*Amer.*	22
NEW Fogón	*Mex.*	-
NEW Frontier	*Amer./Pub*	-
Z Green Zebra	*Veg.*	26
Habana Libre	*Cuban*	22
Kin	*Japanese/Thai*	-
NEW Leopold	*Belgian*	-
Mexique	*Mex.*	25
Natalino's	*Italian*	23
NEW Ruxbin	*Eclectic*	-
NEW Seadog Sushi	*Japanese*	-
Twisted Spoke	*Pub*	18
West Town	*Amer.*	24

RIVER WEST

NEW Bia for Mia	*Italian*	-
La Scarola	*Italian*	24
Paramount Room	*Amer.*	24
Roti	*Med.*	21
Sushi X	*Japanese*	21
Simply/Thalia	*Asian*	19

UKRAINIAN VILLAGE

Z A Tavola	*Italian*	26
Bite Cafe	*Amer.*	-
Folklore	*Argent./Steak*	-
Jam	*Amer.*	21
Old Oak Tap	*Pub*	20
Sabor Saveur	*French/Mex.*	-

WEST LOOP

Alhambra	*Mideast.*	16
Z Avec	*Med.*	26
NEW Aviary, The	*Eclectic*	-
Bacino's	*Italian*	22
Billy Goat	*Amer.*	17
Z Blackbird	*Amer.*	27
Bombon Café	*Mex.*	-
Butterfly	*Japanese/Thai*	22
Carmichael's	*Steak*	22
De Cero	*Mex.*	21
Felony Franks	*Hot Dogs*	-
Flat Top	*Asian*	20
NEW Girl/The Goat	*Amer.*	-
NEW Haymarket Pub	*Pub*	-
Ina's	*Amer.*	23
NEW Ing	*Amer.*	-
Jaipur	*Indian*	-
NEW La Lagartija	*Mex.*	-
La Sardine	*French*	24

LM	*French/Sandwiches*	22
NEW Mac/Min's	*Southern*	-
Macello	*Italian*	-
Market	*Amer.*	18
NEW Maude's Liquor	*French*	-
Meiji	*Japanese*	25
Mezé	*Eclectic*	-
Z Moto	*Eclectic*	27
NEW Next	*Eclectic*	-
Nia	*Med.*	-
Z One Sixtyblue	*Amer.*	26
Pasha	*Spanish*	-
Prairie Fire	*Amer.*	-
Province	*Amer.*	23
Z Publican	*Amer.*	25
NEW Saigon Sisters	*Viet.*	-
NEW Sawtooth	*Viet.*	-
Sepia	*Amer.*	24
Z Sushi Wabi	*Japanese*	27
Tasting Room	*Amer.*	20
Trattoria Isabella	*Italian*	26
Veerasway	*Indian*	21
Vivo	*Italian*	24
Wishbone	*Southern*	21

WEST TOWN

NEW Arami	*Japanese*	-
Butterfly	*Japanese/Thai*	22
Chickpea	*Mideast.*	22
NEW Kai Sushi	*Japanese*	-
Makisu/Aha Sushi	*Japanese*	-

Suburbs

SUBURBAN NORTH

Abigail's	*Amer.*	24
Makisu/Aha Sushi	*Japanese*	-
Akai Hana	*Japanese*	21
Bagel	*Deli*	19
Bank Lane	*Amer.*	23
Bar Louie	*Pub*	16
Benihana	*Japanese/Steak*	18
Bistro Bordeaux	*French*	-
Blind Faith	*Veg.*	21
NEW Bluette	*French*	-
Z Bob Chinn's	*Seafood*	23
Bonsai Café	*Asian*	-
Boston Blackies	*Burgers*	19
Cafe Central	*French*	24
Cafe Pyrenees	*French*	21
Campagnola	*Italian*	25
Z Carlos'	*French*	27
Carson's	*BBQ*	22
Cellar/Stained Glass	*Eclectic*	21
Z Cheesecake Factory	*Amer.*	19

Chef's Station	*Amer.*	24
Curry Hut	*Indian/Nepalese*	20
Dave's Italian	*Italian*	17
Davis St. Fish	*Seafood*	19
Del Rio	*Italian*	20
Depot Nuevo	*Nuevo Latino*	18
Di Pescara	*Italian/Seafood*	19
Dixie Kitchen	*Cajun/Southern*	19
NEW Donatella	*Italian/Med.*	-
Edwardo's Pizza	*Pizza*	20
Edzo's	*Burgers*	-
Eggsperience Café	*Amer.*	-
EJ's Pl.	*Italian/Steak*	22
NEW Everest Burger	*Burgers*	-
545 North	*Amer.*	20
Flat Top	*Asian*	20
Flight	*Eclectic*	17
Francesca's	*Italian*	22
Francesco's	*Italian*	24
Froggy's	*French*	22
Z Gabriel's	*French/Italian*	25
Gale St. Inn	*Amer.*	22
Hackney's	*Burgers*	18
Happ Inn	*Amer.*	17
Hecky's	*BBQ*	20
La Casa/Isaac	*Mex.*	20
Jacky's/Prairie	*Eclectic*	21
J. Alexander's	*Amer.*	20
Jilly's Cafe	*Amer./French*	21
Joy Yee	*Asian*	20
Kamehachi	*Japanese*	21
Kansaku	*Japanese*	22
Karma	*Asian*	23
Koi	*Asian*	21
Kuni's	*Japanese*	24
Z Lou Malnati's	*Pizza*	24
Z Lovells	*Amer.*	23
LuLu's	*Asian*	21
Lupita's	*Mex.*	21
L. Woods Tap	*Amer.*	20
Z Maggiano's	*Italian*	20
Main St. Smoke	*BBQ*	-
Manghal	*Kosher/Med.*	-
McCormick/Schmick	*Seafood*	21
Merle's BBQ	*BBQ*	19
Z Michael	*French*	28
Miramar Bistro	*French*	17
Mitchell's	*Seafood*	21
Z Morton's	*Steak*	26
Mt. Everest	*Indian/Nepalese*	22
Myron/Phil Steak	*Steak*	21
Next Door	*Amer./Italian*	23
Z Oceanique	*French/Seafood*	27

Opa! Estiatorio	*Greek*	25
Orange	*Eclectic*	20
Z Original Gino's East	*Pizza*	22
Z Original/Walker Pancake	*Amer.*	24
Penny's Noodle	*Asian*	20
NEW Pensiero	*Italian*	-
Pete Miller	*Seafood/Steak*	22
P.F. Chang's	*Chinese*	20
Philly G's	*Italian*	21
Pine Yard	*Chinese*	18
Pinstripes	*Amer./Italian*	17
Z Pita Inn	*Med./Mideast.*	24
Pomegranate	*Med./Mideast.*	18
Prairie Grass	*Amer.*	22
Quince	*Amer.*	23
RA Sushi	*Japanese*	19
NEW Real Urban BBQ	*BBQ*	-
Z Rosebud	*Italian*	22
Roti	*Med.*	21
Ruby/Siam	*Thai*	23
Z Ruth's Chris	*Steak*	25
San Gabriel	*Mex.*	17
Sarkis Cafe	*Diner*	15
South Gate	*Amer.*	20
Stained Glass	*Amer.*	23
Stir Crazy	*Asian*	19
Z Superdawg	*Burgers/Hot Dogs*	21
Szechwan North	*Chinese*	19
Tamales	*Mex.*	20
Tapas Barcelona	*Spanish*	21
Tapas Gitana	*Spanish*	24
Tramonto's	*Seafood/Steak*	24
Trattoria D.O.C.	*Italian/Pizza*	19
Tub Tim Thai	*Thai*	24
Tuscany	*Italian*	22
Union Pizza	*Pizza*	23
Z Wildfire	*Steak*	23
Wildfish	*Japanese*	21
Yard House	*Amer.*	18
Zapatista	*Mex.*	20
Zhivago	*Continental*	16

SUBURBAN NW

Z Al's Beef	*Sandwich*	23
Aurelio's Pizza	*Pizza*	23
Bar Louie	*Pub*	16
Z Barrington Country	*French*	25
NEW Bauer's Brauhaus	*German*	-
Benihana	*Japanese/Steak*	18
Big Bowl	*Asian*	20
Z Cheesecake Factory	*Amer.*	19
D & J Bistro	*French*	24
Edelweiss	*German*	19

Eggsperience Café | Amer.	-
Francesca's | Italian	22
Gaylord Indian | Indian	22
Hackney's | Burgers	18
☑ India House | Indian	25
Inovasi | Amer.	-
Las Palmas | Mex.	21
La Tasca | Spanish	24
L'Eiffel Bistrot | Crêpes/French	21
☑ Le Titi/Paris | French	26
Le Vichyssois | French	26
☑ Lou Malnati's | Pizza	24
Lucky Monk | Pizza/Pub	-
☑ Maggiano's | Italian	20
McCormick/Schmick | Seafood	21
Melting Pot | Fondue	19
Montarra | Amer.	24
☑ Morton's | Steak	26
Nozumi | Japanese	-
☑ Original Gino's East | Pizza	22
☑ Original/Walker Pancake | Amer.	24
P.F. Chang's | Chinese	20
Pinstripes | Amer./Italian	17
NEW PL8 | Chinese/Japanese	-
Pompei Pizza | Italian	19
Port Edward | Seafood	-
NEW Raj Palace | Indian	-
Retro Bistro | French	23
☑ Rosebud | Italian	22
Russell's BBQ | BBQ	19
☑ Ruth's Chris | Steak	25
Salsa 17 | Mex.	22
Sam/Harry's Steak | Steak	-
Seasons 52 | Amer.	-
1776 | Amer.	22
☑ Shaw's Crab | Seafood	24
Shula's Steak | Steak	21
Stir Crazy | Asian	19
Sushi Ai | Japanese	-
Sushi Para/Sai | Japanese	-
Texas de Brazil | Brazilian	22
Thai Pastry | Thai	23
Todai | Asian	-
Udupi Palace | Indian	23
Weber Grill | BBQ	20
White Fence | Amer.	22
☑ Wildfire | Steak	23
Wildfish | Japanese	21
Woo Lae Oak | Korean	20

SUBURBAN SOUTH

☑ Al's Beef | Sandwich	23
Aurelio's Pizza | Pizza	23
Dixie Kitchen | Cajun/Southern	19
☑ Original/Walker Pancake | Amer.	24

SUBURBAN SW

Al Bawadi Grill | Mideast.	-
☑ Al's Beef | Sandwich	23
Aurelio's Pizza | Pizza	23
Courtright's | Amer.	25
Dan McGee | Amer.	-
Hackney's | Burgers	18
☑ Original/Walker Pancake | Amer.	24
P.F. Chang's | Chinese	20
☑ Tallgrass | French	28
Tin Fish | Seafood	23
Topaz Café | Amer.	23

SUBURBAN WEST

Adelle's | Amer.	25
Amber Cafe | Amer.	22
Antico Posto | Italian	22
Atwater's | Amer./French	20
Aurelio's Pizza | Pizza	23
Bacino's | Italian	22
Bar Louie | Pub	16
Benihana | Japanese/Steak	18
NEW Bistro One West | Amer.	-
Briejo | Amer./Eclectic	14
Brio | Italian	22
NEW Burger Boss | Burgers	-
Cab's Wine Bar | Amer.	24
☑ Capital Grille | Steak	25
Carlucci | Italian	19
☑ Catch 35 | Seafood	24
Chama Gaucha | Brazilian/Steak	-
☑ Cheesecake Factory | Amer.	19
NEW Chef Amaury's | Amer.	-
Chicago Burgerwurks | Burgers	-
Chicago's/Chicken & Waffles | Southern	-
Chinn's Fishery | Seafood	25
CityGate | Amer./Med.	-
Clubhouse | Amer.	21
Costa's | Greek	22
Cucina Paradiso | Italian	20
Czech Plaza | Czech	22
Distinctive Cork | Amer.	21
Ditka's | Steak	22
Duckfat | Amer.	-
Edwardo's Pizza | Pizza	20
Eggsperience Café | Amer.	-
☑ Emilio's Tapas | Spanish	24
Five Guys | Burgers	20

Flat Top	*Asian*	20
Fonda Isabel	*Mex.*	-
Francesca's	*Italian*	22
Gaetano's	*Italian*	24
Z Gibsons	*Steak*	26
Glen Prairie	*Amer.*	23
Gordon Biersch	*Pub*	16
Greek Islands	*Greek*	21
Harry Caray's	*Italian/Steak*	20
Z Heaven/Seven	*Cajun/Creole*	23
Hemmingway's	*Amer./French*	21
Holy Mackerel!	*Seafood*	21
Z Hugo's	*Seafood*	24
Il Poggiolo	*Italian*	19
Z India House	*Indian*	25
Isacco	*Italian*	-
J. Alexander's	*Amer.*	20
Joy Yee	*Asian*	20
Katy's Dumpling	*Chinese*	-
NEW Kinderhook Tap	*Amer.*	-
Klay Oven	*Indian*	20
Z Lao	*Chinese*	24
Laurel	*Med.*	-
Z Lou Malnati's	*Pizza*	24
Z Maggiano's	*Italian*	20
Maijean	*French*	28
Maya Del Sol	*Nuevo Latino*	23
McCormick/Schmick	*Seafood*	21
Melting Pot	*Fondue*	19
Mesón Sabika	*Spanish*	23
Mon Ami Gabi	*French*	22
Z Morton's	*Steak*	26
NEW Nabuki	*Japanese*	-
Nagoya	*Japanese*	-
Niche	*Amer.*	28
Nickson's Eatery	*Amer.*	-

Nosh	*Eclectic*	24
Olive or Twist	*Amer.*	-
Z Original Gino's East	*Pizza*	22
Z Original/Walker Pancake	*Amer.*	24
Z Pappadeaux	*Seafood*	21
Parkers'	*Amer.*	23
Penny's Noodle	*Asian*	20
P.F. Chang's	*Chinese*	20
Pompei Pizza	*Italian*	19
Praga	*Amer./Eclectic*	-
Prasino	*Amer./Veg.*	-
RA Sushi	*Japanese*	19
NEW Redd Herring	*Amer.*	-
Reel Club	*Seafood*	23
Reza's	*Med./Mideast.*	18
Robinson's Ribs	*BBQ*	21
Z Rosebud	*Italian*	22
Russell's BBQ	*BBQ*	19
NEW Smashburger	*Burgers*	-
Stir Crazy	*Asian*	19
Sugartoad	*Amer.*	19
Sullivan's Steak	*Steak*	22
Swordfish	*Japanese*	27
Tango	*Argent.*	22
Trattoria 225	*Italian*	-
Tuscany	*Italian*	22
Uncle Bub's	*BBQ*	-
Viceroy/India	*Indian*	21
Z Vie	*Amer.*	27
Volare	*Italian*	24
Weber Grill	*BBQ*	20
Z Wildfire	*Steak*	23
Wishbone	*Southern*	21
Xni-Pec	*Mex.*	-
Zak's Place	*Amer.*	-

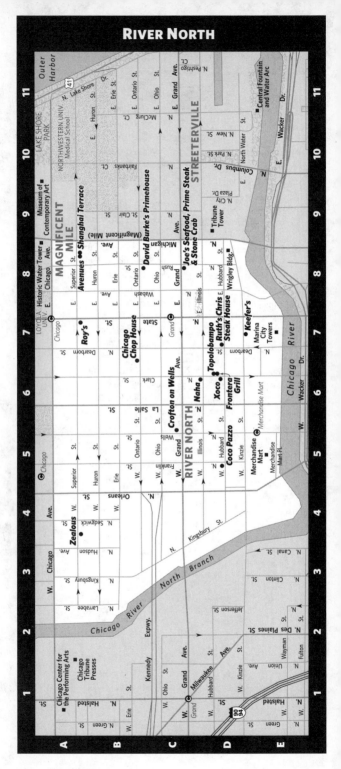

RIVER NORTH

GOLD COAST

LINCOLN PARK

La Salle Dr.

Lincoln Monument

64

Chicago History Museum

W. North Ave.

E. North Ave.

N. Clark St.

W. Burton Pl.

E. Burton Pl.

International Museum of Surgical Science

41

GOLD COAST

St.

N. State St.

Pkwy.

Dearborn

W. Schiller St.

E. Schiller St.

Charnley-Persky House

Clark

E. Banks St.

N.

W. Goethe St.

E. Goethe St.

Astor St.

N.

E. Scott St.

N. Stone St.

Lake Michigan

Clark/Division

W. Division St.

E. Division St.

N. Lake Shore Dr.

W. Elm St.

E. Elm St.

Il Mulino New York

Table Fifty-two

E. Cedar St.

Merlo on Maple

W. Maple St.

Gibsons Bar & Steakhouse

E. Bellevue Pl.

OAK STREET BEACH

Morton's The Steakhouse

Rush St.

E. Oak St.

Hugo's Frog Bar & Fish House

W. Oak St.

41

E. Lake Shore Dr.

One Magnificent Mile

Michigan Ave.

Spiaggia

Café Spiaggia

Le Colonial

State St.

N. Rush St.

E. Walton St.

E. Walton Pl.

WASHINGTON SQ. PARK

N. Ernst Ct.

Seasons

E. Delaware

John Hancock Center

Mies Van Der Rohe Way

N. DeWitt Pl.

CONNORS PARK

E. Chestnut St.

W. Chestnut St.

St.

St.

LOYOLA UNIV.

E. Pearson St.

Water Tower Place

Historic Water Tower

SENECA PARK

Museum of Contemporary Art

W. Chicago Ave.

Chicago

E. Chicago Ave.

Clark

Dearborn

Chicago St.

Ave.

MAGNIFICENT MILE

E. Superior St.

W. Huron St.

N.

N.

State St.

Wabash

E. Huron St.

St.

E. Michigan (Magnificent Mile) Ave.

St. Clair St.

Fairbanks Ct.

W. Erie St.

Rush

E. Erie St.

W. Ontario St.

E. Ontario St.

W. Ohio St.

N.

N.

E. Ohio St.

STREETERVILLE

Grand

W. Grand Ave.

E.

Grand Ave.

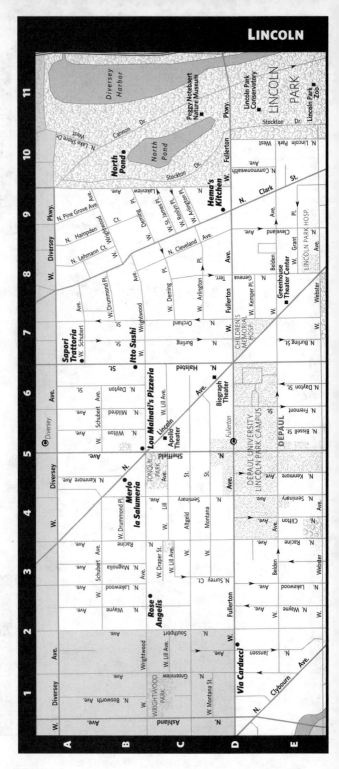

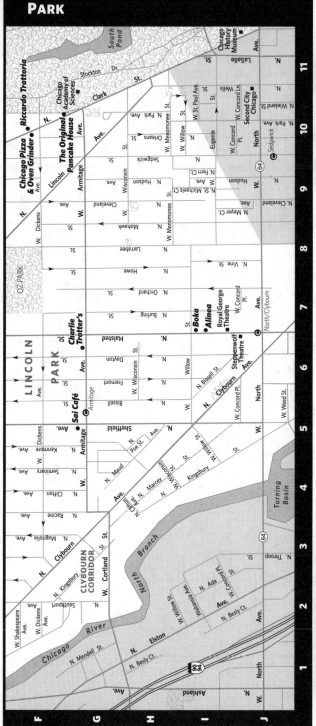

PARK

CHICAGO

MAPS

South Pond

Chicago History Museum

Chicago Academy of Sciences

Stockton Dr.

Clark St.

Ave.

N. LaSalle St.

N. Wells St.

N. St. Paul Ave.

W. Concord Ln.

Second City Chicago

N. Wieland St.

N. Park Ave.

Riccardo Trattoria

Chicago Pizza & Oven Grinder

The Original Pancake House

Lincoln Ave.

N. Park Ave.

W. Menomonee St.

Orleans St.

W. Willow St.

Sedgwick St.

W. Eugenie

N. Concord Pl.

North

Sedgwick

Armitage Ave.

Wisconsin

N. Hudson Ave.

N. St. Michaels Ct.

N. Fern Ct.

Hudson Ave.

W. N. Meyer Ct.

N. Cleveland Ave.

N. Cleveland Ave.

W. Dickens

Cleveland

Mohawk St.

W. Menomonee St.

64

Larrabee St.

Howe St.

N. Orchard St.

N. Vine St.

OZ PARK

Charlie Trotter's

Halsted St.

N. Burling St.

Boka

Alinea

Royal George Theatre

W. Concord Pl.

N. Chicago

North/Clybourn

LINCOLN PARK

Sai Café

Armitage Ave.

Dayton

Fremont

N. Wisconsin St.

Willow

N. Bissell St.

Steppenwolf Theatre

Clybourn Ave.

W. Concord Pl.

North

W. Weed St.

W. Dickens

N. Kenmore Ave.

W. Seminary Ave.

N. Clifton Ave.

N. Racine Ave.

Magnolia Ave.

Sheffield Ave.

N. Maud

N. Poe St.

N. Wisconsin St.

W. Willow St.

Kingsbury

N. Marcey

N. Clifton Ave.

Turning Basin

Clybourn St.

W. Cortland St.

CLYBOURN CORRIDOR

N. Kingsbury

North Branch

W. Willow St.

Wabansia Ave.

N. Ada St.

W. Concord Pl.

N. Throop St.

64

W. Shakespeare Ave.

W. Dickens Ave.

Southport Ave.

Chicago River

Elston

N. Mendell St.

N. Besly Ct.

90 94

N. Ashland Ave.

North Ave.

F

G

H

I

J

1 2 3 4 5 6 7 8 9 10 11

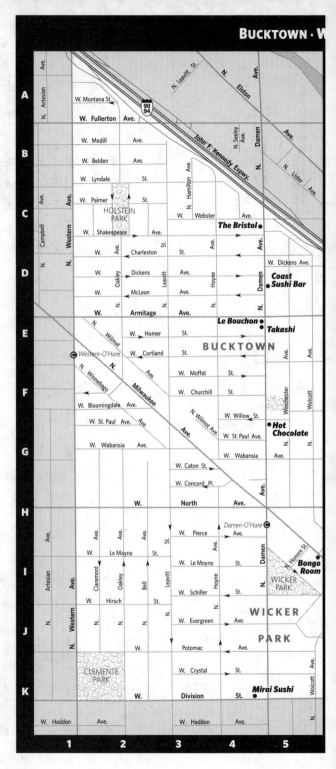

WICKER PARK

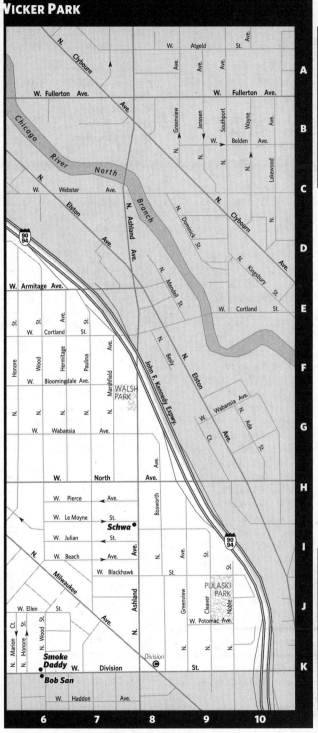

Special Features

Listings cover the best in each category and include names, locations and Food ratings. Multi-location restaurants' features may vary by branch.

ADDITIONS

(Properties added since the last edition of the book)

Abiquiù | **Lakeview** ⌐

A 'Cappella | **S Loop** ⌐

Ace Bar | **Lincoln Pk** ⌐

Acre | **Andersonville** ⌐

Act One Pub | **Rogers Pk** ⌐

Al Bawadi Grill | **Bridgeview** ⌐

Antico | **Bucktown** ⌐

Aquitaine | **Lincoln Pk** ⌐

Arami | **W Town** ⌐

Ara On | **Loop** ⌐

Aroy | **Lincoln Sq** ⌐

Aviary, The | **W Loop** ⌐

Awash | **Edgewater** ⌐

Bad Apple | **North Ctr/St. Ben's** ⌐

Ba Le Sandwich | **Uptown** ⌐

Bangers/Lace | **Wicker Pk** ⌐

Bauer's Brauhaus | **Palatine** ⌐

Bedford | **Wicker Pk** ⌐

Bento Box | **Bucktown** ⌐

Bia for Mia | **River W** ⌐

Big & Little's | **River N** ⌐

Big Stuff | **Lincoln Pk** ⌐

Bistronomic | **Gold Coast** ⌐

Bistro One West | **St. Charles** ⌐

Bite Cafe | **Ukrainian Vill** ⌐

Bivona | **Lincoln Pk** ⌐

Blokes/Birds | **Lakeview** ⌐

Bluette | **Wilmette** ⌐

Boiler Room | **Logan Sq** ⌐

Bombon Café | **W Loop** ⌐

Bourgeois Pig | **Lincoln Pk** ⌐

Burger Bar | **Lincoln Pk** ⌐

Burger Boss | **Elmwood Pk** ⌐

Calabruzzi's | **Bridgeport** ⌐

Caminito | **Lincoln Pk** ⌐

Cantonesia | **Chinatown** ⌐

Chama Gaucha | **Downers Grove** ⌐

Chef Amaury's | **Aurora** ⌐

Chez Violette | **Rogers Pk** ⌐

Chicago Burgerwurks | **Brookfield** ⌐

Chicago Cut | **River N** ⌐

Chicago Q | **Gold Coast** ⌐

Chicago's/Chicken & Waffles | **multi.** ⌐

Chikurin Sushi | **Wicker Pk** ⌐

Chizakaya | **Lakeview** ⌐

Choppers | **Wicker Pk** ⌐

Cho Sun Ok | **North Ctr/St. Ben's** ⌐

City Provisions | **Ravenswood** ⌐

Cumin | **Wicker Pk** ⌐

Currents/River | **Loop** ⌐

Danzón | **Logan Sq** ⌐

Davanti | **Little Italy/University Vill** ⌐

Del Seoul | **Lakeview** ⌐

Demera | **Uptown** ⌐

DiSotto | **Streeterville** ⌐

D'Noche/Café Con Leche | **Logan Sq** ⌐

Donatella | **Evanston** ⌐

Due Lire | **Lincoln Sq** ⌐

Eatt | **River N** ⌐

Eggsperience Café | **multi.** ⌐

Everest Burger | **Glencoe** ⌐

Fin Sushi | **Ravenswood** ⌐

Fish Bar | **Lakeview** ⌐

Florentine | **Loop** ⌐

Fogón | **Noble Sq** ⌐

Fork | **Lincoln Sq** ⌐

Frances' Deli | **Lincoln Pk** ⌐

Frontier | **Noble Sq** ⌐

Gaztro-Wagon | **Edgewater** ⌐

Gene & Jude's | **O'Hare Area** ⌐

George St. Pub | **Lakeview** ⌐

Girl/The Goat | **W Loop** ⌐

Gosu | **Logan Sq** ⌐

Grahamwich | **River N** ⌐

GT Fish/Oyster | **River N** ⌐

Gyu-Kaku | **Streeterville** ⌐

Haymarket Pub | **W Loop** ⌐

Henri | **S Loop** ⌐

Hoyt's | **Loop** ⌐

Hubbard Inn | **River N** ⌐

Ing | **W Loop** ⌐

IPO | **Loop** ⌐

Ja' Grill | **Lincoln Pk** ⌐

Joey's Shrimp | **Humboldt Pk** ⌐

Kai Sushi | **W Town** ⌐

Kanela | **Lakeview** ⌐

Katy's Dumpling | **multi.** ⌐

Kinderhook Tap | **Oak Pk** ⌐

Kingfisher | **Andersonville** ⌐

La Cantina Grill | **S Loop** ⌐

La Lagartija | **W Loop** ⌐

Lao You Ju | **Chinatown** ⌐

La Taberna | **University Vill** ⌐

Leopold | **Noble Sq** ⌐

Letizia's Fiore | **Logan Sq** ⌐

Lillie's Q | **Bucktown** ⌐

Lure Izakaya | **Chinatown** ⌐

Mac/Min's | **W Loop** ⌐

Mastro's Steak | **River N** ⌐

Maude's Liquor | **W Loop** ⌐

MC Bistro | **Wicker Pk** ⌐

Meatyballs | **Location Varies** ⌐

Mia Figlia | **NW Side** ⌐

MingHin | **Chinatown** ⌐

Nabuki | **Hinsdale** ⌐

Nana | **Far S Side** ⌐

Nano Sushi | **NW Side** ⌐

Next | **W Loop** ⌐

Nickson's Eatery | **La Grange** ⌐

Nozumi | **S Barrington** ⌐

Olive or Twist | **Berwyn** ⌐

One.Six One |
Little Italy/University Vill ⌐

Original Five | **University Vill** ⌐

Owen/Engine | **Logan Sq** ⌐

Paris Club | **River N** ⌐

Pensiero | **Evanston** ⌐

Perennial Virant | **Lincoln Pk** ⌐

Pizza Rustica | **Wrigleyville** ⌐

PL8 | **Barrington** ⌐

Pork Shoppe | **Avondale** ⌐

Portage | **NW Side** ⌐

Port Edward | **Algonquin** ⌐

Pret A Manger | **Loop** ⌐

Prince Crepe | **Albany Pk** ⌐

Prix Fixe | **Lincoln Sq** ⌐

Public House | **River N** ⌐

Raj Palace | **Schaumburg** ⌐

Real Urban BBQ | **Highland Pk** ⌐

Redd Herring | **Clarendon Hills** ⌐

Redflame | **Lincoln Pk** ⌐

Rewster's Café | **Logan Sq** ⌐

Rice Bistro | **Lakeview** ⌐

Rosded | **Lincoln Sq** ⌐

Rub BBQ | **W Rogers Pk** ⌐

Rudy's B&G | **Loop** ⌐

Ruxbin | **Noble Sq** ⌐

Saigon Grill | **Jefferson Pk** ⌐

Saigon Sisters | **W Loop** ⌐

Sakura | **Logan Sq** ⌐

Salatino's/Doughboys |
Little Italy/University Vill ⌐

Sawtooth | **W Loop** ⌐

Seadog Sushi | **Noble Sq** ⌐

Semiramis | **Albany Pk** ⌐

Silom 12 | **Bucktown** ⌐

Smak-Tak | **NW Side** ⌐

Smashburger | **Batavia** ⌐

Smokey Bears BBQ | **Albany Pk** ⌐

Snarf's | **River N** ⌐

Sono | **Lincoln Pk** ⌐

South Branch | **Loop** ⌐

Southern/Mac |
Location Varies ⌐

Stax Café |
Little Italy/University Vill ⌐

Sticky Rice | **North Ctr/St. Ben's** ⌐

Sun Wah BBQ | **Uptown** ⌐

Sushi Para/Sai | **multi.** ⌐

Taco Joint | **Lincoln Pk** ⌐

Three Aces |
Little Italy/University Vill ⌐

Todai | **Schaumburg** ⌐

Ukai | **Lakeview** ⌐

Uncle Bub's | **Westmont** ⌐

Uptowner | **Lincoln Pk** ⌐

Vincent | **Andersonville** ⌐

Wasabi | **Logan Sq** ⌐

Wolcott's | **Ravenswood** ⌐

Xni-Pec | **Brookfield** ⌐

Yindee | **Lakeview** ⌐

Yuca Café | **Wicker Pk** ⌐

Zodiac Room | **Streeterville** ⌐

BREAKFAST

(See also Hotel Dining)

Ann Sather | **multi.** 21

Bagel | **multi.** 19

Bite Cafe | **Ukrainian Vill** ⌐

Bongo Room | **multi.** 24

Breakfast Club | **Near W** 20

Café Selmarie | **Lincoln Sq** 23

Chicago Diner | **Lakeview** 22

Depot/Diner | **Far W** ⌐

Flo | **Noble Sq** 22

Ina's | **W Loop** 23

Jam | **Ukrainian Vill** 21

Julius Meinl | **Lakeview** 21

Kitsch'n/K-Cafe | **Roscoe Vill** 19

Lou Mitchell's | **multi.** 23

🚾 Lula Cafe | **Logan Sq** 26

Manny's | **multi.** 23

M Henry/Henrietta |
Andersonville 25

Milk/Honey | **Wicker Pk** 23

Nookies | **multi.** 20

Nosh | **Geneva** 24

Oak Tree Bakery and Restaurant |
Gold Coast 17

🚾 Original/Walker Pancake |
multi. 24

Over Easy	**Ravenswood**	27
Z Phoenix	**Chinatown**	23
Tempo	**Gold Coast**	20
Toast	**multi.**	22
Tre Kronor	**Albany Pk**	23
Uncommon Ground	**Lakeview**	22
Victory's Banner	**Roscoe Vill**	24
Wishbone	**multi.**	21
Yolk	**S Loop**	22

BRUNCH

Ann Sather	**Andersonville**	21
Bakin' & Eggs	**Lakeview**	19
Balsan	**Gold Coast**	-
Big Jones	**Andersonville**	21
Bistro 110	**Gold Coast**	21
Bite Cafe	**Ukrainian Vill**	-
Bongo Room	**multi.**	24
Bristol	**Bucktown**	23
Cafe 28	**North Ctr/St. Ben's**	26
Erwin	**Lakeview**	23
Feast	**multi.**	19
Flo	**Noble Sq**	22
Z Frontera Grill	**River N**	27
Z Gage	**Loop**	22
Hearty	**Lakeview**	-
Z Heaven/Seven	**multi.**	23
Hot Chocolate	**Bucktown**	24
Kitsch'n/K-Cafe	**Roscoe Vill**	19
Lobby	**River N**	28
Mercadito	**River N**	22
M Henry/Henrietta	**Andersonville**	25
Milk/Honey	**Wicker Pk**	23
Nightwood	**Pilsen**	23
Z Nomi Kitchen	**Gold Coast**	-
Z North Pond	**Lincoln Pk**	25
Orange	**multi.**	20
Over Easy	**Ravenswood**	27
NEW Perennial Virant	**Lincoln Pk**	-
Prairie Grass	**Northbrook**	22
Z Publican	**W Loop**	25
Puck's/MCA	**Streeterville**	20
Z RL	**Gold Coast**	23
Salpicón	**Old Town**	26
Z Seasons	**Gold Coast**	27
Z Sixteen	**River N**	22
State/Lake	**Loop**	21
Toast	**multi.**	22
Uncommon Ground	**multi.**	22
Wishbone	**multi.**	21
Yoshi's Café	**Lakeview**	25

BUFFET

(Check availability)

NEW Act One Pub	**Rogers Pk**	-
Andies	**Andersonville**	18
Aurelio's Pizza	**multi.**	23
Chicago Curry	**S Loop**	25
Chief O'Neill's	**NW Side**	18
Clubhouse	**Oak Brook**	21
NEW Cumin	**Wicker Pk**	-
Curry Hut	**Highwood**	20
Deca	**Streeterville**	-
Demera	**Uptown**	-
Drake Bros.'	**Gold Coast**	-
Edwardo's Pizza	**Oak Pk**	20
Fogo de Chão	**River N**	24
Gale St. Inn	**Jefferson Pk**	22
Gaylord Indian	**multi.**	22
Hemmingway's	**Oak Pk**	21
Z India House	**multi.**	25
Indian Garden	**multi.**	21
ItaliAsia	**River N**	-
Ja' Grill	**Lincoln Pk**	-
Karyn's	**Lincoln Pk**	20
Klay Oven	**multi.**	20
La Fonda/Grill	**Andersonville**	-
Las Tablas	**Lakeview**	20
Lobby	**River N**	28
Mandarin Kitchen	**Chinatown**	-
Mesón Sabika	**multi.**	23
Miramar Bistro	**Highwood**	17
Mt. Everest	**Evanston**	22
Nagoya	**Naperville**	-
Z Nomi Kitchen	**Gold Coast**	-
Pizza D.O.C.	**Lincoln Sq**	23
Port Edward	**Algonquin**	-
Puck's/MCA	**Streeterville**	20
NEW Raj Palace	**Schaumburg**	-
Reza's	**multi.**	18
Ringo	**Lincoln Pk**	-
R.J. Grunts	**Lincoln Pk**	19
Robinson's Ribs	**Oak Pk**	21
Ruby/Siam	**multi.**	23
Z Seasons	**Gold Coast**	27
Z Shaw's Crab	**multi.**	24
Z Signature Room	**Streeterville**	18
Z Sixteen	**River N**	22
Stanley's	**Lincoln Pk**	18
Tango	**Naperville**	22
Thai Classic	**Lakeview**	23
Tiffin	**W Rogers Pk**	21
Todai	**Schaumburg**	-
Udupi Palace	**Schaumburg**	23

Viceroy/India | **multi.**	21
Zed 451 | **River N**	21

BUSINESS DINING

Abigail's | **Highland Pk**	24
Ai Sushi | **River N**	24
aja | **River N**	-
☑ Alinea | **Lincoln Pk**	29
NEW Ara On | **Loop**	-
Aria | **Loop**	24
Atwood Cafe | **Loop**	22
☑ Avenues | **River N**	26
Balsan | **Gold Coast**	-
Benny's Chop | **River N**	-
☑ Blackbird | **W Loop**	27
NEW Bluette | **Wilmette**	-
Café/Architectes | **Gold Coast**	24
☑ Capital Grille | **Streeterville**	25
Carlucci | **Downers Grove**	19
Carlucci | **Rosemont**	20
Carmichael's | **W Loop**	22
☑ Catch 35 | **Loop**	24
Chama Gaucha | **Downers Grove**	-
☑ Charlie Trotter's | **Lincoln Pk**	27
☑ Chicago Chop | **River N**	25
NEW Chicago Cut | **River N**	-
C-House | **Streeterville**	21
Cibo Matto | **Loop**	24
CityGate | **Naperville**	-
☑ Coco Pazzo | **River N**	25
☑ Crofton on Wells | **River N**	26
NEW Currents/River | **Loop**	-
Custom House | **Printer's Row**	25
☑ David Burke Prime | **River N**	25
Deca | **Streeterville**	-
Devon Seafood | **River N**	21
Ditka's | **Gold Coast**	22
Elate | **River N**	21
Epic | **River N**	-
Erie Cafe | **River N**	22
☑ Everest | **Loop**	27
NEW Fish Bar | **Lakeview**	-
Fleming's | **Lincolnshire**	23
NEW Florentine | **Loop**	-
Fogo de Chão | **River N**	24
Fred's | **Gold Coast**	19
Fulton's | **River N**	19
☑ Gage | **Loop**	22
☑ Gene/Georgetti | **River N**	24
☑ Gibsons | **multi.**	26
Glen Prairie | **Glen Ellyn**	23
Grill on Alley | **Streeterville**	21
Grillroom | **Loop**	15
NEW Gyu-Kaku | **Streeterville**	-

Harry Caray's | **multi.**	20
NEW Henri | **S Loop**	-
NEW Hoyt's | **Loop**	-
Il Mulino | **Gold Coast**	25
Inovasi | **Lake Bluff**	-
NEW IPO | **Loop**	-
ItaliAsia | **River N**	-
Jacky's/Prairie | **Evanston**	21
☑ Japonais | **River N**	24
☑ Joe's Sea/Steak | **River N**	26
Karma | **Mundelein**	23
☑ Keefer's | **River N**	25
Kinzie Chop | **River N**	22
Lawry's | **River N**	24
Le Colonial | **Gold Coast**	24
☑ Les Nomades | **Streeterville**	29
☑ Le Titi/Paris | **Arlington Hts**	26
Lockwood | **Loop**	19
☑ L2O | **Lincoln Pk**	-
McCormick/Schmick | **Gold Coast**	21
☑ Michael | **Winnetka**	28
☑ MK | **Near North**	27
☑ Morton's | **multi.**	26
☑ Naha | **River N**	27
NEW Next | **W Loop**	-
Nick's Fishmarket | **Rosemont**	23
☑ Nine Steakhouse | **Loop**	24
☑ Nomi Kitchen | **Gold Coast**	-
Nozumi | **S Barrington**	-
☑ One Sixtyblue | **W Loop**	26
Palm | **Loop**	24
Park 52 | **Hyde Pk**	19
Park Grill | **Loop**	20
NEW Perennial Virant | **Lincoln Pk**	-
Phil Stefani's | **River N**	24
Piccolo Sogno | **Near W**	24
Port Edward | **Algonquin**	-
Prairie Fire | **W Loop**	-
Prasino | **La Grange**	-
Province | **W Loop**	23
Quince | **Evanston**	23
RB Grille | **River N**	-
Rhapsody | **Loop**	20
Ria | **Gold Coast**	-
☑ RL | **Gold Coast**	23
Roy's | **River N**	25
☑ Ruth's Chris | **multi.**	25
Sable | **River N**	-
Saloon Steak | **Streeterville**	23
Sam/Harry's Steak | **Schaumburg**	-
☑ Seasons | **Gold Coast**	27

Sepia | **W Loop**	24
🅱 Shaw's Crab | **multi.**	24
🅱 Sixteen | **River N**	22
Smith/Wollensky | **River N**	23
NEW South Branch | **Loop**	-
🅱 Spiaggia | **Gold Coast**	27
State/Lake | **Loop**	21
Sugartoad | **Naperville**	19
Sullivan's Steak | **multi.**	22
Tavern/Park | **Loop**	20
312 Chicago | **Loop**	21
🅱 Topolobampo | **River N**	28
Vivere | **Loop**	22
Vivo | **W Loop**	24
Weber Grill | **River N**	20
Zak's Place | **Hinsdale**	-

BYO

NEW Abiquiù | **Lakeview**	-
Amitabul | **NW Side**	21
Andalous | **Lakeview**	22
Ann Sather | **multi.**	21
Antica Pizza | **Andersonville**	23
Aroy | **Lincoln Sq**	-
Art of Pizza | **Lakeview**	22
Belly Shack | **Humboldt Pk**	23
NEW Bento Box | **Bucktown**	-
Birchwood | **Bucktown**	23
Bite Cafe | **Ukrainian Vill**	-
NEW Bluette | **Wilmette**	-
🅱 Bonsoirée | **Logan Sq**	26
Butterfly | **multi.**	22
Café 103 | **Far S Side**	-
NEW Caminito | **Lincoln Pk**	-
Chickpea | **W Town**	22
Chilam Balam | **Lakeview**	25
Coast Sushi/South Coast | **Bucktown**	24
Conoce/Panama | **Logan Sq**	-
Co-Si-Na | **Andersonville**	-
Crêpe Crave | **Wicker Pk**	-
Crêpe Town | **Lakeview**	-
NEW Danzón | **Logan Sq**	-
Dee's Place | **Wicker Pk**	-
NEW Donatella | **Evanston**	-
Dorado | **Lincoln Sq**	23
Double Li | **Chinatown**	-
Estrella Negra | **Logan Sq**	-
NEW Fin Sushi | **Ravenswood**	-
NEW Gaztro-Wagon | **Edgewater**	-
NEW Gosu | **Logan Sq**	-
Great Lake | **Andersonville**	23
Habana Libre | **Noble Sq**	22
Han 202 | **Bridgeport**	25

HB Home Bistro | **Lakeview**	25
Hema's Kitchen | **multi.**	22
Hot Woks | **NW Side**	23
Icosium Kafe | **multi.**	19
Irazu | **Bucktown**	22
Isla Filipino | **Lincoln Sq**	-
Jam | **Ukrainian Vill**	21
Joy Yee | **multi.**	20
NEW Kai Sushi | **W Town**	-
NEW Kanela | **Lakeview**	-
Kan Zaman | **River N**	-
Karyn's | **Lincoln Pk**	20
NEW Kingfisher | **Andersonville**	-
Kin | **Noble Sq**	-
Knew | **Logan Sq**	-
🅱 La Gondola | **Lakeview**	-
Lan's Bistro | **Old Town**	-
NEW Mac/Min's | **W Loop**	-
NEW MC Bistro | **Wicker Pk**	-
Melting Pot | **River N**	19
M Henry/Henrietta | **multi.**	25
Mixteco Grill | **Lakeview**	25
Mon Ami Gabi | **Lincoln Pk**	22
Mythos | **Lakeview**	23
NEW Nano Sushi | **NW Side**	-
90 Miles | **multi.**	22
Nookies | **multi.**	20
Orange | **multi.**	20
Over Easy | **Ravenswood**	27
Parrot Cage | **Far S Side**	-
Penny's Noodle | **multi.**	20
Pizza Capri | **Lincoln Pk**	20
Pizza Rustica | **Wrigleyville**	-
NEW Prince Crepe | **Albany Pk**	-
Real Tenochtitlán | **Logan Sq**	20
NEW Rewster's Café | **Logan Sq**	-
NEW Rice Bistro | **Lakeview**	-
Robinson's Ribs | **multi.**	21
Rolis | **Uptown**	-
Rollapalooza | **Lakeview**	-
Rosded | **Lincoln Sq**	-
Ruby/Siam | **multi.**	23
NEW Ruxbin | **Noble Sq**	-
Sabor Saveur | **Ukrainian Vill**	-
NEW Saigon Grill | **Jefferson Pk**	-
NEW Sakura | **Logan Sq**	-
Sanook | **North Ctr/St. Ben's**	-
Sapore/Napoli | **Lakeview**	20
🅱 Schwa | **Wicker Pk**	29
NEW Seadog Sushi | **Noble Sq**	-
Semiramis | **Albany Pk**	-
Sikia | **Far S Side**	-
NEW Silom 12 | **Bucktown**	-

Vote at ZAGAT.com

Simply It	**Lincoln Pk**	22
Spoon Thai	**Lincoln Sq**	23
Spring World	**Chinatown**	-
Sticky Rice	**North Ctr/St. Ben's**	-
Sushi Para/Sai	**multi.**	-
Sushi X	**River W**	21
Tango Sur	**Lakeview**	24
Tanoshii	**Andersonville**	-
Terragusto	**Roscoe Vill**	25
Thai Classic	**Lakeview**	23
Thai Pastry	**multi.**	23
Simply/Thalia	**Loop**	19
Tre Kronor	**Albany Pk**	23
Udupi Palace	**multi.**	23
NEW Ukai	**Lakeview**	-
Urbanbelly	**Logan Sq**	24
NEW Wasabi	**Logan Sq**	-
NEW Yindee	**Lakeview**	-
Yolk	**multi.**	22
NEW Yuca Café	**Wicker Pk**	-

CELEBRITY CHEFS

Domenico Acampora
Accanto | **Logan Sq** — -

Grant Achatz
Z Alinea | **Lincoln Pk** — 29
NEW Aviary, The | **W Loop** — -
NEW Next | **W Loop** — -

Geno Bahena
NEW Danzón | **Logan Sq** — -
Real Tenochtitlán | **Logan Sq** — 20

Jimmy Bannos Jr.
Purple Pig | **River N** — -

Rick Bayless
Z Frontera Grill | **River N** — 27
Z Topolobampo | **River N** — 28
Xoco | **River N** — 25

Graham Elliot Bowles
Graham Elliot | **River N** — 24
NEW Grahamwich | **River N** — -

Laurent Branlard
LB Bistro/Patisserie | **Streeterville** — -

George Bumbaris & Sarah Stegner
Prairie Fire | **W Loop** — -
Prairie Grass | **Northbrook** — 22

Homaro Cantu
NEW Ing | **W Loop** — -
Z Moto | **W Loop** — 27

Michael Carlson
Z Schwa | **Wicker Pk** — 29

Suzy Crofton
Z Crofton on Wells | **River N** — 26

Danny Grant
Balsan | **Gold Coast** — -
Ria | **Gold Coast** — -

Jose Garces
Z Mercat | **S Loop** — 26

Susan Goss
West Town | **Noble Sq** — 24

Koren Grieveson
Z Avec | **W Loop** — 26

John Hogan
Z Keefer's | **River N** — 25

Stephanie Izard
NEW Girl/The Goat | **W Loop** — -

Jean Joho
Z Everest | **Loop** — 27

Paul Kahan
Big Star | **Wicker Pk** — 23
Z Blackbird | **W Loop** — 27
Z Publican | **W Loop** — 25

Yoshi Katsumura
Yoshi's Café | **Lakeview** — 25

Michael Kornick
DMK Burger | **Lakeview** — 22
NEW Fish Bar | **Lakeview** — -
Z MK | **Near North** — 27

Joncarl Lachman
HB Home Bistro | **Lakeview** — 25
NEW Vincent | **Andersonville** — -

Michael Lachowitz
Z Michael | **Winnetka** — 28

Dale Levitski
Sprout | **Lincoln Pk** — 28

Michael Maddox
Z Le Titi/Paris | **Arlington Hts** — 26

Tony Mantuano
Z Spiaggia | **Gold Coast** — 27
Terzo Piano | **Loop** — 21

Shawn McClain
Z Green Zebra | **Noble Sq** — 26

Michael McDonald
Z One Sixtyblue | **W Loop** — 26

Carrie Nahabedian
Z Naha | **River N** — 27

Martial Noguier
NEW Bistronomic | **Gold Coast** — -

Tony Priolo
Piccolo Sogno | **Near W** — 24

Arun Sampanthavivat
Z Arun's | **NW Side** — 28

CHICAGO

SPECIAL FEATURES

Marcus Samuelsson	
C-House | **Streeterville**	21
Giuseppe Scurato	
Ceres' Table | **Uptown**	–
Mindy Segal	
Hot Chocolate | **Bucktown**	24
Bruce Sherman	
☑ North Pond | **Lincoln Pk**	25
Art Smith	
Table Fifty-two | **Gold Coast**	24
Dan Smith	
Hearty | **Lakeview**	–
Brendan Sodikoff	
Gilt Bar | **River N**	–
NEW Maude's Liquor | **W Loop**	–
Michael Taus	
Zealous | **River N**	25
Giuseppe Tentori	
Boka | **Lincoln Pk**	25
NEW GT Fish/Oyster | **River N**	–
Charlie Trotter	
☑ Charlie Trotter's | **Lincoln Pk**	27
Paul Virant	
NEW Perennial Virant | **Lincoln Pk**	–
☑ Vie | **W Springs**	27
Takashi Yagihashi	
☑ Takashi | **Bucktown**	26
Randy Zweiban	
Province | **W Loop**	23

CHILD-FRIENDLY

(Alternatives to the usual fast-food places; * children's menu available)

American Girl | **Streeterville**	16
Ann Sather* | **multi.**	21
Antico Posto* | **Oak Brook**	22
Artopolis | **Greektown**	22
Bandera* | **Streeterville**	22
Benihana* | **multi.**	18
Berghoff | **O'Hare Area**	18
Big Bowl* | **multi.**	20
☑ Bob Chinn's* | **Wheeling**	23
Breakfast Club | **Near W**	20
Café Selmarie* | **Lincoln Sq**	23
Carson's* | **River N**	22
☑ Cheesecake Factory* | **multi.**	19
Chicago Pizza | **Lincoln Pk**	23
Dave's Italian | **Evanston**	17
Davis St. Fish* | **Evanston**	19
Depot/Diner | **Far W**	–
Ed Debevic's* | **River N**	15

Edwardo's Pizza* | **multi.**	20
Flat Top | **multi.**	20
Foodlife | **Streeterville**	19
Hackney's* | **multi.**	18
Hard Rock* | **River N**	12
Harry Caray's* | **multi.**	20
☑ Heaven/Seven* | **multi.**	23
☑ Hot Doug's | **NW Side**	27
Ina's | **W Loop**	23
John's Pl.* | **Lincoln Pk**	18
Joy Yee | **multi.**	20
Kansaku | **Evanston**	22
Kitsch'n/K-Cafe* | **Roscoe Vill**	19
Lawry's* | **River N**	24
Leo's Coney Island* | **Wrigleyville**	–
☑ Lou Malnati's* | **multi.**	24
Lou Mitchell's* | **multi.**	23
LuLu's | **Evanston**	21
☑ Maggiano's* | **multi.**	20
Manny's* | **SW Side**	23
☑ Margie's Candies* | **Bucktown**	22
Mity Nice* | **Streeterville**	17
Oak Tree Bakery and Restaurant | **Gold Coast**	17
Opa! Estiatorio* | **Vernon Hills**	25
☑ Original Gino's East* | **multi.**	22
☑ Original/Walker Pancake* | **multi.**	24
Pegasus | **SW Side**	20
P.F. Chang's | **River N**	20
Pizza Capri | **Lincoln Pk**	20
Pizza D.O.C. | **Lincoln Sq**	23
Pizzeria Uno/Due* | **River N**	22
☑ Potbelly Sandwich | **multi.**	19
R.J. Grunts* | **Lincoln Pk**	19
Robinson's Ribs* | **multi.**	21
Russell's BBQ* | **Elmwood Pk**	19
Sapore/Napoli | **Lakeview**	20
Sapori Trattoria | **Lincoln Pk**	23
Scoozi!* | **River N**	19
☑ Smoque BBQ* | **NW Side**	26
Stanley's* | **Lincoln Pk**	18
Stir Crazy* | **multi.**	19
Tempo | **Gold Coast**	20
Toast* | **multi.**	22
Trattoria D.O.C. | **Evanston**	19
Tufano's Tap | **Little Italy/University Vill**	20
Twin Anchors* | **Old Town**	23
Uncle Julio's* | **Old Town**	18
Uncommon Ground* | **Lakeview**	22
White Fence* | **Romeoville**	22
Wishbone* | **multi.**	21

DANCING

Alhambra | **W Loop** 16
NEW Frontier | **Noble Sq** –
Gale St. Inn | **Mundelein** 22
Z Nacional 27 | **River N** 23
Pasha | **W Loop** –
Rosebud Trattoria | **River N** 22
Rumba | **River N** 23
Sayat Nova | **Streeterville** 23
Zhivago | **Skokie** 16

DELIVERY/TAKEOUT

(D=delivery, T=takeout)
Adobo | T | **Old Town** 21
Akai Hana | D, T | **Wilmette** 21
Aladdin's Eatery | D, T |
  Lincoln Pk 18
A La Turka | T | **Lakeview** 20
Andies | D, T | **Andersonville** 18
Athena | T | **Greektown** 21
Bella Notte | D, T | **Noble Sq** 21
Benihana | T | **multi.** 18
Berghoff | T | **multi.** 18
Bijan's | T | **River N** 19
Z Bob Chinn's | T | **Wheeling** 23
Cafe Ba-Ba-Reeba! | T |
  Lincoln Pk 22
Z Café Spiaggia | T | **Gold Coast** 25
Coco Pazzo | T | **Streeterville** 22
Z Crofton on Wells | T | **River N** 26
D & J Bistro | T | **Lake Zurich** 24
Davis St. Fish | T | **Evanston** 19
Don Juan's | T | **Edison Pk** 20
Z Emilio's Tapas | T | **multi.** 24
Erwin | T | **Lakeview** 23
Filippo's | T | **Lincoln Pk** 24
Foodlife | D, T | **Streeterville** 19
Francesca's | D, T | **multi.** 22
Gale St. Inn | D, T | **multi.** 22
Z Gene/Georgetti | T | **River N** 24
Z Gibsons | T | **multi.** 26
Gioco | T | **S Loop** 25
Z Heaven/Seven | D, T | **multi.** 23
Hema's Kitchen | D, T |
  Lincoln Pk 22
Z Japonais | T | **River N** 24
Z Joe's Sea/Steak | T | **River N** 26
Z Keefer's | T | **River N** 25
La Sardine | T | **W Loop** 24
La Scarola | T | **River W** 24
La Tasca | T | **Arlington Hts** 24
Z Le Colonial | D, T |
  Gold Coast 24
Z Lula Cafe | T | **Logan Sq** 26

L. Woods Tap | T | **Lincolnwood** 20
Z Maggiano's | T | **multi.** 20
Mesón Sabika | T | **Naperville** 23
Z Mia Francesca | T | **Lakeview** 26
Mirai Sushi | T | **Wicker Pk** 25
Mon Ami Gabi | T | **multi.** 22
Old Jerusalem | D, T | **Old Town** 19
Parthenon | T | **Greektown** 21
Pierrot Gourmet | T | **River N** 20
Z Potbelly Sandwich | D, T |
  multi. 19
R.J. Grunts | T | **Lincoln Pk** 19
Rosal's | T |
  Little Italy/University Vill 26
Z Rosebud | D, T | **multi.** 22
Saloon Steak | D, T |
  Streeterville 23
San Soo Gab San | D, T |
  Lincoln Sq 21
Scoozi! | T | **River N** 19
Z Shaw's Crab | D, T | **multi.** 24
Smith/Wollensky | T | **River N** 23
Sullivan's Steak | T | **River N** 22
Sushi Naniwa | T | **River N** 23
Z Sushi Wabi | D, T | **W Loop** 27
Swordfish | T | **Batavia** 27
Tapas Gitana | T | **Northfield** 24
Tarantino's | T | **Lincoln Pk** 22
Trattoria Roma | T | **Old Town** 21
Twin Anchors | T | **Old Town** 23
Village | D, T | **Loop** 21
Volare | D, T | **Streeterville** 24
Yoshi's Café | T | **Lakeview** 25

DINING ALONE

(Other than hotels and places with
counter service)
Amitabul | **NW Side** 21
Ann Sather | **multi.** 21
Bar Louie | **multi.** 16
Bin | **River N** 21
Bite Cafe | **Ukrainian Vill** –
Blind Faith | **Evanston** 21
Breakfast Club | **Near W** 20
Chicago Diner | **Lakeview** 22
Eleven City | **S Loop** 19
Flat Top | **multi.** 20
Foodlife | **Streeterville** 19
Gold Coast | **Loop** 19
Heartland Cafe | **Rogers Pk** 16
Z Hot Doug's | **NW Side** 27
Indie Cafe | **Edgewater** 24
Kinzie Chop | **River N** 22
Koi | **Evanston** 21
Kroll's | **S Loop** 19

Lucky Monk | **S Barrington**	-
Z Lula Cafe | **Logan Sq**	26
Maiz | **Humboldt Pk**	23
Manny's | **S Loop**	23
Meiji | **W Loop**	25
Moody's Pub | **Edgewater**	19
Mrs. Murphy | **North Ctr/St. Ben's**	22
Nookies | **multi.**	20
Oak Tree Bakery and Restaurant | **Gold Coast**	17
Penny's Noodle | **multi.**	20
Puck's/MCA | **Streeterville**	20
Reza's | **multi.**	18
Taco Fuego | **Lakeview**	-
Toast | **multi.**	22
Tweet | **Uptown**	22
Viand Bar | **Streeterville**	22
Z Wiener's Circle | **Lincoln Pk**	21

ENTERTAINMENT

(Call for days and times of performances)

A La Turka | belly dancing | **Lakeview**	20
Z Catch 35 | piano | **Loop**	24
Z Chicago Chop | piano | **River N**	25
Chief O'Neill's | Irish | **NW Side**	18
Costa's | piano | **Oakbrook Terr**	22
Cyrano's Bistrot | cabaret | **River N**	22
Edelweiss | German | **Norridge**	19
Geja's Cafe | flamenco/guitar | **Lincoln Pk**	21
Irish Oak | rock | **Wrigleyville**	19
Kit Kat | celebrity impersonators | **Lakeview**	16
Lobby | jazz | **River N**	28
Mesón Sabika | flamenco | **Naperville**	23
Myron/Phil Steak | karaoke/piano | **Lincolnwood**	21
Z Nacional 27 | varies | **River N**	23
Parkers' | jazz/piano | **Downers Grove**	23
Philly G's | piano | **Vernon Hills**	21
Rumba | jazz | **River N**	23
Sabatino's | piano | **NW Side**	24
Sayat Nova | DJ | **Streeterville**	23
Z Shaw's Crab | jazz | **multi.**	24
Z Signature Room | jazz | **Streeterville**	18
Z Smoke Daddy | varies | **Wicker Pk**	24
Sullivan's Steak | jazz | **multi.**	22

Tapas Gitana | guitar | **Northfield**	24
Uncommon Ground | varies | **Lakeview**	22

FIREPLACES

NEW Abiquiù | **Lakeview**	-
NEW A 'Cappella | **S Loop**	-
NEW Ace Bar | **Lincoln Pk**	-
NEW Acre | **Andersonville**	-
Adelle's | **Wheaton**	25
Ai Sushi | **River N**	24
Andies | **Andersonville**	18
Ann Sather | **Lakeview**	21
Athena | **Greektown**	21
Atwater's | **Geneva**	20
Bacino's | **Loop**	22
NEW Bedford | **Wicker Pk**	-
Bistrot Margot | **Old Town**	20
NEW Bivona | **Lincoln Pk**	-
NEW Blokes/Birds | **Lakeview**	-
Bluebird | **Bucktown**	20
Bourgeois Pig | **Lincoln Pk**	-
Brio | **Lombard**	22
Carlucci | **Downers Grove**	19
Carson's | **Deerfield**	22
Chens | **Wrigleyville**	22
Chicago Firehouse | **S Loop**	20
Chief O'Neill's | **NW Side**	18
Clubhouse | **Oak Brook**	21
Costa's | **Oakbrook Terr**	22
Courtright's | **Willow Spgs**	25
Dee's | **Lincoln Pk**	19
Deleece Grill | **Lakeview**	20
Devon Seafood | **River N**	21
Edelweiss | **Norridge**	19
EJ's Pl. | **Skokie**	22
Erie Cafe | **River N**	22
NEW Fork | **Lincoln Sq**	-
1492 | **River N**	21
Francesca's | **multi.**	22
Froggy's | **Highwood**	22
NEW Frontier | **Noble Sq**	-
Gale St. Inn | **Mundelein**	22
Z Gene/Georgetti | **River N**	24
Z Gibsons | **multi.**	26
Greek Islands | **multi.**	21
Hackney's | **Lake Zurich**	18
Half Shell | **Lakeview**	24
Hecky's | **Evanston**	20
NEW Hubbard Inn | **River N**	-
Il Mulino | **Gold Coast**	25
Inovasi | **Lake Bluff**	-
Z Japonais | **River N**	24
Jerry's | **Wicker Pk**	22

John's Pl. | **Lincoln Pk**	18
🔲 Keefer's | **River N**	25
Koi | **Evanston**	21
La Madia | **River N**	23
🔲 Les Nomades | **Streeterville**	29
Le Vichyssois | **Lakemoor**	26
🔲 Lovells | **Lake Forest**	23
Maijean | **Clarendon Hills**	28
McCormick/Schmick | **Gold Coast**	21
Melting Pot | **Schaumburg**	19
Milk/Honey | **Wicker Pk**	23
Moody's Pub | **Edgewater**	19
Mrs. Murphy | **North Ctr/St. Ben's**	22
🔲 North Pond | **Lincoln Pk**	25
Old Oak Tap | **Ukrainian Vill**	20
🔲 Original/Walker Pancake | **Lake Zurich**	24
Oysy | **S Loop**	20
Parkers' | **Downers Grove**	23
Park Grill | **Loop**	20
Pelago | **Streeterville**	26
Penny's Noodle | **multi.**	20
🆕 Pensiero | **Evanston**	-
🆕 Perennial Virant | **Lincoln Pk**	-
Prairie Grass | **Northbrook**	22
Quartino | **River N**	21
Quince | **Evanston**	23
Red Brick | **Lakeview**	-
Revolution Brewing | **Logan Sq**	-
Reza's | **River N**	18
Ribs 'n' Bibs | **Hyde Pk**	21
🔲 RL | **Gold Coast**	23
Robinson's Ribs | **Lincoln Pk**	21
Rockit B&G | **Wrigleyville**	19
Russell's BBQ | **Rolling Meadows**	19
🔲 Ruth's Chris | **Northbrook**	25
Sai Café | **Lincoln Pk**	25
Santorini | **Greektown**	21
Smak-Tak | **NW Side**	-
Sola | **Lakeview**	25
Sullivan's Steak | **Lincolnshire**	22
Sunda | **River N**	23
Swordfish | **Batavia**	27
🔲 Tallgrass | **Lockport**	28
Tavern/Park | **Loop**	20
33 Club | **Old Town**	20
Trattoria Gianni | **Lincoln Pk**	26
Udupi Palace | **W Rogers Pk**	23
Uncommon Ground | **multi.**	22
🔲 Vie | **W Springs**	27
Weber Grill | **multi.**	20
Webster Wine | **Lincoln Pk**	20

FOOD TRUCKS

🆕 Gaztro-Wagon | **Edgewater**	-
🆕 Meatyballs | **Location Varies**	-
Southern/Mac | **Location Varies**	-

HISTORIC PLACES

(Year opened; * building)

1800 | Chief O'Neill's* | **NW Side**	18
1800 | Il Mulino* | **Gold Coast**	25
1847 | Mesón Sabika* | **Naperville**	23
1865 | Crofton on Wells* | **River N**	26
1870 | Depot Nuevo* | **Wilmette**	18
1880 | Bourgeois Pig* | **Lincoln Pk**	-
1880 | Leopold* | **Noble Sq**	-
1880 | West Town* | **Noble Sq**	24
1881 | Twin Anchors* | **Old Town**	23
1887 | Merlo* | **Gold Coast**	24
1890 | Pasta Palazzo* | **Lincoln Pk**	22
1890 | Pizzeria Uno/Due* | **River N**	22
1890 | Sapori Trattoria* | **Lincoln Pk**	23
1890 | Webster Wine* | **Lincoln Pk**	20
1892 | Francesca's* | **Naperville**	22
1897 | Tallgrass* | **Lockport**	28
1900 | Antica Pizza* | **Andersonville**	23
1900 | Duchamp* | **Bucktown**	17
1900 | Vivo* | **W Loop**	24
1901 | Bank Lane* | **Lake Forest**	23
1901 | South Gate* | **Lake Forest**	20
1905 | Carnivale* | **Loop**	23
1905 | Chicago Firehouse* | **S Loop**	20
1910 | Bauer's Brauhaus* | **Palatine**	-
1911 | Haymarket Pub* | **W Loop**	-
1912 | Eleven City* | **S Loop**	19
1920 | Chef's Station* | **Evanston**	24
1920 | Drake Bros.' | **Gold Coast**	-
1921 | Margie's Candies | **Bucktown**	22
1922 | Del Rio* | **Highwood**	20
1923 | Lou Mitchell's | **Loop**	23
1927 | La Cantina Chop* | **Loop**	21
1927 | Village* | **Loop**	21
1927 | Vivere* | **Loop**	22

Year	Restaurant	Location	Rating
1928	IPO*	Loop	-
1930	Russell's BBQ	**Elmwood Pk**	19
1930	Tufano's Tap*	**Little Italy/University Vill**	20
1933	Bruna's	**SW Side**	26
1933	Cape Cod Room	**Streeterville**	22
1934	Billy Goat	**multi.**	17
1935	Duckfat*	**Forest Pk**	-
1938	Al's Beef	**multi.**	23
1938	Frances' Deli	**Lincoln Pk**	-
1939	Hackney's	**multi.**	18
1940	Due Lire*	**Lincoln Sq**	-
1940	L2O*	**Lincoln Pk**	-
1941	Gene/Georgetti	**River N**	24
1942	Manny's	**S Loop**	23
1947	Cantonesia*	**Chinatown**	-
1948	Superdawg	**NW Side**	21
1950	Gene & Jude's	**O'Hare Area**	-
1950	Miller's Pub	**Loop**	17
1954	White Fence	**Romeoville**	22
1955	Pizzeria Uno/Due	**River N**	22
1959	Aurelio's Pizza	**multi.**	23
1959	Moody's Pub	**Edgewater**	19
1960	Moon Palace	**Chinatown**	22
1960	Original/Walker Pancake	**Wilmette**	24

HOTEL DINING

Affinia Chicago Hotel
C-House | **Streeterville** 21

Allegro, Hotel
312 Chicago | **Loop** 21

Arista, Hotel
Sugartoad | **Naperville** 19

Belden-Stratford Hotel
◪ L2O | **Lincoln Pk** -
Mon Ami Gabi | **Lincoln Pk** 22

Blackstone Hotel
◪ Mercat | **S Loop** 26

Burnham, Hotel
Atwood Cafe | **Loop** 22

Crowne Plaza Glen Ellyn
Glen Prairie | **Glen Ellyn** 23

Dana Hotel & Spa
aja | **River N** -

Doubletree Libertyville
Karma | **Mundelein** 23

Doubletree Magnificent Mile
Markethouse | **Streeterville** 21

Doubletree O'Hare
◪ Gibsons | **Rosemont** 26

Drake Hotel
Cape Cod Room | **Streeterville** 22
Drake Bros.' | **Gold Coast** -

Elysian, The
Balsan | **Gold Coast** -
Ria | **Gold Coast** -

Embassy Suites Hotel
◪ Original Gino's East | **Deerfield** 22
P.J. Clarke's | **Streeterville** 17

Fairmont Chicago Hotel
Aria | **Loop** 24

Felix, Hotel
Elate | **River N** 21

Four Seasons Hotel
◪ Seasons | **Gold Coast** 27

Hard Rock Hotel
China Grill | **Loop** 22

Herrington Inn
Atwater's | **Geneva** 20

Hilton Garden Inn
Weber Grill | **River N** 20

Holiday Inn Chicago Downtown
Aurelio's Pizza | **Loop** 23

Holiday Inn Chicago Mart Plaza
ItaliAsia | **River N** -

Holiday Inn Chicago O'Hare Airport
Bar Louie | **O'Hare Area** 16

Holiday Inn Mount Prospect
Bar Louie | **Mt. Prospect** 16

Holiday Inn North Shore
Bar Louie | **Skokie** 16

Homestead Hotel
Quince | **Evanston** 23

Hotel 71
NEW Hoyt's | **Loop** -

James Chicago Hotel
◪ David Burke Prime | **River N** 25

JW Marriott Chicago
NEW Florentine | **Loop** -

Margarita Inn
NEW Pensiero | **Evanston** -

Monaco, Hotel
South Water | **Loop** 16

Palmer House Hilton
Lockwood | **Loop** 19

Palomar, Hotel
Sable | **River N** -

Vote at ZAGAT.com

Park Hyatt Chicago
☑ Nomi Kitchen | **Gold Coast** ‑⅃

Park View Hotel
NEW Perennial Virant | ‑⅃
Lincoln Pk

Peninsula Hotel
☑ Avenues | **River N** 26
Lobby | **River N** 28
Pierrot Gourmet | **River N** 20
☑ Shanghai Terrace | **River N** 25

Raffaello Hotel
Pelago | **Streeterville** 26

Red Roof Inn
Coco Pazzo | **Streeterville** 22

Renaissance North Shore Hotel
☑ Ruth's Chris | **Northbrook** 25

Renaissance Schaumburg Hotel
Sam/Harry's Steak | ‑⅃
Schaumburg

Ritz-Carlton Hotel
Deca | **Streeterville** ‑⅃

Seneca Hotel
Francesca's | **Streeterville** 22
Saloon Steak | **Streeterville** 23

Sheraton Chicago Hotel
LB Bistro/Patisserie | ‑⅃
Streeterville
Shula's Steak | **Streeterville** 21

Sheraton Four Points Hotel
Sushi Taiyo | **River N** ‑⅃

Sofitel Chicago Water Tower
Café/Architectes | 24
Gold Coast

Swissôtel
Palm | **Loop** 24

theWit Hotel
Cibo Matto | **Loop** 24
State/Lake | **Loop** 21

Tremont Hotel
Ditka's | **Gold Coast** 22

Trump Int'l Hotel
☑ Sixteen | **River N** 22

W Chicago Lakeshore
Wave | **Streeterville** 13

W City Center Hotel
NEW IPO | **Loop** ‑⅃

Westin Chicago North Shore
Tramonto's | **Wheeling** 24

Westin Chicago NW
Shula's Steak | **Itasca** 21

Westin Lombard
Harry Caray's | **Lombard** 20
Holy Mackerel! | **Lombard** 21

Westin Michigan Ave.
Grill on Alley | **Streeterville** 21

Westin River North
Kamehachi | **River N** 21

Whitehall Hotel
Fornetto Mei | **Gold Coast** 20

Write Inn
Hemmingway's | **Oak Pk** 21

Wyndham Blake
Custom House | **Printer's Row** 25

JACKET REQUIRED

☑ Carlos' | **Highland Pk** 27
☑ Charlie Trotter's | **Lincoln Pk** 27
☑ Les Nomades | **Streeterville** 29
☑ Spiaggia | **Gold Coast** 27
☑ Tru | **Streeterville** 28

LATE DINING

(Weekday closing hour)

NEW Ace Bar | 12 AM | ‑⅃
Lincoln Pk
NEW Acre | varies | ‑⅃
Andersonville
☑ Al's Beef | varies | **multi.** 23
Artopolis | 12 AM | **Greektown** 22
Athena | 12 AM | **Greektown** 21
☑ Avec | 12 AM | **W Loop** 26
NEW Bangers/Lace | 2 AM | ‑⅃
Wicker Pk
Bar Louie | varies | **multi.** 16
NEW Bauer's Brauhaus | ‑⅃
varies | **Palatine**
NEW Bedford | varies | ‑⅃
Wicker Pk
Big Star | 2 AM | **Wicker Pk** 23
Bijan's | 3:30 AM | **River N** 19
Billy Goat | varies | **River N** 17
NEW Blokes/Birds | 2 AM | ‑⅃
Lakeview
Bluebird | varies | **Bucktown** 20
Blue 13 | 12 AM | **River N** 24
NEW Boiler Room | 2 AM | ‑⅃
Logan Sq
Café Iberico | 11:30 PM | 22
River N
Carmine's | 12 AM | **Gold Coast** 22
Ciao Napoli | varies | **Logan Sq** ‑⅃
Coast Sushi/South Coast | 24
12 AM | **Bucktown**
NEW DiSotto | varies | ‑⅃
Streeterville
NEW D'Noche/Café Con ‑⅃
Leche | varies | **Logan Sq**
Dos Diablos | varies | **River N** ‑⅃
Drawing Room | 4 AM | 23
Gold Coast

NEW Eatt	varies	**River N**	–
Emperor's Choice	12 AM	**Chinatown**	23
Fifty/50	1 AM	**Wicker Pk**	21
NEW Fish Bar	12 AM	**Lakeview**	–
NEW Frontier	varies	**Noble Sq**	–
Gene & Jude's	varies	**O'Hare Area**	–
NEW George St. Pub	1 AM	**Lakeview**	–
Z Gibsons	varies	**multi.**	26
Gilt Bar	12 AM	**River N**	–
Z Giordano's	varies	**multi.**	23
Gold Coast	varies	**multi.**	19
Greek Islands	varies	**Greektown**	21
Half Shell	12 AM	**Lakeview**	24
Hard Rock	12 AM	**River N**	12
NEW Haymarket Pub	varies	**W Loop**	–
Hop Häus	varies	**multi.**	19
NEW Hubbard Inn	3 AM	**River N**	–
Hub 51	12 AM	**River N**	21
Z Hugo's	varies	**multi.**	24
Itto Sushi	12 AM	**Lincoln Pk**	24
Kamehachi	varies	**Old Town**	21
NEW Kinderhook Tap	varies	**Oak Pk**	–
Z Kuma's	1 AM	**Avondale**	26
Lan's Bistro	12 AM	**Old Town**	–
Z Lao	varies	**Chinatown**	24
NEW Lao You Ju	2 AM	**Chinatown**	–
Little Bucharest	2 AM	**NW Side**	–
Longman/Eagle	1 AM	**Logan Sq**	–
Lou Mitchell's	varies	**O'Hare Area**	23
NEW Lure Izakaya	2 AM	**Chinatown**	–
Luxbar	1:30 AM	**Gold Coast**	20
Z Margie's Candies	varies	**Bucktown**	22
NEW Mastro's Steak	varies	**River N**	–
NEW Maude's Liquor	2 AM	**W Loop**	–
Melting Pot	varies	**multi.**	19
Mercadito	varies	**River N**	22
Mezé	2 AM	**W Loop**	–
Miller's Pub	2 AM	**Loop**	17
NEW MingHin	2 AM	**Chinatown**	–
Moody's Pub	1 AM	**Edgewater**	19
Old Oak Tap	12 AM	**Ukrainian Vill**	20
NEW Paris Club	varies	**River N**	–
Parthenon	12 AM	**Greektown**	21
Pegasus	varies	**multi.**	20
Pete Miller	varies	**Evanston**	22
Pingpong	12 AM	**Lakeview**	20
Pizzeria Uno/Due	varies	**River N**	22
NEW Public House	1 AM	**River N**	–
Quartino	1 AM	**River N**	21
Revolution Brewing	12 AM	**Logan Sq**	–
Reza's	varies	**Andersonville**	18
Ribs 'n' Bibs	12 AM	**Hyde Pk**	21
Rockit B&G	1:30 AM	**multi.**	19
Roditys	12 AM	**Greektown**	21
Rootstock	1 AM	**Humboldt Pk**	24
NEW Rudy's B&G	varies	**Loop**	–
Sable	varies	**River N**	–
NEW Sakura	12 AM	**Logan Sq**	–
San Soo Gab San	24 hrs.	**Lincoln Sq**	21
Santorini	12 AM	**Greektown**	21
NEW Seadog Sushi	12 AM	**Noble Sq**	–
Silver Seafood	1 AM	**Uptown**	23
Southern/Mac	varies	**Bucktown**	–
Z Superdawg	varies	**NW Side**	21
Sushisamba Rio	1 AM	**River N**	21
Taco Fuego	3 AM	**Lakeview**	–
Tasting Room	12 AM	**W Loop**	20
Tavern/Rush	12 AM	**Gold Coast**	21
Tempo	24 hrs.	**Gold Coast**	20
NEW Three Aces	varies	**Little Italy/University Vill**	–
Three Happiness	6 AM	**Chinatown**	21
Twisted Spoke	1 AM	**Noble Sq**	18
Village	11:30 PM	**Loop**	21
Vintage 338	varies	**Lincoln Pk**	–
Webster Wine	12:30 AM	**Lincoln Pk**	20
Z Wiener's Circle	4 AM	**Lincoln Pk**	21
NEW Wolcott's	1 AM	**Ravenswood**	–

MEET FOR A DRINK

(Most top hotels and the following standouts)

NEW Act One Pub | **Rogers Pk**	-
aja | **River N**	-
Alhambra | **W Loop**	16
NEW Ara On | **Loop**	-
Bandera | **Streeterville**	22
NEW Bauer's Brauhaus | **Palatine**	-
Benny's Chop | **River N**	-
Bijan's | **River N**	19
Bin | **multi.**	21
Bistro 110 | **Gold Coast**	21
NEW Blokes/Birds | **Lakeview**	-
NEW Boiler Room | **Logan Sq**	-
Boka | **Lincoln Pk**	25
Broadway Cellars | **Edgewater**	21
NEW Burger Bar | **Lincoln Pk**	-
Cab's Wine Bar | **Glen Ellyn**	24
Café/Architectes | **Gold Coast**	24
Z Carnivale | **Loop**	23
Z Catch 35 | **Loop**	24
Chama Gaucha | **Downers Grove**	-
NEW Chef Amaury's | **Aurora**	-
Chicago Burgerwurks | **Brookfield**	-
NEW Chicago Cut | **River N**	-
Chief O'Neill's | **NW Side**	18
China Grill | **Loop**	22
NEW Chizakaya | **Lakeview**	-
Coobah | **Lakeview**	17
NEW Currents/River | **Loop**	-
NEW Davanti | **Little Italy/University Vill**	-
Deca | **Streeterville**	-
Di Pescara | **Northbrook**	19
NEW DiSotto | **Streeterville**	-
Distinctive Cork | **Naperville**	21
Ditka's | **Gold Coast**	22
Drawing Room | **Gold Coast**	23
NEW Eatt | **River N**	-
Epic | **River N**	-
Fleming's | **Lincolnshire**	23
Flight | **Glenview**	17
Fountainhead | **Ravenswood**	-
Fred's | **Gold Coast**	19
Z Frontera Grill | **River N**	27
Fuego | **Logan Sq**	24
Fulton's | **River N**	19
Z Gage | **Loop**	22
NEW George St. Pub | **Lakeview**	-
Z Gibsons | **multi.**	26
NEW Girl/The Goat | **W Loop**	-
Glen Prairie | **Glen Ellyn**	23
Goose Island | **multi.**	17
Gordon Biersch | **Bolingbrook**	16
Graham Elliot | **River N**	24
NEW Gyu-Kaku | **Streeterville**	-
Harry Caray's | **multi.**	20
NEW Haymarket Pub | **W Loop**	-
NEW Henri | **S Loop**	-
NEW Hoyt's | **Loop**	-
Hub 51 | **River N**	21
ItaliAsia | **River N**	-
Z Japonais | **River N**	24
Z Joe's Sea/Steak | **River N**	26
Z Keefer's | **River N**	25
Landmark | **Lincoln Pk**	20
NEW Lao You Ju | **Chinatown**	-
NEW Leopold | **Noble Sq**	-
Longman/Eagle | **Logan Sq**	-
Lucky Monk | **S Barrington**	-
NEW Lure Izakaya | **Chinatown**	-
Luxbar | **Gold Coast**	20
Market | **W Loop**	18
Markethouse | **Streeterville**	21
NEW Mastro's Steak | **River N**	-
NEW Maude's Liquor | **W Loop**	-
McCormick/Schmick | **multi.**	21
Mercadito | **River N**	22
Miramar Bistro | **Highwood**	17
Z MK | **Near North**	27
Moody's Pub | **Edgewater**	19
Z Nacional 27 | **River N**	23
NEW Next | **W Loop**	-
Nickson's Eatery | **La Grange**	-
Z Nine Steakhouse | **Loop**	24
Z Nomi Kitchen | **Gold Coast**	-
Nozumi | **S Barrington**	-
Old Oak Tap | **Ukrainian Vill**	20
Old Town Social | **Old Town**	18
Olive or Twist | **Berwyn**	-
Z One Sixtyblue | **W Loop**	26
Osteria/Pizzeria Via Stato | **River N**	23
NEW Owen/Engine | **Logan Sq**	-
NEW Paris Club | **River N**	-
Park 52 | **Hyde Pk**	19
NEW Perennial Virant | **Lincoln Pk**	-
Port Edward | **Algonquin**	-
Prairie Fire | **W Loop**	-
Prairie Grass | **Northbrook**	22
Prosecco | **River N**	24
Province | **W Loop**	23
Z Publican | **W Loop**	25
NEW Public House | **River N**	-

CHICAGO

SPECIAL FEATURES

Purple Pig | **River N**	–
Quartino | **River N**	21
Revolution Brewing | **Logan Sq**	–
Rhapsody | **Loop**	20
☑ RL | **Gold Coast**	23
Rockit B&G | **River N**	19
Rosebud Prime/Steak | **Streeterville**	25
Rosebud Trattoria | **River N**	22
NEW Rudy's B&G | **Loop**	–
Rumba | **River N**	23
Sable | **River N**	–
NEW Sawtooth | **W Loop**	–
Scoozi! | **River N**	19
Sepia | **W Loop**	24
☑ Shaw's Crab | **multi.**	24
☑ Signature Room | **Streeterville**	18
☑ Sixteen | **River N**	22
Smith/Wollensky | **River N**	23
NEW South Branch | **Loop**	–
Southern/Mac | **Bucktown**	–
South Water | **Loop**	16
Stained Glass | **Evanston**	23
State/Lake | **Loop**	21
Sugartoad | **Naperville**	19
Sullivan's Steak | **River N**	22
Sunda | **River N**	23
Sura | **Lakeview**	20
Sushisamba Rio | **River N**	21
Tasting Room | **W Loop**	20
Tavern/Park | **Loop**	20
Tavern/Rush | **Gold Coast**	21
33 Club | **Old Town**	20
NEW Three Aces | **Little Italy/University Vill**	–
312 Chicago | **Loop**	21
Tocco | **Bucktown**	12
Topaz Café | **Burr Ridge**	23
Trader Vic's | **Gold Coast**	17
Tramonto's | **Wheeling**	24
Trattoria No. 10 | **Loop**	24
Twisted Spoke | **Noble Sq**	18
Vintage 338 | **Lincoln Pk**	–
Volo | **Roscoe Vill**	–
Wave | **Streeterville**	13
Webster Wine | **Lincoln Pk**	20
NEW Wolcott's | **Ravenswood**	–
Zak's Place | **Hinsdale**	–
Zapatista | **S Loop**	20
Zocalo | **River N**	20

MICROBREWERIES

Goose Island | **multi.**	17
Gordon Biersch | **Bolingbrook**	16
NEW Haymarket Pub | **W Loop**	–
Lucky Monk | **S Barrington**	–
Piece | **Wicker Pk**	23
RB Grille | **River N**	–
Revolution Brewing | **Logan Sq**	–

OUTDOOR DINING

(G=garden; P=patio; S=sidewalk; T=terrace; W=waterside)

Athena | G | **Greektown**	21
Atwater's | P | **Geneva**	20
Big Jones | P | **Andersonville**	21
Big Star | P | **Wicker Pk**	23
☑ Bistro Campagne | G | **Lincoln Sq**	25
Bistro 110 | S | **Gold Coast**	21
☑ Blackbird | S | **W Loop**	27
Boka | P | **Lincoln Pk**	25
Cafe Ba-Ba-Reeba! | P | **Lincoln Pk**	22
Café Touché | S | **Edison Pk**	25
Carmine's | P | **Gold Coast**	22
Chez Joël | P | **Little Italy/University Vill**	24
Chicago Firehouse | P | **S Loop**	20
Coco Pazzo | P | **Streeterville**	22
NEW Currents/River | W | **Loop**	–
☑ David Burke Prime | S | **River N**	25
Dinotto | P | **Old Town**	19
Duchamp | P | **Bucktown**	17
Elate | **River N**	21
Erie Cafe | T, W | **River N**	22
Feast | G, S | **multi.**	19
Fred's | T | **Gold Coast**	19
Fulton's | P, W | **River N**	19
☑ Gage | P | **Loop**	22
NEW Girl/The Goat | **W Loop**	–
Hackney's | G, P, S, T | **multi.**	18
NEW Henri | P | **S Loop**	–
NEW Hoyt's | P | **Loop**	–
☑ Japonais | P | **River N**	24
☑ Keefer's | S | **River N**	25
☑ Le Colonial | S, T | **Gold Coast**	24
Longman/Eagle | **Logan Sq**	–
☑ Lula Cafe | S | **Logan Sq**	26
Mercadito | P | **River N**	22
☑ Mercat | S | **S Loop**	26
Mesón Sabika | G, P | **multi.**	23
☑ Mia Francesca | P | **Lakeview**	26
Miramar Bistro | S | **Highwood**	17
Moody's Pub | G | **Edgewater**	19
☑ Naha | S | **River N**	27
Nightwood | P | **Pilsen**	23

Z Nomi Kitchen | G | **Gold Coast** _−_

Z Oceanique | S | **Evanston** 27

Opa! Estiatorio | P | **Vernon Hills** 25

NEW Paris Club | P | **River N** _−_

Park Grill | P | **Loop** 20

Parrot Cage | P | **Far S Side** _−_

Pegasus | T | **Greektown** 20

Pelago | P | **Streeterville** 26

NEW Pensiero | T | **Evanston** _−_

NEW Perennial Virant | P | **Lincoln Pk** _−_

Piccolo Sogno | G | **Near W** 24

Pizzeria Uno/Due | P | **River N** 22

Port Edward | P, W | **Algonquin** _−_

Puck's/MCA | P, W | **Streeterville** 20

Purple Pig | P | **River N** _−_

Rhapsody | P | **Loop** 20

Riva | P, W | **Streeterville** 20

Z RL | P | **Gold Coast** 23

Z Rosebud | P | **Streeterville** 22

Salpicón | S | **Old Town** 26

Z Shanghai Terrace | T | **River N** 25

Z Sixteen | **River N** 22

Smith/Wollensky | G, P, T, W | **River N** 23

NEW South Branch | P | **Loop** _−_

Sushisamba Rio | S | **River N** 21

Tavern/Park | P | **Loop** 20

Tavern/Rush | P, S | **Gold Coast** 21

Terzo Piano | P | **Loop** 21

Topo Gigio | G, S | **Old Town** 23

Twisted Spoke | P | **Noble Sq** 18

Uncommon Ground | S | **Edgewater** 22

PEOPLE-WATCHING

Adobo | **Old Town** 21

aja | **River N** _−_

Alhambra | **W Loop** 16

American Girl | **Streeterville** 16

NEW Ara On | **Loop** _−_

Z Avec | **W Loop** 26

NEW Bangers/Lace | **Wicker Pk** _−_

Benny's Chop | **River N** _−_

Bin | **River N** 21

Bistro 110 | **Gold Coast** 21

Z Blackbird | **W Loop** 27

NEW Blokes/Birds | **Lakeview** _−_

Boka | **Lincoln Pk** 25

Bongo Room | **Wicker Pk** 24

Carmine's | **Gold Coast** 22

Z Carnivale | **Loop** 23

Z Chicago Chop | **River N** 25

NEW Chicago Cut | **River N** _−_

NEW Chizakaya | **Lakeview** _−_

C-House | **Streeterville** 21

Coobah | **Lakeview** 17

NEW Davanti | **Little Italy/University Vill** _−_

Deca | **Streeterville** _−_

DMK Burger | **Lakeview** 22

Drawing Room | **Gold Coast** 23

NEW Eatt | **River N** _−_

Epic | **River N** _−_

Fifty/50 | **Wicker Pk** 21

NEW Fish Bar | **Lakeview** _−_

Fred's | **Gold Coast** 19

Z Gibsons | **Gold Coast** 26

NEW Girl/The Goat | **W Loop** _−_

Graham Elliot | **River N** 24

Z Green Zebra | **Noble Sq** 26

NEW Gyu-Kaku | **Streeterville** _−_

Hamburger Mary's | **Andersonville** 17

Happ Inn | **Northfield** 17

Harry Caray's | **River N** 20

Hearty | **Lakeview** _−_

NEW Henri | **S Loop** _−_

Hub 51 | **River N** 21

Il Mulino | **Gold Coast** 25

NEW Ing | **W Loop** _−_

Z Japonais | **River N** 24

Z Keefer's | **River N** 25

Landmark | **Lincoln Pk** 20

NEW Lao You Ju | **Chinatown** _−_

Z Le Colonial | **Gold Coast** 24

NEW Leopold | **Noble Sq** _−_

NEW Lure Izakaya | **Chinatown** _−_

Luxbar | **Gold Coast** 20

Manny's | **S Loop** 23

Market | **W Loop** 18

NEW Mastro's Steak | **River N** _−_

NEW Maude's Liquor | **W Loop** _−_

Mercadito | **River N** 22

Z Mercat | **S Loop** 26

Mezé | **W Loop** _−_

Mirai Sushi | **Wicker Pk** 25

Miramar Bistro | **Highwood** 17

Z MK | **Near North** 27

Z Naha | **River N** 27

NEW Next | **W Loop** _−_

Z Nine Steakhouse | **Loop** 24

Niu | **Streeterville** 19

Z Nomi Kitchen | **Gold Coast** _−_

Nozumi | **S Barrington** _−_

Old Town Social | **Old Town** 18
Osteria/Pizzeria Via Stato | **River N** 23
NEW Owen/Engine | **Logan Sq** –
NEW Paris Club | **River N** –
Park 52 | **Hyde Pk** 19
NEW Perennial Virant | **Lincoln Pk** –
NEW Pret A Manger | **Loop** –
Prosecco | **River N** 24
Province | **W Loop** 23
Z Publican | **W Loop** 25
NEW Public House | **River N** –
Purple Pig | **River N** –
Quartino | **River N** 21
Z Rosebud | **multi.** 22
Rosebud Prime/Steak | **Streeterville** 25
Sable | **River N** –
NEW Sawtooth | **W Loop** –
Scoozi! | **River N** 19
Z Sixteen | **River N** 22
Southern/Mac | **Bucktown** –
State/Lake | **Loop** 21
Sugartoad | **Naperville** 19
Sunda | **River N** 23
Sura | **Lakeview** 20
Sushisamba Rio | **River N** 21
Tavern/Rush | **Gold Coast** 21
Terzo Piano | **Loop** 21
33 Club | **Old Town** 20
NEW Three Aces | **Little Italy/University Vill** –
Tocco | **Bucktown** 12
Topaz Café | **Burr Ridge** 23
Trader Vic's | **Gold Coast** 17
Tramonto's | **Wheeling** 24
Wave | **Streeterville** 13
Zaleski/Horvath | **Kenwood** –
Zapatista | **S Loop** 20
Zhivago | **Skokie** 16

POWER SCENES

Z Alinea | **Lincoln Pk** 29
Z Avenues | **River N** 26
Benny's Chop | **River N** –
Z Blackbird | **W Loop** 27
Z Capital Grille | **Streeterville** 25
Z Charlie Trotter's | **Lincoln Pk** 27
Z Chicago Chop | **River N** 25
NEW Chicago Cut | **River N** –
Z Coco Pazzo | **River N** 25
Custom House | **Printer's Row** 25
Z David Burke Prime | **River N** 25
Epic | **River N** –

Z Everest | **Loop** 27
Fred's | **Gold Coast** 19
Fulton's | **River N** 19
Z Gene/Georgetti | **River N** 24
Z Gibsons | **multi.** 26
NEW Girl/The Goat | **W Loop** –
NEW GT Fish/Oyster | **River N** –
Z Hugo's | **Gold Coast** 24
Il Mulino | **Gold Coast** 25
Z Joe's Sea/Steak | **River N** 26
Z Keefer's | **River N** 25
Z Les Nomades | **Streeterville** 29
Z L2O | **Lincoln Pk** –
NEW Mastro's Steak | **River N** –
Z MK | **Near North** 27
Z Morton's | **multi.** 26
Z Naha | **River N** 27
NEW Next | **W Loop** –
Z Nomi Kitchen | **Gold Coast** –
Ria | **Gold Coast** –
Z RL | **Gold Coast** 23
Z Rosebud | **Little Italy/University Vill** 22
Rosebud Prime/Steak | **multi.** 25
Z Ruth's Chris | **multi.** 25
Z Seasons | **Gold Coast** 27
Z Sixteen | **River N** 22
Smith/Wollensky | **River N** 23
Z Spiaggia | **Gold Coast** 27
State/Lake | **Loop** 21
Z Tru | **Streeterville** 28

PRIVATE ROOMS

(Restaurants charge less at off times; call for capacity)

Z Alinea | **Lincoln Pk** 29
Athena | **Greektown** 21
Ben Pao | **River N** 21
Z Carnivale | **Loop** 23
Z Catch 35 | **multi.** 24
Z Charlie Trotter's | **Lincoln Pk** 27
Z Chicago Chop | **River N** 25
Club Lucky | **Bucktown** 19
Costa's | **Oakbrook Terr** 22
Edwardo's Pizza | **multi.** 20
Z Everest | **Loop** 27
Francesca's | **multi.** 22
Z Frontera Grill | **River N** 27
Z Gabriel's | **Highwood** 25
Z Gene/Georgetti | **River N** 24
Z Gibsons | **multi.** 26
Gioco | **S Loop** 25
Goose Island | **multi.** 17
Greek Islands | **multi.** 21

🅉 Joe's Sea/Steak | **River N**	26
Kamehachi | **multi.**	21
🅉 Keefer's | **River N**	25
Lockwood | **Loop**	19
L. Woods Tap | **Lincolnwood**	20
🅉 Mercat | **S Loop**	26
Mesón Sabika | **Naperville**	23
🅉 MK | **Near North**	27
🅉 Naha | **River N**	27
🅉 Nine Steakhouse | **Loop**	24
🅉 Nomi Kitchen | **Gold Coast**	–
🅉 One Sixtyblue | **W Loop**	26
Park Grill | **Loop**	20
NEW Pensiero | **Evanston**	–
Pete Miller | **multi.**	22
🅉 Rosebud | **multi.**	22
Russian Tea | **Loop**	22
🅉 Ruth's Chris | **multi.**	25
Scoozi! | **River N**	19
Sepia | **W Loop**	24
🅉 Shanghai Terrace | **River N**	25
🅉 Shaw's Crab | **multi.**	24
🅉 Spiaggia | **Gold Coast**	27
Sushisamba Rio | **River N**	21
🅉 Tallgrass | **Lockport**	28
312 Chicago | **Loop**	21
🅉 Topolobampo | **River N**	28
Trattoria Roma | **Old Town**	21
Vivo | **W Loop**	24
🅉 Wildfire | **multi.**	23

PRIX FIXE MENUS

(Call for prices and times)

🅉 Arun's | **NW Side**	28
🅉 Avenues | **River N**	26
Bank Lane | **Lake Forest**	23
Bistro 110 | **Gold Coast**	21
🅉 Carlos' | **Highland Pk**	27
🅉 Charlie Trotter's | **Lincoln Pk**	27
Courtright's | **Willow Spgs**	25
Cyrano's Bistrot | **River N**	22
D & J Bistro | **Lake Zurich**	24
🅉 Everest | **Loop**	27
Froggy's | **Highwood**	22
🅉 Gabriel's | **Highwood**	25
La Sardine | **W Loop**	24
🅉 Les Nomades | **Streeterville**	29
🅉 MK | **Near North**	27
🅉 Moto | **W Loop**	27
🅉 North Pond | **Lincoln Pk**	25
🅉 Oceanique | **Evanston**	27
Roy's | **River N**	25
Salpicón | **Old Town**	26

🅉 Seasons | **Gold Coast**	27
🅉 Spiaggia | **Gold Coast**	27
🅉 Tallgrass | **Lockport**	28
🅉 Tru | **Streeterville**	28

QUICK BITES

Aladdin's Eatery | **Lincoln Pk**	18
Art of Pizza | **Lakeview**	22
Artopolis | **Greektown**	22
Azucar | **Logan Sq**	22
Bagel | **multi.**	19
Bakin' & Eggs | **Lakeview**	19
Ba Le Sandwich | **Uptown**	–
Bar Louie | **multi.**	16
Belly Shack | **Humboldt Pk**	23
NEW Bento Box | **Bucktown**	–
Berghoff | **O'Hare Area**	18
Big & Little's | **River N**	–
Big Bowl | **multi.**	20
Big Jones | **Andersonville**	21
Big Star | **Wicker Pk**	23
NEW Big Stuff | **Lincoln Pk**	–
Bijan's | **River N**	19
Billy Goat | **multi.**	17
Bin | **multi.**	21
Birchwood | **Bucktown**	23
Bombon Café | **W Loop**	–
Bonsai Café | **Evanston**	–
Bourgeois Pig | **Lincoln Pk**	–
Bristol | **Bucktown**	23
NEW Burger Boss | **Elmwood Pk**	–
Café Selmarie | **Lincoln Sq**	23
Chicago Burgerwurks | **Brookfield**	–
Chicago Pizza | **Lincoln Pk**	23
C-House | **Streeterville**	21
NEW City Provisions | **Ravenswood**	–
Crêpe Crave | **Wicker Pk**	–
Crêpe Town | **Lakeview**	–
Deca | **Streeterville**	–
NEW Del Seoul | **Lakeview**	–
Distinctive Cork | **Naperville**	21
DMK Burger | **Lakeview**	22
Drawing Room | **Gold Coast**	23
Edzo's | **Evanston**	–
Eleven City | **S Loop**	19
Epic | **River N**	–
Epic Burger | **Loop**	22
NEW Everest Burger | **Glencoe**	–
Felony Franks | **W Loop**	–
Five Guys | **multi.**	20
Flat Top | **multi.**	20
Foodlife | **Streeterville**	19

Frankie's Scaloppine | **Gold Coast**	18
Franks 'N' Dawgs | **Lincoln Pk**	-
NEW Gaztro-Wagon | **Edgewater**	-
Gene & Jude's | **O'Hare Area**	-
Gold Coast | **multi.**	19
Ƶ Hannah's Bretzel | **Loop**	23
Honey 1 BBQ | **Bucktown**	20
Hot Chocolate | **Bucktown**	24
Ƶ Hot Doug's | **NW Side**	27
Ja' Grill | **Lincoln Pk**	-
Jerry's | **Wicker Pk**	22
NEW Joey's Shrimp | **Humboldt Pk**	-
J. Wellington's | **Wicker Pk**	-
Katy's Dumpling | **multi.**	-
NEW La Lagartija | **W Loop**	-
Lem's BBQ | **Far S Side**	25
Leo's Coney Island | **Wrigleyville**	-
NEW Lillie's Q | **Bucktown**	-
LM | **W Loop**	22
NEW Mac/Min's | **W Loop**	-
Maiz | **Humboldt Pk**	23
Mana | **Wicker Pk**	27
Manny's | **multi.**	23
M Burger | **Streeterville**	-
NEW Meatyballs | **Location Varies**	-
Ƶ Mercat | **S Loop**	26
Mundial | **Pilsen**	-
Nia | **W Loop**	-
90 Miles | **Logan Sq**	22
Noon-O-Kabab | **Albany Pk**	25
Oak Tree Bakery and Restaurant | **Gold Coast**	17
Old Jerusalem | **Old Town**	19
Old Oak Tap | **Ukrainian Vill**	20
Old Town Social | **Old Town**	18
NEW Original Five | **University Vill**	-
NEW Owen/Engine | **Logan Sq**	-
Pegasus | **SW Side**	20
Penny's Noodle | **multi.**	20
Perry's Deli | **Loop**	26
Pierrot Gourmet | **River N**	20
Piggery | **Lakeview**	-
Pomegranate | **Evanston**	18
Pompei Pizza | **multi.**	19
NEW Pork Shoppe | **Avondale**	-
Ƶ Potbelly Sandwich | **multi.**	19
NEW Pret A Manger | **Loop**	-
Puck's/MCA | **Streeterville**	20
Purple Pig | **River N**	-

Quartino | **River N**	21
Rootstock | **Humboldt Pk**	24
Roti | **River W**	21
NEW Rub BBQ | **W Rogers Pk**	-
Russell's BBQ | **Elmwood Pk**	19
Sarkis Cafe | **Evanston**	15
NEW Smokey Bears BBQ | **Albany Pk**	-
NEW Snarf's | **River N**	-
Southern/Mac | **Location Varies**	-
Stained Glass | **Evanston**	23
State/Lake | **Loop**	21
Stir Crazy | **multi.**	19
Ƶ Superdawg | **NW Side**	21
Taco Fuego | **Lakeview**	-
NEW Taco Joint | **Lincoln Pk**	-
Tapas Las Ramblas | **Andersonville**	23
Tasting Room | **W Loop**	20
Tempo | **Gold Coast**	20
Trattoria Trullo | **Lincoln Sq**	23
Uncle Bub's | **Westmont**	-
Uncle John's BBQ | **Far S Side**	-
Uncommon Ground | **Lakeview**	22
NEW Uptowner | **Lincoln Pk**	-
Urbanbelly | **Logan Sq**	24
Viand Bar | **Streeterville**	22
Webster Wine | **Lincoln Pk**	20
Ƶ Wiener's Circle | **Lincoln Pk**	21
Xoco | **River N**	25
Zaleski/Horvath | **Kenwood**	-

QUIET CONVERSATION

Akai Hana | **Wilmette**	21
Al Bawadi Grill | **Bridgeview**	-
Amitabul | **NW Side**	21
Aria | **Loop**	24
Ƶ Arun's | **NW Side**	28
Ƶ A Tavola | **Ukrainian Vill**	26
NEW Awash | **Edgewater**	-
Bank Lane | **Lake Forest**	23
Ƶ Barrington Country | **Barrington**	25
Bistro Bordeaux | **Evanston**	-
Café Bernard | **Lincoln Pk**	19
Café/Architectes | **Gold Coast**	24
Café 103 | **Far S Side**	-
Cafe Pyrenees | **Libertyville**	21
Café Selmarie | **Lincoln Sq**	23
Ƶ Café Spiaggia | **Gold Coast**	25
Cape Cod Room | **Streeterville**	22
Ƶ Carlos' | **Highland Pk**	27
Ƶ Charlie Trotter's | **Lincoln Pk**	27

Vote at ZAGAT.com

NEW Chef Amaury's | **Aurora**	-
Cibo Matto | **Loop**	24
Cité | **Streeterville**	20
D & J Bistro | **Lake Zurich**	24
Erwin | **Lakeview**	23
☑ Everest | **Loop**	27
Gaetano's | **Forest Pk**	24
Gale St. Inn | **Mundelein**	22
Gaylord Indian | **Schaumburg**	22
Geja's Cafe | **Lincoln Pk**	21
Glen Prairie | **Glen Ellyn**	23
Inovasi | **Lake Bluff**	-
Itto Sushi | **Lincoln Pk**	24
Jacky's/Prairie | **Evanston**	21
Jilly's Cafe | **Evanston**	21
Klay Oven | **River N**	20
La Crêperie | **Lakeview**	21
☑ La Gondola | **Lakeview**	-
Lawry's | **River N**	24
Le P'tit Paris | **Streeterville**	20
☑ Les Nomades | **Streeterville**	29
☑ Le Titi/Paris | **Arlington Hts**	26
Le Vichyssois | **Lakemoor**	26
☑ Lovells | **Lake Forest**	23
☑ North Pond | **Lincoln Pk**	25
☑ Oceanique | **Evanston**	27
Olive or Twist | **Berwyn**	-
One North | **Loop**	15
NEW Pensiero | **Evanston**	-
Pierrot Gourmet | **River N**	20
Prairie Fire | **W Loop**	-
Quince | **Evanston**	23
Rhapsody | **Loop**	20
☑ RL | **Gold Coast**	23
Russian Tea | **Loop**	22
☑ Seasons | **Gold Coast**	27
1776 | **Crystal Lake**	22
☑ Shanghai Terrace | **River N**	25
☑ Signature Room | **Streeterville**	18
South Gate | **Lake Forest**	20
South Water | **Loop**	16
Table Fifty-two | **Gold Coast**	24
☑ Tallgrass | **Lockport**	28
Tasting Room | **W Loop**	20
Terzo Piano | **Loop**	21
Trattoria No. 10 | **Loop**	24
Tre Kronor | **Albany Pk**	23
☑ Tru | **Streeterville**	28
Village | **Loop**	21
Vinci | **Lincoln Pk**	21
Vivere | **Loop**	22
Zaleski/Horvath | **Kenwood**	-
Zealous | **River N**	25

RAW BARS

Balsan | **Gold Coast**	-
Benny's Chop | **River N**	-
☑ Bob Chinn's | **Wheeling**	23
C-House | **Streeterville**	21
Davis St. Fish | **Evanston**	19
Deca | **Streeterville**	-
NEW GT Fish/Oyster | **River N**	-
Half Shell | **Lakeview**	24
NEW Henri | **S Loop**	-
Mitchell's | **Glenview**	21
☑ Nine Steakhouse | **Loop**	24
Niu | **Streeterville**	19
Riva | **Streeterville**	20
☑ Shaw's Crab | **multi.**	24
Tin Fish | **Tinley Park**	23

ROMANTIC PLACES

Abigail's | **Highland Pk**	24
NEW Acre | **Andersonville**	-
Ai Sushi | **River N**	24
aja | **River N**	-
Alhambra | **W Loop**	16
NEW Ara On | **Loop**	-
☑ Avenues | **River N**	26
Azucar | **Logan Sq**	22
Balsan | **Gold Coast**	-
☑ Barrington Country | **Barrington**	25
Bistro Bordeaux | **Evanston**	-
☑ Bistro Campagne | **Lincoln Sq**	25
Bistrot Margot | **Old Town**	20
Blue 13 | **River N**	24
NEW Bluette | **Wilmette**	-
Boka | **Lincoln Pk**	25
Briejo | **Oak Pk**	14
Browntrout | **North Ctr/St. Ben's**	24
Café Absinthe | **Bucktown**	23
☑ Carlos' | **Highland Pk**	27
Ceres' Table | **Uptown**	-
☑ Charlie Trotter's | **Lincoln Pk**	27
NEW Chef Amaury's | **Aurora**	-
Chez Joël | **Little Italy/University Vill**	24
NEW Chizakaya | **Lakeview**	-
Cibo Matto | **Loop**	24
Cité | **Streeterville**	20
☑ Coco Pazzo | **River N**	25
Courtright's | **Willow Spgs**	25
☑ Crofton on Wells | **River N**	26
D & J Bistro | **Lake Zurich**	24
NEW Davanti | **Little Italy/University Vill**	-

Restaurant	Rating
NEW Donatella | **Evanston**	–
Drawing Room | **Gold Coast**	23
Elate | **River N**	21
Epic | **River N**	–
Z Everest | **Loop**	27
Fiorentino's | **Lakeview**	22
NEW Florentine | **Loop**	–
NEW Fork | **Lincoln Sq**	–
Gaetano's | **Forest Pk**	24
Geja's Cafe | **Lincoln Pk**	21
Gioco | **S Loop**	25
Glen Prairie | **Glen Ellyn**	23
NEW Gyu-Kaku | **Streeterville**	–
NEW Henri | **S Loop**	–
Il Mulino | **Gold Coast**	25
NEW Ing | **W Loop**	–
Z Japonais | **River N**	24
Jilly's Cafe | **Evanston**	21
Kiki's | **Near North**	25
Kith/Kin | **Lincoln Pk**	–
La Crêperie | **Lakeview**	21
Landmark | **Lincoln Pk**	20
Lan's Bistro | **Old Town**	–
NEW Lao You Ju | **Chinatown**	–
Le Bouchon | **Bucktown**	24
Z Le Colonial | **Gold Coast**	24
L'Eiffel Bistrot | **S Barrington**	21
NEW Leopold | **Noble Sq**	–
Le P'tit Paris | **Streeterville**	20
Z Les Nomades | **Streeterville**	29
Z Le Titi/Paris | **Arlington Hts**	26
Le Vichyssois | **Lakemoor**	26
LM | **Lincoln Sq**	22
Lokal | **Bucktown**	–
Z L2O | **Lincoln Pk**	–
Maijean | **Clarendon Hills**	28
Marigold | **Uptown**	23
NEW Maude's Liquor | **W Loop**	–
Melanthios | **Lakeview**	–
Mercadito | **River N**	22
Mezé | **W Loop**	–
Z MK | **Near North**	27
Mon Ami Gabi | **multi.**	22
Mythos | **Lakeview**	23
Z Nacional 27 | **River N**	23
Z Naha | **River N**	27
Natalino's | **W Town**	23
NEW Next | **W Loop**	–
Niche | **Geneva**	28
Z Nomi Kitchen | **Gold Coast**	–
Nozumi | **S Barrington**	–
Z Oceanique | **Evanston**	27
Olive or Twist | **Berwyn**	–
NEW Owen/Engine | **Logan Sq**	–
Pane Caldo | **Gold Coast**	23
Paramount Room | **River W**	24
NEW Paris Club | **River N**	–
Pasha | **W Loop**	–
Pelago | **Streeterville**	26
NEW Pensiero | **Evanston**	–
Piccolo Sogno | **Near W**	24
NEW PL8 | **Barrington**	–
Prairie Fire | **W Loop**	–
Prasino | **La Grange**	–
Prosecco | **River N**	24
Purple Pig | **River N**	–
Quince | **Evanston**	23
Rhapsody | **Loop**	20
Z Riccardo | **Lincoln Pk**	27
Z RL | **Gold Coast**	23
Sable | **River N**	–
NEW Sawtooth | **W Loop**	–
Z Seasons | **Gold Coast**	27
Sepia | **W Loop**	24
Z Shanghai Terrace | **River N**	25
Z Signature Room | **Streeterville**	18
Z Sixteen | **River N**	22
Sola | **Lakeview**	25
Southern/Mac | **Bucktown**	–
Sprout | **Lincoln Pk**	28
Stained Glass | **Evanston**	23
Sugartoad | **Naperville**	19
Sunda | **River N**	23
Sushi Taiyo | **River N**	–
Table Fifty-two | **Gold Coast**	24
Z Tallgrass | **Lockport**	28
Tasting Room | **W Loop**	20
Taxim | **Wicker Pk**	22
Topo Gigio | **Old Town**	23
Trattoria Trullo | **Lincoln Sq**	23
Trattoria 225 | **Oak Pk**	–
Z Tru | **Streeterville**	28
NEW Ukai | **Lakeview**	–
Vermilion | **River N**	22
NEW Vincent | **Andersonville**	–
Vinci | **Lincoln Pk**	21
Vintage 338 | **Lincoln Pk**	–
Vivo | **W Loop**	24
Wave | **Streeterville**	13
Webster Wine | **Lincoln Pk**	20
Wildfish | **Arlington Hts**	21
Zak's Place | **Hinsdale**	–
Zhivago | **Skokie**	16
Zocalo | **River N**	20

SENIOR APPEAL

Andies | **Ravenswood**	18
Ann Sather | **multi.**	21
Bacchanalia | **SW Side**	24
Bagel | **multi.**	19
Berghoff | **Loop**	18
Bruna's | **SW Side**	26
Café 103 | **Far S Side**	-
Cape Cod Room | **Streeterville**	22
Carson's | **River N**	22
Czech Plaza | **Berwyn**	22
Dave's Italian | **Evanston**	17
Davis St. Fish | **Evanston**	19
Del Rio | **Highwood**	20
Edelweiss | **Norridge**	19
Francesco's | **Northbrook**	24
Frances' Deli | **Lincoln Pk**	-
Gale St. Inn | **multi.**	22
Hackney's | **multi.**	18
Jacky's/Prairie | **Evanston**	21
La Cantina Chop | **Loop**	21
❷ La Gondola | **Lakeview**	-
Lawry's | **River N**	24
Le P'tit Paris | **Streeterville**	20
Le Vichyssois | **Lakemoor**	26
Lou Mitchell's | **Loop**	23
❷ Margie's Candies | **Bucktown**	22
Melting Pot | **multi.**	19
Miller's Pub | **Loop**	17
Mirabell | **NW Side**	21
Myron/Phil Steak | **Lincolnwood**	21
Nagoya | **Naperville**	-
Next Door | **Northbrook**	23
Nick's Fishmarket | **Rosemont**	23
Oak Tree Bakery and Restaurant | **Gold Coast**	17
❷ Original/Walker Pancake | **multi.**	24
Rist. al Teatro | **Pilsen**	-
❷ Rosebud | **Loop**	22
Russell's BBQ | **Elmwood Pk**	19
Russian Tea | **Loop**	22
Sabatino's | **NW Side**	24
Sarks/Park | **Lincoln Pk**	-
Smak-Tak | **NW Side**	-
South Gate | **Lake Forest**	20
Todai | **Schaumburg**	-
Tre Kronor | **Albany Pk**	23
Tufano's Tap | **Little Italy/University Vill**	20
Village | **Loop**	21
White Fence | **Romeoville**	22

Zhivago | **Skokie**	16
Zodiac Room | **Streeterville**	-

SINGLES SCENES

Adobo | **Old Town**	21
Bar Louie | **multi.**	16
Boka | **Lincoln Pk**	25
Café Iberico | **River N**	22
❷ Carnivale | **Loop**	23
Clubhouse | **Oak Brook**	21
Ditka's | **Gold Coast**	22
Drawing Room | **Gold Coast**	23
Fleming's | **Lincolnshire**	23
❷ Gibsons | **multi.**	26
Landmark | **Lincoln Pk**	20
Luxbar | **Gold Coast**	20
Market | **W Loop**	18
Moody's Pub | **Edgewater**	19
❷ Nine Steakhouse | **Loop**	24
Old Town Social | **Old Town**	18
P.J. Clarke's | **Gold Coast**	17
NEW Public House | **River N**	-
Rockit B&G | **River N**	19
Scoozi! | **River N**	19
Stanley's | **Lincoln Pk**	18
Sullivan's Steak | **multi.**	22
Sushisamba Rio | **River N**	21
Tavern/Rush | **Gold Coast**	21
33 Club | **Old Town**	20
Trader Vic's | **Gold Coast**	17
Wave | **Streeterville**	13
Zaleski/Horvath | **Kenwood**	-

SLEEPERS
(Good food, but little known)

Blue Ocean | **Ravenswood**	23
Café Touché | **Edison Pk**	25
Czech Plaza | **Berwyn**	22
Drawing Room | **Gold Coast**	23
Evergreen | **Chinatown**	23
Filippo's | **Lincoln Pk**	24
Habana Libre | **Noble Sq**	22
Han 202 | **Bridgeport**	25
Kansaku | **Evanston**	22
Lem's BBQ | **Far S Side**	25
Maijean | **Clarendon Hills**	28
Maiz | **Humboldt Pk**	23
Montarra | **Algonquin**	24
Nosh | **Geneva**	24
Paramount Room | **River W**	24
Pasta Palazzo | **Lincoln Pk**	22
Ras Dashen | **Edgewater**	23
Rumba | **River N**	23
Shui Wah | **Chinatown**	24

CHICAGO

SPECIAL FEATURES

Swordfish | **Batavia**	27
Tango | **Naperville**	22
Tapas Las Ramblas | **Andersonville**	23
Topaz Café | **Burr Ridge**	23
Trattoria Isabella | **W Loop**	26
Tub Tim Thai | **Skokie**	24
Victory's Banner | **Roscoe Vill**	24

TEEN APPEAL

Ann Sather | **multi.**	21
Aurelio's Pizza | **multi.**	23
Bacino's | **multi.**	22
Ba Le Sandwich | **Uptown**	-
Bandera | **Streeterville**	22
Big Bowl | **multi.**	20
🆕 Burger Bar | **Lincoln Pk**	-
🆕 Burger Boss | **Elmwood Pk**	-
ⓩ Cheesecake Factory | **multi.**	19
Chicago Burgerwurks | **Brookfield**	-
Chicago Pizza | **Lincoln Pk**	23
Choppers | **Wicker Pk**	-
Ciao Napoli | **Logan Sq**	-
Counter | **Lincoln Pk**	20
DMK Burger | **Lakeview**	22
Edwardo's Pizza | **multi.**	20
Edzo's | **Evanston**	-
Eggsperience Café | **multi.**	-
EJ's Pl. | **Skokie**	22
Epic Burger | **Loop**	22
🆕 Everest Burger | **Glencoe**	-
Felony Franks | **W Loop**	-
Five Guys | **Rogers Pk**	20
Flat Top | **multi.**	20
Gene & Jude's | **O'Hare Area**	-
ⓩ Giordano's | **multi.**	23
Gold Coast | **multi.**	19
Grand Lux | **River N**	20
Hackney's | **multi.**	18
ⓩ Hannah's Bretzel | **Loop**	23
Hard Rock | **River N**	12
Harry Caray's | **River N**	20
ⓩ Heaven/Seven | **multi.**	23
ⓩ Hot Doug's | **NW Side**	27
Hub 51 | **River N**	21
Ina's | **W Loop**	23
Joy Yee | **multi.**	20
Kroll's | **S Loop**	19
Leo's Coney Island | **Wrigleyville**	-
ⓩ Lou Malnati's | **multi.**	24
Lou Mitchell's | **Loop**	23
LuLu's | **Evanston**	21

L. Woods Tap | **Lincolnwood**	20
ⓩ Margie's Candies | **Bucktown**	22
Melting Pot | **multi.**	19
Mity Nice | **Streeterville**	17
Nookies | **multi.**	20
ⓩ Original Gino's East | **multi.**	22
ⓩ Original/Walker Pancake | **multi.**	24
Penny's Noodle | **multi.**	20
Pizzeria Uno/Due | **River N**	22
Pizzeria Serio | **Lakeview**	-
Pompei Pizza | **multi.**	19
ⓩ Potbelly Sandwich | **multi.**	19
R.J. Grunts | **Lincoln Pk**	19
Robinson's Ribs | **multi.**	21
Russell's BBQ | **Elmwood Pk**	19
Sarkis Cafe | **Evanston**	15
🆕 Smashburger | **Batavia**	-
Stanley's | **Lincoln Pk**	18
Stir Crazy | **Northbrook**	19
ⓩ Superdawg | **NW Side**	21
Tamales | **Highland Pk**	20
Tempo | **Gold Coast**	20
Toast | **multi.**	22
Trader Vic's | **Gold Coast**	17
Uncle Julio's | **Old Town**	18
ⓩ Wiener's Circle | **Lincoln Pk**	21
Wishbone | **multi.**	21

TRENDY

🆕 Ace Bar | **Lincoln Pk**	-
🆕 Arami | **W Town**	-
🆕 Ara On | **Loop**	-
ⓩ Avec | **W Loop**	26
Belly Shack | **Humboldt Pk**	23
Big Star | **Wicker Pk**	23
ⓩ Blackbird | **W Loop**	27
Blue 13 | **River N**	24
🆕 Boiler Room | **Logan Sq**	-
Boka | **Lincoln Pk**	25
ⓩ Bonsoirée | **Logan Sq**	26
Bourgeois Pig | **Lincoln Pk**	-
Bristol | **Bucktown**	23
🆕 Burger Bar | **Lincoln Pk**	-
ⓩ Carnivale | **Loop**	23
Ceres' Table | **Uptown**	-
🆕 Chicago Q | **Gold Coast**	-
🆕 Chikurin Sushi | **Wicker Pk**	-
ⓩ David Burke Prime | **River N**	25
DMK Burger | **Lakeview**	22
🆕 D'Noche/Café Con Leche | **Logan Sq**	-
Drawing Room | **Gold Coast**	23

Duchamp | **Bucktown**	17
Elate | **River N**	21
Epic | **River N**	-
Folklore | **Ukrainian Vill**	-
NEW Fork | **Lincoln Sq**	-
Fred's | **Gold Coast**	19
Z Frontera Grill | **River N**	27
NEW Frontier | **Noble Sq**	-
NEW Gaztro-Wagon | **Edgewater**	-
Gemini Bistro | **Lincoln Pk**	21
Z Gibsons | **Gold Coast**	26
Gioco | **S Loop**	25
NEW Girl/The Goat | **W Loop**	-
NEW Gosu | **Logan Sq**	-
Graham Elliot | **River N**	24
Great Lake | **Andersonville**	23
Z Green Zebra | **Noble Sq**	26
NEW Gyu-Kaku | **Streeterville**	-
Hearty | **Lakeview**	-
Hot Chocolate | **Bucktown**	24
Z Hot Doug's | **NW Side**	27
Hub 51 | **River N**	21
Isacco | **St. Charles**	-
Jam | **Ukrainian Vill**	21
Z Japonais | **River N**	24
Kin | **Noble Sq**	-
Kith/Kin | **Lincoln Pk**	-
La Madia | **River N**	23
Landmark | **Lincoln Pk**	20
NEW Lao You Ju | **Chinatown**	-
NEW Leopold | **Noble Sq**	-
Longman/Eagle | **Logan Sq**	-
NEW Lure Izakaya | **Chinatown**	-
Luxbar | **Gold Coast**	20
Mana | **Wicker Pk**	27
Marigold | **Uptown**	23
Mercadito | **River N**	22
Z Mercat | **S Loop**	26
Z Mia Francesca | **Lakeview**	26
NEW MingHin | **Chinatown**	-
Mirai Sushi | **Wicker Pk**	25
Miramar Bistro | **Highwood**	17
Z MK | **Near North**	27
NEW Nabuki | **Hinsdale**	-
Z Naha | **River N**	27
NEW Nano Sushi | **NW Side**	-
Nightwood | **Pilsen**	23
Z Nine Steakhouse | **Loop**	24
Z Nomi Kitchen | **Gold Coast**	-
Nozumi | **S Barrington**	-
NEW One.Six One | **Little Italy/University Vill**	-
Z One Sixtyblue | **W Loop**	26
Osteria/Pizzeria Via Stato | **River N**	23
Paramount Room | **River W**	24
Park 52 | **Hyde Pk**	19
NEW Perennial Virant | **Lincoln Pk**	-
NEW PL8 | **Barrington**	-
NEW Pork Shoppe | **Avondale**	-
Prosecco | **River N**	24
Province | **W Loop**	23
Z Publican | **W Loop**	25
Purple Pig | **River N**	-
Quartino | **River N**	21
Real Tenochtitlán | **Logan Sq**	20
Revolution Brewing | **Logan Sq**	-
Rootstock | **Humboldt Pk**	24
NEW Ruxbin | **Noble Sq**	-
Sable | **River N**	-
NEW Sawtooth | **W Loop**	-
Z Schwa | **Wicker Pk**	29
Sepia | **W Loop**	24
Sola | **Lakeview**	25
Southern/Mac | **multi.**	-
Spacca Napoli | **Ravenswood**	23
Sprout | **Lincoln Pk**	28
State/Lake | **Loop**	21
Sunda | **River N**	23
Sura | **Lakeview**	20
Sushisamba Rio | **River N**	21
Z Sushi Wabi | **W Loop**	27
Taxim | **Wicker Pk**	22
Tocco | **Bucktown**	12
NEW Ukai | **Lakeview**	-
Urbanbelly | **Logan Sq**	24
Veerasway | **W Loop**	21
NEW Wasabi | **Logan Sq**	-
Zapatista | **S Loop**	20

VIEWS

Athena | **Greektown**	21
Atwater's | **Geneva**	20
Z Avenues | **River N**	26
NEW Bauer's Brauhaus | **Palatine**	-
NEW Bistro One West | **St. Charles**	-
NEW Chicago Cut | **River N**	-
Chief O'Neill's | **NW Side**	18
Ciao Napoli | **Logan Sq**	-
Cité | **Streeterville**	20
Courtright's | **Willow Spgs**	25
Deca | **Streeterville**	-
Drake Bros.' | **Gold Coast**	-
Z Everest | **Loop**	27
Fred's | **Gold Coast**	19

Fulton's	**River N**	19
Z Gage	**Loop**	22
NEW Kanela	**Lakeview**	–
Lobby	**River N**	28
Z Mercat	**S Loop**	26
Z Nomi Kitchen	**Gold Coast**	–
Z North Pond	**Lincoln Pk**	25
Opa! Estiatorio	**Vernon Hills**	25
Park Grill	**Loop**	20
Port Edward	**Algonquin**	–
Puck's/MCA	**Streeterville**	20
Riva	**Streeterville**	20
Z Rosebud	**Naperville**	22
Z Seasons	**Gold Coast**	27
Z Shanghai Terrace	**River N**	25
Z Signature Room	**Streeterville**	18
Z Sixteen	**River N**	22
Smith/Wollensky	**River N**	23
Z Spiaggia	**Gold Coast**	27
Z Superdawg	**Wheeling**	21
Tasting Room	**W Loop**	20
Tavern/Rush	**Gold Coast**	21
Terzo Piano	**Loop**	21
Zed 451	**River N**	21
Zodiac Room	**Streeterville**	–

VISITORS ON EXPENSE ACCOUNT

aja	**River N**	–
Z Alinea	**Lincoln Pk**	29
Z Arun's	**NW Side**	28
Z Avenues	**River N**	26
Z Blackbird	**W Loop**	27
Z Bob Chinn's	**Wheeling**	23
Cape Cod Room	**Streeterville**	22
Z Capital Grille	**Streeterville**	25
Z Carlos'	**Highland Pk**	27
Z Catch 35	**Loop**	24
Z Charlie Trotter's	**Lincoln Pk**	27
Z Chicago Chop	**River N**	25
NEW Chicago Cut	**River N**	–
C-House	**Streeterville**	21
Cibo Matto	**Loop**	24
Z Coco Pazzo	**River N**	25
Courtright's	**Willow Spgs**	25
Z Crofton on Wells	**River N**	26
Custom House	**Printer's Row**	25
Z David Burke Prime	**River N**	25
Epic	**River N**	–
Z Everest	**Loop**	27
NEW Florentine	**Loop**	–
Fred's	**Gold Coast**	19
Z Gene/Georgetti	**River N**	24
Z Gibsons	**multi.**	26

Graham Elliot	**River N**	24
NEW Gyu-Kaku	**Streeterville**	–
NEW Henri	**S Loop**	–
Il Mulino	**Gold Coast**	25
NEW Ing	**W Loop**	–
Z Joe's Sea/Steak	**River N**	26
Z Keefer's	**River N**	25
Lawry's	**River N**	24
Z Le Colonial	**Gold Coast**	24
Z Les Nomades	**Streeterville**	29
Z Le Titi/Paris	**Arlington Hts**	26
Lobby	**River N**	28
Lockwood	**Loop**	19
Z L2O	**Lincoln Pk**	–
Z MK	**Near North**	27
Z Morton's	**multi.**	26
Z Naha	**River N**	27
NEW Next	**W Loop**	–
Z Nine Steakhouse	**Loop**	24
Z Nomi Kitchen	**Gold Coast**	–
Z North Pond	**Lincoln Pk**	25
Z Oceanique	**Evanston**	27
Z One Sixtyblue	**W Loop**	26
Palm	**Loop**	24
Ria	**Gold Coast**	–
Z RL	**Gold Coast**	23
Rosebud Prime/Steak	**Streeterville**	25
Roy's	**River N**	25
Z Ruth's Chris	**multi.**	25
Saloon Steak	**Streeterville**	23
Z Seasons	**Gold Coast**	27
Z Shanghai Terrace	**River N**	25
Z Shaw's Crab	**multi.**	24
Z Signature Room	**Streeterville**	18
Z Sixteen	**River N**	22
Smith/Wollensky	**River N**	23
Z Spiaggia	**Gold Coast**	27
Z Takashi	**Bucktown**	26
Z Tallgrass	**Lockport**	28
Z Topolobampo	**River N**	28
Trader Vic's	**Gold Coast**	17
Z Tru	**Streeterville**	28
Vivere	**Loop**	22
Zealous	**River N**	25

WINE BARS

Z Avec	**W Loop**	26
Bin	**Wicker Pk**	21
Broadway Cellars	**Edgewater**	21
Cab's Wine Bar	**Glen Ellyn**	24
Café Bernard	**Lincoln Pk**	19
Cafe Pyrenees	**Libertyville**	21
Cyrano's Bistrot	**River N**	22

Vote at ZAGAT.com

NEW Davanti | Little Italy/University Vill	-
Devon Seafood | River N	21
NEW DiSotto | Streeterville	-
Fleming's | Lincolnshire	23
Flight | Glenview	17
Fontana Grill | Uptown	-
Frasca Pizza | Lakeview	20
Quartino | River N	21
NEW Redd Herring | Clarendon Hills	-
Rhapsody | Loop	20
Rootstock | Humboldt Pk	24
Ropa | Rogers Pk	-
San Gabriel | Bannockburn	17
NEW Sono | Lincoln Pk	-
South Water | Loop	16
Stained Glass | Evanston	23
Tasting Room | W Loop	20
Vintage 338 | Lincoln Pk	-
Volo | Roscoe Vill	-
Webster Wine | Lincoln Pk	20

WINNING WINE LISTS

Z Alinea | Lincoln Pk	29
Z Arun's | NW Side	28
Z Avec | W Loop	26
Z Avenues | River N	26
Bin | multi.	21
Bistro Bordeaux | Evanston	-
Bistrot Margot | Old Town	20
Z Blackbird | W Loop	27
Bluebird | Bucktown	20
Boka | Lincoln Pk	25
Bristol | Bucktown	23
Cab's Wine Bar | Glen Ellyn	24
Campagnola | Evanston	25
Z Capital Grille | Streeterville	25
Z Carlos' | Highland Pk	27
Chalkboard | Lakeview	22
Z Charlie Trotter's | Lincoln Pk	27
NEW Chicago Cut | River N	-
C-House | Streeterville	21
Cibo Matto | Loop	24
Courtright's | Willow Spgs	25
Custom House | Printer's Row	25
Cyrano's Bistrot | River N	22
Del Rio | Highwood	20
Distinctive Cork | Naperville	21
Duchamp | Bucktown	17
Elate | River N	21
Epic | River N	-
Z Everest | Loop	27
Fleming's | Lincolnshire	23
Flight | Glenview	17
Fogo de Chão | River N	24
Fornetto Mei | Gold Coast	20
Z Gabriel's | Highwood	25
Geja's Cafe | Lincoln Pk	21
Glen Prairie | Glen Ellyn	23
Graham Elliot | River N	24
Z Green Zebra | Noble Sq	26
NEW Henri | S Loop	-
Jacky's/Prairie | Evanston	21
Z Japonais | River N	24
Koda | Far S Side	-
La Madia | River N	23
La Sardine | W Loop	24
Le P'tit Paris | Streeterville	20
Z Les Nomades | Streeterville	29
Z Le Titi/Paris | Arlington Hts	26
Lockwood | Loop	19
Z L2O | Lincoln Pk	-
Z Michael | Winnetka	28
Miramar Bistro | Highwood	17
Z MK | Near North	27
Z Moto | W Loop	27
Z Naha | River N	27
NEW Next | W Loop	-
Niche | Geneva	28
Z Nomi Kitchen | Gold Coast	-
Z North Pond | Lincoln Pk	25
Z Oceanique | Evanston	27
Z One Sixtyblue | W Loop	26
Pane Caldo | Gold Coast	23
NEW Pensiero | Evanston	-
NEW Perennial Virant | Lincoln Pk	-
Piccolo Sogno | Near W	24
Prosecco | River N	24
Province | W Loop	23
Z Publican | W Loop	25
Purple Pig | River N	-
Quince | Evanston	23
Rhapsody | Loop	20
Ria | Gold Coast	-
Salpicón | Old Town	26
Sam/Harry's Steak | Schaumburg	-
Z Seasons | Gold Coast	27
Sepia | W Loop	24
1776 | Crystal Lake	22
Z Signature Room | Streeterville	18
Z Sixteen | River N	22
Smith/Wollensky | River N	23
Z Spiaggia | Gold Coast	27
Stained Glass | Evanston	23

MILWAUKEE

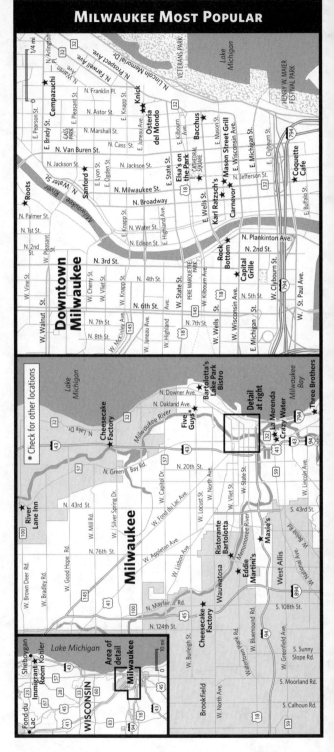

MILWAUKEE MOST POPULAR

★ Cempazuchi
★ Knick
Osteria del Mondo
Bacchus
Mason Street Grill
E. Wisconsin St.
E. Michigan St.
★ Coquette Cafe
Elsa's on the Park
Karl Ratzsch's
Carnevor
★ Roots
Sanford
Rock Bottom
Capital Grille

Downtown Milwaukee

Milwaukee River

Bartolotta's Lake Park Bistro
★ Three Brothers
Detail at right
La Merenda
Crazy Water
Five Guys *
Cheesecake Factory
★ River Lane Inn

Milwaukee

Ristorante Bartolotta
Maxie's
Eddie Martini's
Cheesecake Factory
West Allis
Wauwatosa

* Check for other locations

WISCONSIN
Immigrant Room Kohler
Sheboygan
Lake Michigan
Area of detail
Milwaukee
Fond du Lac
Brookfield

272   Vote at ZAGAT.com

Top Ratings

MOST POPULAR

1. Sanford | *American*
2. Bartolotta's Lake Park | *French*
3. Coquette Cafe | *French*
4. Eddie Martini's | *Steak*
5. Bacchus | *American*
6. Karl Ratzsch's | *German*
7. Capital Grille | *Steak*
8. Mason St. Grill | *American*
9. La Merenda | *Eclectic*
10. Rist. Bartolotta | *Italian*
11. Cheesecake Factory | *American*
12. Maxie's* | *Creole*
13. Rock Bottom* | *American*
14. Five Guys | *Burgers*
15. Immigrant Room* | *American*
16. Osteria del Mondo* | *Italian*
17. Carnevor | *Steak*
18. Cempazuchi* | *Mexican*
19. Crazy Water* | *Eclectic*
20. Knick* | *Eclectic*
21. Three Brothers* | *Serbian*
22. Elsa's on the Park | *American*
23. Roots* | *Californian*
24. River Lane Inn | *Seafood*

TOP FOOD

29 Roots | *Californian*
   Sanford | *American*
   Eddie Martini's | *Steak*
28 Bartolotta's Lake Park | *French*
   Osteria del Mondo | *Italian*

   Rist. Bartolotta | *Italian*
27 La Merenda | *Eclectic*
26 River Lane Inn | *Seafood*
   Coquette Cafe | *French*
   Hinterland Erie St. | *American*

BY CUISINE

AMERICAN (NEW)

29 Sanford
26 Hinterland Erie St.
25 Bacchus

AMERICAN (TRAD.)

24 Original Pancake
23 Mason St. Grill
   Elsa's on Park

ECLECTIC

27 La Merenda
25 Crazy Water
21 Knick

FRENCH

28 Bartolotta's Lake Park
26 Coquette Cafe

ITALIAN

28 Osteria del Mondo
   Rist. Bartolotta
24 Mimma's Café

STEAKHOUSES

29 Eddie Martini's
25 Capital Grille
   Five O'Clock Steak

BY LOCATION

DOWNTOWN

28 Osteria del Mondo
25 Capital Grille
   Bacchus

EAST SIDE

29 Sanford
28 Bartolotta's Lake Park
24 Original Pancake

Excludes places with low votes, unless otherwise indicated; * indicates a tie with restaurant above

OUTLYING AREAS

24 Original Pancake
23 Fleming's
   Immigrant Room

THIRD WARD

26 Coquette Cafe
   Hinterland Erie St.
20 Palms∇

WAUWATOSA

29 Eddie Martini's
28 Rist. Bartolotta
20 Maggiano's

TOP DECOR

28 Bartolotta's Lake Park
27 Roots
   Sanford
26 Eddie Martini's
   Bacchus

25 Rist. Bartolotta
   Hinterland Erie St.
24 Capital Grille
   Mason St. Grill
23 Karl Ratzsch's

TOP SERVICE

29 Sanford
28 Eddie Martini's
27 Bartolotta's Lake Park
   Rist. Bartolotta
26 River Lane Inn

25 Osteria del Mondo
   Capital Grille
   Immigrant Room
   Bacchus
24 Crazy Water

BEST BUYS

In order of Bang for the Buck rating.

1. Potbelly Sandwich
2. Five Guys
3. Original Pancake
4. Elsa's on Park
5. Edwardo's Pizza
6. Cubanitas
7. Cempazuchi
8. Rock Bottom
9. La Merenda
10. Maxie's

MILWAUKEE RESTAURANT DIRECTORY

☒ Bacchus ☒ *American*

25 | 26 | 25 | $61

Downtown | Cudahy Tower | 925 E. Wells St. (Prospect Ave.) |
414-765-1166 | www.bacchusmke.com

With a "fabulous" Cudahy Tower setting (including a glassed-in
conservatory with lake views) as a backdrop for chef Adam Siegel's
"wonderful" American fare brought by a "marvelous staff", this
Downtown sibling of Lake Park Bistro and Ristorante Bartolotta is
built to "impress"; while some surveyors "save" it "for a special
night out", others "keep coming back" for an "experience" they
deem "worth the price"; N.B. dinner only.

☒ Bartolotta's Lake Park Bistro *French*

28 | 28 | 27 | $55

East Side | Lake Park Pavilion | 3133 E. Newberry Blvd. (Lake Dr.) |
414-962-6300 | www.lakeparkbistro.com

A "beautiful view of Lake Michigan" and the park from the historic
Lake Park Pavilion provides the setting "for romance" – and
Milwaukee's top-rated Decor – at this East Side "French gem" where
the "world-class" cuisine of chef Adam Siegel "matches any in Chicago
or New York City" and is accompanied by "outstanding service" and
an "attainable wine list"; fans of this "beauty" from restaurateur Joe
Bartolotta feel transported "to the French countryside."

Benihana *Japanese/Steak*

18 | 18 | 20 | $36

Downtown | 850 N. Plankinton Ave. (bet. Kilbourn Ave. & Wells St.) |
414-270-0890 | www.benihana.com

See review in Chicago Directory.

NEW Blue's Egg *American*

- | - | - | M

West Side | 317 N. 76th St. (Bluemound Rd.) | 414-299-3180 |
www.bluesegg.com

This West Side sister to Maxie's Southern Comfort offers Traditional
American breakfast and lunch favorites – including stuffed hash
browns, omelets and sandwiches – enhanced with a few global
twists and served in a space outfitted with art deco touches and its
very own Statue of Liberty replica; prices are moderate and it serves
beer, wine and cocktails too.

Bosley on Brady ☒ *Seafood/Steak*

- | - | - | M

East Side | 815 E. Brady St. (bet. Cass & Marshall Sts.) | 414-727-7975 |
www.bosleyonbrady.com

A "casual" "Key West theme" stokes the "inviting atmosphere"
of this "neighborly", moderately priced East Sider on "trendy
Brady Street", where a "well-trained, enthusiastic staff" ferries
"luscious, fresh and creative" seafood and steakhouse fare; the
"upbeat" decor is "delightfully warm", and there's also alfresco
sidewalk seating in summer.

Buckley's Kiskeam Inn *American*

- | - | - | M

Downtown | 801 N. Cass St. (Wells St.) | 414-277-1111 |
www.buckleyskiskeaminn.com

Despite its name, this midpriced Downtown pub offers Traditional
American eats with a few global touches (including Irish, of course);

an antique dark-wood bar frames the dining room where locals enjoy monthly beer and wine dinners and occasional live music.

Café Manna ☒ Vegetarian

| - | - | - | M |

Brookfield | Sendik's Towne Ctr. | 3815 N. Brookfield Rd.
(bet. San Fernando & Thomson Drs.) | 262-790-2340 |
www.cafemanna.com

From eco-friendly digs to biodegradable carry-out containers, every facet of this affordable Brookfield vegetarian is green; the voluminous menu features salads, soups, sandwiches and more, including a number of raw, vegan and gluten-free options alongside beer and organic wines; P.S. the patio is dog-friendly.

☒ Capital Grille Steak

| 25 | 24 | 25 | $63 |

Downtown | 310 W. Wisconsin Ave. (4th St.) | 414-223-0600 |
www.thecapitalgrille.com
See review in Chicago Directory.

Carnevor ☒ Steak

| 24 | 21 | 23 | $63 |

Downtown | 724 N. Milwaukee St. (Mason St.) | 414-223-2200 |
www.carnevor.com

Milwaukee Street moguls take meat-ings at this Downtown "steakhouse with a nightclub vibe", a "business-dinner heaven" where ribeyes and Kobe beef are among the "excellent" offerings served in a "modern", earth-toned setting; of course you'll "dig deep" into your wallet, but carnivores concur the portions are "huge" enough to leave them "in a vegetative state"; N.B. valet parking is a necessity.

Cempazuchi Ⓜ Mexican

| 23 | 18 | 19 | $27 |

East Side | 1205 E. Brady St. (Franklin Pl.) | 414-291-5233 |
www.cempazuchi.com

"Beautiful mole sauces" – including a different one served weekly over turkey – are a highlight of the "incredible, simply prepared dishes" offered at this East Side Mexican also known for "authentic fish tacos" and some of the "best margaritas in Milwaukee"; the *"Dia de los Muertos* decor" adds to the "friendly, bustling" atmosphere, and in summer, the "cozy setting" spills onto the sidewalk for people-watching "trendy Brady Street"–style.

Centro Café ⊅ Italian

| - | - | - | I |

Riverwest | 808 E. Center St. (bet. Bremen & Fratney Sts.) |
414-455-3751 | www.centrocaferiverwest.com

This intimate Riverwest Italian is reminiscent of a cozy European cafe, serving inexpensive antipasto, pasta and sandwiches in a casual dining area boasting an open kitchen and banquettes crafted from church pews; P.S. warm weather brings sidewalk alfresco dining.

Cheesecake Factory American

| 19 | 19 | 18 | $28 |

Glendale | Bayshore Mall | 5799 N. Bayshore Dr. (Port Washington Rd.) |
414-906-8550
Wauwatosa | 2350 N. Mayfair Rd. (North Ave.) | 414-258-8512
www.thecheesecakefactory.com
See review in Chicago Directory.

	FOOD	DECOR	SERVICE	COST

Comet Café *American*

| - | - | - | I |

East Side | 1947 N. Farwell Ave. (Irving Pl.) | 414-273-7677 |
www.thecometcafe.com

East Side hipsters haunt this casual, affordable American known for healthy helpings of homestyle comfort food that satisfies meat lovers and meatphobes alike; just be prepared for a wait as the cozy digs can get crowded during peak hours.

☒ Coquette Cafe *French*

| 26 | 22 | 24 | $38 |

Third Ward | 316 N. Milwaukee St. (St. Paul Ave.) | 414-291-2655 |
www.coquettecafe.com

"Lovely" French bistro fare is *"la différence"* at this "wonderful" "Third Ward gem" of "real integrity" that draws Francophiles for "romantic dinners for two" and "lunch with clients" with its "superb steak frites" and other "terrific" items; the "cute" dining room is like being "in Paris" (except for "no attitude" from the staff) with "reasonable prices"; P.S. owner Sanford D'Amato passed the reins to two former protégés post-Survey, which is not reflected in the scores.

Crawdaddy's Ⓜ *Cajun/Creole*

| ▽ 16 | 18 | 17 | $29 |

Southwest Side | 6414 W. Greenfield Ave. (bet. 64th & 65th Sts.) |
414-778-2228 | www.crawdaddysrestaurant.com

Cajun-Creole fare brings a touch of N'Awlins to the Southwest Side at this "general all-around good-time place" that dishes out "delightful" crawfish étouffée, gumbo and other regional bites; naturally it's "noisy" in the "big" room decorated with Louisiana artwork, and disappointed diners declare the "menu seems tired and the staff even more so", but at least it won't break the bank with its moderate prices.

Crazy Water *Eclectic*

| 25 | 18 | 24 | $40 |

Walker's Point | 839 S. Second St. (Walker St.) | 414-645-2606 |
www.crazywaterrestaurant.com

"Once a bar", this "cozy" Walker's Point Eclectic "off the beaten path" has a "homey feeling" and a "great vibe" say locals who "watch" chef-owner Peggy Magister "working in her tiny makeshift kitchen"; a "casualness that's not intimidating" extends to the staff as well as moderate prices, so patrons profess it deserves "all the accolades."

Cubanitas Ⓢ *Cuban*

| 20 | 16 | 16 | $21 |

Downtown | 728 N. Milwaukee St. (bet. Mason St. & Wisconsin Ave.) |
414-225-1760 | www.getcubanitas.com

"Casual, tasty" Cuban fare is "at the heart of" this "hip, affordable" "slice of Havana" Downtown (little sister of Italian Osteria del Mondo) that fans call a "real treat"; though some speculate it "needs a shakeup" (especially in the service area), mojitos and summer sidewalk seating on modish Milwaukee Street up the pleasure quotient.

Dream Dance Steak ⓈⓂ *American/Steak*

| - | - | - | E |

Downtown | Potawatomi Bingo Casino | 1721 W. Canal St. (16th St.) |
414-847-7883 | www.paysbig.com

An "incredible" 600-label wine list caps off the experience at this over-21-only steakhouse in Downtown's Potawatomi Bingo Casino where the Wisconsin-inflected New American cuisine receives a "deft, skilled presentation", coaxing cognoscenti to whisper it's a "best-kept secret"; a staff that's "attentive" but not "overbearing" also gets kudos, though surveyors are "tempted to hit the slots afterward to make up for the outsize bill"; N.B. there's a separate restaurant entrance.

☑ Eddie Martini's ☒ *Seafood/Steak*

| 29 | 26 | 28 | $65 |

Wauwatosa | 8612 W. Watertown Plank Rd. (86th St.) | 414-771-6680 | www.eddiemartinis.com

"Forget the image of a smoke-filled supper club", this Wauwatosa "standout" is "elegant" say fans who call the clubby classic their "all-time favorite" (and show it with improved scores) for "huge steaks" (e.g. the 22-ounce bone-in rib-eye) and "wonderfully fresh, inventive" seafood; sure it's expensive but "you get what you pay for", and an "attentive", "knowledgeable staff" seals the deal for "a special night."

Edwardo's Natural Pizza *Pizza*

| 20 | 11 | 15 | $19 |

West Side | 10845 W. Bluemound Rd. (Hwy. 100) | 414-771-7770 | www.edwardos.com

See review in Chicago Directory.

Elsa's on the Park ◑ *American*

| 23 | 22 | 21 | $24 |

Downtown | 833 N. Jefferson St. (Wells St.) | 414-765-0615 | www.elsas.com

An "interesting crowd" fills this "Milwaukee tradition" situated in a Downtown building dating to 1890, where the decor is "sleek" and "modern" and the "reasonably priced" roster of "inventive" American bar bites includes "pork-chop sandwiches" and "burgers worth the trip"; it's open for lunch, dinner and late-night" noshing, just be sure to "dress to be seen" at this "upscale" Karl Kopp–owned spot.

Envoy *American*

| - | - | - | M |

Downtown | Ambassador Hotel | 2308 W. Wisconsin Ave. (bet. 23rd & 24th Sts.) | 414-345-5015 | www.envoymilwaukee.com

Situated inside the painstakingly "restored" Ambassador Hotel (from 1927), this Downtown New American benefits from the "beautiful architecture" of its "art deco" surroundings and decor; a "helpful staff" adds to the "pleasant experience" even if the mid-priced menu draws mixed reviews ("average" vs. "reliable").

Five Guys *Burgers*

| 20 | 10 | 16 | $11 |

East Side | 2907 N. Oakland Ave. (Locust St.) | 414-964-5303
Glendale | Bayshore Town Ctr. | 5800 N. Bayshore Dr. (Glen Bay Ave.) | 414-962-3560
Delafield | Shoppes at Nagawaukee | 2900 Golf Rd. (Rte. 83) | 262-646-4897
Pewaukee | Pewaukee Commons | 1279 Capitol Dr. (Willow Grove Dr.) | 262-691-7566
www.fiveguys.com

See review in Chicago Directory.

	FOOD	DECOR	SERVICE	COST

Five O'Clock Steakhouse 🗷Ⓜ *Steak*   25 | 18 | 21 | $48

Central City | 2416 W. State St. (24th St.) | 414-342-3553 |
www.fiveoclocksteakhouse.com

"Ordering dinner" at the bar "before you're seated" is part of the
"old-school" experience at this "reliable" Central City steakhouse
"straight from the '40s", where carnivores "step back in time" with
"classic" touches like a "relish tray" complementing "succulent cuts of
meat" with a "crispy blackened edge"; the dark wood might give it the
ambiance of a "guys' place", but it's considered "one of Milwaukee's
finest" by "ladies too"; N.B. the suburban Chicago branch has closed.

Fleming's Prime Steakhouse &   23 | 23 | 22 | $60
Wine Bar   *Steak*

Brookfield | Brookfield Square Mall | 15665 W. Bluemound Rd.
(Moorland Rd.) | 262-782-9463 | www.flemingssteakhouse.com
See review in Chicago Directory.

NEW Harbor House   *Seafood*   - | - | - | E

Downtown | 550 N. Harbor Dr. (Michigan St.) | 414-395-4900 |
www.harborhousemke.com

A Downtown relative to Bacchus and Bartolotta's Lake Park Bistro, this
New England–style seafood salon serves up a frequently changing
menu of fresh fish and shellfish (including a raw bar), plus pasta and
more; the spacious dining area includes banquettes, counter seats
and high-tops in the bar and boasts beautiful views of the lakefront.

Heaven City 🗷Ⓜ *American*   - | - | - | M

Mukwonago | S91 W27850 National Ave./Hwy. ES (Edgewood Ave.) |
262-363-5191 | www.heavencity.com

Ghost hunters and history buffs feast at this Mukwonago blend of
the past and present; the art deco decor smacks of Prohibition times
(and infamous mobster Al Capone, who is said to have hidden out
here), while the midpriced menu (bone-in rib-eye, sashimi-grade
tuna) is up-to-date New American; N.B. the long-established Tapas
Tuesday features live flamenco music.

Hinterland   26 | 25 | 24 | $51
Erie Street Gastropub 🗷 *American*

Third Ward | 222 E. Erie St. (Water St.) | 414-727-9300 |
www.hinterlandbeer.com

Admirers of this "creative" New American situated in a Third Ward
storefront call its "expensive" seasonal menu emphasizing fish and
local game "superbly crafted" and give service a thumbs-up too; the
wood-filled modern quarters include a lounge that's an "excellent
spot to grab a cocktail", and there's sidewalk dining in summer.

Honeypie   *American*   - | - | - | M

Bay View | 2643 S. Kinnickinnic Ave. (Potter Ave.) | 414-489-7437 |
www.honeypiecafe.com

Traditional American breakfast fare, creative sandwiches and imag-
inatively iced cupcakes – along with pie, of course – earn fans for
this Bay View favorite known for its from-scratch cooking and local

sourcing; the "Up North" Wisconsin theme threads through the interior, which displays taxidermy animals and maps of the area.

Il Mito Enoteca M *Italian* ∇ 25 | 18 | 21 | $36

Wauwatosa | 6913 W. North Ave. (69th St.) | 414-443-1414 | www.ilmito.com

"Wonderful", "affordable" fare from "enthusiastic" chef-owner Michael Feker "dazzles with flair" at this Wauwatosa Italian where a staff that's "attentive but not pushy" navigates the warm, wood-filled, exposed-beam quarters; N.B. a cooking school is adjacent.

Immigrant Room & Winery ⊠ M *American* 23 | 22 | 25 | $59

Kohler | American Club | 419 Highland Dr. (School St.) | 920-457-8888 | www.destinationkohler.com

Diners feel as if they've "stepped back in time" at this New American "tucked away" in the "dark" downstairs of a historic building at Kohler's American Club resort, where the "expensive", "superb" cuisine is "presented with a modern twist" by staffers who are "masters of hospitality"; the six dining rooms are decorated in different ethnic themes honoring the original immigrant tenants, and there's also a winery bar with a regional cheese room; N.B. jackets are required in the dining room area.

Jackson Grill ⊠ M *American* ∇ 23 | 18 | 22 | $42

South Side | 3736 W. Mitchell St. (38th St.) | 414-384-7384 | www.jacksongrillmilwaukee.com

The "time machine back to the 1950s" stops at this South Side American "classic", a "quintessential urban supper club" "chock-full of regulars" who regard it as the "friendliest, homiest place in Milwaukee"; everything on the menu (including steaks and ribs) is "first-rate, properly prepared and lovingly dished out" in "copious servings" that embody "what Wisconsin is all about."

Jake's ⊠ *Steak* - | - | - | E

Pewaukee | 21445 Gumina Rd. (Capitol Dr.) | 262-781-7995 | www.jakes-restaurant.com

"On a winter day", patrons procure a table near the "huge fireplace" at this more than 40-year-old Pewaukee "steak haunt" where the "classic comfort-food menu" (including the "much-imitated, never-surpassed onion rings") includes "selections for more modern tastes"; to "longtime fans", it feels "comfortably like the bar down the street."

⊠ Karl Ratzsch's ⊠ *German* 25 | 23 | 24 | $41

Downtown | 320 E. Mason St. (bet. B'way & Milwaukee St.) | 414-276-2720 | www.karlratzsch.com

For a "sauerbraten and spaetzle fix", this Downtown "classic" is a "destination of choice" dishing out "substantial" portions of "excellent", "hearty" "old-world" German "favorites" including "wonderful roast goose" in a Bavarian-inspired room that "oozes gemütlichkeit"; the ski-lodge decor is "a little over-the-top" ("where else can you dine under chandeliers made from antlers?") and some find prices a bit "high for comfort food", but good service helps make it "worth the trip"; P.S. a pianist performs on weekends.

	FOOD	DECOR	SERVICE	COST

Kilawat Restaurant *American* ▽ 21 | 23 | 18 | $47

Downtown | InterContinental Milwaukee Hotel | 139 E. Kilbourn Ave. (Water St.) | 414-291-4793 | www.kilawatcuisine.com

Located in the InterContinental Hotel near the Milwaukee Repertory Theater, this "upscale" New American is a "perfect" choice for "well-prepared", "tasty" fare (including lobster pot pie) before catching a "Downtown show"; the "bar is a spot to see and be seen" before heading to the colorful orange-and-lime dining room, where a few find the service "too casual."

King & I *Thai* ▽ 20 | 17 | 19 | $25

Downtown | 830 N. Old World Third St. (bet. Kilbourn Ave. & Wells St.) | 414-276-4181 | www.kingandirestaurant.com

Thai "with some ingenuity" draws loyal subjects to this affordable Downtowner whose roster of dishes (pad Thai, curry) is "consistent" and "satisfying"; patrons preach "when they say 'hot', they mean it", but that adds to the "adventure"; N.B. there's a weekday lunch buffet.

Knick, The ❶ *Eclectic* 21 | 21 | 22 | $33

Downtown | Knickerbocker Hotel | 1028 E. Juneau Ave. (Astor St.) | 414-272-0011 | www.theknickrestaurant.com

"One of the New York-iest spots in town", this Downtowner at the Knickerbocker Hotel is "always a good bet" for "sophisticated" Eclectic fare that's offered from lunch through "the late-hour munchies" and delivered by a staff that "goes out of its way to please"; moderate tabs and modern decor are other reasons fans "love hanging out here."

La Merenda ▣ *Eclectic* 27 | 19 | 22 | $32

Walker's Point | 125 E. National Ave. (1st St.) | 414-389-0125 | www.lamerenda125.com

"Not much on decor" but still "festive", this "warm and comfortable" Walker's Point "little neighborhood gem" provides "outstanding", "well-presented" "international tapas" on an Eclectic menu of "creative" small plates; prices are "well within budget reach" "for larger groups", though it's also "perfect for a first date" or a "quick bite."

Le Rêve Patisserie & Café ▣ *Dessert/French* ▽ 27 | 19 | 22 | $29

Wauwatosa | 7610 Harwood Ave. (Menomonee River Pkwy.) | 414-778-3333 | www.lerevecafe.com

Francophiles feel the "formidable" pull of this "perfect little French cafe" from the "luscious pastries in the counter display case" to the "freakishly high ceiling" and "European decor" that make "you think you're in Paris" (rather than a restored century-old Wauwatosa bank building); the "excellent", "reasonably priced" bistro bites (e.g. crêpes, quiche, steak frites) are made even better by the "brisk but friendly white-aproned service."

Maggiano's Little Italy *Italian* 20 | 19 | 21 | $32

Wauwatosa | Mayfair Mall | 2500 N. Mayfair Rd. (North Ave.) | 414-978-1000 | www.maggianos.com
See review in Chicago Directory.

	FOOD	DECOR	SERVICE	COST

Mangia 🗷Ⓜ *Italian*

▽ 25 | 17 | 22 | $42

Kenosha | 5717 Sheridan Rd. (bet. 57th & 58th Sts.) | 262-652-4285 | www.kenoshamangia.com

Italian fare that's "excellent" and "consistent" makes this Kenosha trattoria "worth the drive", and its "interesting menu" – including seasonal selections and an antipasto bar – is delivered by a "friendly, knowledgeable staff" under the eye of co-owner Tony Mantuano; the rustic scene includes an outdoor patio, prompting patrons to praise it as a "perfect" "meeting place" between Milwaukee and Chicago.

☒ Mason Street Grill *American*

23 | 24 | 24 | $55

Downtown | Pfister Hotel | 425 E. Mason St. (bet. Jefferson & Milwaukee Sts.) | 414-298-3131 | www.masonstreetgrill.com

"Excellent steaks and chops" coupled with "good value" and "knowledgeable service" draw meat eaters to this American in Downtown's historic Pfister Hotel, where the "seafood is top-rate too", making for an all-around "solid stop"; patrons "grab a counter seat" facing the kitchen to "see how the food is prepared" or head for the "sleek", "upscale" dining room to spend a "pleasant" "evening lingering"; P.S. for the lounge lizards, there's live music.

Maxie's Southern Comfort *Cajun/Creole*

23 | 18 | 22 | $30

West Side | 6732 W. Fairview Ave. (68th St.) | 414-292-3969 | www.maxies.com

"Bustling" and "boisterous", this West Side "value" offers a "solid menu" of Cajun-Creole fare dished out "on the site of an old butcher shop" kitted out with bordello-red walls; the Southern charm extends to a "helpful staff", while a raw bar adds "flair in a meat-and-potatoes town" and "happy-hour specials" fuel the "festive" vibe.

Meritage 🗷Ⓜ *Eclectic*

- | - | - | E

West Side | 5921 W. Vliet St. (60th St.) | 414-479-0620 | www.meritage.us

Pilgrims who venture "off the beaten path" to the West Side proclaim this Washington Heights Eclectic a "delicious destination" for chef-owner Jan Kelly's dishes "using an abundance of local and organic ingredients" in a "creative menu" that blends "tastes from all over the world"; P.S. the "outdoor patio is a summertime must."

Milwaukee Chophouse *Steak*

▽ 22 | 22 | 22 | $48

Downtown | Hilton Milwaukee | 633 N. Fifth St. (bet. Michigan St. & Wisconsin Ave.) | 414-226-2467 | www.milwaukeechophouse.com

The "old Milwaukee steakhouse legends" have nothing on this Downtowner, the fine-dining hub of the Hilton Milwaukee City Center where cuts are "cooked spot-on"; count in the "comfortable", "relaxed" feel and "knowledgeable staff" and this beef boutique is "worth a special trip"; N.B. there's also a 30-seat private dining room.

Mimma's Café *Italian*

24 | 19 | 24 | $35

East Side | 1307 E. Brady St. (Arlington Pl.) | 414-271-7337 | www.mimmas.com

With Brady Street as a backdrop, this East Side Italian stalwart makes patrons "feel at home" with chef-owner Mimma Megna

FOOD DECOR SERVICE COST

"sending out little surprises" alongside "excellent pasta" and "outstanding specials" at moderate prices; while some call the elegantly casual decor featuring marble columns "adorable", others contest it's "seen better days"; N.B. the wine list offers 300 labels.

Mo's: A Place for Steaks 🅢 *Steak* | 23 | 23 | 24 | $62 |

Downtown | 720 N. Plankinton Ave. (Wisconsin Ave.) | 414-272-0720 | www.mosrestaurants.com

"Big-city" flair accompanies the "fantastic" fare at this Downtown steakhouse that carnivores claim "would fit right into" the Chicago scene; in addition to "exceptional" cuts such as filet mignon and ribeye plus a long list of sides, the "quality" extends to the service in the traditional wood-filled digs (and is reflected in improved scores in all areas), so naturally it comes with "high tabs."

Mr. B's: A Bartolotta Steakhouse *Steak* | ▽ 26 | 20 | 25 | $53 |

Brookfield | 18380 W. Capitol Drive (bet. Brookfield Rd. & Mountain Dr.) | 262-790-7005 | www.mrbssteakhouse.com

Surveyors sate their "carnivorous side" at this "traditional" chophouse in Brookfield offering "quality" steaks and other "hearty" fare along with the "touches we have come to expect" from its parent, Bartolotta Restaurant Group (Bacchus, Lake Park Bistro, Ristorante Bartolotta), including "excellent service" for a meal that's "wonderful from start to finish"; N.B. a post-Survey move (not reflected in the Decor score) has netted more seating and parking (plus a patio), while keeping the trademark green-checked tablecloth ambiance.

North Star American Bistro *American* | 22 | 18 | 21 | $31 |

Shorewood | Cornerstone Bldg. | 4518 N. Oakland Ave. (Kensington Blvd.) | 414-964-4663
Brookfield | 19115 W. Capitol Dr. (Brookfield Rd.) | 262-754-1515 www.northstarbistro.com

These "unpretentious", moderately priced Brookfield and Shorewood American siblings offer "lots of choices" including "interesting" creations (e.g. bourbon salmon, lamb shank) that work for a "special meal" or "family" dining in "casual" "neighborhood bistro" settings; N.B. the monthly wine club offers savings on featured wines.

NSB Bar and Grill *American* | 19 | - | 19 | $35 |

North Shore | River Point Vill. | 8649 N. Port Washington Rd. (Brown Deer Rd.) | 414-351-6100 | www.northshorebistro.com

This North Shore "neighborhood hangout" underwent a major facelift post-Survey, shrinking the banquet hall–like dining room to a small, intimate space with richly colored walls and cozy banquettes; its midpriced New American menu remains "reliable" for salad, burger and sandwich fans, and has been hipped up with new nightly specials (to wit: shrimp boil, prime rib).

Original Pancake House, The *American* | 24 | 16 | 20 | $17 |

East Side | 2621 N. Downer Ave. (E. Belleview Pl.) | 414-431-5055
Brookfield | 16460 W. Bluemound Rd. (Dechant Rd.) | 262-797-0800 www.originalpancakehouse.com
See review in Chicago Directory.

	FOOD	DECOR	SERVICE	COST

☑ Osteria del Mondo ☒ *Italian* — 28 | 21 | 25 | $53

Downtown | Knickerbocker Hotel | 1028 E. Juneau Ave. (Astor St.) | 414-291-3770 | www.getosteria.com

Chef/co-owner Marc Bianchini's Northern Italian "standards with flair" are "as close to authentic as you'll find in the Midwest" at this Downtown "favorite" (and sibling of Cubanitas) that's been "consistent over the years" for "fine dining" in a "comfortable" Tuscan-themed setting; "sure it's expensive – especially for Milwaukee", but acolytes advise "trust the server" and "enjoy"; P.S. there's an outdoor patio too.

Palms Bistro & Bar Ⓜ *American* — ▽ 20 | 18 | 19 | $32

Third Ward | 221 N. Broadway (bet. Buffalo & Chicago Sts.) | 414-298-3000 | www.palmsbistrobar.com

Situated inside a late-19th-century Cream City brick building, this "pearl of the Third Ward" is known for its salads as well as its "unique approach with seafood dishes" and other New American fare served in a bistro setting with local artwork lining the walls; the "open-air" dining at sidewalk tables appeals in summertime, but "friendly service" and "solid value" are year-round staples; N.B. extensive happy-hour specials run Tuesday–Friday.

NEW Parkside 23 ☒ *American* — - | - | - | M
(aka PS23)

Brookfield | 2300 Pilgrim Square Dr. (North Ave.) | 262-784-7275 | www.parkside23.com

Using locally sourced ingredients – including some grown on its own farm – this Brookfield American from the owners of Eddie Martini's offers a wide-ranging menu arranged primarily by cost, not course; beer flights and cocktails crafted from housemade syrups accompany the hearty fare, and it's all served in a cozy, casual setting at moderate prices.

Pasta Tree *Italian* — ▽ 20 | 19 | 23 | $35

East Side | 1503 N. Farwell Ave. (Curtis Pl.) | 414-276-8867 | www.pastatreerestaurant.com

"Excellent pastas and sauces" at moderate prices lure loyalists to this "*romantico*" more than 30-year-old Italian in the East Side, where a pair of dining rooms with tin ceilings and antique chandeliers are the setting for "quiet, intimate meals"; N.B. in summer, a secluded garden patio offers additional tables.

NEW Pastiche ☒ *French* — - | - | - | M

Bay View | 3001 S. Kinnickinnic Ave. (Rusk Ave.) | 414-482-1446 | www.pastichebistro.com

Suffusing the sunny warmth of Provence into an unassuming corner storefront in Bay View, this casual newcomer with butter-colored walls and Gallic posters features chef-owner Michael Engel's French bistro cuisine; the neighborhood's rich stew of residents and workers from its eclectic businesses dig into hearty classics like cassoulet and escargots, all washed down with wines whose prices are as affordable as the fare.

	FOOD	DECOR	SERVICE	COST

P.F. Chang's China Bistro *Chinese*
20 | 19 | 19 | $31

Wauwatosa | Mayfair Mall | 2500 N. Mayfair Rd. (North Ave.) | 414-607-1029 | www.pfchangs.com
See review in Chicago Directory.

Polonez Ⓜ *Polish*
- | - | - | I

South Side | 4016 S. Packard Ave. (Tesch St.) | 414-482-0080 | www.foodspot.com/polonez

Diners decamp at this off-the-beaten-path South Sider for "true, European, old-world" Polish specialties ("mmm, sausages and pierogi"); the affordable, "excellent" menu meanders into *czarnina* (duck-blood soup) and bigos (Hunter's stew) territory, the bar stocks *Polski* beer and a mural of folk costumes adds color to the otherwise functional decor; N.B. live accordion music enlivens the Sunday all-you-can-eat brunch.

Potbelly Sandwich Shop *Sandwiches*
19 | 13 | 17 | $10

Downtown | 135 W. Wisconsin Ave. (Plankinton Ave.) | 414-226-0014
Brookfield | 17800 W. Bluemound Rd. (bet. Brookfield & Calhoun Rds.) | 262-796-9845
www.potbelly.com
See review in Chicago Directory.

☑ Ristorante Bartolotta *Italian*
28 | 25 | 27 | $55

Wauwatosa | 7616 W. State St. (Harwood Ave.) | 414-771-7910 | www.bartolottaristorante.com

"Awesome" Italian flavors make it easy to "pretend you are in a small bistro in Rome" rather than "Downtown Wauwatosa" (in an old Pabst Brewery saloon, no less) at this "charming, noisy trattoria" that also offers an "extensive wine list" (all Italian labels) and "well-trained staff"; old family photos lining the walls provide a contrast with the "upscale sensibility" that surveyors expect from "the [Joe] Bartolotta empire" (which includes Bartolotta's Lake Park Bistro and Bacchus).

River Lane Inn ☒ *Seafood*
26 | 18 | 26 | $42

North Shore | 4313 W. River Ln. (Brown Deer Rd.) | 414-354-1995

While the look of this longtime North Shore seafood specialist located inside a late-1800s building may be "dark and unchanged", its repertoire of moderately priced seafood items – many listed on the chalkboard roster of daily specials – is "fresh and creatively prepared"; fin fans say "you can't go wrong with anything on the menu", and further adding to its "steady-as-she-goes" status is the "experienced staff" and "friendly bartenders who pour an ample drink."

Riversite, The ☒ *American*
- | - | - | E

Mequon | 11120 N. Cedarburg Rd. (Mequon Rd.) | 262-242-6050 | www.riversiterestaurant.com

In its peaceful setting along the Milwaukee River, this Mequon American offers "stylish, inventive and delicious" cuisine from longtime chef Thomas Peschong to loyal patrons who especially "love the seafood and creative starters"; the room boasts 20-ft. ceilings

	FOOD	DECOR	SERVICE	COST

and chandeliers, making for an upscale experience that's always "worth a visit"; N.B. a tapas menu is featured on Tuesday nights.

Rock Bottom Brewery *American*

17	17	17	$24

Downtown | 740 N. Plankinton Ave. (bet. Wells St. & Wisconsin Ave.) | 414-276-3030 | www.rockbottom.com

"It's all about" the "hearty" "appetizers and beer" for some patrons of this Downtown Traditional American "neighborhood hangout", but its "diverse" menu offers "something for everyone" too; the "brewery warehouse" atmosphere is "adult and family-friendly at the same time", and though foes find it "chain-ish" and "mediocre throughout", fans call it a "good sports bar for the price"; P.S. there's seasonal patio seating.

☑ Roots Restaurant & Cellar *Californian*

29	27	22	$38

Brewers Hill | 1818 N. Hubbard St. (Vine St.) | 414-374-8480 | www.rootsmilwaukee.com

You can "see the staff snipping herbs" at this green-minded Brewers Hill Californian – voted No. 1 for Food in the Milwaukee Survey – that's a "must-go" for chef John Raymond's "exceptional" midpriced menu using "local ingredients" (some "homegrown") in "adventurous", "seasonal" creations; the "cozy" yet "fabulous digs" include a two-level patio, gracious gardens and a "beautiful view of the Downtown skyline", and the "reliable wine list" is another "step up"; P.S. the lower-level Cellar offers casual options.

NEW Ryan Braun's Graffito ● *Italian*

-	-	-	M

Third Ward | 102 N. Water St. (Erie St.) | 414-727-2888 | www.ryanbraungraffito.com

Star Brewers left-fielder Ryan Braun lends his name to this midpriced Third Ward 'from scratch' Italian, where chef Dominic Zumpano (ex Umami Moto) makes everything in-house using fresh, local ingredients; the setting features Milwaukee River views and bright graffitilike murals of local landmarks, including Miller Park.

Sake Tumi *Asian*

-	-	-	M

Downtown | 714 N. Milwaukee St. (bet. Mason St. & Wisconsin Ave.) | 414-224-7253 | www.sake-milwaukee.com

"Diverse little Restaurant Row" (Milwaukee Street) is the setting for this Downtown Asian, where "excellent rolls and sushi" ("tasty" Korean creations too) are served in a narrow, contemporary space; romantics say it suits "for a date", plus "you can hit the bars on Water Street afterwards to round out the evening"; N.B. since parking "can be a deterrent", consider valet.

Sala da Pranzo ☒ *Italian*

-	-	-	M

East Side | 2613 E. Hampshire Ave. (Downer Ave.) | 414-964-2611 | www.sala-dapranzo.com

Locals and profs from the nearby university call this "family-owned and -operated" East Side trattoria where eclectic artwork adorns the walls a "real hidden gem" for saltimbocca, pastas and other midpriced Italian fare.

Z Sanford ☒ *American*   29 | 27 | 29 | $74

East Side | 1547 N. Jackson St. (Pleasant St.) | 414-276-9608 |
www.sanfordrestaurant.com

Co-owner and chef Sanford D'Amato's nationally recognized New
American, residing in the East Side storefront home of his family's
old grocery store, is "as impressive as any top New York restaurant"
say surveyors who vote it Most Popular and No. 1 for Service in
Milwaukee; "superb and imaginative", this "little neighborhood
gem" pays "attention to every detail", from its "marvelous" cuisine –
including a seven-course surprise tasting menu – to its "down-to-
earth, professional" service to decor that mixes "modern" (a single
chartreuse wall) and historical (old black-and-white family photos);
while not cheap, it's a "great value considering what you get."

Sebastian's ☒ *American*   - | - | - | M

Caledonia | 6025 Douglas Ave. (5 Mile Rd.) | 262-681-5465 |
www.sebastiansfinefood.com

This casual midpriced New American has been pleasantly "surprising" patrons for the last decade in quiet Caledonia; the "nice
Midwestern" staff serves signature potato-crusted grouper and dry-
aged meats in a dining room with high ceilings and hardwood
floors – nothing fancy because this off-the-beaten-path place is all
"about the food."

Singha Thai *Thai*   - | - | - | I

West Side | 2237 S. 108th St. (Lincoln Ave.) | 414-541-1234 |
www.singhathaimilwaukee.com

This West Side Thai serves up "some extraordinary dishes in every
category" on its "huge menu" (the noodle dishes alone "are worth a
drive"); service and ambiance are another story, but the lackluster
"strip-mall location" just "simplifies" the decision to order "carryout."

Smyth *American*   ▽ 24 | 27 | 26 | $44

Walker's Point | Iron Horse Hotel | 500 W. Florida St. (6th St.) |
414-831-4615 | www.theironhorsehotel.com

Rustic 100-year-old warehouse decor including Cream City brick
is the backdrop for "smitten" surveyors at this "stylish" Walker's
Point New American "'in' place" located inside the motorcycle-
friendly Iron Horse Hotel, where the "energy is electrifying";
while the cuisine is both "innovative and comforting", the
"interesting wine list" and "knowledgeable staff" make the meal
even "more special"; N.B. the Food score may not reflect a chef
change post-Survey.

Tess Ⓜ *Eclectic*   - | - | - | E

East Side | 2499 N. Bartlett Ave. (Bradford Ave.) | 414-964-8377

"Cozy rooms in winter" and a "wonderful summer patio" (with
both open-air and heated spots) attract East Siders to this
"neighborhood charmer" with a small, "quirky, casual" storefront setting; "outstanding" Eclectic dishes such as Madeira
beef tenderloin and equally impressive service help justify the
slightly pricey tabs.

	FOOD	DECOR	SERVICE	COST

Third Ward Caffe Ⓜ *Italian*
| - | - | - | M |

Third Ward | 225 E. St. Paul Ave. (bet. B'way & Water St.) | 414-224-0895 | www.thirdwardcaffe.com

Located in historically significant Commission Row, this Third Ward "stalwart" for "pre-theater dining" offers Northern Italian fare including over 20 kinds of pasta and seasonal specials in a trattoria atmosphere; sidewalk seating adds to the appeal.

Three Brothers Ⓜ⇄ *Serbian*
| 24 | 12 | 20 | $32 |

South Side | 2414 S. St. Clair St. (Russell Ave.) | 414-481-7530

"Crowds of lifelong" loyalists "still" fill this 60-year-old South Side family-owned "must"-go where borek and other "excellent", "authentic" midpriced Serbian fare is served in a historic former Schlitz tavern by a staff displaying "warm hospitality"; the atmosphere is "lively", though regulars warn "don't go in a hurry as this food takes time" – but it's an "experience you won't forget."

Triskele's ⓈⓂ *American*
| - | - | - | M |

Walker's Point | 1801 S. Third St. (Maple St.) | 414-837-5950 | www.triskelesrestaurant.com

For "delightful" "comfort food" "at comfortable prices", try this Walker's Point "up-and-comer" dishing out New American fare including housemade chicken sausage and Tuesday night all-you can-eat mussels; the setting includes booth seating and has a "neighborhood" vibe underscored by "friendly service."

Umami Moto Ⓢ *Asian*
| ∇ 24 | 25 | 19 | $50 |

Downtown | 718 N. Milwaukee St. (bet. Mason St. & Wisconsin Ave.) | 414-727-9333 | www.umamimoto.com

"Pretty people" populate this sleek Milwaukee Street place "to be seen" with an "amazing" interior design boasting wavelike walls, river-stone pillars and pale-green tile as a backdrop for the "imaginative", "beautifully prepared" Asian fusion menu; though it's costly, the fare "hits all the high points for taste" ("love the sliders"), plus service is "friendly" and "helpful."

Ward's House of Prime ●Ⓢ *Steak*
| - | - | - | E |

Downtown | 540 E. Mason St. (bet. Jackson & Jefferson Sts.) | 414-223-0135 | www.wardshouseofprime.com

This Downtown meating place offers all that steak lovers crave (including prime rib in three sizes) and rounds out the pricey menu with seafood, flatbreads, pastas and more; dark wood and leather chairs give it an upscale, masculine feel, befitting the suits who congregate here; P.S. valet parking alleviates the limited street parking situation, and a more casual bar menu is served until 1 AM.

Wasabi Sake Lounge *Japanese*
| - | - | - | M |

Brookfield | 15455 W. Bluemound Rd. (bet. Fairway Dr. & Moorland Rd.) | 262-780-0011 | www.wasabisakelounge.com

"Fresh" sushi and sashimi attract a fish-loving following to this moderately priced Brookfield Japanese located in a strip mall; the open setting aims for Downtown New York style, and patrons are gregariously greeted by sushi chefs when they arrive.

Zarletti ⊠ *Italian*   22 | 19 | 18 | $42

Downtown | 741 N. Milwaukee St. (Mason St.) | 414-225-0000 |
www.zarletti.net

The pre-show and pre-nightlife crowd gathers at this "bustling Milwaukee Street" Downtowner dispensing "delicious" Italian fare "from cocktails to desserts" for slightly pricey tabs; "attentive" servers work the modern space that some call "beautiful", others "sterile", and "sidewalk dining" is an added attraction in "decent weather."

MILWAUKEE
INDEXES

Cuisines

Includes names, locations and Food ratings.

AMERICAN

Z Bacchus | **Downtown**	25
NEW Blue's Egg | **W Side**	-
Buckley's Kiskeam Inn | **Downtown**	-
Cheesecake Factory | **multi.**	19
Comet Café | **E Side**	-
Dream Dance | **Downtown**	-
Elsa's/Park | **Downtown**	23
Envoy | **Downtown**	-
Heaven City | **Mukwonago**	-
Hinterland | **Third Ward**	26
Honeypie | **Bay View**	-
Immigrant Room | **Kohler**	23
Jackson Grill | **S Side**	23
Kilawat | **Downtown**	21
Z Mason St. Grill | **Downtown**	23
North Star | **multi.**	22
NSB B&G | **N Shore**	19
Original/Walker Pancake | **multi.**	24
Palms Bistro | **Third Ward**	20
NEW Parkside 23 | **Brookfield**	-
Riversite | **Mequon**	-
Rock Bottom | **Downtown**	17
Z Sanford | **E Side**	29
Sebastian's | **Caledonia**	-
Smyth | **Walker's Point**	24
Triskele's | **Walker's Point**	-

ASIAN

Umami Moto | **Downtown**	24

BURGERS

Elsa's/Park | **Downtown**	23
Five Guys | **multi.**	20

CAJUN

Crawdaddy's | **SW Side**	16
Maxie's | **W Side**	23

CALIFORNIAN

Z Roots | **Brewers Hill**	29

CHINESE

P.F. Chang's | **Wauwatosa**	20

COFFEE SHOPS/ DINERS

Original/Walker Pancake | **multi.**	24

CREOLE

Crawdaddy's | **SW Side**	16
Maxie's | **W Side**	23

CUBAN

Cubanitas | **Downtown**	20

DESSERT

Honeypie | **Bay View**	-
Le Rêve | **Wauwatosa**	27

ECLECTIC

NEW Blue's Egg | **W Side**	-
Crazy Water | **Walker's Point**	25
Knick | **Downtown**	21
La Merenda | **Walker's Point**	27
Meritage | **W Side**	-
Tess | **E Side**	-

FRENCH

Le Rêve | **Wauwatosa**	27

FRENCH (BISTRO)

Z Bartolotta's Lake Park | **E Side**	28
Z Coquette Cafe | **Third Ward**	26
NEW Pastiche | **Bay View**	-

GASTROPUB

Hinterland | Amer. | **Third Ward**	26

GERMAN

Z Karl Ratzsch's | **Downtown**	25

ITALIAN

(N=Northern)

Centro Café | **Riverwest**	-
Edwardo's Pizza | **W Side**	20
Il Mito | **Wauwatosa**	25
Maggiano's | **Wauwatosa**	20
Mangia | **Kenosha**	25
Mimma's Café | **E Side**	24
Z Osteria/Mondo | N | **Downtown**	28
Pasta Tree | N | **E Side**	20
Z Rist. Bartolotta | **Wauwatosa**	28
NEW R. Braun's Graffito | **Third Ward**	-
Sala/Pranzo | **E Side**	-
Third Ward | N | **Third Ward**	-
Zarletti | N | **Downtown**	22

JAPANESE

(* sushi specialist)

Benihana | **Downtown**	18
Sake Tumi* | **Downtown**	-
Wasabi* | **Brookfield**	-

KOREAN

(* barbecue specialist)

Sake Tumi* | **Downtown** -|

MEXICAN

Cempazuchi | **E Side** 23|

PIZZA

Edwardo's Pizza | **W Side** 20|

POLISH

Polonez | **S Side** -|

SANDWICHES

Potbelly Sandwich | **multi.** 19|

SEAFOOD

Bosley/Brady | **E Side** -|
Z Eddie Martini's | **Wauwatosa** 29|
NEW Harbor House | **Downtown** -|
River Ln. Inn | **N Shore** 26|

SERBIAN

Three Brothers | **S Side** 24|

SOUTHERN

Maxie's | **W Side** 23|

STEAKHOUSES

Benihana | **Downtown** 18|
Bosley/Brady | **E Side** -|
Z Capital Grille | **Downtown** 25|
Carnevor | **Downtown** 24|
Dream Dance | **Downtown** -|
Z Eddie Martini's | **Wauwatosa** 29|
Five O'Clock Steak | **Central City** 25|
Fleming's | **Brookfield** 23|
Jackson Grill | **S Side** 23|
Jake's | **Pewaukee** -|
Milwaukee Chop | **Downtown** 22|
Mo's: Steak | **Downtown** 23|
Mr. B's: Steak | **Brookfield** 26|
Ward's House | **Downtown** -|

THAI

King & I | **Downtown** 20|
Singha Thai | **W Side** -|

VEGETARIAN

Café Manna | **Brookfield** -|

MILWAUKEE

CUISINES

Locations

Includes names, cuisines and Food ratings.

Milwaukee Metro Area

BAY VIEW

Honeypie	*Amer.*	-
NEW Pastiche	*French*	-

BREWERS HILL

Z Roots	*Cal.*	29

CENTRAL CITY

Five O'Clock Steak	*Steak*	25

DOWNTOWN

Z Bacchus	*Amer.*	25
Benihana	*Japanese/Steak*	18
Buckley's Kiskeam Inn	*Amer.*	-
Z Capital Grille	*Steak*	25
Carnevor	*Steak*	24
Cubanitas	*Cuban*	20
Dream Dance	*Amer./Steak*	-
Elsa's/Park	*Amer.*	23
Envoy	*Amer.*	-
NEW Harbor House	*Seafood*	-
Z Karl Ratzsch's	*German*	25
Kilawat	*Amer.*	21
King & I	*Thai*	20
Knick	*Eclectic*	21
Z Mason St. Grill	*Amer.*	23
Milwaukee Chop	*Steak*	22
Mo's: Steak	*Steak*	23
Z Osteria/Mondo	*Italian*	28
Potbelly Sandwich	*Sandwich*	19
Rock Bottom	*Amer.*	17
Sake Tumi	*Asian*	-
Umami Moto	*Asian*	24
Ward's House	*Steak*	-
Zarletti	*Italian*	22

EAST SIDE

Z Bartolotta's Lake Park	*French*	28
Bosley/Brady	*Seafood/Steak*	-
Cempazuchi	*Mex.*	23
Comet Café	*Amer.*	-
Five Guys	*Burgers*	20
Mimma's Café	*Italian*	24
Original/Walker Pancake	*Amer.*	24
Pasta Tree	*Italian*	20
Sala/Pranzo	*Italian*	-
Z Sanford	*Amer.*	29
Tess	*Eclectic*	-

GLENDALE

Cheesecake Factory	*Amer.*	19
Five Guys	*Burgers*	20

NORTH SHORE

NSB B&G	*Amer.*	19
River Ln. Inn	*Seafood*	26

RIVERWEST

Centro Café	*Italian*	-

SHOREWOOD

North Star	*Amer.*	22

SOUTH SIDE

Jackson Grill	*Amer.*	23
Polonez	*Polish*	-
Three Brothers	*Serbian*	24

SOUTHWEST SIDE

Crawdaddy's	*Cajun/Creole*	16

THIRD WARD

Z Coquette Cafe	*French*	26
Hinterland	*Amer.*	26
Palms Bistro	*Amer.*	20
NEW R. Braun's Graffito	*Italian*	-
Third Ward	*Italian*	-

WALKER'S POINT

Crazy Water	*Eclectic*	25
La Merenda	*Eclectic*	27
Smyth	*Amer.*	24
Triskele's	*Amer.*	-

WAUWATOSA

Cheesecake Factory	*Amer.*	19
Z Eddie Martini's	*Seafood/Steak*	29
Il Mito	*Italian*	25
Le Rêve	*Dessert/French*	27
Maggiano's	*Italian*	20
P.F. Chang's	*Chinese*	20
Z Rist. Bartolotta	*Italian*	28

WEST SIDE

NEW Blue's Egg	*Amer.*	-
Edwardo's Pizza	*Pizza*	20
Maxie's	*Cajun/Creole*	23
Meritage	*Eclectic*	-
Singha Thai	*Thai*	-

Vote at ZAGAT.com

Outlying Areas

BROOKFIELD

Café Manna | *Veg.* | -
Fleming's | *Steak* | 23
Mr. B's: Steak | *Steak* | 26
North Star | *Amer.* | 22
Original/Walker Pancake | *Amer.* | 24
NEW Parkside 23 | *Amer.* | -
Potbelly Sandwich | *Sandwich* | 19
Wasabi | *Japanese* | -

CALEDONIA

Sebastian's | *Amer.* | -

DELAFIELD

Five Guys | *Burgers* | 20

KENOSHA

Mangia | *Italian* | 25

KOHLER

Immigrant Room | *Amer.* | 23

MEQUON

Riversite | *Amer.* | -

MUKWONAGO

Heaven City | *Amer.* | -

PEWAUKEE

Five Guys | *Burgers* | 20
Jake's | *Steak* | -

MILWAUKEE

LOCATIONS

Special Features

Listings cover the best in each category and include names, locations and Food ratings. Multi-location restaurants' features may vary by branch.

ADDITIONS

(Properties added since the last edition of the book)

Blue's Egg | **W Side**	–
Buckley's Kiskeam Inn | **Downtown**	–
Café Manna | **Brookfield**	–
Centro Café | **Riverwest**	–
Comet Café | **E Side**	–
Harbor House | **Downtown**	–
Honeypie | **Bay View**	–
Parkside 23 | **Brookfield**	–
Pastiche | **Bay View**	–
R. Braun's Graffito | **Third Ward**	–
Ward's House | **Downtown**	–

BRUNCH

Z Bartolotta's Lake Park | **E Side**	28
Knick | **Downtown**	21
Polonez | **S Side**	–
Z Roots | **Brewers Hill**	29

BUSINESS DINING

Z Bacchus | **Downtown**	25
Z Bartolotta's Lake Park | **E Side**	28
Carnevor | **Downtown**	24
Z Coquette Cafe | **Third Ward**	26
Z Eddie Martini's | **Wauwatosa**	29
Envoy | **Downtown**	–
NEW Harbor House | **Downtown**	–
Jake's | **Pewaukee**	–
Z Karl Ratzsch's | **Downtown**	25
Kilawat | **Downtown**	21
Knick | **Downtown**	21
Z Mason St. Grill | **Downtown**	23
Milwaukee Chop | **Downtown**	22
Mo's: Steak | **Downtown**	23
Mr. B's: Steak | **Brookfield**	26
North Star | **Brookfield**	22
NSB B&G | **N Shore**	19
NEW Parkside 23 | **Brookfield**	–
Z Rist. Bartolotta | **Wauwatosa**	28
River Ln. Inn | **N Shore**	26
Riversite | **Mequon**	–
Z Roots | **Brewers Hill**	29
Smyth | **Walker's Point**	24
Umami Moto | **Downtown**	24
Ward's House | **Downtown**	–

CELEBRITY CHEFS

Marc Bianchini

Z Osteria/Mondo | **Downtown**	28

Sandy D'Amato

Z Sanford | **E Side**	29

Mike Engel

NEW Pastiche | **Bay View**	–

Michael Feker

Il Mito | **Wauwatosa**	25

Jimmy Jackson

Jackson Grill | **S Side**	23

JoLinda Klopp

Triskele's | **Walker's Point**	–

Adam Lucks

Comet Café | **E Side**	–
Honeypie | **Bay View**	–

Peggy Magister

Crazy Water | **Walker's Point**	25

Mimma Megna

Mimma's Café | **E Side**	24

Joe Muench

NEW Blue's Egg | **W Side**	–
Maxie's | **W Side**	23

Tom Peschong

Riversite | **Mequon**	–

Mark Weber

Z Mason St. Grill | **Downtown**	23

Dominic Zumpano

NEW R. Braun's Graffito | **Third Ward**	–

CHILD-FRIENDLY

(Alternatives to the usual fast-food places; * children's menu available)

Benihana* | **Downtown**	18
Cempazuchi | **E Side**	23
Edwardo's Pizza* | **W Side**	20
Z Karl Ratzsch's* | **Downtown**	25
Knick | **Downtown**	21
Maggiano's* | **Wauwatosa**	20
Mangia* | **Kenosha**	25
Palms Bistro | **Third Ward**	20
Pasta Tree | **E Side**	20
P.F. Chang's | **Wauwatosa**	20
Rock Bottom* | **Downtown**	17
Tess | **E Side**	–
Third Ward* | **Third Ward**	–

DELIVERY/TAKEOUT

(D=delivery, T=takeout)

Benihana | T | **Downtown**	18
Cempazuchi | T | **E Side**	23
Crawdaddy's | T | **SW Side**	16
Elsa's/Park | T | **Downtown**	23
Knick | T | **Downtown**	21
Maggiano's | T | **Wauwatosa**	20
Mimma's Café | T | **E Side**	24
NSB B&G | T | **N Shore**	19
Palms Bistro | T | **Third Ward**	20
Pasta Tree | T | **E Side**	20
Polonez | T | **S Side**	⌐
Potbelly Sandwich | D, T | **multi.**	19
River Ln. Inn | T | **N Shore**	26
Rock Bottom | T | **Downtown**	17
⚡ Roots | T | **Brewers Hill**	29
Singha Thai | T | **W Side**	⌐
Third Ward | T | **Third Ward**	⌐

DINING ALONE

(Other than hotels and places with counter service)

⚡ Bartolotta's Lake Park | **E Side**	28
Benihana | **Downtown**	18
Cempazuchi | **E Side**	23
⚡ Coquette Cafe | **Third Ward**	26
Cubanitas | **Downtown**	20
NSB B&G | **N Shore**	19
Potbelly Sandwich | **Downtown**	19
Rock Bottom | **Downtown**	17
Singha Thai | **W Side**	⌐

ENTERTAINMENT

(Call for days and times of performances)

Immigrant Room | piano | **Kohler**	23
⚡ Karl Ratzsch's | piano | **Downtown**	25
NSB B&G | jazz | **N Shore**	19

FIREPLACES

Heaven City | **Mukwonago**	-
Jake's | **Pewaukee**	⌐
Palms Bistro | **Third Ward**	20
Pasta Tree | **E Side**	20
Sebastian's | **Caledonia**	⌐

GAME IN SEASON

Dream Dance | **Downtown**	⌐
Hinterland | **Third Ward**	26
Immigrant Room | **Kohler**	23
Jake's | **Pewaukee**	⌐
Smyth | **Walker's Point**	24

HISTORIC PLACES

(Year opened; * building)

1875 | Third Ward* | **Third Ward**	⌐
1890 | Elsa's/Park* | **Downtown**	23
1890 | Three Brothers* | **S Side**	24
1893 | Mason St. Grill* | **Downtown**	23
1900 | Rist. Bartolotta* | **Wauwatosa**	28
1900 | River Ln. Inn* | **N Shore**	26
1904 | Karl Ratzsch's | **Downtown**	25
1918 | Immigrant Room* | **Kohler**	23
1927 | Envoy* | **Downtown**	⌐
1948 | Five O'Clock Steak | **Central City**	25
1960 | Jake's | **Pewaukee**	⌐

HOTEL DINING

Ambassador Hotel	
Envoy | **Downtown**	⌐
Hilton Milwaukee	
Milwaukee Chop | **Downtown**	22
InterContinental Hotel	
Kilawat | **Downtown**	21
Iron Horse Hotel	
Smyth | **Walker's Point**	24
Knickerbocker Hotel	
Knick | **Downtown**	21
⚡ Osteria/Mondo | **Downtown**	28
Pfister Hotel	
⚡ Mason St. Grill | **Downtown**	23

JACKET REQUIRED

Immigrant Room | **Kohler**	23

LATE DINING

(Weekday closing hour)

Elsa's/Park | 1 AM | **Downtown**	23
Knick | 12 AM | **Downtown**	21
NEW R. Braun's Graffito | varies | **Third Ward**	⌐
Ward's House | 1 AM | **Downtown**	⌐

MEET FOR A DRINK

(Most top hotels and the following standouts)

⚡ Bacchus | **Downtown**	25
⚡ Bartolotta's Lake Park | **E Side**	28
Bosley/Brady | **E Side**	⌐
Buckley's Kiskeam Inn | **Downtown**	⌐
Carnevor | **Downtown**	24
Cempazuchi | **E Side**	23
Comet Café | **E Side**	⌐
⚡ Coquette Cafe | **Third Ward**	26
Crawdaddy's | **SW Side**	16

Crazy Water | **Walker's Point**	25
Cubanitas | **Downtown**	20
Z Eddie Martini's | **Wauwatosa**	29
Elsa's/Park | **Downtown**	23
Envoy | **Downtown**	-
NEW Harbor House | **Downtown**	-
Honeypie | **Bay View**	-
Il Mito | **Wauwatosa**	25
Jackson Grill | **S Side**	23
Knick | **Downtown**	21
Z Mason St. Grill | **Downtown**	23
Maxie's | **W Side**	23
Mo's: Steak | **Downtown**	23
North Star | **multi.**	22
NSB B&G | **N Shore**	19
Z Osteria/Mondo | **Downtown**	28
Palms Bistro | **Third Ward**	20
NEW Parkside 23 | **Brookfield**	-
NEW Pastiche | **Bay View**	-
Rock Bottom | **Downtown**	17
NEW R. Braun's Graffito | **Third Ward**	-
Sake Tumi | **Downtown**	-
Smyth | **Walker's Point**	24
Tess | **E Side**	-
Triskele's | **Walker's Point**	-
Umami Moto | **Downtown**	24
Ward's House | **Downtown**	-
Zarletti | **Downtown**	22

OUTDOOR DINING

(P=patio; S=sidewalk; T=terrace; W=waterside)

Edwardo's Pizza | P | **W Side**	20
Knick | P | **Downtown**	21
Maggiano's | P | **Wauwatosa**	20
Mangia | P | **Kenosha**	25
NSB B&G | P | **N Shore**	19
Z Osteria/Mondo | P | **Downtown**	28
Palms Bistro | S | **Third Ward**	20
Pasta Tree | P | **E Side**	20
P.F. Chang's | P | **Wauwatosa**	20
Potbelly Sandwich | P, S | **multi.**	19
Z Rist. Bartolotta | S | **Wauwatosa**	28
River Ln. Inn | P | **N Shore**	26
Riversite | P, W | **Mequon**	-
Rock Bottom | P, W | **Downtown**	17
Z Roots | P, T | **Brewers Hill**	29
Tess | P | **E Side**	-
Third Ward | S | **Third Ward**	-

PEOPLE-WATCHING

Z Bacchus | **Downtown**	25
Buckley's Kiskeam Inn | **Downtown**	-

Carnevor | **Downtown**	24
Centro Café | **Riverwest**	-
Comet Café | **E Side**	-
Z Coquette Cafe | **Third Ward**	26
Cubanitas | **Downtown**	20
Z Eddie Martini's | **Wauwatosa**	29
Elsa's/Park | **Downtown**	23
Envoy | **Downtown**	-
NEW Harbor House | **Downtown**	-
Honeypie | **Bay View**	-
Kilawat | **Downtown**	21
Knick | **Downtown**	21
Le Rêve | **Wauwatosa**	27
Maggiano's | **Wauwatosa**	20
Z Mason St. Grill | **Downtown**	23
Maxie's | **W Side**	23
Mimma's Café | **E Side**	24
Mo's: Steak | **Downtown**	23
NSB B&G | **N Shore**	19
Palms Bistro | **Third Ward**	20
NEW Parkside 23 | **Brookfield**	-
Pasta Tree | **E Side**	20
P.F. Chang's | **Wauwatosa**	20
Z Rist. Bartolotta | **Wauwatosa**	28
River Ln. Inn | **N Shore**	26
Rock Bottom | **Downtown**	17
NEW R. Braun's Graffito | **Third Ward**	-
Sake Tumi | **Downtown**	-
Z Sanford | **E Side**	29
Smyth | **Walker's Point**	24
Three Brothers | **S Side**	24
Umami Moto | **Downtown**	24
Ward's House | **Downtown**	-

POWER SCENES

Z Bacchus | **Downtown**	25
Z Bartolotta's Lake Park | **E Side**	28
Carnevor | **Downtown**	24
Z Eddie Martini's | **Wauwatosa**	29
Envoy | **Downtown**	-
NEW Harbor House | **Downtown**	-
Z Mason St. Grill | **Downtown**	23
Mo's: Steak | **Downtown**	23
Mr. B's: Steak | **Brookfield**	26
North Star | **Brookfield**	22
Ward's House | **Downtown**	-

PRIVATE ROOMS

(Restaurants charge less at off times; call for capacity)

Z Coquette Cafe | **Third Ward**	26
Z Eddie Martini's | **Wauwatosa**	29
Edwardo's Pizza | **W Side**	20

Heaven City | **Mukwonago** —
Immigrant Room | **Kohler** 23
Maggiano's | **Wauwatosa** 20
Mangia | **Kenosha** 25
Mimma's Café | **E Side** 24
Mr. B's: Steak | **Brookfield** 26
🄲 Osteria/Mondo | **Downtown** 28
Polonez | **S Side** —
River Ln. Inn | **N Shore** 26
Riversite | **Mequon** —
Rock Bottom | **Downtown** 17
Sebastian's | **Caledonia** —

PRIX FIXE MENUS

(Call for prices and times)
🄲 Bartolotta's Lake Park | **E Side** 28
Immigrant Room | **Kohler** 23
🄲 Sanford | **E Side** 29

QUICK BITES

🄽🄴🅆 Blue's Egg | **W Side** —
Comet Café | **E Side** —
Cubanitas | **Downtown** 20
Edwardo's Pizza | **W Side** 20
Elsa's/Park | **Downtown** 23
Honeypie | **Bay View** —
Knick | **Downtown** 21
Le Rêve | **Wauwatosa** 27
Maxie's | **W Side** 23

QUIET CONVERSATION

Bosley/Brady | **E Side** —
Dream Dance | **Downtown** —
🄲 Eddie Martini's | **Wauwatosa** 29
Envoy | **Downtown** —
Jake's | **Pewaukee** —
🄲 Karl Ratzsch's | **Downtown** 25
Kilawat | **Downtown** 21
Milwaukee Chop | **Downtown** 22
North Star | **Brookfield** 22
🄲 Osteria/Mondo | **Downtown** 28
Pasta Tree | **E Side** 20
🄽🄴🅆 Pastiche | **Bay View** —
Polonez | **S Side** —
Riversite | **Mequon** —
🄲 Sanford | **E Side** 29
Third Ward | **Third Ward** —

ROMANTIC PLACES

🄲 Bartolotta's Lake Park | **E Side** 28
Centro Café | **Riverwest** —
Crazy Water | **Walker's Point** 25
Heaven City | **Mukwonago** —
Il Mito | **Wauwatosa** 25

Immigrant Room | **Kohler** 23
Mimma's Café | **E Side** 24
🄲 Osteria/Mondo | **Downtown** 28
Pasta Tree | **E Side** 20
🄽🄴🅆 Pastiche | **Bay View** —
Riversite | **Mequon** —
Third Ward | **Third Ward** —
Three Brothers | **S Side** 24
Zarletti | **Downtown** 22

SENIOR APPEAL

🄽🄴🅆 Blue's Egg | **W Side** —
Buckley's Kiskeam Inn | **Downtown** —
Envoy | **Downtown** —
Immigrant Room | **Kohler** 23
Jake's | **Pewaukee** —
🄲 Karl Ratzsch's | **Downtown** 25
North Star | **multi.** 22
🄽🄴🅆 Pastiche | **Bay View** —
Polonez | **S Side** —
Riversite | **Mequon** —
Three Brothers | **S Side** 24

SINGLES SCENES

Carnevor | **Downtown** 24
Comet Café | **E Side** —
Crawdaddy's | **SW Side** 16
Cubanitas | **Downtown** 20
Elsa's/Park | **Downtown** 23
Fleming's | **Brookfield** 23
Knick | **Downtown** 21
Mo's: Steak | **Downtown** 23
Palms Bistro | **Third Ward** 20
Rock Bottom | **Downtown** 17
🄽🄴🅆 R. Braun's Graffito | **Third Ward** —
Sake Tumi | **Downtown** —
Umami Moto | **Downtown** 24

SLEEPERS

(Good food, but little known)
Il Mito | **Wauwatosa** 25
Jackson Grill | **S Side** 23
Le Rêve | **Wauwatosa** 27
Mangia | **Kenosha** 25
Milwaukee Chop | **Downtown** 22
Mr. B's: Steak | **Brookfield** 26
Smyth | **Walker's Point** 24
Umami Moto | **Downtown** 24

TRENDY

🄲 Bacchus | **Downtown** 25
🄲 Bartolotta's Lake Park | **E Side** 28
Carnevor | **Downtown** 24
Cempazuchi | **E Side** 23
Comet Café | **E Side** —

Cubanitas | **Downtown** 20

Z Eddie Martini's | **Wauwatosa** 29

Elsa's/Park | **Downtown** 23

Honeypie | **Bay View** -

Kilawat | **Downtown** 21

Maggiano's | **Wauwatosa** 20

Mo's: Steak | **Downtown** 23

Palms Bistro | **Third Ward** 20

Z Rist. Bartolotta | **Wauwatosa** 28

NEW R. Braun's Graffito | **Third Ward** -

Sake Tumi | **Downtown** -

Z Sanford | **E Side** 29

Umami Moto | **Downtown** 24

Zarletti | **Downtown** 22

VIEWS

Z Bacchus | **Downtown** 25

Z Bartolotta's Lake Park | **E Side** 28

NEW Harbor House | **Downtown** -

Knick | **Downtown** 21

Riversite | **Mequon** -

Z Roots | **Brewers Hill** 29

NEW R. Braun's Graffito | **Third Ward** -

Sebastian's | **Caledonia** -

VISITORS ON EXPENSE ACCOUNT

Z Bacchus | **Downtown** 25

Z Bartolotta's Lake Park | **E Side** 28

Carnevor | **Downtown** 24

Z Eddie Martini's | **Wauwatosa** 29

Z Mason St. Grill | **Downtown** 23

Z Rist. Bartolotta | **Wauwatosa** 28

Z Sanford | **E Side** 29

Zarletti | **Downtown** 22

WINNING WINE LISTS

Z Bacchus | **Downtown** 25

Z Bartolotta's Lake Park | **E Side** 28

Carnevor | **Downtown** 24

Z Coquette Cafe | **Third Ward** 26

Dream Dance | **Downtown** -

NEW Harbor House | **Downtown** -

Mangia | **Kenosha** 25

Z Mason St. Grill | **Downtown** 23

Milwaukee Chop | **Downtown** 22

Z Osteria/Mondo | **Downtown** 28

NEW Pastiche | **Bay View** -

Z Rist. Bartolotta | **Wauwatosa** 28

Z Sanford | **E Side** 29

Smyth | **Walker's Point** 24

Ward's House | **Downtown** -

WORTH A TRIP

Caledonia
  Sebastian's -

Kenosha
  Mangia 25

Kohler
  Immigrant Room 23

Mukwonago
  Heaven City -

Wine Vintage Chart

This chart is based on our 0 to 30 scale. The ratings (by U. of South Carolina law professor **Howard Stravitz**) reflect vintage quality and the wine's readiness to drink. A dash means the wine is past its peak or too young to rate. Loire ratings are for dry whites.

Whites	95	96	97	98	99	00	01	02	03	04	05	06	07	08	09
France:															
Alsace	24	23	23	25	23	25	26	23	21	24	25	24	26	25	25
Burgundy	27	26	22	21	24	24	24	27	23	26	27	25	26	25	25
Loire Valley	-	-	-	-	-	-	-	26	21	23	27	23	24	24	26
Champagne	26	27	24	23	25	24	21	26	21	-	-	-	-	-	-
Sauternes	21	23	25	23	24	24	29	24	26	21	26	24	27	25	27
California:															
Chardonnay	-	-	-	-	22	21	25	26	22	26	29	24	27	25	-
Sauvignon Blanc	-	-	-	-	-	-	-	-	-	26	25	27	25	24	25
Austria:															
Grüner V./Riesl.	22	-	25	22	25	21	22	25	26	25	24	26	25	23	27
Germany:	21	26	21	22	24	20	29	25	26	27	28	25	27	25	25

Reds	95	96	97	98	99	00	01	02	03	04	05	06	07	08	09
France:															
Bordeaux	26	25	23	25	24	29	26	24	26	25	28	24	23	25	27
Burgundy	26	27	25	24	27	22	24	27	25	23	28	25	25	24	26
Rhône	26	22	23	27	26	27	26	-	26	25	27	25	26	23	26
Beaujolais	-	-	-	-	-	-	-	-	-	-	27	24	25	23	27
California:															
Cab./Merlot	27	25	28	23	25	-	27	26	25	24	26	23	26	23	25
Pinot Noir	-	-	-	-	-	-	25	26	25	26	24	23	27	25	24
Zinfandel	-	-	-	-	-	-	25	23	27	22	24	21	21	25	23
Oregon:															
Pinot Noir	-	-	-	-	-	-	-	26	24	26	25	24	23	27	25
Italy:															
Tuscany	25	24	29	24	27	24	27	-	25	27	26	26	25	24	-
Piedmont	21	27	26	25	26	28	27	-	24	27	26	25	26	26	-
Spain:															
Rioja	26	24	25	-	25	24	28	-	23	27	26	24	24	-	26
Ribera del Duero/ Priorat	26	27	25	24	25	24	27	-	24	27	26	24	26	-	-
Australia:															
Shiraz/Cab.	24	26	25	28	24	24	27	27	25	26	27	25	23	-	-
Chile:	-	-	-	-	25	23	26	24	25	24	27	25	24	26	-
Argentina:															
Malbec	-	-	-	-	-	-	-	-	25	26	27	25	24	-

ZAGATMAP

Chicago Transit Map

Chicago's Most Popular Restaurants

Map coordinates follow each name. For chains, only flagship or central locations are plotted. Sections A-H show places in the city of Chicago (see adjacent map). Sections I-P show nearby suburbs of Chicago (see reverse side of map).

1 Frontera Grill (E-4)

2 Alinea (C-2)

3 Topolobampo (E-4)

4 Charlie Trotter's (B-2)

5 Gibsons (D-4)

6 Joe's Sea/Steak (E-4)

7 Blackbird (F-3)

8 Wildfire † (L-2)

9 Morton's † (D-4)

10 Tru (E-5)

11 Spiaggia (D-5)

12 Everest (G-4)

13 Avec (F-3)

14 Shaw's (E-4, L-2)

15 Lou Malnati's † (E-4)

16 MK (D-3)

17 Chicago Chop House (E-4)

18 L2O (A-3)

19 Capital Grille † (E-5)

20 Giordano's † (G-3)

21 Gene & Georgetti (E-3)

22 Publican (F-2)

23 Maggiano's † (E-4)

24 Hugo's (D-4, P-1)

25 Bob Chinn's (K-4)

26 Hot Doug's (M-6)

27 Café Spiaggia (D-5)

28 Ruth's Chris* † (E-4)

29 Original Gino's † (E-5)

30 Gage (F-4)

31 Original/Walker Pancake † (D-4)

32 Les Nomades (E-5)

33 Japonais (E-3)

34 Coco Pazzo (E-3)

35 Catch 35 (F-4, P-1)

36 Cheesecake Factory † (D-5)

37 Arun's (M-6)

38 Rosebud* † (H-1)

39 David Burke's (E-4)

40 Francesca's † (H-1)

41 Café Ba-Ba-Reeba! (B-2)

42 Naha (E-4)

43 Bistro 110 (D-4)

44 Harry Caray's* † (E-4)

45 Heaven on Seven* † (F-4)

46 Pizzeria Due/Uno (E-4)

47 North Pond (A-3)

48 Le Colonial (D-4)

49 Atwood Cafe (F-4)

50 Mercat a la Planxa (G-4)

---

*Indicates tie with above   † Indicates multiple branches